KRAKATOA

KRAKATOA

THE DAY THE WORLD EXPLODED
27 AUGUST 1883

SIMON WINCHESTER

VIKING
an imprint of
PENGUIN BOOKS

VIKING

Published by the Penguin Group

Penguin Books Ltd, 80 Strand, London WC2R 0RL, England
Penguin Putnam Inc., 375 Hudson Street, New York, New York 10014, USA
Penguin Books Australia Ltd, 250 Camberwell Road, Camberwell, Victoria 3124, Australia
Penguin Books Canada Ltd, 10 Alcorn Avenue, Toronto, Ontario, Canada M4V 3B2
Penguin Books India (P) Ltd, 11 Community Centre,
Panchsheel Park, New Delhi – 110 017, India
Penguin Books (NZ) Ltd, Cnr Rosedale and Airborne Roads,
Albany, Auckland, New Zealand
Penguin Books (South Africa) (Pty) Ltd, 24 Sturdee Avenue,
Rosebank 2196, South Africa

Penguin Books Ltd, Registered Offices: 80 Strand, London WC2R 0RL, England

www.penguin.com

First published 2003

1

The publisher is grateful for permission to reproduce the following extracts:
'For the Time Being' by W. H. Auden, courtesy of Faber and Faber Ltd;
'Jakarta 1' from the album *Camellia 1* by Ebiet G. Ade, copyright © Jackson Records, 1979

Frederic Edwin Church's *Sunset over the Ice on Chaumont Bay, Lake Ontario* – painted on 28 December 1883 and showing a sunset tinted with the vivid crepuscular colours known to have been caused by Krakatoan dust in the upper atmosphere (credit: courtesy of Powerstock)

Set in 11/14.25pt Monotype Bell
Typeset by Rowland Phototypesetting Ltd, Bury St Edmunds, Suffolk
Printed in Great Britain by Clays Ltd, St Ives plc

A CIP catalogue record for this book is available from the British Library

HARDBACK ISBN 0–670–91126–7/0–670–91430–4
TRADE PAPERBACK ISBN 0–670–91428–2

I dedicate this book,
with pleasure and with thanks,
to my mother and father

At any given instant
All solids dissolve, no wheels revolve,
And facts have no endurance –
And who knows if it is by design or pure inadvertence
That the Present destroys its inherited self-importance?
from 'For the Time Being', W. H. Auden

CONTENTS

LIST OF ILLUSTRATIONS AND MAPS

South-East Asia.

South-East Asia, with the western islands of the immense archipelago of what is now Indonesia, formerly the Dutch East Indies.

VERLATEN I.

LANG I.

PERBOEWATAN

DANAN

KRAKATOA

RAKATA

0   6 km

The islands of the Krakatoa group, as known before the 1883 eruption.

PRELUDE

He also had one volcano that was extinct. But, as he said, 'One never knows!' So he cleaned out the extinct volcano, too. If they are well cleaned out, volcanoes burn slowly and steadily, without any eruptions. Volcanic eruptions are like fires in a chimney.

On our earth we are much too small to clean out our volcanoes. That is why they bring no end of trouble upon us.

– from *The Little Prince* by Antoine de Saint-Exupéry, 1944

It was early on a warm summer's evening in the 1970s, as I stood in a palm plantation high on a green hillside in western Java, that I saw for the first time, silhouetted against the faint blue hills of faraway Sumatra, the small gathering of islands that is all that remains of what was once a mountain called Krakatoa.

There was a high peak to the left of the group, its pyramid shape cut off sharply by its vertical northern cliff. A couple of low islands hugged the horizon to the right. In between them was one small and perfectly formed, absolutely symmetrical low cone, from which rose a thin wisp of smoke. The smoke left a blackish, greyish trail that first rose vertically and then, as it caught the trade winds a few hundred feet above the darkening surface of the sea, was whisked off to the left, melting away until it became no more than a slow-fading stain against the salmon glow of the sunset.

I must have stood there, enraptured, until it got quite dark. And then I turned away for the drive back to Jakarta. This, I remembered thinking during the endless night of the flight back west, had been a scene of impeccable beauty. And all the more so because it presented a distant prospect of a place where the processes of the world were at work, a place of elemental significance, and a disastrous place once – but these days quiet again, serenely biding its time.

It was almost another quarter of a century before I found myself back in Java. Most of the work I was doing now kept me in the island's centre, in towns like Jogjakarta and Solo and Semarang. But just before I was due to fly away, and because I had a free evening until my plane left, I decided on a whim to make my way back across to the western edge of the island. I drove down to the coast road, just as I had in the seventies.

I wanted to go back for no other reason than to take what I thought would be one final look at a place that, though few beyond the East Indies knew exactly where it was or what it looked like or just what had happened there, had a name – Krakatoa – that had for decades been firmly annealed into the world's collective consciousness. There was a famous film (which admittedly placed the island on the wrong side, the east side, of Java). There was a much loved children's book (which admittedly placed the island in a different ocean, the Pacific, rather than in the Indian). The name had become part of the world's cultural lexicon – it had a vaguely exotic familiarity about it, a certain indefinable resonance. It was a word that people seemed to like, both to say and to have said to them. And now here I was, so close to the volcano that the chance of seeing it once more seemed an opportunity that I shouldn't pass up.

When I reached the best viewpoint on the corniche, it was evening, perhaps a little later than before, and so rather darker than when I had been there last. This time the enormous iron lighthouse near the port of Anjer – built by the Dutch to replace the one that had been torn away in the terrible waves caused by the great eruption – was sweeping its beam calmly across the unruffled waters of the Sunda Strait, beginning its night on sentry-go.

The group of islands was there, just as before, now black against the vivid deep pinks of the western sky. The giant peak to the left of the group was just as I remembered; the low islands too, this time merging with the evening clouds. And in the middle of them all, its summit seemingly lipped with a curious orange fire, rose the pyramid-shape of the one active remnant of the great disaster. As I looked through my glasses, I could clearly see that the orange was indeed fire, and that from it rose smoke, just as before, only this time a tumble of black billows that towered straight up into the windless late-evening sky.

But there was one obvious difference. The pyramid – which I now knew to be called *Anak* locally, which is Malay for *the child* of what had once existed there before the great eruption – seemed this time somehow bigger, sturdier, much taller than I had remembered.

I blinked hard, looked again. I measured it as best I could against the big peak to the left – trying to recall where the smaller mountain had stood in relation to that cliff wall. It was higher up now, surely. Yes, there was no doubt. Memory does play tricks in situations like this, to be sure: but, as I stared long and hard, I became ever more certain. The volcano, *the child of Krakatoa*, had grown very much larger during the twenty-five years that I had been away.

*

When I got back to the maps, I checked, and could see in short order that the modern surveys all agreed. The small island-mountain, which had been born out of the sea forty-odd years after the very explosion that destroyed and vaporized its parent, was now itself growing fast, thrusting upwards at an extraordinary rate. By looking at the old charts and maps that had been published down the years since the last week of June 1927, when it was first seen above the waves, it was possible to calculate that it had been growing taller, fairly steadily, at an average rate of about five inches a week.

True, there had been some fits and starts – a lava flow here, a wild eruption there – but generally Anak Krakatoa had enlarged itself by twenty or so inches each month since 1927. Every year since its birth it had become higher by twenty feet, and somewhere near forty feet wider. And if this was indeed still so – I checked my figures once again – then it meant that my mountain was not simply taller: it was fully *five hundred feet* taller than when I had last seen it.

Which is why this sturdy stripling of a volcano has captivated me ever since. It is a volcano that absolutely and very visibly refuses to die. It is a volcano that seems to me to possess a wonderfully seductive combination of qualities, being beautiful and dangerous, unpredictable and unforgettable. And more: though what happened in its former life was unutterably dreadful, the realities of geology and seismicity and the peculiar tectonics of Java and Sumatra will make sure that what occurred back then will without a doubt one day repeat itself, and in precisely the same way.

No one can be sure exactly when. Probably it will be very many years – many years, that is, before anything will befall the world that could possibly be as terrible as what took place during the historic paroxysmal moment that reached its extraordinary climax at exactly two minutes past ten on the morning of Monday, 27 August 1883.

*

The explosion itself was terrific, a monstrous thing that still attracts an endless procession of superlatives. It was the greatest detonation, the loudest sound, the most devastating volcanic event in modern recorded human history, and it killed more than 36,000 people.

Geological evidence from around the world admits of a number of bigger and more devastating volcanoes, true. Krakatoa is reckoned today to be only the fifth most explosive in the planet's certain geological history – Mounts Toba and Tambora in the East Indies, Taupo in New Zealand and Katmai in Alaska are all thought to have been very much larger, at least in terms of the amount of material they hurled into the sky and the height to which all that material is thought to have soared.

But these were all eruptions quite lost to antiquity, with rather little direct effect on human society. When Krakatoa exploded it was 1883, and the world was a profoundly different place. Sophisticated human beings were on hand to see this volcano's convulsions, they were able to investigate the event, and they were able to attempt to understand the processes that had caused such dreadful violence. And yet, as it happens, their observations, painstaking and precise as science demanded, collided head on with a most discomfiting reality: that while in 1883 the world was becoming ever more scientifically advanced, it was in part because of these same advances that its people found themselves in a strangely febrile and delicately balanced condition, which an event like Krakatoa did much to unsettle.

The communications technology of the time, for example – the advances of telegraphy, the building of undersea cables, the flourishing of news agencies – ensured that the world's more advanced peoples learned about the eruption within moments of its happening. But at the time the limited, and only slowly unfolding, geological knowledge then to hand did not give the audience an explanation of the events that was sufficient to soothe their fears about all they were learning. Hearing of the event baffled people thousands of miles away from where it happened, and left faraway populations bewildered and, in some cases, more than a little frightened.

Moreover, religious dogma still held a powerful grip on millions, even in societies whose scientific understanding was advancing so rapidly. Tribal ancestors might have explained away an eruption like Krakatoa's: it was simply a matter of the gods being angry. But the luxury of such a facile explanation was not available to the more modern people of 1883, whose growing sophistication meant they both knew so much about an event like this and yet at the same time actually knew so little. They had sufficient knowledge of the facts – the news agencies saw to that – but it was knowledge coupled with an insufficiency of understanding. Many people worried in consequence that the eruption of Krakatoa meant something infinitely more dreadful than it did: that their world was being torn asunder, and perhaps even, as the Bible had foretold, was coming to an end.

Fretful and fascinated people around the world, in cities as distant from Java and from each other as Boston and Bombay and Brisbane, all came to know of the event in an instant – and they did so quite simply because this was the world's first major catastrophe to have taken place in the aftermath of the invention of the submarine telegraph. The newspapers were full of it, the descriptions of the happenings made all the more enthralling because they were so perfectly up to date. Words and phrases that had hitherto been utterly unfamiliar – *Java, Sumatra*, the *Sunda Strait, Batavia* – became in one mighty flash of eruptive light part of the common currency of all.

And in learning of these places and of the terrible events that occurred there, so the world's people suddenly became part of a new brotherhood of knowledge – in a sense it was that day in August 1883 that the modern phenomenon known as *the global village* was born, in part through the agency of this enormous explosion. The word *Krakatoa*, despite being a word misspelled and mangled by the imperfect arts of Victorian telegraphy and journalism, became in one awful ear-splitting moment a byname for cataclysm, paroxysm, death and disaster. And the disaster left a trail of practical consequences – political, religious, social, economic, psychological, scientific consequences among them. Even today curious and chilling echoes of those consequences are still faintly and worryingly discernible, both in Java and around the globe.

In all sorts of other observable ways the impact of Krakatoa on the world's consciousness was profound, and immensely more so than in the case of the eruption of the four technically greater volcanoes of earlier times. Krakatoa had an impact on climate, for example: the airborne debris hurled into the skies lowered the planet's temperature; it changed the appearance of the entire world's sky; it set barometers and tide-meters to flailing wildly thousands of miles away; it panicked American firefighters into battling what they thought were raging infernos, but that were in truth violent sunsets caused by the roiling clouds of Krakatoan dust.

Because of all the painstaking and precise work that was begun in the immediate aftermath of the eruption, we know today just why it was that Krakatoa erupted, and we understand only too well the nature of the forces that caused it. An entirely new science has come along to pare away the old and myth-making mysteries of the event, and to render this volcano, and indeed all other volcanoes, readily explicable.

Now, from a palm plantation high on a green hillside, Krakatoa looks peaceful and serene, with just a thin column of white or grey or on occasion black smoke easing up from its summit. But looks are deceptive: all the while the child-mountain is growing steadily and rapidly, as the elemental fires that created the world rage deep inside.

1

'AN ISLAND WITH A POINTED MOUNTAIN'

Volcanic Eruption Area: *Owing to volcanic eruption this area is considered unsafe for shipping . . .*

Pulau Anakrakata: *(6°06'S, 105°25'E), an islet, appearing midway between Pulau Sertung and Pulau Rakata Kecil in 1928, where formerly a bank with a depth of 27m was charted. In 1929, this islet disappeared again, but resurfaced by eruptions in 1930, and after heavy eruptions in February 1933, appeared to have increased in size. In 1935 this islet was almost circular in shape, with a diameter of about 1200m, and a height of 63m, and in 1940 it was 125m high. In 1948 there were a few casuarina trees on the N extremity of the islet; in 1955 the islet had an elevation of 155m and, viewed from the S, was devoid of vegetation. In 1959 it was in eruption and emitted thick black smoke to a height of 600m. Volcanic activity on Pulau Anakrakata was last observed in 1993.*

Danger Signal: *In the event of threatened eruption within the Krakatau area, Jakarta Radio will broadcast the necessary warning in Indonesian and English. (See Admiralty List of Radio Signals.)*

– from 'Admiralty Sailing Directions', NP36, *Indonesia Pilot*, Volume 1, London, 1999

Though we think first of Java as an eponym for coffee (or, to some today, a computer language), it is in fact the trading of aromatic tropical spices on which the fortunes of the great island's colonizers and Western discoverers were first founded. And initially supreme among those spices was the one rather ordinary variety that remains the most widely used today: pepper.

*Piper nigrum, Syzygium aromaticum** and *Myristica fragrans* – pepper, clove and nutmeg – were the original holy trinity of the Asian spice trade. Each was familiar to, and used by, the Ancients. Two hundred years before the birth of Christ, for instance, the Chinese of the Han Dynasty demanded that their courtiers address their emperors only when their breath had been sweetened with a mouthful of Javanese cloves, the 'odoriferous pistils', as they were later more widely known. There is some vague evidence that Roman priests may have employed nutmeg as an incense; it was definitely in use as a flavouring in ninth-century Constantinople, since the terrifyingly Orthodox St Theodore the Studite – the scourge of the image-smashing Iconoclasts – famously allowed his monks to sprinkle it on the pease pudding they were obliged to eat on days when monastery meat was forbidden. And in Elizabethan times a nutmeg pomander was an essential for keeping foul ailments at bay: the notion that nutmeg could ward off the plague survived longer than many another old wives' tale.

Pepper, though, was of infinitely more moment to the Ancients than to be merely a topping, nostrum or cachou. The Romans used it in abundance: Gibbon wrote of pepper being 'a favourite ingredient of the most expensive Roman cookery' and added his authority to the widely held idea that Alaric, the rambunctious king of the Visigoths, had demanded more than a ton of it from

---

* Some botanists regard the clove as more properly *Eugenia caryophyllata*, though all agree it is part of the family *Myrtaceae*, of which the evergreen myrtle is the best known.

the Romans as ransom when he laid siege to the city in AD 410. The *aureus* and the *denarius*, the gold and silver coins of the Empire, became the preferred currency of the Spice Route, and the Indian pepper merchants of Cochin and Malacca and the ports of southern Ceylon were said to be impressed that the denomination of coins was indicated by the number engraved upon them, not by their size.

Syzygium aromaticum,
the clove.

However they may have been denominated, the coins must have been paid out in enormous numbers. Pepper was so precious and costly and so much in demand that the cost of it all had Pliny the Elder fulminating. 'There was no year in which India' – and by this he meant *the Indies,* since pepper traded came both from the Malabar Coast and from western Java – 'does not drain the Roman empire of fifty million sesterces.' So dearly, he added drily, 'do we pay for our luxury and our women.'

(There is a pleasing symmetry about Pliny's involvement in this part of the story of Krakatoa, even if he appears in only a walk-on role. Although this rich and well-connected former soldier – he was a cavalry officer in Roman Germany – happily took on a variety of official duties on behalf of his emperors, Pliny was above all else a naturalist. He was a savant, or a student as he once famously put it, of 'the nature of things, that is, life'. His reputation is based largely on his 37-volume *Natural History,* an immense masterpiece in which, among countless other delights, is the first use of the word from which we derive today's *encyclopedia.*

It was during the late summer of AD 79, while pursuing his official task of investigating piracy in the Bay of Naples, that Pliny was persuaded to explore a

Nutmeg and mace.

Piper nigrum, pepper.

peculiar cloud formation that appeared to be coming from the summit of the local mountain, Vesuvius. He was duly rowed ashore, visited a local village to calm the panicked inhabitants – and was promptly caught up in a massive eruption. He died of asphyxiation by volcanic gases on 24 August, leaving behind him a vast reputation and, as memorial, a single word in the lexicon of modern vulcanology, *Plinian*. A Plinian eruption is now defined as an almighty, explosive eruption that all but destroys the entire volcano from which it emanates. And the most devastating Plinian event of the modern era occurred 1,804 years, almost to the day, after Pliny the Elder's death: at Krakatoa.)

Pepper has a confused reputation. There is no truth, for example, in the widely held belief that it was once used to hide the taste of putrefying meat; this charming thought perhaps derives from the equally delightful notion, still recognized by pharmacists today, that pepper can be used as a carminative, a potion that expels entrapped flatulence. But it was very much used as a preservative, and more commonly still as a seasoning. By the tenth century it was being imported into England; the Guild of Pepperers, one of the most ancient of London's city guilds, was established at least before 1180, which was when the body was first recorded (they were in court for some minor infraction); by 1328 the Guild had been formally registered as an importer of spices in large, or *gross*, amounts: its members were called *grossarii*, from which comes the modern word 'grocer'.

Joseph Conrad caught the obsession, in *Lord Jim*:

The seventeenth-century traders went there for pepper, because the passion for pepper seemed to burn like a flame of love in the breast of Dutch and English adventurers about the time of James the First.*

* 1603–25.

Where wouldn't they go for pepper! For a bag of pepper they would cut each other's throats without hesitation, and would forswear their souls, of which they were so careful otherwise: the bizarre obstinacy of that desire made them defy death in a thousand shapes; the unknown seas, the loathsome and strange diseases; wounds, captivity, hunger, pestilence, and despair. It made them great! By heavens! it made them heroic . . .

The Western appetite for the trinity of flavourings increased almost exponentially during the fourteenth and fifteenth centuries – the trade being dominated, at least after the Papal Donation of 1493, by the only serious maritime power of the day in the Orient, the Portuguese.* Vasco da Gama, who opened up the East and made it as far as Calicut, was said to be exultant at finding out that the pepper he knew would sell for eighty ducats a hundredweight back in Venice (which was the European centre for the trade) could be bought in India for only three. A steady stream of Portuguese merchantmen and explorers promptly left the Tagus for the Orient – one of them, Pedro Alvarez Cabral,

---

* The Papal Donation in essence 'gave' the exploitation of the Western world to Spain and of the East to Portugal. The Spaniards, who were seamen and navigators of equal skill, had under papal supervision agreed with the Portuguese on the division of the conquerable planet – drawing Pope Julius II's so-called Tordesillas Line along the meridian 370 leagues to the west of the Cape Verde Islands (approximately 48 degrees west of Greenwich). To the west of the Line, Spain had a free hand – hence Mexico, Chile, California; to its east – which crucially included the coast of Brazil – Portugal could freely operate its caravels. And since Africa, Asia and the islands of the Spice Route lay similarly to the east of the Tordesillas Line, so Portugal dominated the exploration of the East and, for a while, the European pepper trade too. The antimeridian of the Tordesillas Line appears in the East too, of course, at around 129 degrees east of Greenwich. Spain colonized the Philippines as a consequence; and Portugal won parts of New Guinea and Timor. The Papal Donation, which had its origins in a ruling from Pope Alexander VI in 1493, cast a very long shadow indeed.

The very vague placement of the antimeridian of the Tordesillas Line
essentially allowed the Portuguese free rein over the entire Indian Ocean
– their possessions are marked. The line snakes around the eastern Pacific
margin of the map, with the islands to the north-east of Borneo – the
Philippines – by papal right Spanish.

discovering and then claiming Brazil on the way – and for a while
the Portuguese entirely dominated the business. The ancient
overland route, ships to Arabia, camels to the Mediterranean,
was utterly changed; now it was massive sailing ships all the way,
via West Africa and the Cape. And in just the same way as
Roman currency became the common coin of the old route, so the
Portuguese language became the lingua franca of the new.

But slowly time and technology intervened: by the sixteenth
century the Dutch and the English, now with all the skills for
shipbuilding finely tuned, with all the oak they needed for their
hulls and all the flax they wanted for their sails and all the
cannonry their foundries could produce and the navigating
wherewithal for making long journeys fast and safely, found they

could outrun and outgun the fine vessels from Lisbon. More than a few Dutch ships, flagged with the Portuguese *bandhera* to get around the royal prohibition on non-Iberians trading in the Orient, were now coming home and whetting the appetites of the Amsterdam merchants for pepper and for profit. And so slowly, under the force of these various imperatives, the balance of maritime power in the East started to change. The Portuguese from the warm and lazy south were slowly driven out and replaced by doughty Europeans from the cold and more ruthless north.

The change began somewhat inauspiciously in late June of 1596, when a ragged flotilla of four Dutch vessels dropped anchor in the roads off the north-western Javanese pepper port of Banten and invited the Portuguese spice merchants, whose godowns had long lined the shore, to come aboard. The voyage had been sponsored by the nine merchant-adventurers of the Compagnie van Verre of Amsterdam – in translation simply 'The Long Distance Company' – who had been inspired by the idea of blazing a spice trade-route to the Indies. It had not gone at all well.

Cornelis de Houtman, who commanded the venture, turned out to be both an inept navigator and a cantankerous martinet. Not that he had been wanting of preparation: along with his brother Frederik he had already spent two years in Lisbon gathering intelligence on the Portuguese operations in the East.* His expedition was grandly titled *Eerste Scheepvart*, 'The First Ship Sailing'. It excited much attention as, with 249 men aboard, it swept out into the Zuider Zee and, after provisioning at the merchant docks inshore of Texel, fell away from the roads on the morning of 2 April 1595. It promptly ran into a whole sea of troubles.

---

* Both had been imprisoned for their pains. They were alleged to have stolen a number of Portuguese *portolanos*, the secret charts and sailing directions carried on all expeditions. No doubt, given the furtive nature of their employment as 'commercial representatives' of the van Verre group, they were guilty as charged.

The provisioning had been too hasty. After a matter of only a few weeks scurvy broke out, with sailors suffering such rending stomach pains among their other symptoms that the Dutch still have a word for it, *scheurbuik*, 'tearing-belly'. Disputes raged between the on-board merchants and the ships' masters: one merchant was locked in his cabin in chains for the entire voyage, another was poisoned in India, a master fell victim to a mutiny. De Houtman proved himself to be no more than 'a boaster and a ruffian'. A short stopover in Madagascar for the convoy to catch its breath turned into a six-month death-watch, during which so many crewmen died that there is still a Madagascan bay called the Dutch Cemetery. By the time the venture reached Banten* only a hundred Dutchmen were still alive.

The surprised Portuguese at first made them welcome, probably assuming that so wretched a gaggle of starving men could hardly pose much of a challenge to the might of Lisbon. The head of the entrepôt sent a message to his immediate superior in Goa, on the Indian coast, though more for reasons of diplomatic propriety than of disquiet. He then introduced the visitors to the local Banten sultan, who was sufficiently impressed with them to enter into a treaty: the first formal document between Dutchmen and Javanese, whose relationship of three and a half centuries would prove to be one of repression, exploitation and too often most cruel colonization. 'We are well content,' the sultan wrote, 'to have a permanent league of alliance and friendship with His Highness the Prince† and with you, gentlemen.'

The contentedness would not long survive. Some indication of what would evolve into a deeply unhappy relationship between the

* In many accounts this small north-west Javan port-city appears with its original Portuguese-given spelling, 'Bantam', which suggests, probably not wholly accurately, that the small and eponymous chickens that are actually believed to have first come from Japan originated there.
† Maurice of Nassau, after whom another Dutch-settled island, Mauritius, was named.

Dutch and their soon-to-be subject people came good and early, during the subsequent sojourn of the de Houtman expedition.

Much of Sumatra and Java had already become widely Islamicized (the earliest-known Muslim grave on Java dates from 1419, after which the creed took hold rapidly), and the local people and their leaders were acutely sensitive to the strange ways of the European infidels. The Portuguese had seemingly shown a measure of tact; the Dutch, on the other hand, had a reputation for being crass and insensitive in their dealings with the 'primitives' they met. Cornelis de Houtman himself insulted the Banten sultan – contemporary accounts are not specific and speak only of de Houtman's 'rude behaviour' – and was ordered to leave port.

De Houtman's flotilla sailed east. It was then attacked by pirates off Surabaya, a dozen more of his crew were killed, and one of the ships had to be abandoned and set ablaze because there were too few hands to work it. In retribution for the piracy he ordered a brief campaign of systematic rape and pillage off the coast of Madura. But by the time he reached Bali he had calmed, just as many others find themselves similarly soothed.

He found that the king of Bali was 'a good-natured fat man who had two hundred wives, drove a chariot pulled by two white buffalos and owned fifty dwarves'. He was, perhaps understandably given his location, not the best informed of monarchs. When de Houtman, keen to impress him with Holland's importance, drew him a map of Europe showing the Dutch borders lying improbably close to Venice and Moscow, the old man did not for a moment even raise a sceptical eyebrow.

The crew liked the place hugely; only one sailor deserted. But there were yet more rows, and before they left an ill-tempered de Houtman almost had to be forced to accept a cargo of a few pots of peppercorns, which the expedition took back to Amsterdam. Their return voyage, by way of Java's south coast, was every bit as miserable, and almost as time-consuming, as the outbound. And seven more sailors dropped dead almost as soon as they

reached home, their stomachs reacting violently to the change
back to civilized rations.

But for all the blundering tragedy of that first Dutch expedition, the achievement could hardly be gainsaid: for it did
bring back those few pots of precious black Java pepper. And that,
it seemed to the nine sponsoring merchants of Amsterdam, was
all that really counted. The Portuguese stranglehold on Oriental
spice trading could in theory at long last be broken. Other, better-
furnished expeditions could now venture out and obtain more
pepper, clove and nutmeg (and its attendant aril, called mace, as
well as the cinnamon that grew close by) and thus help make the
mercantile barons of Holland richer than could be imagined.

One might have expected a spirited reaction from the Portuguese. They did indeed react – but then managed to blunder even
more calamitously than had the Dutch. The Portuguese ran their
Estado da India from Goa, on the western coast of India. Their
viceroy there had received news of the de Houtman expedition
from his agents and promptly decided he would see to it that no
such impertinence happened again. He dispatched a specially built
fleet* south to Banten, but the admiral he chose for the mission,
a still-infamous-in-Lisbon figure named Don Lourenzo de Brito,
took such a long time to get there that the Dutch whom he had
planned to confront had already upped and sailed back to (and at
the time were in fact comfortably ensconced in) Amsterdam.

So the admiral, apoplectic, turned his fury on the Bantenese –
despite his chief in Goa having ordered him specifically to do no
such thing. He tried to teach them a lesson for having dared to
be hospitable to his masters' rivals – and was promptly outfoxed
by the Javanese sailors' battling techniques. He lost two of his
four ships and withdrew, humbled, to Malacca to lick his wounds.

* Included were a pair of Mediterranean-style rowing galleys, surely inconveniently lumbering beasts for handling in the open waters of the Bay of
Bengal.

No one – not the admiral or the viceroy or King Philip back home – recognized the import of the moment: that the skirmish between the Bantenese and the tiny fleet from Goa marked the beginning of the end for Portugal's imperial role in the East. It took a while for it to be wholly extinguished (the reversion of Macau from Portuguese to Chinese rule in 1999 marked the final drawing-down of blinds); but the lights began to go out from that time. 'Look at the Portuguese,' noted the British ambassador to India, Sir Thomas Roe. 'In spite of all their fine settlements they are beggared by the maintenance of military forces; and even their garrisons are only mediocre.' Within half a century only Goa, Macau, Mombasa, the ports of Mozambique and, in the Indies, Flores and Timor remained. The power of the old Iberian empires was suddenly waning; new trading empires, directed by men from the chilly north European capitals of Amsterdam and London, were about to be born.

From the moment of the return of that first unhappy excursion to Java and beyond, shoals of Dutch fleets, each backed by packs of excited adventurers, began coursing across the ocean, bound for Banten and the fast-opening Oriental universe beyond. In May 1598 a fleet twice the size of de Houtman's, under the command of the more competent and distinguished sea-captain Jacob van Neck, left Texel for Banten, reached there in half the time and sailed away with enough pepper for its backers to realize no less than a 400 per cent return on their investment. The floodgates then opened, once and for all.

Before the end of 1601 fourteen fleets had gone East – a total of sixty-five vessels. Most had passed along the conventional route via the Cape of Good Hope. Others, keen to be first to reach the spice-rich islands on the eastern side of the archipelago, took the much riskier path south-westwards across the open Atlantic, through the newly discovered, but windy and reef-strewn, Strait of Magellan and then across the entire Pacific Ocean. It was an

extraordinary, boisterous, devil-may-care time, and the docks in
Hoorn and Enkhuizen and Amsterdam were frantic with shipping,
always leaving, leaving, leaving. Some of the more sobersided
Hollanders sniffed over their glasses of genever and accused the
adventurers of indulging what they termed *the wild navigation.*
And wild it may well have been – but the commercial results were
obvious. The Hollanders were on to something big.

Banten itself – though it was once the largest city in South-East
Asia and one of the most famous of the world's seventeenth-
century's ports – is these days anything but big. The garrison
that the local sultan permitted the Dutch to build, Fort Speelwijk,
still stands: with its ten-foot-thick walls, its worn machicolations
and breastworks, its muddy tunnels and embrasures now greasy
with tropic mould, it is a melancholy reminder of how mighty
and ambitious the Dutch had once been. The sea that their vigilant
sentries scanned for approaching enemy sails now laps a full mile
away beyond the fort's curtain-walls: silt oozing from the river
started to choke the estuary in the nineteenth century, and before
long had rendered Banten port unusable for vessels much larger
than whalers and large canoes. Its rise was spectacular; its fall –
like the fall of empires more generally – slow and inevitable. It
has long since been abandoned as a port; nowadays Banten is
little more than a collection of shanties and ruins, with a lane of
shops selling Muslim caps and boxes of locally grown dates.
There are no local pepper plantations: western Java has turned
its plantations to tapioca and coffee, and it is Sumatra that now
produces about a sixth of the world's 200,000 yearly tons of *Piper
nigrum.*

  Yet Banten still makes its own contribution to the economic
well-being of the islands. Just beside the old Dutch fort, at the
entrance to the maze of lanes that lead to the former sultan's
ruined palace, stands a curious trio of immense and very ugly

cement towers. They look mysterious and rather sinister. They are formidably well guarded with razor-wire, attack dogs and civilian guards (one of them a young woman who contentedly suckled her infant when I inquired – in vain – if I might go inside). They look as if they might be kin to Fort Speelwijk, fortresses of a kind too, a protection for a population fretful about some nameless and more contemporary disaster.

In fact they are nothing of the kind. The towers are man-made homes for the local birds called swiftlets, members of the genus *Collocalia*, whose saliva is the basis for that most celebrated Cantonese aphrodisiac, bird's nest soup. The towers' owner is a Chinese restaurateur from Jakarta. He thinks it most un-likely that any client would ever realize that the soup he serves comes not from nests plucked in the traditional manner from dangerous clifftops in Thailand, but from those farmed weekly inside a cement blockhouse in a former Dutch pepper port. He is reputed to be one of the wealthiest Chinese in all of modern Java. He remains blissfully unaware that he made his fortune in the town that had once made other outsiders, the entirely dissimilar burghers of seventeenth-century Amsterdam, extremely wealthy too.

With the advent of those Dutch, whose maritime traditions had already spawned legions of cartographers, came maps: good, beautiful, accurate and before too long utterly magnificent maps. With the making of maps came the observed and calculated details of place. With details of place came names – and among them, quite early in the process, the first naming of the tiny island that is the subject of this story.

For 1,500 years the notion of the great Greek astronomer Ptolemy, published in his definitive *Geography*, was that Africa and Asia were one, connected by a land-bridge across the southern Indian Ocean. It took a very long while to discredit this idea. But by the fourteenth century, on the basis of reports from early explorers (such as Marco Polo) and intelligence gathered from Arab travellers and traders, cartographers in Europe began to suppose the existence of a number of peninsulas and discrete islands littering the ocean between China and Africa. The dangling appendages of India and the Malayan peninsula began to appear on maps first; and then three of the largest supposed islands, today's Borneo, Sumatra and Java, started to be depicted on charts printed in the sixteenth century (though there was a long period when lozenge-shaped Sumatra was confused with its not-too-distant neighbour, pearl-drop-shaped Ceylon).

Martin Behaim's globe of 1492 – his *erdapfel*, or 'earth-apple', as this solid wooden sphere was charmingly called – shows painted on its surface the islands of Java and Sumatra, part of a ragged chain of land between a quite distinct Malayan peninsula and a body of vaguely determinate shape that is just recognizable as Borneo. And Martin Waldseemüller, the German mapmaker who, in 1507, was the first to put the name *America* on to a world map, clearly indicates on one of the same woodcut's dozen sheets an island, to which he gives the name *Java Minor*, quite separate from another island to its west.

And even before these, there were prescient maps made elsewhere. Early Thai, Indian and Korean maps, often delightfully fanciful, indicate bodies of land that could well be the two huge islands. There is also a copy of a fourth-century Roman road map from England to India (with the distances variously measured out in Roman miles, Gallic leagues and Persian parasangs) showing Ceylon as a decidedly insular *insula Taprobane* at its bottom right-hand corner, but which could, from its size and familiar shape, easily be mistaken for Sumatra.

Once the Italian, Spanish and Portuguese sailor-adventurers began to penetrate to the east of Malacca, this imprecision vanished. Sumatra and Java are by then named and shown to exist, most assuredly, separated by a body of water called the Strait of

Sunda. Far to their east the nutmeg island of Banda* finds its way on to a map of 1516, as well as a proper (and more or less properly spelled) Borneo, located five years before Magellan's expeditions reached it on history's first (and for Magellan, tragic and fatal) circumnavigation. The Moluccas, Timor, the Celebes and the Philippines likewise all begin to appear on maps and *portolanos* and charts as well, their positions and their dimensions depicted ever more accurately – such that by the end of the sixteenth century, when the Dutch were poised to sail in from Texel to try to wrest the spice monopoly from the stranglehold of the Mediterranean powers, every major island between the Maldives and the coast of China was illustrated, reasonably correct in outline, place and size.

And then, with the turn of the century, and as those first commercial fleets began their laborious voyages out from Texel, so along with the merchants went the Dutch cartographic masters. These were men possessed of formidable naval knowledge, great artistic brilliance and still unrivalled mapmaking skills, who would push back the boundaries of world cartographic knowledge further and even further, and also add to their newly developed picture of the planet a wonderful measure of beauty and style. Their maps are treasures, awesome in both utility and aspect. And it was one of these mapmakers, Jan Huyghen van Linschoten, who was to make the first positive identification of the volcano-island that would cause such mischief in the years ahead.

Van Linschoten was a curious and energetic traveller, a man afflicted by wanderlust centuries before the ailment was properly known. 'My heart is longing day and night for voyages to faraway

---

* Known also because one of its neighbour islands, Pulau Ran, was seized by the British and later swapped for a Dutch-held North American island, Pulau Manhattan.

lands,' his journals note in an entry for 1587. His travels were prodigious. He was keenly interested in the Arctic, and his numerous journeys there – to the lonely supra-Russian island of Novaya Zemlya, for example, to which he went with the Dutchman who named the Barents Sea – were recounted in a hugely popular book that inspired both the English and the Dutch to try to forge a sea-route through the ice to India (they never did).

But it was for the maps he created as a by-product of his six years in service to the Portuguese that he remains best known today. He had travelled East via Africa and the Cape across to the administrative capital of Goa, in western India, working as bookkeeper to the Portuguese Catholic archbishop. He spent the six years from 1583 in the immense province, travelling with the divine, noting furiously details of every place and peoples he visited (though we do not know if he actually visited Java and the islands to its east). In 1595 he published his account of it all – the *Itinerario*, one of the most detailed travel guides ever known. Bound into the volume were a number of remarkable maps – some by Portuguese mapmakers, some by Spaniards, and one exquisite map of the Far East drawn by van Linschoten himself.

The map itself has a curious history: it was executed by a Dutchman, based on information that van Linschoten admits was 'from the most correct charts that the Portuguese pilots nowadays make use of' and later handed over and republished for the English. The custom was for these four powers jealously to guard such information; yet in the case of this one beautiful creation – with great cartouches, sea-monsters, rhumb lines, the arms of Portugal and a flourish of compass roses – it was allowed to be seen by the navigating hierarchs of all four competing nations.

On the map much is recognizable – China, the Mekong, Malaya, Luzon. The islands of Java and Sumatra are also named and shaped more or less as they should be (though the island of Sulawesi near by is a strange 'paramecium' shape, according to one critic). Between Sumatra and what van Linschoten called

Java Major is a narrow strait, and within it a tangled mess of unnamed islands. But though they are anonymous on the map, there is, and crucially for this story, the text from the *Itinerario*, which acts as vade mecum for any Java-bound navigators using this map, whom it duly advises:

to reach the mouth of the Sunda Strait stay close to the mainland of Sumatra, always keeping a good eye out for the mountains and cliffs, of which there are many ahead, for one does not know where one will find the mouth of the Strait except only by the knowledge of the islands; look for a high island located straight across from the land tip on the north side of Sumatra, which with the island of Java Major forms the Strait that ends here. On the northwest side of the coast are two or three small islands about one mile away from land. On the island closest to land a ship with Frenchmen was run aground once. Its guns went to the king of the Island Bantam, and the one from Calapa. And a mile from land towards the south is an island with a high top or pointed mountain.

There can be no doubt at all, despite van Linschoten's failure to name the island on either his chart or in the *Itinerario*, that this is Krakatoa.

He probably never saw it; though he travelled widely from Goa, there is no certainty that he visited the archipelago itself; all his reports come from his immense network of Portuguese pilots. But there simply is no other island in the Strait that fits his description (or, rather, until 1883 there *was* no other such island in the Strait, for since that August morning the original island has essentially not existed at all). There is no 'pointed mountain' in van Linschoten's reported position at the northern end of the Strait or, for that matter, anywhere else near by.

Other early Dutch cartographers are revered along with van Linschoten: Blaeu, Lodewijcksz, Hondius, Visscher and, equally important in this one context, Lucas Janszoon Waghenaer. For though van Linschoten writes briefly of his island with its pointed

Jan Huyghen van Linschoten's 1595 map of the Far East, which shows a
dusting of islets and skerries in the strait between *Sumatra* and *Java
Mayor*. Krakatoa – seen for the first time ever on a European chart – is
probably the large island marked opposite *Palimbam*.

summit in 1595, and though a year later Willem Lodewijcksz
records so many small islands in the Strait that one crew said
they had difficulty finding a channel along its western side, it was
the Waghenaer map that first depicted the island and properly
captioned it with an approximation of a soon-to-be-familiar name.

Lucas Janszoon Waghenaer was a Dutch pilot who almost
single-handedly revolutionized the entire business of sea-borne
maps. Until his publication in 1583 of a *rutter*, a mass-produced
collection of navigational notes and charts that a mariner might
use to help plan a voyage in unfamiliar waters, such maps as a
ship's captain had taken on board were hand-made, singly produced and often ultra-secret. Waghenaer decided instead that
ships' charts should be printed, using wooden or engraved metal

blocks. They should be made by the hundreds, the better to encourage men to sail, to explore and to discover.

His maps are many, and among the finest ever made. They are colourful, filled, like van Linschoten's, with elaborate cartouches, ships in full sail, fabulous sea-monsters and a host of devices – compasses, scales, indications of deeps and shallows – that are still in use on charts today. His name was Anglicized to *Waggoner*, and so popular and respected did his works become that the word is still heard in some of the older chandleries and appears in recent dictionaries of the sea; Dalrymple's famous chart-book was once known colloquially as *The English Waggoner*.

His exquisite chart of the Sunda Strait was published in 1602, seven years after the *Itinerario*. Engraved on the map, halfway between the immense body of land called *Suma. Pars.* and its equally immense eastern neighbour, *Javae Pars.*, is a group of what appear to be four small islands – a trinity of larger bodies, partially enclosing a fourth. The inscription says simply *Pulo Carcata*.

It was half a century before the island was named in a prose work. In October 1658 a Dutch doctor, Wouter Schouten, noted in his travelogue that he passed the 'high tree-covered island Krakatau' – the first mention of the island by its currently accepted name.

As to the origin of this name, it sometimes seems that there are almost as many theories as there are geographers. The word *Pulau* that appeared on the Waghenaer chart remains, since it is the modern *bahasa Indonesia* for 'island'. But Carcata? Or Krakatau? Or something in between? Both the idea of what should be the spelling and the etymologies of its various names are an enduring mystery.

There is an early and linguistically alluring report by a French Jesuit priest, Guy Tachard, suggesting that it was an onomatopoeia. Tachard passed the island eighty years after the Dutch cartographers, and wrote in his log that 'we made many Tacks to double the island of Cacatoua, so-called because of the white Parrots that are upon that Isle, and which incessantly repeat the name'. It sounds improbable, not least because of the difficulty that any mariner might experience trying to hear the call of land-based birds from high on the windy deck of a passing ship.

Others subsequently thought that Krakatoa, or the more common local form Krakatau, derives essentially from one of three words, *karta-karkata, karkataka* or *rakata*, which are the Sanskrit and, according to some, the Old Javan words meaning 'lobster' or 'crab'. Then there is a Malay word, *kelakatoe*, which means 'flying white ant'. Since crabs and parrots belong on the island – or since they did, at least, until that dire August morning in 1883 – any one of the two last lexical explanations seems reasonably acceptable.* White ants only occur in the eastern part of the archipelago, rendering this theory rather less credible; though perhaps rather more credible than the notion, briefly popular in Batavia, that an Indian ship's captain had asked a local boatman what name was given to the pointed mountain he could see, prompting the local to reply *Kaga tau*, meaning 'I don't know'.†

*

* Modern navigational charts call what remains of the island Pulau Anakrakata. The official details of its ever changing condition can be found in this chapter's epigraph.

† As to why Krakatoa, and not the more properly Javanese Krakatau, it is said – but not proven – that this was a spelling mistake made in an early telegraphic cable to London – a spelling error that, thanks to British domination of so much nineteenth-century science and geography, came to be accepted for many years after as the preferred (but technically incorrect) spelling. Robert Cribb, editor of *The Historical Atlas of Indonesia*, wonders if the ending -*oa* simply sounded, to the British ear, more euphonious and charmingly like an idyll in the South Pacific. I shall revisit what is to some a very vexing matter in Chapter Six, when I look in more detail at those first telegraphic messages about the eruption.

The effect of the eastward onrush of armadas of Dutch sailing vessels, their captains now well equipped with their bound collections, their *rutters*, of the region's new-printed charts, was immediate and profound. Such Portuguese as remained were soon overwhelmed and dismissed. They were eventually and officially sent packing from the Banten pepper port in 1601. In 1605 the Dutch seized all the eastern islands of the Moluccas, which included the nutmeg and clove islands of the Banda Sea. The fort at Solor fell in 1613, and Malacca, the great trading station on the western side of the Malay peninsula, passed from the control of Goa to that of Amsterdam in 1641. The Dutch speedily assumed power across fully forty-five degrees of eastern longitude, and before long effective control of what were to be called the East Indies was almost (aside from tenacious Portuguese holdouts on the islands of Flores and Timor, and fast-fading competition from the British in a variety of tempting places) entirely theirs.*

In 1602 the Dutch took a step of profound importance. It was a move that, as well as hugely improving their own merchants' fortunes in the East, helped to create a business model for the

---

* I have no wish to belabour a historical nicety that will be familiar to most, but it seems worth while pausing to underline the fine irony of the coming change of power-centres in the East. Since the early sixteenth century the Netherlands were in fact under Spanish control, as a province of the Spanish branch of the Hapsburgs. A revolt led by William of Orange ensured that the seven most northerly districts – including the best known, Holland, Zeeland and Friesland – became independent in 1579. In 1648, under the terms of the Treaty of Westphalia, Spain recognized the independence of these seven and an additional southern group of provinces as what was then called the Republic of the Netherlands, headed by members of the Orange-Nassau family as *stadhouders*, or governors. The Netherlands only became a monarchy – as it remains today – in 1815. What is now the Kingdom of Belgium – those additions that were to be known colloquially as the 'Spanish Netherlands' – split back away in 1830. The sudden rush of Dutch colonial energies and anti-Iberian zeal in the 1600s came just after their first emergence from under the yoke of Spain.

foundations of all of modern capitalism. The government formally
chartered a company, the Vereenigde Oost-Indische Compagnie,
known to this day as the VOC, to act in concert, and as a
monopoly, in all trading matters to the east of the Cape of Good
Hope. And not just trading: the VOC was given exclusive and
quasi-sovereign rights to enter into treaties with local princes, to
build forts, to maintain armed forces and to set up administrative
systems of government whose officials pledged loyalty to the
government of the Netherlands.

The idea of officially sanctioned trading cooperatives was far
from new. The British had had the Merchant Adventurers and
the Merchant Staplers; they had created the Muscovy Company
in 1555 and the Turkey Company in 1583. The Plymouth Company and the Massachusetts Bay Company were established at
the beginning of the seventeenth century, to settle colonists. The
Hudson's Bay Company, set up half a century later solely to trade,
remains today: the Bay, its flagship department stores, can be
found in all of Canada's cities (and in not a few more isolated
Arctic settlements), and its owner, a cheerfully eccentric peer
called Ken Thomson, lives modestly and happily in a suburb of
Toronto.

But there was a difference about the VOC. Right from its
beginnings, it was cleverly constructed as a joint-stock company.
The good burghers of Holland who had initially sent out their
own small fleets decided to band together to back a much larger,
much more ambitious company, with each backer owning a 'share'
of this company's value, with the value of each share depending
on the amount by which each shareholder backed it. This new
concept, of a joint-stock company, with in this case a start-up
capital of six and a half million guilders, was to become the model
for all the thousands upon thousands of publicly traded firms that
are listed on the world's bourses and stock exchanges today, and
whose *raison d'être*, the sharing of risk and sharing of reward, lies
now at the beating heart of the modern capitalist system.

The 'Gentlemen Seventeen' who were the directors of the VOC may have been ultimately responsible to the Dutch parliament; but they were also financially responsible to those who bought shares in the Compagnie, to the merchants and the bankers who had taken the bold and revolutionary view that such a costly undertaking – impossibly expensive for any one Dutch company to afford – might, in time, win vast profits for them if they supported it collectively and backed it in concert. The VOC may be best known to historians for having ruled most of the East Indies for two centuries, from 1602 until its collapse in a welter of ignominy and corruption in 1799; but students of finance know it best for its seminal effect on the making of the model for an institution that underpins much of the prosperous West's current way of economic life.

The first steps were modest enough: a renewal of the pepper treaty with the sultan of Banten; the takeover of spice factories on the Banda Islands, in Aceh, in central Sumatra and at a number of small ports on the Malay peninsula; the rebuilding of a conquered Portuguese fort in Ambon in the Spice Islands that was to become the first permanent Dutch military base in the region and that would protect (from the newly predatory English, mainly) their fleets, which were now carrying cinnamon, cloves and nutmeg home in enormous tonnages.

Before long, however, it became evident to the stockholders back in the Netherlands that there might be much more money to be made if at least some of the ships stationed out East began actually to trade within the East – taking goods not just from Java to Holland but from Java to Sumatra, say, or from Galle in Ceylon to Macassar in the Celebes. The local people weren't fully exploiting their potential for trading, so why shouldn't the Dutch – who had the ships and the growing navigational knowledge, confidence and skill – trade for themselves? And so the practice known as 'country trading' began, with skippers from faraway Holland sailing along the immense coastlines of an archipelago that is now known to embrace more than 17,000 islands, bringing cargoes from merchant to merchant and carrying not a small tonnage of their own goods, by the sale of which some became extremely wealthy men.

Just one warning was sounded during those early, braggartly, optimistic days. It was a warning that would sound intermittently through all the succeeding years of Dutch rule in the East, that would find echoes in the rule of other European powers beyond Europe, that would extend past and become surprisingly important locally immediately after the explosion of Krakatoa, and that would reverberate across the world, with varying intensity and degree, right through to modern times.

And this tocsin note was the suspicious and on occasion the openly hostile relationship that developed between the Dutch and those local people who were, and already for the two past centuries had been, as the papers of the day called them, *Muhammadans.*

From the very moment the Dutch admirals met with the sultans of Ambon and Banda, the easy-going arrogance of the visiting Christian Dutch sat uneasily with the rigid formalisms of Islamic belief. An entire spectrum of antipathy developed: almost from the beginning there was a suspicion, disdain and contempt felt and expressed on both sides. Relations between Muslim and Christian, in the East Indies and throughout the Eastern world, presents a discordant *continuo* in the telling of the tale of Krakatoa.

Surviving portraits usually show Jan Pieterszoon Coen hatless and crop-headed, with a menacingly thin moustache and goatee, and invariably dressed in the frills and furbelows of the time: a soft lace millstone ruff, a heavily embroidered black doublet, an elaborate system of belts and buckles holding up a silver-handled Toledo sword. He never smiles, or looks in any way genial.

Jan Pieterszoon Coen.

To those who painted him he seemed always stern, forbidding, ruthless. Whether he did indeed look that way, or whether the portraitists simply reflected the abiding perception of the man, we cannot know. But everyone in the Netherlands and in the East seemed to know only too well that Coen, the founding father of the Dutch empire in the Orient, was not by any stretch of the imagination a kindly man.

No doubt his Calvinist roots – he was born in the small, religious and conservative fishing-town of Hoorn on the Zuider Zee – had much to do with his attitude. The fact that he witnessed an early slaughter of Dutchmen at the hands of Spice Islanders – the admiral in command of his first voyage to the East and fifty of his men were killed in the Banda group in a massacre that Coen long vowed he would avenge – was maybe of even more influence. Whatever the roots of his disdain, by the time the 'Gentlemen Seventeen' saw fit, in 1618, to promote him as the fourth and most famous of their governors-general of the East Indies, Coen was a man in a mood to go out East only to enforce, expand, discipline and punish. And to lay the foundations for what would in due course become a world-class trading empire – an empire that would have at its epicentre a world-class capital city, as Rome and Athens and Venice had in their turn been before.

The directors back in Amsterdam recognized early on the need for a regional headquarters – a place from where they might administer their Indies,* somewhere where they might victual and water and rest their imperial adventurers, somewhere where they might repair their warships or build new trading sloops, somewhere from where they might pause to reflect on the vast territory they were fast acquiring and learn about its subtleties and plan its future course. The existing major centres, Malacca and Banten, had problems, Malacca still being run by the Portuguese and Banten ruled by a sultan whose congeniality was capricious, to say the least.

The only site that tempted Coen, when he became governor-general in 1618, was the tiny fort that the Banten sultan had allowed the Dutch to build on the right bank of a greasy and slow-flowing river called the Ciliwung, on Java's north coast, opposite a village called Jayakarta. The only obvious disadvantage was the local presence of a fair number of British adventurers and would-be colonizers. Ever since Sir Francis Drake, on his great circumnavigation, had arrived in the Moluccas in 1579, there had been a British presence, and men like Sir Thomas Cavendish and James Lancaster had enjoyed some success with the local chiefs, presenting themselves as potential enemies of the Portuguese. The British colonial intentions for Java and Sumatra were formless and lacked direction; but British engineers had built a fort on the left bank of the Ciliwung River, beside Jayakarta, at least to protect their traders. Coen, aware of their potential rivalry and sure that they meant, in time, to become a local imperial power, decided to toss them out.

---

* And well beyond – Dutch outposts in Japan, Formosa, India, Burma, Laos, Thailand, Cambodia, Vietnam, Mauritius, Ceylon, even the Cape Colony in southern Africa were all, at various times, run from this Javanese HQ.

It looked likely to be a tougher task than he at first supposed. The British Army garrison was larger than his, and the Royal Navy squadron had fourteen vessels, while Coen had only eight. He wrote beseechingly to the directors in Amsterdam, asking for reinforcements. His request was ignored. He promptly left town in high dudgeon – 'I swear to you that . . . the Company has no enemies who more hinder and harm it here than the ignorance and thoughtlessness which reigns among Your Excellencies and defies understanding' – and sailed off to the Dutch fort in Ambon, hoping that he might find reinforcements there.

By doing so he missed such action as then took place – which wasn't much, and most of which descended rapidly into farce. The British laid half-hearted siege to the tiny Dutch fort, irritating the Dutch storekeeper, a Mr van den Broecke, by forcing him to build barricades out of the very costly bolts of silk and batik cloth he had waiting for export. Then a row broke out between the Britons and a local junior sultan, over how the spoils of the coming fight, if won, would be divided. Next the sultan of Banten brought in his fleet, to make sure that neither the British nor the junior sultan should benefit from Dutch weakness. The upshot of all this noise and tumult was the opening of four-way negotiations, the sudden abandonment of the scene by the British and the overthrow of the junior sultan by the sultan of Banten.

All of a sudden, by dint less of savage and courageous fighting than of unseemly argument among their many foes, the Dutch found that they had won. Their fort was unscathed and secure. Mr van den Broecke could take down his precious bolts and bales and send them back to the godown. And when Jan Pieterszoon Coen returned home from the Moluccas, shipless and much delayed – but that is quite another story – he found to his surprise and (considering he was such a bellicose man, always spoiling for a fight) some small dismay that his men and his little fortress were all safe and sound. He also discovered that in a moment of relief, celebration and sentimental rapture the men he had left behind him had on 12 March 1619 realized they were now free to transform their fortress into their planned regional headquarters, and so they had given their tiny settlement what they considered a properly dignified Dutch name: Batavia.

Jan Pieterszoon Coen, the founder of the Dutch East Indies, can take credit for much. But the naming of the capital that he founded is an honour that belongs to an unsung and quite forgotten soldier, and decidedly not to Coen. And yet to whomever the glory of foundation belongs, the coming role of this city is undeniable: a great Oriental conurbation was soon to be in the making here, a headquarters for a gathering of Europeans that would all be key to the enginework of a great colonial capital. There would soon be small armies of Dutchmen working in Batavia as merchants, traders, bankers, surveyors, soldiers, farmers, engineers, tax-collectors, teachers, accountants, spies, philosophers, historians and scientists, and in a whole host more of other professions and trades.

It was the particular concentration in the city of scientists, however, that is most important to this story. For there would soon be men, institutes and laboratories dotted around Jan Pieterszoon Coen's capital specifically charged with keeping under close scrutiny the East's manifest natural peculiarities – peculiarities that included on more than one occasion the spectacularly unpredictable nature of her geology, especially that which was readying itself to erupt so terrifyingly in the narrow body of water that lay quietly off to the west, less than a hundred miles away.

2

THE CROCODILE IN THE CANAL

Dust lies hot on streets
Clearly empty of love and pity;
It's not like my green village
Here.

– Ebiet G. Ade, from his song
'Jakarta 1', the album
Camellia 1, 1979

The name Batavia had a kind of easy, silky poetry to it. The Dutch, who were exceptionally proud of having created their great administrative super-city for the Orient from scratch – a somewhat less than altogether accurate claim, as the equally proud Javanese are still eager to point out – liked to think of it as their 'Queen of the East'. The choice of the name was a nicely sentimental notion. Batavia was the old name for Holland, later the Netherlands more generally, the Batavi having been a tribe, first recognized by the Romans, who inhabited a muddily fertile peninsula between the Rhine and the Waal, some few miles south of what is now the city of Utrecht.

One of the world's first corporate logos, that of Holland's *Vereenigde Oost-Indische Compagnie.*

There had in fact been a village beside the muddy seepings of the Ciliwung River long before the men of the VOC had planted their corporate flag with its distinctive logo (one of the world's first ever, used on colonial coins and public buildings too) beside their silk and spice warehouses. What would be known as Batavia until the Dutch were compelled to leave it in 1949 had hitherto been known by its more appropriately Javanese name, Jayakarta, which meant 'victorious and prosperous'. In 1949, as capital of the newly independent Indonesia, the city reverted to what its new leaders thought of as its happily suitable old name, though they modernized it a little to today's *Jakarta.* There are many, and not simply elderly Dutchmen of nostalgic temperament, who still think Batavia a sweeter sound.

And generally speaking old Batavia was, outwardly at least, and for much of its history, a very much sweeter place than now. Today more than seventeen million people cluster around the Ciliwung's long-cemented and mostly vanished river banks, clambering and jostling and polluting in the kind of cheerful huggermugger mayhem that marks many a modern Asian city. Jakarta is not at all a pretty place, and for a visitor stuck stickily in an interminable traffic jam, between gaudy hotels, gimcrack office blocks and tarpaper shanties, it is difficult to imagine it ever enjoying a queenly status or ever having been a favoured place for posting or employment.

But though Batavia has had more than her share of urban wretchedness, there was a golden era, most especially so around the time that Krakatoa exploded, when it was very much a queen among cities, and a place for which many felt great fondness.

Less so, however, during those formative, early Company

years, when the VOC was feeling its way into the East. The first settlers were by and large rather frightened men, understandably bewildered by the environment they found themselves in, and not at all sure whether they were in Batavia to lay the foundations of a great city, or simply to build a hasty confection of a town that could serve as Company headquarters, while somewhere more agreeable was waiting to be discovered.

They did their best, however, to turn the sultry and fetid estuary that Jan Pieterszoon Coen had chosen as his base into somewhere that might remind them, at least a little, of their home. They built their fortress, a prison, an armoury, a treasury, a Protestant church and a modest palace for their governor-general* on a sandspit out in the roads. With quiet and deliberate speed, all of this complex became landlocked, as more and more of the lagoon was dredged, more and more real estate was reclaimed, and more and more houses were thrown up around it.

A network of narrow streets (Amsterdam-straat, Utrecht-straat) and sixteen canals (the evocatively named DeLeeuwinen-gracht, Bacharachtsgracht and Stadsbinnengracht among them) was then built in the jungle. The canals in particular, lined with flowering tamarind trees, were also intended to remind the settlers of home; but in fact, since local crocodiles got into the disagreeable habit of sauntering carelessly along them and poking their noses into the residents' doorways, the gesture had for a while rather the opposite effect.

Across the Ciliwung River, which was straightened and given high earthen embankments, an engineer constructed a classic Dutch drawbridge: the kind of double-sided bridge with struts and wires and T-shaped wooden beams that is still found spanning the canals in Amsterdam today, but of which the most famous is

---

* The governor-general soon took on airs: he used to walk around town with an umbrella-carrier, a dozen halberdiers and a detachment of sentries armed with muskets.

actually at Arles in southern France, because a homesick Vincent
van Gogh had painted the specimen there. The very first Batavia
bridge still exists: it is called Hoenderpasarbrug – the 'Chicken
Market Bridge' – and is one of the more powerful reminders, of
only a very few that have survived, that the Dutch did ever hold
sway over this bustling modern city. In some evening lights, if
one can forget the sight and sound of the choking traffic, there is
a touch of Rembrandt to the scene, a hint of van Gogh among the
diesel fumes.

Because the early Dutch were petrified of attacks from the Javanese – from the often hostile sultan of Banten near by and his
opposite number at Mataram in the island's centre – they also
built themselves a wall. They did so at least in part because there
was a particular fear abroad, especially among some of those
Dutchmen who knew a little of the ways of India, Malaya and
Arabia, that they were at risk of being murdered in their beds by
fanatical Muslims. But, as it turned out, the Dutch in Java had
precious little cause to be so apprehensive.

The Javanese sultans were indeed Muslims, as were their
followers; and if Islamic orthodoxy was being strictly obeyed,
then they were men who were perhaps in theory likely to be
ill-disposed towards the pale-skinned infidel invaders. But here
the theory simply did not apply. In the seventeenth and eighteenth
centuries, at the very time the Dutch were arriving and setting
up colonial camp, the old orthodoxies of Islam were hardly being
obeyed at all. The faraway mullahs of Araby were not being
heeded. Nor were their teachings: a home-grown, locally brewed
version of the creed was proving immensely more popular.

The Islam that had swept so furiously through Sumatra and Java
in the fifteenth century had evolved, rather swiftly, into a gentler
amalgam of beliefs and passions, and become very different from
the rigorous pursuits of the desert-dried Arabs. Here in Java, in
particular, on an island in the lush and fecund tropics, a place where

there was colour and gaiety and a tradition of vibrant animist religions and curious and long-revered local gods, and where sex was *fun*, and girls went half naked and were unlikely ever to wish to veil themselves, Islam took on a very different form. One of the great scholars of the period, Snouck Hurgronje, observed in an essay written in 1906 that the Javanese 'render in a purely formal manner due homage to the institutions ordained of Allah, which are everywhere as sincerely received in theory as they are ill-observed in practice'. Java, in short, was a place where Islam was amiably syncretic, more or less well disposed to everyone – whether a Christian from Europe, a Hindu from the Malabar Coast, or a Buddhist Chinese from Amoy – who happened by.

Very much later – indeed, at about the exact time of the Krakatoa eruption in the late nineteenth century – this was all to change. Orthodox Islam, its revival in part triggered by tragic events such as the great cataclysm, was totally transformed in Java during the nineteenth century, with fundamentalism, militancy and profound hostility to non-Muslims its watchwords. But that was later. At the time of the building of early Batavia, the Dutch had little reason to be fearful of the Javanese *as Muslims*. They had other reasons to be uncertain, true; but it was not the thought of a *fatwah* or a *jihad* that made most of them jumpy. They built their fortress Batavia for more mundane reasons, bowing to the kind of unspoken fears such as anyone camped in an unfamiliar jungle might experience, and that might prompt him to mount a picket, light a bonfire or be ready with a gun. Or to construct a wall.

At first the Dutch created a series of high wooden palisades around their little town; but after thirty years of growing insecurity the governor-general agreed to raise funds to enclose an area of about a mile square within a formidable laager of stone. In some places this was simply provided by the massive outer walls of the dockside spice warehouses; elsewhere sappers built a twelve-foot-high masonry structure, with embrasures, barbicans, donjons, battlements, a moat and a sentry-walk. Beyond it stretched the jungles, hot, dense, soggy and ever hostile, alive with animals: the tiger and the panther, the tapir and the one-horned rhino, black apes and giant rats, a range of giant pythons and venomous cobras together with a gaudy wealth of cockatoos, parrots and birds of paradise.

Inside the walls grew up the curiously compounded population of this quintessentially Company town. Dutchmen were at first reluctant to come – the 'scum of the earth', complained Coen, were the ones who wanted to settle – and in the early years only a vanishingly small number of Dutch women appeared on the scene. In fact there were so few females that Coen was forced to appeal to Holland: 'Everyone knows that the male sex cannot exist without women ... if your Excellencies cannot get any honest married people, do not neglect to send underage young girls: thus do we hope to do better than with older women.'

At first only Company servants from the other Asian outposts of the VOC would deign to work in Batavia: Company employees, their slaves (for slavery, usually of men from faraway islands or from elsewhere in Asia, was permitted, and was extraordinarily widespread in the early years of Dutch rule in the East), a motley garrison of soldiers (with troops from as far away as Japan and the Philippines brought to do guard-duty under their bewildered Dutch officers), and, on occasion outnumbering everyone else, a very large number of Chinese.

There had been Chinese in Java long before the Dutch, long before the Portuguese. Along with squadrons of coolies hired to perform the hard work, scores of Chinese merchants had sailed down from the southern ports of Fujian province and set up a prosperous agriculture on the Javan shore. They cultivated sugar and made gallons of the coco-palm toddies and rice-and-jaggery arracks that so beguiled (and rendered happily insensible) genera-tions of visiting Western sailors.

Coen immediately spotted their usefulness. He insisted they

Vlechten van Hoeden.

A milliner weaves topis and bonnets from alang-alang grass, the better to keep off the sun and the flies.

stay and become part of his new community – offering them (unlike his fellow Dutchmen) the right to trade privately, and to take pepper and birds' nests and sea-cucumbers, all of which were readily available in Java, back to their homes across the South China Sea without interference from the monopoly of the Company. 'They are an uncommonly clever, courteous, industrious and obliging people,' wrote one of Coen's colleagues. 'There is nothing you can imagine that they do not undertake and practise . . . Many keep eating-houses or tea-houses . . . or earn money fishing or carrying or conveying people.' It has been 400 years since this was written. So far as the impression offered by the diaspora of overseas Chinese is concerned, very little seems to have changed.

Slowly the community was born and struggled to its feet, matured and began to grow. At first no Javanese were allowed to live within the city walls – and no Javanese were employed as slaves, lest they band together and conspire against the Dutch. But by the middle of the seventeenth century the ban had been relaxed somewhat, and a census in 1673 records the presence within the walls of 27,000 inhabitants, of whom 1,300 were classed as 'Moors and Javanese'. Two thousand were Dutch, nearly 3,000 Chinese and 5,000 were members of a curious group called *Mardijkers*, who were Portuguese-speaking Asians, most of them freed slaves from Malacca and India who had been converted to Protestant Christianity.* The result was that Batavia had a cosmopolitan air of the most exotic stripe: there were turbaned Macasserese and long-haired Ambonese, Chinese with festoons of black queues, Balinese Hindus, 'black Portuguese' vegetable hawkers, Moors from Kerala, Tamils, Burmese, a few soldiers from Japan. And overseeing them all, with the haughty disdain that is born of vague fear, were the stout and pale-skinned burghers from Holland and Zeeland and Friesland and elsewhere in the flat and cold European north.

And then there were the others, now nearly 16,000 of this counted population of 1673, the slaves. Their use (which remained legal until abolition in 1860†) made life exquisitely comfortable for some. Since no one would risk having slaves from Java, they had to be brought in by ship from elsewhere – an efficient process, one slave-pedlar complained, after noting that of a consignment of 250 slaves sent down to him from the Arakan hills of Burma, only 114 had been delivered. And some slaves did flee over the

---

* And who under the peculiar rules of the VOC were, as Christians, permitted to wear hats: the only non-whites in Batavia allowed to do so.
† When slavery was abolished in the Dutch East Indies it was still widespread in America. Indeed the final slave ship, the *Clothilde*, had arrived in Alabama's Mobile Bay with her grim cargo only a few months before.

city wall, gathered into gangs that lived in the jungle and raided parties of wandering Dutch; one, a Balinese named Surapati, had a band of rogues so large and powerful he formed his own fiefdom in east Java, which was ruled as an independent state for more than a century.

The wealthier Europeans in seventeenth-century Batavia might own a hundred or more slaves, and the town's main slave-market was from the beginning a bustling, crowded place. These Malays, Indians, Burmese and Balinese workers were trained to occupy the tiniest of niches in the household labour structure – advertisements spoke of a need for lamplighters, coachmen, pageboys, tea-makers, bakers, seamstresses and, most specialized of all, makers of a spicy side-dish known as *sambal*.

The ladies' maid-slaves would be put to work as masseuses or hairdressers; these girls were skilled in fashioning hair into the bun-shaped style known as the *conde*, much favoured in the salons of the time. Since they were so plentiful and so cheap, slaves frequently had little to do and sat around gambling their days away. But if they ever tried to escape, or, worse, if they ran *amok* – the word is Malay for a state of frenzy and was used as a legal term in the VOC courts – punishment was severe: they could be whipped or imprisoned. A Dutchman who shot one of his slaves dead and injured three others was merely told to leave Batavia, and not to do any further business with the VOC for the rest of his days.

Though the townsfolk in those closing years of the seventeenth century did not yet know it, their neighbour island of Krakatoa was itself also, and for the first time within their sight, about to run amok.

No one had yet noticed that the island in the Sunda Strait had any potential for trouble. None of the navigators who had passed northwards into the Java Sea and gazed, as seamen do, at the island with the 'pointed mountain' on their port beam had supposed that one day it might do something quite terrifyingly

and world-shatteringly dramatic. They, like the citizens of their
destination-city, were blissful in their ignorance of the tectonic
complications then beginning to unravel many miles beneath
their feet. They carried on instead with the serious business of
colonial life, with a magnificent insouciance that was to be their
motif for the next two centuries – right up to the moment of the
cataclysm that engulfed their lives when the tiny parrot-filled
and palm-covered island finally went mad.

But on the eve of this first recorded volcanic throat-clearing,
life for the European men and women who lived eighty-three
miles east in Batavia had assumed an atmosphere of near-settled
urbanity. Perhaps the frantic gaiety that would characterize life in
the nineteenth century was not yet apparent: seventeenth-century
eve-of-eruption life tended to the more formal, strict, luxurious
and, at times, terrifyingly cruel.

The buildings that were being constructed in mid century were
by now quite substantial affairs. The warehouses were massive
with teak and mahogany. The grand mansions along the Jacatra
Weg that were built for the pepper planters and ship-dealers,
with their ornate wrought-iron gates, their gilded carvings and
delft tiles, moved an otherwise forgotten Mr Speenhoff to song:

> At long last I enjoyed myself
> Outside Batavia
> Along the green heather
> On the Jaketra road.

And the great Town Hall was first built during this rather sedate
and pompous period:* a cupola, shutters, columns and the porte
cochère all part of the standard architecture of the East.

This building served a myriad of functions: the magistrates'
bench was here, licences were issued, slaves were freed, ships

* The third and present incarnation of the Batavia Stadhuis, built in 1707,
remains intact, serving as the Jakarta History Museum.

were sold. On the cobbled square outside was a set of stocks, with miscreants frequently seen locked into them. Inside and below ground there were dungeons, and many are the stories of how the VOC security officers, who ran their Company town with a ferocious rectitude, resorted to torture to extract confessions. A visiting German soldier named Christopher Schweitzer wrote an account of the harshness he saw:

The 29th. Four Seamen were publicly Beheaded at Batavia (which is here the common Death of Criminals) for having killed a Chinese. At the same time, six Slaves that had Murthered their master in the night were broke upon the Wheel. A Mulatto (as they call those that are betwixt a Black-a-Moor and a White) was Hang'd for Theft. Eight other Seamen were Whipt for Stealing, and running away, and were besides this Burnt on the Shoulder with the Arms of the East India Company. Two Dutch Soldiers that had absented themselves from the Guard two days, ran the Gauntlet. A Dutch Schoolmaster's Wife that was caught in Bed with another Man (it being her frequent Practice) was put in the Pillory, and Condemn'd to 12 years Imprisonment in the Spinhuys, the women's prison.

Christopher Schweitzer's account is dated 1676. It is suggestive of a certain public unhappiness, of a draconian degree of Dutch response, of a current of distemper in the land.

And then, four years later, with the situation between rulers and ruled still uneasy, Krakatoa very noisily awakened its slumbering self. It was an event that astonished and perhaps even briefly terrified the new European arrivals. Yet most Javanese, long immersed in a balm of myth and legend relating to their volcanoes, would later say that with all the evident unhappiness abroad, they could have seen it coming.

Orang Alijeh, the Javan god and mountain ghost whose task is to superintend the emissions of smoke and fire into the eastern heavens, is said to breathe sulphur from his nostrils when all is less than well on his earthly dominions. Krakatoa, which, along with Tambora and Merapi and Merbapu and Bromo, was one of his most potent mountains, had been blessedly quiet, or comparatively so,* for at least the previous 1,200 years. The only event that some might say had taken place to tax his patience was that foreigners, white men from far away, had now come by sea to rule over the people of Java. This, not a few Javan mystics liked to say, was one of the reasons why volcanoes occasionally made their fire, the more forcefully to display the degree of Orang Alijeh's grave displeasure.

Yet, however displeased Alijeh might have been, what followed was by all accounts not the greatest of pyrotechnic performances. And no one who witnessed what happened ever came forward to write a first-person account. All we know comes essentially from one man, a Dutch silver assayer from the western Sumatran mining town of Salida, named Johan Vilhelm Vogel.

Vogel, who was said to be so 'pious and studious a servant of the Compagnie' that he eventually became mayor of Salida, first passed Krakatoa in the usual way en route from Holland to Batavia – thus with the island to his port side – aboard the long-range packet *Hollandsche Thuyn* in June 1679. He waited ten weeks in town, then left Batavia for Sumatra in September aboard the yacht *Wapen van ter Gos*, this time Krakatoa passing by to starboard. He saw nothing that struck him as remarkable.

But then in due course he fell ill. The Company, sedulous in caring for their more valuable employees, ordered him to visit their doctors in Batavia, and he left the Sumatran port of Padang in January 1681 aboard the yacht *de Zijp*. This time the Krakatoa he saw presented a very different aspect.

---

* Evidence both geological (fresh lava flows on the island) and anecdotal (references in Javanese oral histories) suggests that Krakatoa had erupted as many as ten times prior to whatever happened in 1680. Few of the dates of these previous eruptions can be pinned down with any certainty.

I saw with amazement that the island Cracketovv, on my first trip to Sumatra completely green and healthy with trees, lay completely burned and barren in front of our eyes and that at four locations was throwing up large chunks of fire.

. . . the ship's Captain told me this had happened in May 1680. That time also he had made the trip from Bengal, had run into a heavy storm, and about ten miles away from the island had experienced an earthquake. This was followed by a tremendous thundering crash which had made him think that an island or otherwise a piece of land had split apart . . . He and the whole ship's population had smelled a strong and very fresh sulphur odour. Also the sailors had retrieved with water pails from the sea some very lightweight rocks, very much resembling pumice stone, which had been thrown from the island. They were scooped up as a rarity. He showed me a piece of the island. He showed me a piece of it a little larger than a fist.

By checking the port records of vessels sailing in and out of Batavia, we can see that the captain of the *de Zijp* had indeed travelled between Batavia and the port of Bengalen* in May 1680 aboard the cutter *Aardenburgh*. The story, in this respect, does thus seem to tally. If it is true, then this long-forgotten and so far anonymous sea-captain and his crew were the first Europeans ever either to see the volcano of Krakatoa erupt or to see the results of its recent eruption. The *Aardenburgh*'s log, however, has never been found; and the day-register of Batavia Castle, an official journal that records all ship movements in and out of the harbour and any pertinent comments from the vessels' various masters, is silent.

A writer named Elias Hesse then wrote a vivid account of an eruption, suggesting that it was continuing in November 1681 when he and Mayor Vogel left together aboard a Sumatra-bound

* Or he may have been on international duty, journeying to and from the British possessions in India: the record is not clear as to whether the *Aardenburgh*'s destination was Bengal or a Sumatran port named Bengalen.

ship called the *Nieuw-Middelburgh*. He first mentions passing an island he calls Zibbesie (today's Sebesi, a couple of miles north of Krakatoa) and being unable to sleep because of the crying of ghosts (which the apparently rather more sober Vogel later reported were orang-utans, 'which produce a terrible howling, often when the weather is about to change'). He continues:

then still north of the island Cracatou, which erupted about a year ago and is also uninhabited. The rising smoke column of this island can be seen from miles away; we were with our ship very close to shore and could see the trees sticking out high on the mountain, and which looked completely burned, but we could not see the fire itself.

Later the *Nieuw-Middelburgh* and its crew of company servants and miners were forced to heave to in the Sunda Strait, where they experienced heavy sea-quakes and learned of an earthquake that, Hesse reported, 'did considerable damage to the buildings of the Company'.

A close study of the records of other ships passing through the Strait at the time – and for a variety of reasons there were very many – shows no other suggestion of an eruption or earthquake in 1681. And further – the day-register has no information even in May 1680 of anything of interest having taken place in the Sunda Strait. The register reports the most mundane occurrences of city life: a tiger found outside the walls, crocodiles captured in the city streets, a comet seen in the sky, servants running amok. Yet nowhere in 1680 or 1681 is there any mention at all of an eruption on an island that was passed by scores of Company ships every week.

From this dearth of information it is perhaps fair to conclude only three things: first, that Elias Hesse was an inventive fantasist and probably made up his entire account of volcanic activity in November 1681. Second, that the silver assayer and sobersided mayor Johan Vogel was similarly afflicted, and that his suggestion

.

of seeing 'large chunks of fire' at 'four locations' on Krakatoa in February 1681 is also fictional. He did, however, probably see evidence – burned trees, barren plains of ash – that some disaster had befallen Krakatoa a while before. And third, the captain of the *de Zijp* and the *Aardenburgh* almost certainly did see something of an eruption in May 1680. But since no other passing vessel did, and since no mention was made of anything grave having occurred to the ever vigilant bureaucrats in the Castle, whatever had happened was small beer indeed, and the captain had, like many men of the sea, made the story into a considerably better one the moment he stepped ashore.

3

CLOSE ENCOUNTERS
ON THE WALLACE LINE

Southeast Asia is probably the finest natural geological laboratory in the world . . . It is a spectacular region in which the manifestations and processes of plate collision can be observed at present and in which their history is recorded. It is a region which must be understood if we are to understand mountain belts, arc development, marginal basin evolution and, more generally, the behaviour of the lithosphere in collision settings . . . Furthermore the region is developing rapidly . . .

– from the introduction to *Tectonic Evolution of Southeast Asia*, R. Hall and D. J. Blundell (eds.), London, 1996

1. Delineation

On a bleak December evening shortly before Christmas in 1857, in the severely elegant lecture theatre of what was then biology's sanctum sanctorum, the Linnean Society in Burlington House on London's Piccadilly, a young man named Philip Lutley Sclater rose to present a paper that, though all but overlooked by most biologists today, was to lead steadily to a revolution in scientific thinking about the history of the world.

Philip Sclater may have been only twenty-eight years old when he stood before the assembled worthies, but already he had won an awesome reputation. He had been to Winchester and Christ Church, Oxford, and was inordinately clever. He was unusually well travelled (Argentina, Malaysia, India, Australia and most of the states of America), and was both a superb artist and – the basis of his near-legendary reputation among his few followers today – a brilliant ornithologist.

He specialized in the exotic, the colourful, the tropical, the odd. He came to know all there was to know about the South American finch-like birds called tanagers and the country neighbours of theirs that were called ovenbirds, because they built their nests out of clay in the shape of ovens. He would write definitive books about Passeriformes, that huge class of rather less unusual perching birds; he had a lark named after him; he founded the British Ornithologists' Club and was for many years secretary of the Zoological Society of London. And he gave the name *Lemuria** to a landmass he believed (wrongly) had in Eocene times connected the Malayan peninsula with Madagascar, and on the remaining peaks of which now sits the enormous mid-Indian Ocean, British-owned and American-leased military base of Diego Garcia.

Crucially for this Krakatoa story, Philip Sclater was also a specialist in a new science that was growing apace during late

---

* Helena Blavatsky, the creator of the genial Hindu–Buddhist religion called Theosophy, seized upon Lemuria as the likely home for a people she insisted were the Third Root of Mankind. As she described them, they lacked classical beauty: they were fifteen feet tall, brown-skinned hermaphrodites with four arms, some possessing a third eye in the back of the skull. Their feet had protruding heels enabling them to walk either forward or backward, and their eyes were sited so they could see sideways.

Victorian times, and that has been called variously either bio-
geography or zoogeography. As more and more specimens of
animals, insects, plants and birds were collected, classified and
catalogued, so it became steadily more apparent that geography
had a major influence on zoology and botany – that certain living
creatures were peculiar to certain parts of the world and not
merely to certain climatic zones. One might find precisely the
same climate in Uganda and Queensland, for example, but because
Africa and Australia were so far away from each other, their
native inhabitants had developed without ever making contact
with one another. In the same way their flora and fauna were now
entirely separate, different and peculiar to each of the two places.
The polar populations are another obvious example of zoogeographical reality: polar bears and people inhabit the north, penguins
and albatrosses the south, even though the climatic environment
in each place is essentially identical.

The birth of the study of such regional differences in populations of plants and animals – of the *biota*, to use the proper if
rather unattractive word – was a natural by-product of the frenetic
pace of exploration of the time; and Dr Sclater, an explorer of the
old school, had by the middle of the nineteenth century a keenly
developed interest and expertise in the topic.

The paper he presented to the Linneans that winter's night
was on precisely this subject: 'On the General Geographical
Distribution of the Members of the Class Aves', with a particular
interest 'in the islands around New Guinea'. And Sclater offered
what to his listeners was a remarkable and startling discovery.
He had observed what seemed to be a rigid zoogeographical
distinction deep within the islands of the East Indies.

The kind of dramatic geographical variation that might be seen
on the two sides of a vast body of water – the measure of difference
between African birds and Brazilian birds, for example, separated
by the whole of the South Atlantic – might not be expected within
the continuum of an archipelago as closely knit as the East Indies.

But here, astonishingly, there was. In months of research that took him right along the 2,000-mile volcanic chain stretching from Sumatra to the Trobriand Islands, Sclater found the occurrence of a huge, unanticipated and very sudden change: the jungles in the west of the archipelago, for example, sported birds that were akin to those found in India, while those to the east of a vaguely imagined line were alive with an avian fauna that was to be found only in Australia.

Sclater had not completed enough research to be able to draw a firm demarcation line between the two populations. All he could say for certain was what he had seen. Certain birds – say, parrots – found in wild abundance in the eastern, Australian end of the archipelago were, quite literally, *rarae aves* on the western, Indian side. There are barely any parrots on Java; but there is every imaginable kind in Sulawesi, Irian and Timor. Not a single cockatoo is to be found in the west; but two entire families each of cockatoos and lories – this last a kind of parrot with a brush-like tongue – are found in the east.

Barely any thrushes are to be found on the islands to the east of Bali. In the western half of the archipelago there are woodpeckers, barbets, trogons, paradise flycatchers and paradise shrikes, minivets, blue drongoes, pheasants and jungle fowl – but none of these, just like the humble thrush, is to be found in the east. The forests of this eastern end of the chain, on the other hand, are populated uniquely with legions of showy and exotic birds that one might just as easily find in Queensland and New South Wales: honey-suckers and birds of paradise, cassowaries and emus.

Any traveller with half an eye and half an ear open will realize simply from the colours and the birdsong that something profound is going on. In making an eastward journey from Sumatra to Irian, though he may not once pass out of sight of land, the traveller will have most decidedly left one world and entered another one utterly different.

Alfred Russel Wallace.

It would be forty more years before Sclater, working then with his son, would draw a map with the formal delineation, as the pair saw it, that separated the two avian worlds. But his work, which culminated in the reading of his 1857 paper outlining but not quite delineating their meeting-place, excited the interest of a much older, bolder and less well-educated Briton who was then living in the Indies. It was Alfred Russel Wallace who came swiftly to understand that it was not simply birds who inhabited two quite different worlds: plants and animals did also. And, just like the birds, they all met – collided, even – somewhere among the maze of jungles of the myriad islands of the Dutch East Indies.

Alfred Russel Wallace – who at the time was collecting, studying and living on the spice-rich island of Ternate in a grass hut – would take the observations of this young naturalist and, adding a vast amount of information from his own observations and collections, transform them into a theory and a grand carto-graphic creation that would survive to this very day. It has a name that remains its architect's most familiar memorial: the Wallace Line.

Philip Lutley Sclater, learned, patrician and well connected, might have thought he had some vague right to have this 2,000 miles of tracery named after him, in recognition of his pioneering work on the region's bird-geography. But the honour was eventually to be given to his very much more capable successor, the lowly born, hugely tall genius from the town of Usk in south Wales, remembered today mainly for having imagined and then drawn this vast and invisible line in the sea. Mainly, but not solely: Alfred Russel* Wallace has a trench off Java named after him too, as well as a 13,300-foot peak in the Sierra Nevada, a garden in Wales, an aviary in Bristol, a bird of paradise, biology prizes in both Kansas and Australia, countless lecture theatres and university halls, and craters on both Mars and the Moon.

Whoever named a lunar crater in his honour was a man with a mordant wit, or an ear for the laboured pun. For many years Wallace had been known, perhaps more widely than anything else, as *Darwin's Moon*✝ – the lesser body that was bound by the Fates to dance in constant attendance around the orbit of the greater. For although the Wallace Line has yet some importance, and though it has a singular connection to this story of Krakatoa, any account of Wallace himself must make mention of the more important reasons for such fame as he still has – and that is that Alfred Russel Wallace, alongside Charles Darwin but always as his satellite, is the other true but largely unremembered pioneer of the science of evolution.

His birth in Usk in 1823, as the seventh child of a librarian, was into a threadbare but intellectually respectable family. He started his own life as a Leicestershire schoolteacher, but one

* The spelling was an error by Usk's Registrar of Births; Wallace also long thought, to compound the mistake, that he had been born on 8 January 1822 – it was in fact 1823.
✝ This was the title of a 1966 biography of Wallace by Amabel Williams-Ellis: well known as a Strachey, the editor of a number of science-fiction anthologies for Victor Gollancz, and the wife of the Portmeirion architect and stylish eccentric Clough Williams-Ellis.

whose life was marked from the start by passionate fascinations – in this first case, with the life and times of the *Coleoptera*, those insects with hard coverings for their flight wings that are generally and more prosaically known as beetles. He was also interested in spiritualism, and indeed rediscovered this fascination much later in his life; mercifully for the advance of science, his dabblings into what he called 'phreno-mesmerism' were suddenly nudged back towards worthier pursuits when he stumbled upon a similarly insect-captivated city lad, a hosier's son and sometime warehouse-sweeper named Henry Walter Bates.

This pair, soon inseparable, hunted, collected and catalogued beetles in every corner of Leicestershire and points beyond – with Bates publishing his first paper 'On Coleopterous Insects Frequenting Damp Places', the title telling us perhaps more about Leicestershire than about beetles.

In 1848, three years after meeting and having exhausted the coleopterous delights of the meadows and damp places of the Midlands, this pair of redoubtable young men combined what little savings they had to begin a remarkable scheme: to go off specimen collecting in the wilds of the beetle-rich, insect-rich Amazon rain forest.

For Bates it was the beginning of a lifelong love affair with what he called 'the one uniform, lofty, impervious and humid forest', a love affair that started in the remote Brazilian jungle village of Ega, 1,400 miles upriver. During the six years he lived there he collected and named no fewer than 550 new and distinct species of butterfly (at the time only sixty-six were known throughout the entire British Isles). He travelled thousands of miles in the deepest and most remote corners of the forest, and over the years became a world authority on insect mimicry; and, together with his friend Wallace, ultimately came to be an instigator of the theory of natural selection and an unalloyed supporter of Charles Darwin once *On the Origin of Species* had been published in 1859.

For Wallace, however, the journey to Amazonia was just the start of a fascination that soon ranged around the entire world, but that is most closely associated today with the region he found the richest and most intellectually satisfying: the then Dutch East Indies. Yet his interest did not properly begin until he had been severely tried and tested on his way home from Brazil: the square-rigger *Helen*, in which he was bringing home his valuable collections of Amazon specimens, caught fire and sank in mid Atlantic, and Wallace spent ten days in a longboat before being picked up near Bermuda. He wrote two books on his experiences. Darwin, who trawled through both looking for evidence to bolster his own fast-coalescing ideas on biological variation, natural selection and species origin, found them frustrating. 'Not enough facts,' he harrumphed, cruelly unaware that Wallace had lost not only his notes but his specimens, all gone down with the foundered ship.

In 1854 Wallace set off, alone, for the East Indies – the chain of islands that he, as a geographer, preferred to call the Malay Archipelago, since the thousands of islands were indeed a classic example of an archipelago, and the islands' lingua franca was, in most cases, and to a greater or lesser degree, based on Malay. His keen conviction remained, for all the eight years that he spent there, that evidence to be found in this archipelago would substantiate his two growing beliefs: that geography was highly influential in the development of biology, and that species originated by the natural selection of favoured types from within the variations of any population. He spent the better part of his life seeking to prove both points – and by and large (and in the penumbra of Charles Darwin) he succeeded magnificently.

His collecting zeal was prodigious. He sent back to London, or eventually came back with, a meticulously organized collection of no fewer than 125,660 specimens of the plants, animals, insects and birds of the islands. There were 310 mammals, a hundred reptiles, 83,000 beetles (not surprisingly), 13,000 other insects,

8,000 birds, 13,000 butterflies and 7,500 shells. His study of this
vast number of living things brought him to both of the epiphanies
that he had sought, and at almost the same moment. He suddenly
realized evolution's existence and mechanism, and he immediately
recognized the profound difference between the two basic animal
and plant populations of his chosen archipelago, and he realized
and recognized these two profundities at essentially the same
time: during what for Wallace were the seminal and intellectually
furious years of 1858 and 1859.

Wallace's sudden understanding of evolution is one of the most
romantic tales of modern science, ranking with the sudden
achievements of Archimedes and Galileo, Becquerel and Newton,
Fleming and Marie Curie. The vision came to him not in a
bathtub, or in Pisa, or on a Paddington windowsill, or under an
English apple tree – but in a grass hut on stilts, in a village on
the island of Ternate, during a bout of jungle fever. There are
not a few who believe that it is the Spice Islands, and not the
Galapagos, that one day should come to be recognized as the true
birthplace of the science of evolution.
     At the time, thousands of miles away in Kent, Charles Darwin
was working, with painstaking tardiness, on what he called his
'big book'. He knew he was on to something. He had the core of
an idea as to how and why new species evolved. He had the facts
at hand. He had collected his own beetles; he had bred pigeons;
he had observed and measured and catalogued the tens of thousands of living creatures from his years aboard HMS *Beagle*. And
he was well aware of Alfred Russel Wallace – not least because
in 1855 Wallace, then in Sarawak, wrote a paper entitled 'On the
Law which has Regulated the Introduction of New Species',
which argued that new species arise from within variations in a
population that is somehow (as he was so often seeing in the East
Indies) geographically isolated from other populations of the
same creatures. The paper presented only an incomplete theory,

Charles Darwin.

and it presented no mechanism for this introduction of new species – but it set Darwin once again to pondering, ruminating and (for which he is well known) procrastinating.

And then, just after New Year's Day in 1858, Wallace arrived in those eastern islands that the Dutch called the Moluccas (or Maluku, as they are once again today). During the intervening three years of wanderings between Sumatra and Irian he had had his full share of excitements: headhunters had severely scared him on the island of Lombok, his arms and legs had been badly infected by leeches and biting insects, he had found a ten-foot snake in the ceiling of his hut on Ambon, he had suffered from unremitting dysenteric fever, and he had contracted case after case of malaria. Indeed, it was a particularly nasty attack of this, caught when he was on a brief insect-collecting trip to Halmahera, that prompted him to go back to his little house on Ternate at the end of February. He sat and perspired and wrote and pondered and ruminated – and then, in one of those fascinating manic moments of fever-induced excitability, *he suddenly got it.*

While wondering yet again what it might be that caused the break between one species and the success of a specialized variety that would lead to the creation of a wholly new species

there suddenly flashed upon me the idea of *the survival of the fittest* –
that the individuals removed by these checks must be, on the whole,
inferior to those that survived. Then, considering the variations continually occurring in every fresh generation of animals or plants, and
the changes of climate, of food, of enemies always in progress, the
whole method of specific modification became clear to me, and in the
two hours of my fit I had thought the main points of the theory.
[*My italics.*]

Wallace wrote this account in his book *The Wonderful Century* a
long while later, which might prompt some suspicions. But any
doubts about the legitimacy of his claim to be the first to recognize
both the idea and the mechanism of evolution must be allayed by
his having immediately written a paper and dashed off a letter to
Down House – asking Darwin to forward it for possible publication to the geologist Charles Lyell, whom Wallace thought he
had better impress. It was Darwin who was impressed. The
Wallace paper was, he later said, 'a bolt from the blue'. It deeply
disturbed him. It was the very idea for which he was looking.
It provided the jolt he needed to get on and finish his *big book*.
And when he did, and the book appeared under the now-famous
title *On the Origin of Species*, Wallace's crucial references to 'the
struggle for existence' and the 'survival of the fittest' appear as
the keys to the entire mystery.

   Charles Lyell and Joseph Hooker persuaded Darwin to share
at least some of the glory with Wallace, far away, low born and
an upstart though he may have been. The formal announcement
that the puzzle at the root of the science of evolution had now
been cracked was made at the meeting of the Linnean Society on
1 July 1858: it was a joint announcement, made by the introduction of papers by Darwin and Wallace – with Darwin admitting,
somewhat lamely, that though he had had the very same idea as
Wallace some days before, he had never committed it to paper.
Procrastination had done for him.

But not, it seems, for his reputation. *Darwinism* is the accepted word, invented by Wallace and the title of one of his later books. Wallace never displayed in public a scintilla of bitterness, and contentedly and generously gave Darwin all the credit. His classic, *The Malay Archipelago* (in which Wallace tried to popularize the idea of a zoogeographical division, which so neatly coincides with the phenomenon that gives birth to Krakatoa), is dedicated to Darwin, 'to express my deep admiration for his genius and his work'. He remained loyal, almost servile – the ever revolving little moon around Darwin's glittering and far grander planet.

He did not receive a knighthood, as did so many of his more nobly born contemporaries, like Galton, Huxley, Lyell and Hooker. He did, however, become a member of the Order of Merit, which many in Britain think more worthy. His public standing then went into a long and slow decline, and outside Indonesia, where he is still well known, he has until lately been little recognized in the world.

Perhaps his spell in history's wilderness is now coming to an end. In April 2000 his grave in Dorset was refurbished;* and in November 2001 a plaque was unveiled in what is now the Royal Society's Reynolds Room, noting that a century and a half beforehand the papers of Charles Darwin and Alfred Russel Wallace had been read there, which formally set in motion a whole new science of evolutionary studies.

In recent years there have been kindly new biographies of Wallace, new studies of his contributions to science, fresh examinations of the papers of Darwin, Lyell, Hooker and all the others involved in the evolution of evolutionary thinking. There seems in consequence a growing sympathy these days for the idea that Darwin may have behaved less than fairly to the man who had the same idea as he had, and at the very same time – but who had

* With a descendant of Charles Darwin on hand to observe.

the misfortune of writing everything down almost immediately and shouting the news from the rooftops, of being less gently born and less well connected than the master of Down House, and of spending his declining years more interested in eccentric sciences, out on the fringes of respectability. To some these days, the idea that Wallace's only memorial is merely a line that passes unseen across the sea seems a melancholy insufficiency for all of his many achievements and ideas.

The Wallace Line, however invisible and however controversial (in later years, because of technical arguments among the world's community of zoogeographers), does at least have the merit of being directly relevant to both the makings and the violent unmakings of Krakatoa. It may have played only a marginal role in the development of the theory of evolution of life. But it does play, if unwittingly, a very significant part in the much newer theory of plate tectonics, the evolution of the earth.

Wallace's ideas about it were first made public at the Linnean Society on 3 November 1859 – seventeen months after the famous Linnean Society presentation on evolution and, as then, while he was 5,000 miles away from Burlington House. (He was in Ambon at the time, just back from a half-year in Sulawesi spent indulging in what he incautiously regarded as the 'capital sport' of shooting birds of paradise. He was coming under considerable pressure from his family, who had not seen him for five years, to return home. But he said he felt completely happy and at home in the islands, and was not to come back to England until 1862.) His observations of the distribution of the archipelago's immense stock of animals reflected precisely Philip Sclater's findings on the distribution of birds: the representatives of the Australian kingdom of animals lived in the more easterly islands, and the members of the Indian families to their west.

He was able to show, for example, that in the west there were apes and monkeys: there were none in either Australia or the

The Wallace Line – Australian fauna (cockatoos, kangaroos) to its east,
Indo-European thrushes, monkeys and deer to its west.

Australian-influenced eastern part of the archipelago. Flying lemurs, tigers, wolves, civets, mongooses, polecats, otters, bears, deer, cattle, sheep, tapirs, rhinoceros, elephants, squirrels, porcupines and scaly anteaters were also in the west – and these weren't native to Australia (or, it almost goes without saying, to New Zealand, which was so isolated for so long that it had no native mammals or snakes at all) or to the eastern islands.

Out in those eastern groups, though – where the cloves and nutmegs grow in wild profusion – there were all manner of animals wonderfully unfamiliar to the newcomer from Usk. These included kangaroos, opossums, wombats and the duck-billed platypus. Not an ox or a squirrel, an elephant or a tapir on any of these islands – but instead animals that raise their young in pouches, or hop, or live half in and half out of water, have webbed feet, lay eggs and suckle their young, and flightless birds, and cockatoos.

Alfred Russel Wallace enjoys such fame as he has because he observed all of this bewildering profusion with great care, noted with exactitude where each animal or bird lived – or, just as important, *did not* live – and then drew a long and sinuous line that separated these two very distinct biological regions. The line, which was announced to the Linneans in 1859 and refined in a more substantial speech in 1863, wandered in an approximately north-east to south-west direction. It began to the south of Mindanao, the most southerly of the main Philippine Islands, and snaked to the north of the oddly shaped island now known as Sulawesi, but which was then called the Celebes.* It then swept south through the Strait of Macassar, leaving Borneo on its western, Indian side, and then headed across the Java Sea to the tightest-imaginable division: the 15-mile-wide and very deep strait between the islands of Bali and Lombok.

The contrast is nowhere so abruptly exhibited as on passing from the island of Bali to that of Lombock, where the two regions are in closest proximity. In Bali we have barbets, fruit-thrushes, and woodpeckers; on passing over to Lombock these are seen no more, but we have an abundance of cockatoos, honeysuckers, and brush-turkeys, which are equally unknown in Bali and every island further west. The strait here is 15 miles wide, so that we may pass in two hours from one great division of the earth to another, differing as essentially in their animal life as Europe does from America. If we travel from Java or Borneo, to Celebes or the Moluccas, the difference is still more striking. In the first, the forests abound in monkeys of many kinds, wildcats, deer, civets and otters, and numerous varieties of squirrels are constantly met with. In the latter none of these occur; but the prehensile-tailed opossum is almost the only terrestrial animal seen, except wild pigs, which are found on all the islands, and deer (which have probably been recently introduced) in Celebes and the Moluccas.

What Wallace realized well at the time was that the reason these two biological regions had so nearly merged and yet had

---

* At my school we were more than familiar with at least the shape of the Celebes, since its long, finger-like upper peninsula runs almost exactly along the equator, and thus provided us (as did Belém, at the mouth of the Amazon on the other side of the planet) with an easy way of drawing the line of zero latitude on to any blank map of the world.

remained so distinct was entirely due to geology. 'Facts such as these can only be explained by a bold acceptance of vast changes in the surface of the earth,' he writes, and goes on to speak of a 'great Pacific continent' that had 'probably existed at a much earlier period'. He talks vaguely of submergences and break-ups of masses of land into islands, and other devices that may have caused animals to have existed in isolation and then to have become near, but separated, neighbours.

Four years later, when he presented a much longer paper on the same topic, Wallace was clearly excited, trembling on the brink of a bold new idea.

The nature of the contrast between these two great divisions of the Malay Archipelago could best be understood, he might have said to himself, by considering what would take place if any two of the primary divisions of the earth were brought into equally close contact. Africa and South America, for example, differ very greatly in all their animal forms. On the African side, we have baboons, lions, elephants, buffaloes and giraffes; on the other, American side, spider-monkeys, pumas, tapirs, anteaters and sloths; while among birds, the hornbills, turacos, orioles and honey-suckers of Africa contrast strongly with the toucans, macaws, chatterers and humming-birds of America.

But, he continued to suppose, let us endeavour to imagine that a slow upheaval of the bed of the southern Atlantic takes place, and that earthquake-shocks and volcanic activity on the land-masses on each side of the ocean cause increased volumes of sediment to be poured down the rivers, such that the two contin-ents gradually spread out by the addition of newly formed lands. As a result of these two slow processes, he went on, the Atlantic, which now separates Africa and South America with its thousands of unbridgeable miles of water, would be reduced to an arm of the sea no more than a few hundred miles wide. At the same time we may suppose islands to be upheaved in mid channel; and, as the subterranean forces varied in intensity and shifted their points

of greatest action, these islands would sometimes become connected with the land on one side or the other of the strait, and at
other times be separated from it. The barrier of the ocean all of a
sudden would cease to be a barrier at all . . .

He was floundering here, becoming nervous and stutteringly
prolix, knowing only that somehow he was on the verge of
something, some explanation, some answer to the question posed
by all he had seen. Yes, indeed – some geological process, some
series of events that had something inexplicable to do with movement and submergence and upheaval and spreading and uplift
and earthquakes and volcanoes (for he was a keen and sometimes
very frightened observer of these in his beloved archipelago), had
caused this curious avian and zoological division. But as to what:
we can almost see Wallace dabbing the perspiration from his
brow, as he omits to follow through, as his thinking draws to a
halt, as he fails to come up with the solution, well aware none the
less that the answer he seeks is out there, but has proven too
elusive for him, this time around.

What Wallace was never to realize was that the mechanism
driving all the geology was, in due course, going to be recognized
as the then entirely unimaginable process of plate tectonics. And
of what he had not the least inkling was that the tectonic collision
that had brought his animals and birds together, brought the
cockatoo so close to being snared by the squirrel, and the retro-
mingent tapir so near to encountering the web-footed monotreme
more familiarly known as the platypus, was the selfsame collision
that had brought about Indonesia's reputation as the volcanic
cockpit of the world, with its notoriously dangerous volcano,
Krakatoa, a classic of the kind.

Alfred Russel Wallace knew none of this. But his papers, discoveries and still surviving Line prompted others to begin thinking and pondering too, and to start asking why this encounter
between the animals and birds of Asia and the animals and birds

of Australia might have happened and, much more importantly, since it evidently *had* happened, just how?

The scientific world of the time was in the midst of a terrible ferment, with discoveries and realizations coming at an unseemly rate. To many in the ranks of the conservative and the devout, the new theories of geology and biology were delivering a series of hammer-blows to mankind's own self-regard. Geologists in particular seemed to have gone berserk, to have thrown off all sense of proper obeisance to their Maker.

Men like James Hutton, Charles Lyell and William Smith were fast beginning to suppose that man's existence was, in the grand scheme of the very things that they were delineating, of utter insignificance, his sojourn on the planet temporary and vanishingly brief. Darwin's discoveries (along with those of Wallace, naturally – these very brackets serving to remind us how simple it still is to overlook the dyer's son from Usk) had overturned so much of man's own certainty about his own beginnings. And now, thanks to Wallace's other discoveries in Celebes and Borneo, in Lombok and Bali, the certainties about the very immobile and unyielding solidity of the world itself were being challenged.

Such a series of hammer-blows! Mankind, it seemed, was now suddenly really rather – dare one say it? – insignificant. He may not after all have been, as he had eternally supposed, specially created. The Book of Genesis, believed by so many to be Holy Writ, was perhaps no more than the stuff of myth and ancient legend. And now even the continents themselves, long supposed to be the most reliable and unshifting bedrock of our very existence, had become mobile.

The earth's surface, said this new breed of seers and iconoclasts, was shifting and unstable. The world was not rock-solid at all. Such musings among the scientists were seen variously as dangerous, unsettling, ungodly and evil – and small wonder, after so many centuries of man having been comforted by the certainties

of simpler beliefs. It was a bold man indeed who would now pose
further questions about such matters head-on.

One man who did take the great risk of placing his ponderings
on paper, and who came up with what to many was a highly unwelcome answer (and who suffered mightily as a result) was
Alfred Lothar Wegener.

2. Disputation

Alfred Wegener was German, an Arctic explorer, a meteorologist,* pipe-smoking, taciturn, tenacious – once described simply
as 'the quiet man with a charming smile'. But the theory he
advanced in a book published in 1915 made certain that he became
famous – though for the heresy for which he was famed he was
vilified and, most cruelly, denied his deserved academic reward.
And when he died, at the very early age of fifty, he was a figure
of notoriety and ridicule. Only in the last few decades has the
wheel come full circle, and has Alfred Wegener come to be
regarded as one of the most prescient figures of twentieth-century
science.

The problem that led to Wegener's personal trials was the
very virtue that gave him the insight. He was a generalist,
interested in everything, content to step outside the perimeters
of his chosen science – meteorology – and to dabble in the wide
variety of other unrelated sciences that fascinated him. Scientific
specialists, who still today guard jealously their own fields of
research, attacked him roundly for daring to invade their territories – and never more so than in 1915, when he first published,

* He is memorialized by the names of two rare ice-crystal halo arcs and by
the magnificent eponym of the *Wegener-Bergeron-Findeisen procedure*, the
mechanism that creates the peculiar shape of raindrops, which Wegener
helped to discover.

Alfred Lothar Wegener.

in German, his now-famous book *The Origin of the Continents and Oceans.* In it he used a phrase that was to make him especially notorious: *die Verschiebung der Kontinente*, which translates literally as *continental displacement*, but which by 1926, when it made its first recorded entry into the English language, has transmogrified into what is today's more familiar phrase: *continental drift.*

Wegener's roving attention had first been attracted by a simple Mercator map of the world. He noticed, in a cursory glance that bred a sudden revelation, something that seems perfectly obvious today. He wrote a hurried note to his fiancée: the coastlines of Africa and South America are such – with the huge eastward convexity of Brazil so alluringly similar to the immense eastward concavity between Nigeria and Angola – that *they seem to fit.* Might

it not be, Wegener wondered, that once in some incalculable past
the two continents had actually been joined together? And further
– might it not be possible, since they had been joined and no
longer were, that they had in subsequent years slipped, shifted –
nay, *drifted* – apart?

Others had noticed the congruency of Africa and South
America too – indeed, they would have been blind not to.* The
difference was that only Wegener, a trained planetary astronomer
then working as a weather forecaster, had the temerity to take
the notion and look further. He still had his work to do: he went
on a series of expeditions to Greenland (an island so wonderfully
complicated and instructive that it appears all too often in the
stories of geology and geologists); he flew in balloons† to check
upper-atmosphere jet-streams; he set dozens of high-flying kites
to study the polar weather phenomena.

But though the climate and the atmosphere fascinated him, the
idea that the continents below might have somehow moved was
fast becoming an obsession. He looked for support for the idea.
He examined carefully the observations of other scientists and
the conclusions of their fields – he looked at geology, at palaeon-

---

* Francis Bacon, the philosopher, wrote about the 'fit' as far back as 1620;
the great French naturalist the Comte de Buffon, author of a majestic
36-volume *Natural History*, a pioneering palaeontologist who suggested
that geological history had developed in a series of identifiable stages,
speculated on the reason in 1778; and in 1858 a noted catastrophist named
Antonio Snider-Pellagrini went so far as to propose that a single continent
had once existed and then broken up, its parts torn away from one another
to create today's arrangement. Eduard Seuss, an Austrian, posited the
existence of a Gondwanaland in 1885 – but to create the oceans he imagined
sinking and foundering, not creeping and drifting. An American geologist
named Frank Taylor wrote in 1908 about the likelihood of continents
inching towards the equator. But few of these men are now remembered
for their geology; and Wegener was soon to be rudely rebuffed for his.
† For a while he and his brother Kurt held the world hot-air balloon
endurance record, at 56 hours.

tology, at palaeoclimatology and (most importantly for this story) at Sclater's and Wallace's new-fangled zoogeography and bio-geography. He wanted to see if there was any hard evidence to back his idea that continents had somehow moved from their initial positions to where they are now.

And he found plenty, some of it hard and convincing, some of it circumstantial and tempting, much of it vague and alluring. The easier evidence comprised those existing mountain ranges, coal deposits and fossil appearances that were to be found on the far sides of the oceans, right across from the obvious 'fits': when maps of the continents were pushed together to fit properly. Then the ranges and the outcrops of exploitable minerals and the lines of ammonites and trilobites and skeins of graptolitic shales themselves also slotted together perfectly, like pieces of a gigantic jigsaw puzzle.

To deal with drifting continents where there was no obvious visible fit, instances of which were much more numerous, Weg-ener found it simpler to work backwards. He drew maps of the world's surface as he surmised it might once have been – and then looked to see if there were geological, climatic or biological evidence of possible 'fits' that would back him up.

He created charts based on notions put about by earlier theor-ists. There had once been a great southern continent, Gondwana-land (first named by Eduard Seuss in 1885), and an equally great northern continent, Laurasia, and the pair had been separated by a great sea, the Tethyan Ocean. According to these early theorists the Tethys had originated by way of continental sinking – an ever popular explanation for all manner of earthly mysteries, and which of course remained the basis for such enduring myths as the vanishing of Atlantis.

Wegener plotted on to images of these supercontinents and superseas the fossil evidence of a number of well-known and easily identifiable past events, like the great Permo-Carboniferous Ice Age. Amazingly, the fossil trails, which were so broken and

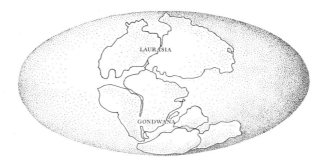

Pangaea is here beginning its division into Laurasia and Gondwanaland,
with the Tethyan Ocean slowly opening up between the two giant
supercontinents, from which all the present-day smaller continental
bodies were born.

discontinuous and almost randomly scattered across the continents today, joined up when the continents were theoretically
pushed together, and huddled around what looked like what once
was the world's 300-million-year-old South Pole.

It all began to look very compelling, with more than enough
evidence of later fossilized events to allow Wegener to follow the
tracks that the chunks of continental crust must have taken across
the surface of the globe to their present positions. Gondwanaland,
for example, could be seen breaking up into the massive bodies
that would in due course become Africa, Antarctica, South
America, Australia, with the peninsulas of India and Arabia
floating off into their own separate existences from within it:
Wegener was able to plot how the fragments moved, when they
moved, where they ended up at different times in the geological
past.

Laurasia had exploded too, fragmenting into wandering lumps
that had the vague appearance of North America, Greenland,
Europe and that part of Asia that today lies north of the Hima-
layan Mountains. Wegener was able also to suggest the paths of
their various intercontinental excursions, and nudge them into
their present shapes and dispositions.

The more that this modest, tweedy weatherman thought and theorized, the more it seemed probable to him that the two early continents of Laurasia and Gondwanaland had themselves in fact been one. This single Ur-continent came to be called Pangaea (though Wegener, who was credited with its invention, never actually used the word: the very Nordic term Pangäa appears in a later edition of his book, though it is not at all clear that he coined this either. The first use of the word comes in a 1924 translation of Wegener's book, by a man named Skerl). Pangaea had then broken apart in some giant mitosis, the Tethyan Ocean had swept in between the superfragments that resulted – and then many tens of millions of years later these two smaller bodies had broken up as well, eventually giving us the world we know and recognize today.

'One day a man visited me whose fine features and penetrating blue-grey eyes I was unable to forget,' the great German geologist Hans Cloos later recalled of his first meeting with Wegener. 'He spun out an extremely strange train of thought about the structure of the Earth and asked me whether I would be willing to help him with geological facts and concepts.' Such was the beginning of Wegener's attempts to get his idea accepted. It was a battle he fought long, and ultimately in vain. The world was simply not ready to accept that its surface moved with such immense drama.

Hans Cloos, who was himself to become a grandee of fundamental geology, with papers on the physics of faulting and the deep-seated deformations of granites, was kindly and sympathetic – though never entirely convinced. Wegener's theory, he wrote, 'placed an easily comprehensible, tremendously exciting structure of ideas upon a solid foundation. It released the continents from the Earth's core and transformed them into icebergs of gneiss on a sea of basalt. It let them float and drift, break apart and converge. Where they broke away, cracks, rifts, trenches remain; where they collided, ranges of folded mountains appear.' It was tempting to believe it – but it was not a temptation to which Cloos, thus far inhabiting a comprehensively proofless world, was quite prepared to yield.

The rest of the academic community was implacably hostile, almost to a man. 'Utter, damned rot!' said the president of the American Philosophical Society. 'If we are to believe this hypothesis we must forget everything we learned in the last seventy years and start all over again,' remarked Thomas Chamberlin, a towering figure in American geology, on hearing Wegener speak in New York in 1923. 'Anyone who valued his reputation for scientific sanity,' said a British geologist, at the same time, when Wegener's ideas were being given wide airing, 'would never dare support such a theory.'

Harold Jeffreys, a giant among early geophysicists, denounced Wegener with indignation and scorn: however powerful the forces that might be brought to bear beneath the earth's crust, none could be sufficiently strong to move it. And what of all the suggestive evidence of the Permo-Carboniferous Ice Age cluster, neatly arranged around Gondwanaland's South Pole – perhaps the strongest piece of evidence that Alfred Wegener had? Mere 'geopoetry', they said, the stuff of little more than idle fantasy.

And so Wegener was pushed out into the cold, like a querulous customer in a bar-room of rowdies. Not a single German university would give him the professorship that his otherwise impeccable pedigree deserved; it was left to the University of Graz, in Austria, to offer him only the chair in meteorology. He was obliged to stand away from the geology that was the business of others.

Alfred Wegener died young, quite convinced that he was right, but with the world beyond equally convinced that he was wrong. His ideas, it was almost universally agreed, were the results of bad science at best, wishful thinking at worst.

He died in his beloved Greenland, contentedly engaged with the problems of what the weather was doing above the earth, rather than worrying over the complex strangulations of what might have happened below. He had helped set up an observation camp 250 miles inland, high up on the ice-cap, to study yet again the Byzantine wonder of the polar climate. He was said by his companions at the time to be deeply happy, blissfully unworried by the firestorm he had ignited among the academic community back to the south.

It was shortly after his fiftieth birthday, on 1 November 1930, that he and his faithful Greenlander companion, Rasmus Villumsen, set off to return to the west coast. It was very cold – recorded temperatures of −58 °F – and dark; the only blessing was that the howling gales were, at least when they left the ice-camp, at their backs.

But neither man was ever seen alive again. The following May an expedition was sent out, and found Wegener's body, fully dressed, lying on a reindeer skin in a sleeping bag. His blue eyes were still open, and he seemed, the expedition report noted, to be smiling. It appeared that he had died of a heart attack; his companion had seemingly pressed on for the sea, but perished in the attempt. His body was never found.

The men who found him erected a 20-foot iron cross above the nameless spot on the glacier where he died. Sometime in the fifties, when another dog-team passed by, the cross had vanished. The glacier ice had moved on and torn itself to pieces, taking Wegener's body with it.

It would be stretching a point to suggest that the ice moved in quite the way the earth did. Indeed, the mechanism for the earth's postulated crustal movement was one of the factors that Wegener did not understand, and could not fully imagine; his inability to do so was one reason why his sceptical foes were so active and effective. But in Greenland the ice moved, and yes, whether it was provable now or sometime in the future, the earth's crust surely moved too. One can almost hear Wegener, calm and pipe-smoking to the end, insisting to those around him who would not believe, and using the very words that Galileo Galilei had used to the Churchmen who had made him recant nearly three centuries before: *'Eppur si muove.'* ('You may force me to say what you wish; you may revile me for saying what I do. *But it moves'.*)

And as with Galileo, so with Alfred Wegener. Aside from the barest murmurs of dissent from groups of present-day fundamentalists, creation scientists and Flat Earthers, the entire scientific world now happily acknowledges that Wegener, whom all once thought a crank, was in essence, and in fact, quite right.

Moreover, in the particular context of this story, it turns out that the very processes that Wegener first and so bravely suggested do indeed happen to underlie, both literally and figuratively, the making and unmaking of all volcanoes − the formidably spectacular eruption of Krakatoa among them.

3. Divination

Yet it was not anywhere near a volcano − and certainly not in the steamy heat of Java or Sumatra − where Wegener's theories first came to be confirmed properly. In the 1960s hard scientific evidence decisively proving the occurrence of continental drift flooded in from a great many sources − some of the most compelling being found fully 10,000 miles and two hemispheres away from Krakatoa, and eighty years after the catastrophe that happened there. Wegener would have savoured this particular irony of geography, since it was early exploration work in the high Arctic snowfields of east Greenland where some of his ideas were first fully tested and shown to be sound.

As it happened (and by a series of strange coincidences that I was not to appreciate fully until the day many years later when I stood watching the sound and light show from Anak Krakatoa), I played a part − a very lowly part but an unforgettable one − in one of the Greenland expeditions where some of those first confirmations of continental drift were gathered in. I was lucky: I happened to be in just the right place at what science has now shown to be just the right time.

It was the summer of 1965, and I was a 21-year-old geology student at Oxford. And though I did not attach any special significance to it then, much of the unravelling of the most profound enigma of the world's volcanoes — *why do some parts of the world erupt, while the rest do not?* — started at the very same moment that I happened to win a place on a small expedition to a wild and unknown part of the east Greenland coast. While I was packing my steel crampons, shark-skinned skis and moleskin salopettes for the journey north, I had not the vaguest thought in my head that this trip might have anything to do with a tropical mountain of which I knew very little, and that lay half a world away.

From the moment I first spotted the Greenland announcement, thumbtacked on to a department noticeboard among offers of second-hand mineralogy textbooks and a former student's barely used Estwing hammer and Brunton compass, I was entranced by the thought of a summer in the cold of the far, far North. I positively yearned to go.

I had long felt a strange compulsion towards high latitudes. As a child I had been raised, quite conventionally for a Briton of my generation, on the heroic imperial stories of Scott and Shackleton, and, less conventionally, on the tall tales of even more heroic foreign figures like Fridtjof Nansen and Peter Freuchen. Much later, and thanks to the peculiar Arctic interests of my Everest-climbing Oxford professor, a tiny but physically and intellectually powerful man named Lawrence Wager, two of the most renowned of Greenland wanderers, Knud Rasmussen and Gino Watkins, became the greatest of my heroes too. Suddenly the chance of being able to take off to spend some time in their Arctic, in the wastes where they had made their names, seemed to me the most noble and romantic of ideas.

Since I had no obvious qualifications for making the team, I decided to teach myself a vaguely appropriate skill that might make me of some potential use. Morse code seemed as good a choice as any, and so I spent a fortnight learning it, and became in short order reasonably competent and fast. I then put the word around Oxford that I might in consequence have something valuable to offer. The ploy evidently worked. Shortly before the expedition was due to set off, and just as I had hoped and schemed, the leader called me for an interview, and, on hearing of my self-professed ability to tell a dot from a dash (he had me tap out the highly rhythmic code for the word 'essences' on his desktop), he signed me up. I was to go along as sled-hauler, because I was reasonably fit and strong; and I was required to add to my duties that of radio operator. Only out on the ice-cap did I discover that the team's radio was in fact set up for voice transmissions alone: there was no Morse key, nothing that would allow me to show off.

What happened that glorious high Arctic summer still remains paramount as the purest of adventures, the dream of every school-boy everywhere. Despite my having subsequently lived a life of fairly unremitting world-wandering, that two-month expedition to the Blosseville Coast, south of the great high Arctic fjord-system (the world's biggest) known as Scoresby Sund, has never once been matched. The memories of those fifty days stay with me yet.

It started with embarkation in Copenhagen, the piles of ex-pedition boxes among the coils of rope and crates of fish, the cold smell of the northern sea and the sweet-sharp aroma of Stockholm tar. It got properly under way a few days later, at the moment when, from the ice-breaker's chilly bridge-wing, we first picked out the luminous glow of the *isblink* on the north horizon of the Denmark Strait, and our little red ship began bucking and cracking her hull through the thick and wind-scoured pack-ice.

Greenland. The vast fjord-system of Scoresby Sund begins halfway up the east coast.

From then on, as we went higher and higher above the Arctic Circle, every subsequent moment, every experience, became vivid, intense, unforgettable. We landed on a remote beach on the iron-bound coast of the immense, mysterious island. We climbed, in brilliant sunshine, the ice-wall and then the crevassed length of a fast-moving, mile-wide glacier. We spent weeks camping high on the ice-cap. We rappelled down sheer walls of black basalt. We skied for scores of miles over snow where none had ever been before.

We learned to speak the Danish–Inuit linguistic blend called Greenlandic, in which the country is called Kalaallit Nunaat, 'our land', in which a snowflake is *qanik*, snow flurries *nittaalaq nalliuttiqattaartuq*, and a good forty-seven other words besides speak of snow or ice and their many varieties. We grew beards, we grew strong, we became bronzed by the perpetual midnight sun. And when the season was ending, and the dark and the cold crept in, so we would thaw our boots out each morning over the Primus stove and watch as our hot washing-water, when we tossed it into the air, fell back as a mist of perfect snowflakes.

There were problems, naturally. We ran out of supplies (except for low-temperature margarine, of which we had a good quarter of a ton), and so I – no great shot at the best of times, but the caretaker of the expedition's only rifle – had to shoot a polar bear for food. It was an aged bear, not at all tasty, and its limbs were riddled with *Planaria*, flatworm parasites that we had to tease from between its thigh muscles. The following day, entirely by chance, I followed the shooting of the bear by bringing down a goose, in flight, with another single shot. From today's perspective, all horribly incorrect things to do – except that we were keenly hungry, and there was nothing else to eat.

We then found ourselves socked in by bad weather, were delayed by two weeks, and our Danish ice-breaker had perforce to leave for Copenhagen without us. We had to risk walking for an endless day, sixty-pound boxes of precious rock samples on our backs, over a crazed sea-carpet of thin and fast-shifting ice-floes in order to reach an Eskimo settlement, and relative safety. We still needed food: we hunted musk-ox with the local men, and then dined with them on young seals, the seals' bellies opened up and filled with roasted sea-birds (to which we added from our near-depleted stores, as the most unfamiliar of condiments, bay leaves).

And we barely got home. The season was changing; the sun was setting earlier and earlier each afternoon; storms were blowing in from the north. The brave Icelandic pilot who came to collect us in a blizzard, in the near-dark, was killed the very next day, flying his Cessna into a cliff in that mythically ghastly part of north

Iceland called the Claw. When we heard the news, we had been celebrating, eating cream cakes in the Savoy in London: we slunk away to our various homes in an awful, sombre silence.

But however memorable Greenland was as an experience, it was as science that our little expedition had its greatest value.

Ours was not the only expedition of its kind. At around the same time Oxford was sending people to Spitzbergen, Arctic Canada, Finnmark and elsewhere in the Arctic, with much the same scientific aims; and other universities and institutions did likewise. There was a great curiosity, particularly among geologists, about what could be discovered in what they called *The Great White*.

What we found out – or, more precisely, what was found out by others in distant laboratories once they had examined the rock samples we brought back – helped to prove a theory that, then still young enough to need the sturdiness of proof, turns out today in its maturity and certainty to have the most profound relevance to Krakatoa and to the key story of this book.

The frigid black-and-white coast of east Greenland may be a very long way from the lushly tropical green islands west of Java. But the two places in fact have a good deal in common, geologically. They are not formed from sandstone, or from shale, or from soft layers of fossil-filled chalk. They owe their origins instead to fire and brimstone. Both Greenland and Java are volcanic places, seared and branded into place by the earth's most elemental processes. And more than that: each was made, and stands where it does on the planet's surface, thanks to the workings of a once mysterious, much derided mechanism that was initially uncovered (or, at least, more than partly confirmed) by those who examined the collections, results and observations that our trifling little expedition and others like it brought back home.

Our collecting boxes (and many that we were obliged by the foul weather to leave behind and collect the following summer

season) were filled with scores upon scores of carefully drilled
and numbered samples of the country-rock of east Greenland.
And that means volcanic rock. At the latitude where we had been
on the island's east coast, Greenland is more or less entirely
underlain by basalt – a dark-grey, fine-grained variety of volcanic
rock that was laid down in layer upon layer during Tertiary
times, thirty million years ago.

Basalt is outwardly an unremarkable rock, generally scenically
unpromising (except in its columnar variety, when it forms
beguiling spectacles like the Giant's Causeway in County Antrim,
or Fingal's Cave on Staffa). On close examination it is not at all
pretty: it does not hold a candle to decorative igneous rocks like
granite or gabbro or varieties of the more exotic porphyries; nor
does it often compete as building stone with Jurassic limestones
or Italian marble. But for the six of us trudging across the snows
that summer, charged with this very particular task, the basalts
did have one uniquely interesting feature, one that may not have
been readily apparent to the casual glance, but that was crucial
for what was then a fledgling programme of geophysical detective
work.

Cooling basalts, it turns out, contain small crystals of iron-
oxide compounds – principally of the cubic spinel mineral magnetite, Fe_3O_4 – that are highly magnetic. During the molten, plastic
phase of their cooling process these crystals tend to act as miniature compasses, swinging hither and yon in the still viscous mix,
in an elegant harmony that is extremely susceptible to the lines
of magnetic force that radiate between the earth's North and
South Poles.

Once the cooling has concluded, and the magma has passed
what is known as the Curie point and become solid (technically
frozen, though the word used here has nothing to do with the
freezing of water and snow, which takes place at a much lower
temperature), the alignment of the swarms of magnetite com-

passes becomes fixed, and is set for all time. And each, crucially, is then aligned to where the North and South Poles were at the time the rocks froze – in this east Greenland case, thirty million years ago. The compasses are thus powerful forensic tools: they tell us where the poles were in relation to the rocks, or the rocks in relation to the poles, a long, long while ago.

Our task – which had been set by a small number of curious laboratories around the world, and whose professors some months before had persuaded a variety of grant-bestowing bodies to give us sufficient money to charter the ice-breaker and buy our Nansen sleds and our pemmican and hard tack and then to set off – was to collect hundreds of samples of these basalts. If and when we

A crystal of magnetite, usually aligned with the poles along its long axis.

got them home, they would be sent off to the researchers, who would measure the strength and the direction of the relict magnetism of the iron-oxide particles contained within them. In truth the strength of the age-old magnetism only claimed their most cursory interest. It was the *direction* of magnetism that beguiled them most – and in connection with that we were asked to note very carefully indeed, while taking the samples, the way they were aligned, relative to the North and South Poles of today.

So we spent hours – day and night, bathed in the Arctic summer's continual sunshine – painstakingly drilling basalt samples out of the sheer walls of the local nunataks. We used a portable power-drill (with a diamond-studded bit that needed to

be cooled by dousing it with bucketfuls of snow) and a very
accurate sun-compass* to make sure we always knew where each
sample lay relative to the present-day poles. The selected cores,
eight inches long, two inches in diameter, were then indelibly
marked with their geological horizon (how high up each had been
found among the other layers of rock) and their sun-compass
orientation, wrapped in plastic and set aside in specially made
boxes of strong and waterproof fibreboard.

The science that required the presence of all those basalt cores
was elegantly simple and, by the standards of the present day,
somewhat mundane. The interested scientists all wanted to work
on the samples to satisfy a suspicion that had been growing during
the early sixties. This burgeoning belief was rooted in an unsay-
able, almost (in some quarters) a heretical view of the making of
the modern world, and held that the magnetic alignments of
crystals in rocks laid down in the past might, just might, be
substantially different from the alignments of the rocks themselves today. This was something that, if it could be demonstrated,
would spawn a profound revolution in contemporary geophysical
knowledge and thinking. If it were to be proved, then the unsay-
able would suddenly become something to preach, and the heresy
would, overnight, become dogma.

And that is just what happened. The rocks we brought back
did eventually (though many months later) prove essentially and
exactly what everyone wanted them to prove. A comparison of
the directions of the spinel compasses (the science of studying
such phenomena had a century before been given the hybrid

---

* This was necessary because of an added complication: the lines of magnetism in very high latitudes in northern North America (of which Greenland is, technically, a part) are so close, and vary so wildly each year, that a
normal magnetic compass is worse than useless. All fishermen and navigators working these waters know this well; we suspected it might be the
case, and decided in Oxford to obtain all our alignment readings via the one
true invariable, the position of the sun.

Greek–Latin name of *palaeomagnetism*) confirmed what a very large number of scientists suspected. There was a very considerable difference between the direction in which the Tertiary magnets were pointing and the position of the poles today. All of the millions of magnets were lined up not towards the present poles at all, but towards a point some fifteen degrees to the east of them. It was a simple realization, but it had a stunning effect.

This meant one of two things: that either the poles had moved in relation to the rocks or the rocks had shifted in relation to the poles. The first was initially the more tempting possibility, since it seemed quite simple for the North Pole, which was after all an invisible and rather mysterious entity, to have somehow shifted itself around by fifteen degrees. But the scientists who were doing the work on our rocks had an advantage, in that they knew this could not be the case. They were already performing palaeomagnetic studies on the other Arctic rocks of the same age, on samples from Spitsbergen and the Faeroes and Norway. What they found was that the computed polar positions suggested by the spinels in these rocks varied wildly – so much so that it looked not like the poles were wandering, but rather like there were scores of North Poles, all existing at the same time.

So if there was no polar wandering, then the alternative could be the only explanation. It was an explanation that proved a *Eureka moment*, a truly life-changing epiphany for many of those researchers back in the sixties. It was the realization from the record of the rocks that *the basalts of east Greenland had moved*. Somehow the basalts of east Greenland had drifted westward, through fifteen longitude degrees or so, in the thirty million years since they had been extruded from the earth.

In other words, the long-imagined (but until this moment, generally discounted) phenomenon of continental drift had – and now, moreover, provably and incontrovertibly – occurred. During Tertiary times the sea-floor beneath the Atlantic Ocean had clearly and demonstrably spread open. Now, from the Greenland basalts, there was powerful evidence to suggest that the theories of continental movement – with the world beginning as one supercontinent, Pangaea, which had then broken up and spread itself over the global surface – which Alfred Wegener had advanced so obsessively and which had been so widely dismissed by the scientific establishment during most of the half century beforehand, had at last been more or less decisively confirmed.

Later in the 1960s, and with a growing amassment of evidence like that from east Greenland now safely in the bag, a great scientific sea-change was in the offing. It first came about un-expectedly. It first came about by accident, and in a much more appropriate piece of geography, off the coast of Java, almost within sight of the island of Krakatoa. And it first came about, as sea-changes are wont to do, at sea.

There were two initial discoveries. One advanced the evidence of sea-floor spreading and the consequent drift of continents from the merely circumstantial into the happily incontrovertible. The other provided sceptics with something that Wegener had never managed to produce: the model for a mechanism that explained how spreading and drift might work.

This first came to light after a series of unrelated experiments conducted off the south coast of Java – quite properly for the present story, and particularly so in that the scientist who performed the work was a Dutchman, from Delft Technical University, by the name of Felix Vening Meinesz.

His initial intellectual interest was quite unrelated to continental drift: Vening Meinesz was solely concerned with the very accurate measurement, at various places on the globe, of the earth's gravity. He was especially concerned with the measurement of gravity in the mysterious world below the very deep oceans. Since gravity is an acceleration, it is extremely difficult to measure from something that is itself moving – like, say, a ship. So Vening

Meinesz had to try out a series of home-made and very specialized measuring devices.

Although the wholesale acceptance of continental drift was not to come about for fully forty years after Wegener's death, Vening Meinesz performed his early work while the unsung pioneer was still alive, between 1923 and 1927. He had taken a crude gravimeter, consisting of a pair of pendulums swinging in opposite directions, and mounted it on gimbals inside the most stable sea-borne vessel he could imagine, a submarine. He then had the Dutch Navy, using submarines with the somewhat unimaginative names of *Her Majesty K II* and *Her Majesty K XIII*,* perform a series of shallow dives off Java – and found to his astonishment that about 190 miles off the southern coasts of both Java and Sumatra, there was a dramatic lowering in the strength of the local gravitational field.

This enormous gravity anomaly coincided precisely with the existence of a tremendously deep and long gash in the sea-floor known as the Java Trench. To appreciate the depth of the Trench, one can imagine someone moving eastwards (driving some seabed crawling machine, if that is not straining credulity too much) two miles beneath the surface of the sea, somewhere off Christmas Island. Without warning the seabed starts to slope downwards at a gradient of 10 per cent or more. It keeps on going down, down, down – until, at the dark and ice-cold bottom of the Trench towards which the slope is heading, the sea is nearly five miles, or 24,440 feet, deep. Then, even more abruptly, the bed begins to climb back up, dipping briefly down, once, and then rising one final time clear up to the continental shelf, the shallows, the fringing reefs and finally the beaches of south Java itself. Within 200 miles of the shore are some of the deepest parts of the world ocean – and

---

* Vening Meinesz was a rather over-large person, uncomfortable in a small submarine. The captain had to remind his crew to draw in their breath every time the good doctor sat down.

directly above them, Vening Meinesz discovered, some of the lowest and weakest gravity accelerations to be found anywhere.

The Dutchman was promptly invited to the United States by a young Princeton scientist named Harry Hess; and, together with two other young men who were to go on to become rising stars in the new field, Maurice Ewing and Teddy (later to be Sir Edward) Bullard, they took off in a boat called the *Barracuda* to see if the Javan anomalies could be found above the submarine trenches known to exist in the Caribbean. They did, spectacularly so. The four excitedly discussed why this might be – with Harry Hess and Vening Meinesz openly speculating that they were caused by some mysterious force dragging the rocks of the seabed downwards and (as it were) dragging the gravity down with them. Hess wrote a seminal paper in 1939:

Recently an important new concept concerning the origins of the negative strip of gravity anomalies . . . has been set forward . . . It is based on model experiments in which . . . by means of horizontal rotating cylinders, convection currents were set up in a fluid layer beneath the 'crust' and a convection cell was formed. A down-buckle in the crust . . . was developed where two opposing currents meet and plunge downwards. So long as the currents are in operation, the down-buckle is maintained . . . the currents would have velocities in nature of one to ten centimetres a year . . .

Perhaps, at last, we had a theoretical mechanism. Perhaps there were currents below the solid surface of the planet, currents that dragged the continents along on top of them and that then plunged downwards, dragging the continents down with them. Continents might thus be moving towards or away from one another at between half an inch and four inches every year – a rate that, miraculously, was entirely consonant (once someone hurriedly did the arithmetic) with what Wegener had proposed for the break-up of Gondwanaland more than twenty years before. But this was 1939, and the world was being enveloped in a

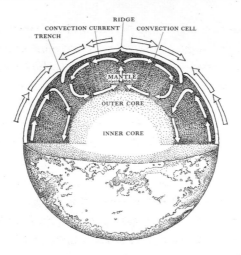

The process of convection inside the earth's mantle, the driving
mechanism behind continental drift and plate movement.

man-made turbulence of a very different kind: Harry Hess and
his bold theory would have to wait until the war was over.

But when it was over, a wholly new and unexpected piece of
evidence for crustal movement came to light – also at sea, but this
time not off Java, but off the north-western United States. And
while the first ground-breaking pre-war study had to do with
anomalies in the earth's gravitational field, this next series of
experiments had to do with a study of the earth's magnetism. More
especially, they were concerned with what was known as the remanent magnetism that might be held in the rocks of the sea-floor,
the old magnetic signatures that we later studied in east Greenland.

The pioneering work on remanent magnetism had been accom-
plished largely by an ebullient red-headed Mancunian named
Keith Runcorn. He was a lateral-thinking geophysicist who wondered out loud if perhaps the magnetic field of the earth somehow
varied over time – if it had perhaps varied in its strength or its
direction. And if it had varied, then perhaps a record of those
variations would be discoverable by examining the remanent

magnetism of rocks laid down during the time that was being
investigated.*

In the early 1950s Runcorn and his colleagues, and associates,
using a range of devices (including a sphere made of thirty-seven
pounds of pure gold, borrowed from a very sceptical British Royal
Mint), studied this fossil magnetism in a variety of rocks of a
variety of ages across Britain. The conclusion to which they came
was published in a paper in 1954. The evidence showed that there
were indeed significant variations in the magnetism held in rocks
of different geological eras, and this could really be accounted for
by only one of two happenings: either the magnetic poles were
wandering about relative to the earth's landmasses, or the earth's
landmasses were wandering about relative to the poles. The latter
was continental drift – and to Keith Runcorn it looked a most
temptingly plausible explanation.

Further compelling evidence to support this notion was soon
to come in. If the rocks on other continents showed the same
remanent magnetic evidence for a wandering of the poles, then it
was likely that yes, the poles themselves had moved. On the other
hand, if the results from continents far away from one another
were different, then it would suggest that it was not the poles
that had moved but the continents. And in 1956 that evidence
came in – showing, to the delight of people like Keith Runcorn
and Harry Hess, widely different degrees of magnetic variation.
The differences could be accounted for only by the continents
having drifted apart from one another. The noose was closing.
Wegener's theories were being resurrected, and fast.

The clincher came quite accidentally, in work that began in

* The idea of remanent magnetism was first put forward by Pierre Curie,
who discovered that rocks that are cooled in a magnetic field assume the
polarity and direction of that field as they do so. The crucial temperature
at which the magnetism is locked in (for study by later geologists) is known
as the Curie point, and varies from rock type to rock type – 582 °C for the
mineral magnetite.

August 1955, in the cold seas between America's most westerly point, Cape Mendocino in California, and the southern tip of Canada's Queen Charlotte Islands. An English geophysicist named Ron Mason, on sabbatical at Caltech, was vaguely aware of highly classified US Government research into underwater magnetism – classified, it was said, because the US Navy was looking at deep-sea hiding places for its long-range submarines.

Over coffee one morning he asked whether it might be possible for him to join Project Magnet, as it was called and, without interfering with the government work, to tow a magnetometer behind the project's ship and make his own maps of any magnetic anomalies he might find down on the sea-floor. The project director agreed: and that summer Mason arranged for a long, floating, fish-like object – known formally, in the kind of language heard in science fiction, as an ASQ-3A fluxgate magnetometer* – to be towed behind the US Coast Guard's ship *Pioneer* as it searched for seemingly more important things on behalf of the Pentagon.

Ron Mason's instruments up in the *Pioneer*'s operations room, hooked by wire to the magnetometer that was trailing behind and below the ship, recorded variations in the strength and direction of the magnetism of the seabed rocks below. The recording paper unrolling from its drum (which in due course was to be superimposed on a topographical map of the sea-floor and the Pacific coastline) indicated the data by way of an intricate trace of lines – with some of the lines showing rocks that had certain properties, and others indicating rocks that had properties that were precisely the opposite.

---

* The instrument was originally designed to be mounted in a low-flying aircraft, with the aim of detecting enemy submarines in the waters below: its acronym, MAD, indicated it was a *magnetic airborne detector*. It was easy enough to modify the instrument so that it could be towed behind a ship in the water itself, by placing it inside a fish-shaped, non-magnetic container.

The magnetic 'zebra stripes' discovered on the seabed of the
north-western Pacific in 1955, which were finally to confirm the idea
of sea-floor spreading.

As the hundreds of miles of ink traces began to plot out on the
screens, Mason could hardly believe what he was seeing. At first
the marks on the ever rolling drum seemed meaningless, no more
than a random mess of indecipherable hieroglyphs. Within a few

hours, however, the traces quite inexplicably began to display an absolutely regular, absolutely consistent pattern. As the ship cut steadily through the water, and as the floating ASQ-3A behind recorded the magnetic fields in the rocks hundreds of fathoms below, so the traces began to arrange themselves in an unmistakable pattern of parallel and linear *stripes*, just like those found on the skin of a zebra or tiger.

The stripes became more and more obvious as, month by month, the little ship worked itself steadily along its recording route. The vessel would scuttle back and forth on its preordained track, the midshipman keeping it at a steady five knots for hour after hour, as it traced and retraced its passage along the specific sector of sea-floor that Ron Mason had decided to measure. And as it did so, so the zebra-stripe pattern from the rocks below steadily built itself up – with the recording paper eventually being covered with long black-and-white patches that alternated from black to white to black and back to white again in an ever more uncannily regular manner.

All of the stripes, moreover, were not simply regular. After just a few passes of the *Pioneer*, their arrangement could be seen: they pointed not merely in parallel but essentially *only to the north and to the south*. Or, to be more accurate, they pointed along the long axis of the ocean in which they were found.

The ship might go east–west, it might go diagonally; it might reverse its voyage – but no matter. Pass after pass after pass, the magnetism in the rocks below was recorded as a series of stripes arranged in long north–south trending patterns that made the plot of the seabed look like an acrylic bed-sheet from Frederick's of Hollywood, or a herd of standing zebras or tigers, rather more exotic than it deserved to be.

And then in a flash everyone realized what it was. The stripes on the paper were noting anomalies that were a record of the reversals that had occurred from time to time in the polarity of the earth's magnetic field.

This was a curious reality that had been dimly recognized by a Frenchman named Jean Brunhes in the early part of the century, then confirmed (by a Japanese geophysicist named Motonari Matuyama) in the 1920s. He showed that there had been a field reversal during the late Pleistocene, 10,000 years ago. Thirty years later his work had been fully confirmed: basalt layers in Iceland showed a series of back-and-forth field reversals in their remanent magnetism. From then on there was no doubt about it.

The work in Iceland and elsewhere showed field reversals to be a standard (if stubbornly inexplicable) feature of the earth's magnetic field, just as can happen in any man-made self-exciting dynamo. Over the last 76 million years, the palaeomagneticists soon reckoned, there had been no fewer than 76 such reversals – and they had continued to a measurable degree right back to the early Jurassic, 150 million years ago (except for a long period between 85 and 110 million years ago when, equally inexplicably, there were no reversals at all, during what has since come to be known as the Cretaceous Quiet Zone).

And now here, at last, was evidence in black and white of reversals in the rocks' magnetic field, and moreover reversals that, when plotted on to a map, seemed to occur along regular lines, following a pattern that was imprinted indelibly on the seabed of the north-eastern Pacific. And, as more and more data was recorded and analysed, something even more astonishing was noticed: that the peculiar intricacies of the stripe pattern on one side of the ocean were almost identical to those that could be seen in the stripe patterns on the other, and that there was a point, or axis, in mid ocean, on which this symmetry seemed to hinge. In an instant the explanation for that became clear too.

The north–south trend of the magnetic stripes suggested that the rocks below were moving outwards, were on each side flowing away from this central point, just like rainwater hitting the ridge-pole of a roof, with some water then going down one side of the roof, some the other.

And the conclusion to be drawn from this turned out to be the single missing part of the mechanism for continental drift, the one that Alfred Wegener had never been able to imagine. The mid-oceanic north–south axis was a place where – presumably, logically, but suddenly somehow astonishingly – *entire tracts of brand new seabed were being created.* The mid-ocean axis was a ridge of making, where the world was welling up from inside itself and spilling out on to the floor, to be carried out and away, thus making ever more room for the making of more.

And as this brand spanking new submarine real estate was being slowly and steadily made over millions of years, and as it spread off away from the deep-sea ridge-pole both to the east and to the west, so the remanent magnetism of its rocks, with the record of the earth's polarity reversing itself every few tens of thousands of years, remained locked there on the sea-floor for all to see. By seeing this, by understanding what it was, scientists were able, at long last, to claim they had evidence of sea-floor spreading that was incontrovertible. Once radiochemical dating techniques had been perfected, then the timing of the spreading, of the making of new seabed, as well as the dating of the continental drift could all be fully established too.

Now that there was a mechanism and a date, the rest suddenly became almost too obvious. The conclusions began rushing in, filling the intellectual void that had so plagued the science for all the decades since Wegener had died forty years before.

In 1962, armed with the new evidence from the *Pioneer* and all the other armadas that dragged schools of fish-shaped magnetometers behind them,* Harry Hess decided he would revisit the nagging question that the war had so rudely interrupted. There was now solid new evidence to underpin his notion that convection

---

* And which showed, for every ocean, ridges where new sea-floor was being made, and giant rafts of magnetized rock moving steadily away from them – the Atlantic Ocean being by far the most spectacularly regular of them all.

currents were at work under the earth's crust, and that the continents were indeed being moved about upon it, like gigantic rafts, colliding and bouncing and plunging down back into the earth's molten heart, in a ceaseless supra-terrestrial dance. 'One may quibble over the details,' he wrote in a paper that year, which is now a classic,* 'but the general picture on palaeomagnetism is sufficiently compelling that it is more reasonable to accept than disregard it.' Continental drift was most assuredly taking place. There could be no doubt – and, indeed, since the publication of Harry Hess's paper, there never has been.

By curious chance, I came to know, if only slightly, both Harry Hess and Keith Runcorn. The encounter with Hess was to provide the more embarrassing memory, at which I blush to this day.

It was the early spring of 1966, and I was approaching twenty-two. I had lately – for reasons of Buggins's turn, rather than any innate talent – been elected president of the Oxford University Geological Society. In that capacity, and because I had often visited America – and Princeton University as well, as it happened – I had managed to persuade Professor Hess to speak to the final, celebratory Society meeting of that Hilary Term. Hess was by then a famous figure, and his acceptance of an invitation written by a mere undergraduate was a signal honour for all. Senior academics from most of Oxford's science departments were eagerly gathering to hear the great man speak.

It is a tradition of the Society that the event's protagonists – including the guest – wear black tie. Accompanied by my lieutenants, I met Hess (he was clothed as requested, though he called it his 'tux' and it looked suitably moth-eaten and academic) at

* 'History of Ocean Basins' in *Petrologic Studies: A Volume in Honor of A. F. Buddington*, Geological Society of America, pp. 599–620.

Oxford railway station. We had decided to give him (and our-selves – we were spending official OUGS funds) a good feed at a well-known riverside inn out in the country, perhaps ten miles from town. So the five of us – Society secretary, treasurer, vice-president, Hess and me – drove off in my 1935 Morris 8, a venerable car much prized by my friends but, as it turned out, of lamentably timed unreliability.

We dined early and very well, beside an immense inglenook-fire, in a building composed of ancient thatch and mid-Jurassic corbels, on soup and lamb and a '59 Aloxe-Corton. Our date with the assembled worthies of the university was at eight thirty, in the Museum. We left at ten minutes to eight – ample time to get to the venue. Harry Hess had enjoyed the Corton, and we had opened, as I recall, three bottles. He was a happy man.

The car, however, was less so. It broke down in some flat and nameless swamp, five miles equidistant from both inn and Oxford. It was foggy, cold and dark. We had no telephone, and no way of finding one. Our only option was to walk, taking a path that our treasurer claimed to recognize and that he laughably described as a short-cut. Well-shone black patent shoes are less than suitable for the Oxfordshire mud. We found a pub, made a telephone call – but the person who answered hadn't heard about any meeting or any museum. Hess had a couple of whiskies.

We arrived back in Oxford at ten o'clock – muddy, wet, cold and, in the case of Harry Hess, agreeably and pleasurably drunk. Our audience had remained, not knowing what else to do. The speech was a disaster. Someone tripped over, and much of what was said was incoherent. Maps fell down. The projector fused. The front row glared at us, deeming us responsible for the supposed slur on this monarch of high academia.

I was not asked to convene any further meetings of the Geo-logical Society; but Harry Hess wrote later to say he could not recall a more amusing or satisfying evening in recent years, and hoped that we would remain in contact – which we did, until he died three years later.

I had known Keith Runcorn well during my time as a reporter in Newcastle-upon-Tyne, where he was professor of geophysics. He had taken me under his wing, seeing me as a local reporter interested in science who might help him publicize his research on deep-ocean tides. He had an arrangement with Cable & Wireless to make use of one of their disused trans-Pacific telegraph cables, and had set up monitoring equipment on Fanning Island, in what is now the Republic of Kiribati, to measure the tiny electrical impulses generated in the cable by the deep-water tidal movements in mid ocean. For readers in the grim and grisly winters of Tyneside, newspaper stories about the blue waters and eternal sunny skies of a South Pacific atoll made a welcome change; I wrote about him often, liked him enormously, and only wished that my paper had the budget to let me go out, as he had often suggested, to spend a season on Fanning, measuring the currents, soaking up the Polynesian Way.

Once I left the north-east of England, Keith Runcorn and I lost touch – one might rightly say that we drifted apart. From time to time I would see his name on various celebratory papers, or on programmes for conferences called to note this anniversary or that, and all to do with the theories of continental drift of which, along with Hess and a small army of others, he was now world-renowned as an architect.

And then, in December 1995, I read that he had been found, brutally murdered, in a hotel room in San Diego. He had been on his way to the annual meeting, in San Francisco, of the American Geophysical Union. He was to give a paper about his new interest, the magnetic fields that were then being measured on the surface of the moon.

4. Definition

It turned out to be but a short step from a wholesale acceptance of the mechanics of continental drift to the creation of the new theory that would be christened *plate tectonics* – that set of abiding planetary principles that today is generally acknowledged to be the first properly global theory to have been adduced and accepted in the history of earth science.

The crucial first mention of the theory came on 24 July 1965, in the British journal *Nature*, under the authorship of the genial Canadian who is now most generally accepted as the 'father' of plate tectonics. Many hundreds of scientists had already spent thousands of man-years working away with their gravimeters and magnetometers, their polarizing microscopes and their hammers, to create a vague and pointillist image of the emerging theory. But it was not fully recognized until that summer's morning in 1965, when the thick, red-covered and always in those days infuriatingly tightly rolled magazine thudded on to desks in geological laboratories across the world. And then, though scores had been involved, no scores seemed to need settling: there was no contest for this particular moment of glory. It was the bluff, genial, approachable and down-to-earth University of Toronto professor J. Tuzo Wilson who, by opening his four-page essay with the following declarative paragraph, in essence created the new science:

Many geologists have maintained that movements of the Earth's crust are concentrated in mobile belts, which may take the form of mountains, mid-ocean ridges or major faults . . . This article suggests that these features are not isolated, that few come to dead ends, but that they are connected into a continuous network of mobile belts about the Earth which divide the surface into several large rigid plates.

His realization was essentially two-fold: the one discovery announced in this seminal 1965 *Nature* paper; the other, inextricably linked to the first and made two years beforehand, when the reacceptance of continental drift was well under way, but in need of as much hard evidence in support as could be found.

The first discovery came when J. Tuzo Wilson looked at the Hawaiian Islands. After thinking about what he saw, he came up with a piece of evidence that added mightily to all the news about tiger-striped remanent magnetics and basalt conveyor-belts on the bed of the ocean. In the tradition of good science – close observation followed by prescient deduction, with in this case the addition of the basilisk glare of his own geophysical insight – he saw something, something that the ancient Hawaiians themselves had suspected for centuries.

The Hawaiian Island chain stretches for more than 2,500 miles, across thirty degrees of Pacific longitude. Most of the islands one would not think of as Hawaiian. Nihoa, Necker, Tern, Disappearing, Laysan, Lisianski, Kittery and Seal Islands, for example, are almost unknown: only Midway and Ocean Islands, at the north-western end of the chain, are household names, and those mainly because of wars and naval battles. What is currently (but technically wrongly) thought of as the Hawaiian Islands is the 400-mile line of just nine bodies of rock and palm reaching from the outermost pinnacle of Kaula, via the north-westernmost (and still privately owned) island of Niihau, to that great chunk of basalt at the south-east called Hawaii, which is known by most non-Polynesian visitors as the Big Island.

Hawaiian legend has long acknowledged what casual visitors may notice too: that the dusty, half-dead island of Niihau looks much wearier and older than the feisty, bubbling and fiery island of Hawaii. The dank black Waialeale swamp at the summit of Kauai – the wettest place on earth, the locals say – looks prehistoric; the fresh crags of Diamond Head on Oahu (the 'diamonds' being glittery and new-looking olivine crystals) look young.

To the ancient Polynesians, who closely examined the islands' soil erosion and vegetation, the difference in age was also self-evident. They incorporated the difference in age into their stories. Pele, the goddess of volcanoes, once lived in Kauai. But then she was attacked by her older sister Namakaokahai, the goddess of the sea. And so she fled, south-east, to Oahu. Namakaokahai attacked again, and Pele moved south-east once more, to Maui. And then a third time, whereupon Pele moved yet again, this time to the Halemaumau Crater of Kilauea, on the summit of Hawaii itself. She had moved 300 miles south-eastwards, hopping from island to island, as one volcano after another exploded and died behind her.

Like many legends, this old yarn has its basis in fact. The sea attacks volcanoes – the waters and the waves erode the fresh-laid rocks. And this is why Pele herself moved, shifting always to the younger and newer volcanoes, and relentlessly away from the older and worn-out islands of the north-west, and down towards their more recently created and unspoiled cousins in the south-east.

It was in 1963, in the cold of faraway Toronto, that J. Tuzo Wilson first looked at these stories, examined the geological maps, peered at the records of the various eruptions and lava flows on the Hawaiian main chain, and came up with an idea. Volcanoes had existed in this area of the world for what seemed a very long period of time. So it seemed likely that, for some reason, there was at this particular point in the earth's mantle a deep and stationary hot spot (geologists have since elided the phrase to form today's *hotspot*).

The heat from this fiercely hot zone partly melted the rocks of the upper mantle lying above it. The magma created by this melting was lighter than the surrounding solid rock; it burst through the remainder of the mantle into and through the crust; and then it erupted through the ocean floor to produce either a sea-mount that would remain always below the surface, or an undersea volcano that would grow until it breached the surface of the sea and emerged as an island.

That part seemed simple and logical. But what Wilson then deduced, both from the Polynesian legends and from his own observations, was that while the hotspot remained static, the upper mantle and crust above had moved, carrying one island at a time away from the hotspot and abruptly stopping the volcanism there. After a while, magma erupted again at a new site that lay in the wake, as it were, of the first moving island, and another fresh island was made altogether. It was rather like moving a baking tray full of batter slowly away from a single intense gas burner, creating a line of ripples and partially cooked batter – the batter cooked at one end of the tray, uncooked at the other, with all the stages in between.

Here in the Pacific, on a grand scale, was a 400-mile-long trail of volcanoes – in various stages of cooking. The older rocks were in this case at the north-western end of the trail, the newer rocks at the south-eastern. If the radiometric dating confirmed this, then it could be incontrovertibly proven that the mantle and crust along the Hawaiian chain was itself moving north-westwards over a hotspot that was now and long had been sited directly under where the Big Island is today.

And the dating of the rocks proved it, precisely. The Kauai basalts were shown to be 5.5 million years old; those on Hawaii itself were on average less than 0.7 million years old; and in the craters where Pele is said now to be lurking, they are still being created, millions of tons of hotspot-induced basaltic melt baked afresh every day.

The dating clinched the idea. Wilson was shown to be exactly right. Science could now add to the evidence of the tiger-stripe magnetic anomalies off Seattle this second indication of the under-sea geological conveyor-belt. The magnetic evidence had been found below the surface; this from Hawaii was by contrast all on the surface. Together they presented science with a sort of gigantic rock-hewn tape-recorder that showed not only the mid-Pacific movement that had been taking place over the last five million

years but also the expansion of the sea-floor, with the continents
on each side of it, undeniably and indisputably, drifting.

The second realization – a true *Eureka!* moment of epiphany –
came after Wilson starting experimenting not with rocks and
magnetic traces or radioactive rubidium, but with paper and a set
of scissors. The title of his famous *Nature* paper, 'A New Class of
Faults and Their Bearing on Continental Drift', suggests why he
was indulging himself so.

John Dewey, who went on from Cambridge to become professor of geology at Oxford, remembers the moment. It was

. . . one early autumn morning in 1964, I was sitting in my room in the
Sedgwick Museum in Cambridge . . . when Toronto's Tuzo Wilson, on
sabbatical leave, sauntered in clearly bursting to tell anyone who
would listen about his new ideas. He had discovered that I was the
new lecturer in structural geology and said: 'Dewey, I have discovered
a new class of fault.' 'Rubbish,' I said, 'we know about the geology and
kinematics of every kind of fault known to mankind.' Tuzo grinned,
and produced a simple coloured folded paper version of his now famous
ridge/transform/ridge model, and proceeded to open and close, open
and close it with that wonderful smile on his face. I was transfixed
both by the realization that I was seeing something profoundly new
and important, and by the fact that I was talking to a very clever and
original man.

Wilson's achievement was to show what would happen if a
geological process caused a fault – in which one body of rock
breaks and slips alongside another – across a ridge that, for some
reason, happened to be spreading open. He was interested
because new bathymetric survey data – the soundings of the sea
– was showing, to everyone's astonishment, that the great ridges
that ran down the centres of both the Atlantic and the Pacific
Oceans were incised by dozens of deep gashes. Geologists initially
thought these gashes were spectacular versions of nothing
more than classic faults, tearing the ridge asunder as they sheared

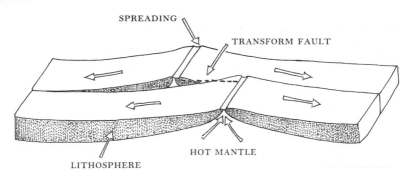

SPREADING

TRANSFORM FAULT

HOT MANTLE

LITHOSPHERE

J. Tuzo Wilson's famous transform fault structure, which finally and
definitively demonstrated exactly what happens when sea-floor spreading
occurs at a mid-ocean ridge.

to the left or to the right as random happenstance directed.

But Tuzo Wilson looked at the bathymetric pictures of these
gashes again and said to himself *no!* – if the ridge in the centre
happened itself to be opening up, for some wholly unconnected
reason, then the directions of the fault slippage would be exactly
the opposite of those that might happen across a line that was
totally stable. He gave a name to the new phenomenon: a normal
left-to-right or right-to-left fault was known as a transcurrent
fault, but he named the fault he was now predicting, which had
never been seen or described before (because no one had ever
imagined a ridge spreading itself open), a *transform fault.*

He drew diagrams of how this should appear – how its oppo-
siteness-from-normal should manifest itself. He created paper-
and-crayon diagrams of the model, cut them out and kept them
in his wallet, showing them to anyone who would give him the
time of day. This friendly Canadian gentleman – scrupulously
dressed, nicely mannered – with his cut-out papers in his pockets
soon became a familiar figure on more than a few university
campuses in the early 1960s.

And, just like John Dewey, everyone who saw Wilson's demonstration knew in an instant that he had it right there, *the proof.*
All that was needed was the test. And for this, the Cold War – of

blessed memory; at least blessed to many scientists – came promptly to the rescue. Just as the US Navy had been happy to tow magnetometers behind the *Pioneer* in the fifties, so in the sixties it was content to let scientists make use of a worldwide seismographic network it had deployed to listen for Soviet and Chinese nuclear weapons tests. It was a system with scores of highly sensitive pieces of seismic equipment scattered around the planet. It was ideally positioned to find out, in addition to the sites of bomb detonations, something that it had never been designed to discern: the direction of slippage along some of the great fault-line gashes in the mid Pacific and the mid Atlantic.

The system worked its magic. The Pentagon agreed the result should be free from military classification, which had so slowed earlier research. And so in 1967, from a laboratory at Columbia University that had examined the numbers, the results came tumbling out: the great faults in the middle of both oceans were *indeed* transform faults, their slip directions were the *exact* opposite of what would be expected had they been standard transcurrent faults. Tuzo Wilson's ideas had been vindicated yet again: first with the evidence from the conveyor-belt island chain of Hawaii, and now with his supposition about the world in general, and what was going on in the unseen middle of its oceans.

And of that, there was now no doubt at all. The rocks underpinning the oceans were most assuredly splitting themselves apart. The academic battle that had been fought for the previous fifty years was now over, for good. The stabilists* – as were

---

* As in an essay by William Dickinson, emeritus professor of geosciences at the University of Arizona: 'In my youth as a geoscientist I was a casual stabilist, assuming that the continents had maintained their relative positions on the globe throughout geologic time. That outmoded stance stemmed less from informed conviction than from sheer ignorance.' Professor Dickinson is now a leading evangelist for the theory, and has as one of his proudest possessions a plate – of china – given to him and adorned with the motto *Hero of Plate Tectonics* and *In Subduction We Trust.*

called those who believed, as most once had, that the world and its continents had always been in approximately the same place – had finally to yield. The day belonged to the mobilists, who had since Wegener's time argued that the continents wandered, with what are now known to be dramatic and highly visible effects – such as the creation of the modern map of the world.

It was, for science, an incredibly exciting time. An odd time too – for geologists soon began to realize they had been studying their earth backwards. It was as though an entomologist had begun studying a bee by looking not at the bee as a whole but at the microscopic structure of the yellow hairs on its abdomen; or as though a botanist had tried to get to know an oak tree by first using an electron microscope to peer at a cross-section of an acorn. It is all a consequence of man's own insignificant size compared to what he is studying, of course. But the fact is, when plate tectonics came along, it was realized that geology had been spending its previous two millennia as a major science looking in great detail at sandstones and gneisses and rift valleys and ammonites – but had never been able to stand back and look at the planet as a whole and then to work out the details, as happens with most sciences where man is generally bigger than whatever it is he is studying.

Plate tectonics offered for the first time an intellectual mechanism for taking the earth and looking at it as an entity – and the fact that its emergence as a brand-new science coincided so nicely with the development of satellites that could look at the planet as a whole was fortuitous, to say the least. One might say that all this meant that, for the first time, geologists were able to begin looking at things *right side up*.

And what a vision was now laid out before them! The oceans were coming apart at the seams. The crust and the upper mantle beneath them were spreading out across the deep-ocean floors, moving in opposite directions on each flank of the mid-ocean ridges. Then, when the mobile material reached the edge of the ocean – the edge of the *plate*, to use Tuzo Wilson's now universally accepted term – it plunged down below whatever it met, readying itself to be recycled in the deepest recesses of the planet, to return to the half-molten underneath of the world and in due course to thrust itself up once more through the oceanic centres and begin the long circular process all over again.

Plate tectonics is, in essence, the way by which the world deals with its steady loss of heat. A vast amount of heat accumulated during the formation of the planet a little over 4,500 million years ago – and natural radioactivity, particularly the decay of isotopes of potassium, uranium and thorium, served only to add to the ferocity of the internal fire. But that heat is now ebbing away, and the means by which it is transferred from the deep interior to the surface tends to be by way of convection currents, just like those one sees working in a vat of vegetable soup simmering on the hob.

The rate of movement of these convection currents is very, very small, generally measured in only a certain number of millimetres each year. Currents of material of the inner earth rise up from the red-hot region, maybe a thousand miles down, pass right through a swimmy, hot, weakly plastic region called the asthenosphere, and then, when they reach a region above this, anywhere from four to twenty miles of the surface, slow, stop and eventually – in classic convection-current, vegetable-soup fashion – turn back downwards once again.

The currents, with the soft, pliable and plastic rocks of which they are composed, turn tail at this point on their upward journey, because they encounter an inconveniently brittle and rigid layer of the earth: the upper part of the mantle and the entirety of the crust, which is today called the lithosphere. And it is in the lithosphere that the tectonic plates themselves exist.

In the oceans the lithosphere is thin – maybe four miles thick – and it is young, no more than 200 million years old. The lithosphere at the continents, with all their long-ago-made lime-stones and granites and shales and gabbros and schists and gneisses piled on top, can on the other hand be as much as twenty miles thick and much, much older – typically, in fact, as much as two *billion* years old. It is from these two kinds of lithosphere that the tectonic plates are made; the convection process that is going on below them, which is slowly cooling the earth to its ultimate frigid darkness, is what drives them to move and shuffle and shunt and bang their way around the surface of the earth. It is a deeply complex subject, the stuff of mathematical modelling and the employment of banks of supercomputers. It is still far from being fully understood.

But out of the early unravelling and understanding of the process was born in those early years yet another new term: *a subduction zone.* This, it seemed, was where the real business of the world was done. This was the comparatively narrow strip of territory below which, at the edges of the plates, the moving material collided, and one plate slipped beneath the other and began to head back downward, to balance the creation of new lithospheric material at the oceanic seams. Most of the plates that converge do in fact display subduction. And so by finding out just where the world's subduction zones were, science could find the boundaries of most of the planet's tectonic plates and, by identifying them, work out what was happening to them, where, how fast and why.

Ever since the beginning of the 1970s – the phrase *subduction zone* appears to have been first used in *Nature* (once again) in the issue of 14 November 1970 – a huge proportion of the world's geophysicists have been engaged in studying their bewildering complexities and their seminal influence on the arrangements of the earth. What happens deep within their hot and roiling mysteries is crucial to an understanding of the processes of the earth's making. All the greatest dramas of the solid world's evolution happen within them.

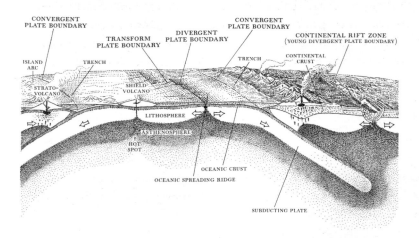

A subduction zone, like that responsible for the Sunda Strait eruption –
and, indeed, for 95 per cent of the world's most violent volcanoes.

And dramas that also include the realization, which was
published in an otherwise obscure book in 1980, that it is

... subduction along the Java Trench, where the Indo-Australian
Plate is moving under the Indonesian island chain . . . that fuelled the
1883 eruption of Krakatoa.

The earth's surface appears to be armoured with between six
and thirty-six of these rigid plates, depending upon how they are
defined and counted. Many of the boundaries between plates
have been drawn on the basis only of educated guesswork; what
happens deep in the interior of China, for instance, where one
plate is thought to meet another, has not yet been fully explained.
Nor is it known what goes on around what is called the Scotia
Arc in the chilly South Atlantic, east of the Falkland Islands.
But, generally speaking, modern tectonics accepts the undisputed
existence of about a dozen major plates. The boundaries between
these, where the mechanics of the planet's architecture are best
exhibited, are by now very well drawn.

Exactly what happens at the boundaries depends on a number of factors. If the plate is entirely of *oceanic material* – that is, basically basalt – and it collides more or less head-on with another plate *of the same type*, then there is an almost randomly decided subduction, with one plate indeed sliding beneath the other. An arc-shaped arrangement of small volcanic islands is usually created, the arc being shaped according to the way the plates move relative to one another. The chain of islands stretching along the International Date Line south of Tonga, for example, is a classic illustration of what happens when two oceanic plates bump into one another. For the purposes of this account, they are best overlooked.

If both plates are, on the other hand, composed mainly of *continental material* – which can best be thought of as a light scum of ancient granites and other sediments and metamorphic rocks lying on top of the oceanic basalts – then their collision may not result in a subduction at all. As the continental material is made up of lighter rocks, it generally resists being thrust down into the earth's subsurface; both plates may instead stay on top in line with one another, and buckle and crumple, forming a chain of mountains that is in most places not volcanic at all. India and Asia are a pair of continental plates that are colliding, for example – with the effect that the earth's crust where they smash into one another has crumpled itself up and more than doubled in thickness, to form the world's highest mountains, the Himalaya.

The Africa Plate is similarly moving slowly northwards and colliding with the Eurasian Plate. The highly unstable mountains of the Caucasus, the earthquake-prone hills of Turkey, the ever restless fracture zone of the Balkans, the ski-slopes of Iran's Mount Damavand are all a consequence of this entirely continental plate collision. But where there is some small amount of subduction, as near Vesuvius and Etna, there are volcanoes. Shallow-focus, very dangerous earthquakes are to be found everywhere along a continental collision zone: volcanoes are more likely where there is subduction.

It is also possible, given the complicated geometry of the earth, that two plates may well not hit each other head-on but *slide alongside one another*, like a tyre sliding past the kerb during a lame attempt at parking. The world's best-known example of this kind of meeting is the San Andreas Fault in California, notorious for what humankind regards as its capricious behaviour (a geologist would not think it capricious at all). It causes earthquakes in abundance and has enabled Hollywood to come up with some heroically awful films about volcanoes in Pasadena, tsunamis – lethally massive sea-waves – scooping surfers off Pebble Beach and faraway politicians uttering such droll slogans as *the Coast is toast.*

The Fault is a classic example of what is known as a *conservative plate boundary*, where there is no collision, no crumpling, no subduction. The immense Pacific Plate is here simply moving northward relative to the North American Plate, sliding along it at about half an inch a year. Extraordinary stresses can build up if this movement is somehow hindered – by friction, for example. And when this stress becomes overwhelming and is suddenly released, terrible earthquakes can and do occur. During the infamous San Francisco Earthquake of 1906 parts of the fault, which in recent years has accelerated its rate of sliding to almost four inches a year, shot past each other a total of twenty-one feet in a matter of twenty seconds!

Finally, and most importantly for the understanding of what happened at Krakatoa, there are those events that occur when two plates of *different types* collide – when one plate that is all oceanic basalt smashes itself into another plate that is loaded up with continental crust. These, so far as this story is concerned, are the important ones.

*

What takes place when plates of different composition run into one another, as might be expected (but was actually not, until that sudden realization made in 1967), is that the heavier of the two, the oceanic basalt plate, dips itself underneath the edge of the lighter continent-laden plate. Immediately it has started to do so, matters directly beneath the point of collision – matters within the classically formed subduction zone, that is – become complicated beyond belief and, to the geophysicist, endlessly fascinating. What takes place within the zone also has a profound effect on the making of the region above and on the lives of the human and animal inhabitants there – not least because, intermittently, the results of the plates' meeting and the making of a subduction zone can be very dangerous indeed.

In essence the process at a subduction zone begins when the colliding oceanic basalt plate begins to head off down back into the earth. It drags some of the continental plate down with it and, in doing so, causes a pinch – a trench – in the bed of the sea. In the case of Java, the five-mile-deep Java Trench, 200 miles off the coast, provides vivid evidence of the oceanic basalt plate as it begins barrelling its way downward. Behind the plate – the coral reefs of Cocos (Keeling) Island, Christmas Island, the flat blue Indian Ocean and, in the far distance, the coast of Australia – all is placid, paradisal, serene. In front of the down-racing plate is the Trench, a line of offshore islands, and then Java and Sumatra – one of the most volcanically unstable pairs of islands ever known.

They are unstable because of a well-understood, if wonderfully complicated, mechanism. The down-racing plate heads into the heat, dragging with it billions upon billions of tons of additional material – and, most crucially of all, water. This it gets from the huge thickness of the waterlogged sediments that are being dragged down from the seabed. Once this waterlogged material is stirred into the mix and reaches a critical depth, quite unexpectedly to those who first noticed the phenomenon, it begins to melt –

doing so because the addition of this water has lowered the melting temperature of the mix.

And so what starts off beneath the seas as cold and solid now moves down towards the hot mantle, and turns viscous and runny; its fluid components begin to 'sweat out' – suddenly bubbling and frothing and coursing and, because they are light and volatile, so rising back up again, passing into the solid mantle through which all the downsliding ingredients had passed. To make matters more complicated still, as they course upwards through this material, they begin to melt that too.

Suddenly a Hadean nightmare is created miles beneath the subducted continental crust: immense volumes of boiling, gaseous, white-hot magma, alive with bubbles and energy and restless muscle, seethe in vaults and chambers of unimaginable size and temperature. The promethean material searches ceaselessly for some weakened spot in the crust above it. Every so often it finds one, a crack, crevice or fault, and then forces its way up into a holding chamber. Before long, the accumulating pressure of the uprushing material becomes too great, and the temperature too high, and the proportion of dissolved gas becomes too large, and it explodes out into the open air in a vicious cannonade of destruction. A type of volcano, which, because of its position at the edge of a subduction zone, is far more explosive and dangerous than any other of the world's many different kinds of volcano, suddenly – and if there are people around, invariably terrifyingly – erupts.

Two points of simple geography remain. The first is a matter of tectonic trivia. The Indo-Australian Plate, the culprit that creates all of the volcanic *tamasha* so notoriously present on Java, on Sumatra and on the tiny island that once lay between them in the Sunda Strait, is moving because the sea-floor south of Australia is spreading open. It is possible to calculate both the speed of that opening and the pole of rotation around which this spreading is taking place.

The speed of the sea-floor spreading, the rate at which the Indo-Australian Plate is moving northwards and colliding with the Eurasian Plate, seems to be about four inches a year, a hundred yards every millennium. Put another way: when Java Man – the *Homo erectus* who first came to these parts from Africa – was living in central Java about 1.7 million years ago, Australia and Asia were rather more than a hundred miles further apart than they are today. They have been moving towards each other ever since, and doing so in a direction that, unusual though it may seem, turns around a pole of rotation that is located a few miles to the south and east of the Egyptian capital, Cairo.

And secondly: there is one delightful symmetry that is noticeable, though imperfect at best and complex in the extreme, as more and more details become known. The tracks of the subduction zones that enfold the islands of Indonesia, the zones that create all the trenches and island arcs and volcanoes and mayhem that goes on among the islands of the archipelago, more or less follow the invisible line of biology and botany that was first hinted at by Philip Sclater in 1857 and drawn a year later by Alfred Russel Wallace.

On one side: Australia, cassowaries, emus and kangaroos. On the other: cows, monkeys, thrushes and elephants. On one side: the Indo-Australian Plate; on the other: the Eurasian Plate. The middle, where the two plates meet, and where they come together very slowly but with immense and unthinkable raw power, is in consequence a serried line of the world's greatest, most dangerous and most predictably unpredictable volcanoes – including, lurking just on the Asian side of an imagined extrapolation of the Wallace Line, the most demonstrably dangerous of them all, the once-great island of Krakatoa. It is an island that has exploded many more times than on the one occasion for which it is now so notorious.

4

THE MOMENTS WHEN
THE MOUNTAIN MOVED

There was a sign from the sun, the like of which had never been seen or reported before. The sun became dark and its darkness lasted for eighteen months. Each day, it shone for about four hours, and still this light was only a feeble shadow. Everyone declared that the sun would never recover its full light again. The fruits did not ripen, and the wine tasted like sour grapes.

– an eleventh-century plagiarism by an Antioch patriarch
called Michael the Syrian, of a document supposedly written
by the sixth-century historian John of Ephesus, describing
the punishing climatic effects of an event that some believe
to have been an early eruption of Krakatoa

Man has been recording his memories for about 30,000 years, in cave-paintings or songs, in carvings or writings, and during this time the small cluster of volcanoes and off-islands that for the last 300 years we have come to call collectively Krakatoa has exploded once, twice, four or even eleven times, depending on just how the runes of geology, myth and circumstance are read and interpreted.

Four of these eruptions are generally accepted to have emerged from the mists of uncertain history into the realms of possible reality. And yet, of these four, one is widely thought of now as most unlikely to have occurred at all; the date of a second is very reluctantly agreed to; a third is known to have been very poorly reported and subject to wanton hyperbole; and only the most recent truly survives as the one of the four that is incontrovertibly regarded as having taken place.

There is some evidence that a very long while before that – perhaps 60,000 years ago or more – there once was a very much larger mountain that some geologists like to call Ancient Krakatoa, which they believe was something like 6,000 feet high and centred on an almost perfectly circular island about nine miles in diameter. But then a gigantic eruption, witnessed only by gibbering hominids and Neanderthals, if indeed by anyone, may have devastated the island and its peak, blowing almost all to smithereens.

Once the dust had settled, what remained of Ancient Krakatoa was a group of four quite small and apparently stable-looking islands. At the northern end of the group were two low and crescent-shaped skerries – one to the east called Panjang, about three miles long, and to the west its larger colleague, four miles long, called Sertung.* Embraced within the parenthesis created by

* Geographical place-names present a problem that is peculiarly endemic to those scores of places that have suffered under history's various colonial yokes, and often result in places having been given three names – the early indigenous name, the colonially applied name and then its post-colonial successor. The islands that make up the Krakatoa group display this complexity: Panjang – the Ur-name – first became Lang Island, and is now Rakata Kecil; Sertung became Verlaten (lonely, forsaken island) during Dutch times, and is currently back to being Sertung. Mercifully for this

these twins was both the Polish Hat, a tiny chunk of the fine-grained volcanic rock known as andesite, and the northern end of the island that we truly once regarded as Krakatoa proper. This was then a lozenge-shaped mass, six miles long by two wide, and half a mile high at its higher southern end. The southern summit was called Rakata; to its north were a pair of smaller crater-peaks. The first of these peaks, roughly in the island's centre, was called Danan; and nudging up into the sky from the island's narrower northern spur was the second, known as Perboewatan.

This main island was found by early visitors to be always well forested, with an abundance of fresh-looking lava flows and steaming hot springs and outcrops of sulphur that were once worked by Batavian dynamite-makers. Over the centuries it had been used variously as a VOC naval reconnaissance station, as a place to build small ships, as a base for a small northern Sunda Strait fishing fleet, and, in 1809 and for the decade following, as a remote and barely accessible Alcatraz for those recalcitrant native prisoners whom the Dutch could not control on the mainland.

A few have suggested that it was an island of evil reputation, a lair for pirates, a place that visitors from Java and Sumatra, who sailed over in their *prahus* to collect wood or wild fruit, found so disenchanting that they failed to leave offerings for Krakatoa's local gods. In fact, there is little evidence of this, however seductive the symbolism and the symmetry – *the island of vile repute that exploded and killed thousands.* From most credible accounts, Krakatoa's real reputation was actually rather the reverse.

For by the reports of most Western visitors, there were from time to time a number of contented, if somewhat impoverished, little settlements on the island. The great English circumnavigating explorer Captain James Cook, for example, stopped on the

---

footnote, which would be further awash in explication, the island in the group that had the English name Polish Hat no longer exists, since it disappeared, a victim of the eruption.

The presumed geological evolution of the Krakatoa islands, viewed from
the north. The original great island – Ancient Krakatoa – is thought to
have exploded some 60,000 years ago.

main island of Krakatoa twice. In January 1771 his colleague
Joseph Banks, the renowned botanist and polymath, noted: 'At
night Anchor'd under a high Island call[ed] in the draughts
Cracatoa and by the Indian *Pulo Racatta* . . . this morn when we
rose we saw that there were many houses and much Cultivation
upon Cracatoa, so that probably a ship might meet with refreshments who chose to touch here.' Six years later, when Cook called
in again, a village and fields of cultivation were still to be found

– pepper was being grown and harvested, as well as other cash crops.

Three years later still, the *Resolution* and the *Discovery* stopped at Krakatoa one further time – but on this occasion, in February 1780, they were without James Cook himself, since he had been bludgeoned to death in Hawaii the previous November. They stopped in the crescent-shaped roads between Krakatoa and Panjang Islands for five days, giving the fleet artist, John Webber, time to make elaborate drawings of the village houses and the luxuriant vegetation – palms, tall grasses, ferns – in the valley on Krakatoa between the two more southerly peaks of Danan and Rakata. The expedition's day-book recorded the details of the party's sojourn on the island:

The *Resolution* refilled its barrels at a stream located at the southern extremity of the little island, a short distance from the shoreline. A little to the south, one finds a heat-source, where the islanders bathe. While we were on a level with the southern extremity of this island the Master went to find an *aiguade*, but he disembarked with difficulty, and returned without finding any sweet water.

The island of Cracatoa is considered very healthy in comparison to those thereabouts. She offers elevated ground which rises little-by-little from the shoreline on all sides; she is covered with trees, except in several places where the islanders have cleared them for growing rice. The population is not very considerable. The chief is subject to the King of Bantam, just as those of the other islands in the Strait. One finds on the coral reef a large quantity of little turtles, refreshments which elsewhere are very rare, and have an enormous price.

The pepper groves had all but disappeared ten years later, when the Dutch administrator visited; such people as lived on Krakatoa were then raising chickens and goats, and made small sums selling firewood, water and food to stopping ships. There may have been people living on the island at the time of each of

The lush coastal jungle of Krakatoa island, drawn by John Webber,
expedition artist for Captain James Cook, during the fleet's visit in 1780.

the early eruptions; at the time of the cataclysm Krakatoa was,
quite widely, vacant. But there is no suggestion that it had an
evil name.

*

The three early occasions that, according to most modern history books, possibly saw eruptions were (according to the Western calendar, only lately adopted in Java) the *anno Domini* years 416, 535 and 1680. There is the vaguest of suggestions that between the ninth and the sixteenth centuries there were also no fewer than seven additional eruptive episodes, and that during the single century when the Buddhist kings of the Cailendra Dynasty were on the throne in central Java* Krakatoa became so notoriously active that it was called 'the fire-mountain'. This figure of seven, when added to the three possible eruptions and the single certain catastrophe, gives the tally of eleven – a number that is rather doubtful, it must be said.

The one subsequent occasion when Krakatoa went wild is the only year that is fixed with total certainty, and that is 1883. Of the three earlier occasions (I am going to dismiss the Cailendra Seven – for want of any evidence at all, other than the somewhat less than illuminating 'fire-mountain' remark in a Buddhist manuscript) we are rather less sure just when or what took place, if indeed anything did at all.

For completeness' sake, though, it is probably worth first exploring something of the shadowy world of old Java, to see if it is possible to establish with any certainty the early volcanic history of the island – if for no other reason than that the establishment of Krakatoa's eruptive past may offer us some useful clue as to her probable future.

The Possible Eruption of AD 416

The most frequently quoted source for the first (and, perhaps, also the second) of these three rather questionable event-dates is

---

* Building among other monuments the immense and ornate temple of Borobudur, the world's largest Buddhist structure.

a monumental modern history written in the nineteenth century, known as the Javanese *Book of Kings*. Its author, a Javanese court poet called Raden Ngabahi Ranggawarsita, was well connected to the Dutch colonial establishment of the day, as well as being a key figure in the most distinguished of traditional circles. He worked in the sultanly estate of Solo, which is unarguably the most refined of all Javanese courts, a place where the gamelan playing, the *wayang kulit* puppetry and the poetry still have few equals for their elegance, style and cultural purity.

But for Ranggawarsita, who was intellectually as much scholar as poet, and who knew the European historical record well, the courtly life was evidently not enough. He had as his principal ambition something more than the fashioning of lyrical poems to mark significant moments in the life of the sultan of Solo. He wanted instead to create something of rather greater and enduring value: a truly comprehensive history of the entire island of Java, a document that could hold up its head alongside the great European tracts about their own countries and peoples. He spent most of his adult years working on the project – and in the 1860s, after decades of what must have been the most thankless toil, he finally achieved his goal, completing and uttering for publication a series of fascinating but undisciplined ramblings that make up what is possibly the world's longest book.* Unfortunately, according to his many critics, most of what he wrote he made up.

That being so, there has been an understandably cautious reaction among scholars who have tried to use Ranggawarsita's tome as the basis for serious historical research. Scientists who have read it have been among the most sceptical of all – and most particularly vulcanologists, who have been both drawn to, and confused by, one highly alluring passage:

* By dint of writing three pages every day for thirty years, he wrote six million words, all in the elaborate language known as Court Javanese. The supposed reference to a possible fifth-century eruption of Krakatoa appears

the whole world was greatly shaken, and violent thundering, accompanied by heavy rain and storms took place, but not only did not this heavy rain extinguish the eruption of the fire of the mountain Kapi, but augmented the fire; the noise was fearful, at last the mountain Kapi with a tremendous roar burst into pieces and sank into the deepest of the earth. The water of the sea rose and inundated the land, the country to the east of the mountain Batuwara, to the mountain Raja Basa, was inundated by the sea; the inhabitants of the northern part of the Sunda country to the mountain Raja Basa were drowned and swept away with all their property . . .

What does it mean? To which mountain – since Kapi is not a name known today – does the passage refer?* And when did whatever happened take place? Geologists, more familiar with gazing at fossils or down microscopes, have pored over this one paragraph of elegant Javanese prose and gone over it with a fine-tooth comb.

It all would have been a good deal more helpful and a sight less confusing if Ranggawarsita had only written once about the supposed great eruption. In fact he went back to it twice. The paragraph quoted above comes from the 1869 version of his book. By the time of his second edition of 1885 he had decided to take another look at it (whatever, wherever and whenever it was), and he wrote about it as follows:†

. . . in the year Saka 338 [i.e. AD 416] a thundering noise was heard from the mountain Batuwara, which was answered by a similar noise

in an early part of Ranggawarsita's history, called 'The Book of Ancient Kings', the 'Pustaka Raja Purwah'.
* By the time Ranggawarsita was writing, the name *Krakatoa*, or at the very least *Krakatau*, was in common use. So it is puzzling that he chose to use the name *Kapi*, unless of course it was a direct transliteration of the original documents he was using for his research.
† According to an English translation published in *Nature* – then awash in narratives of the 1883 eruption of Krakatoa – in August 1889.

coming from the mountain Kapi, lying westward of the modern Bantam. A great glaring fire which reached to the sky came out of the last-named mountain. The whole world was greatly shaken and violent thundering accompanied by heavy rains and storms took place.

But not only did this heavy rain not extinguish the eruption of fire of the mountain Kapi, but it augmented the fire. The noise was fearful. At last the mountain Kapi burst into two pieces with a tremendous roar and sank into the deepest of the earth. The water of the sea rose and inundated the land.

The country to the east of the mountain called Batuwara, to the mountain Kamula, and westward to the mountain Raja Basa, was inundated by the sea.

The inhabitants of the northern part of the Sunda country to the mountain Raja Basa were drowned and swept away with all their property.

After the water subsided the mountain Kapi which had burst into pieces and the surrounding land became sea and the single island [of Java–Sumatra] divided into two parts. The city of Samaskuta, which was situated in the interior of Sumatra, became sea, the water of which was very clear, and which was afterwards called the lake Sinkara. This event was the origin of the separation of Sumatra and Java.

The second of the two passages is more amply filled with geographical detail: the references to Sumatra and Java splitting apart, the identification of 'the Sunda country' and of volcanoes like Kamula – which is now known from other sources to be the western Javan volcano called Gede, south of today's Jakarta – Batuwara, in western Banten, and Rajabasa, which is a 4,000-foot peak at the southern tip of Sumatra, that still bears that name. Given all these circumstantial pieces of cartography, it looks more than likely that 'the mountain Kapi' is in fact Krakatoa.

But there is a small difficulty. The second description, filled as it is with journalistic colour – glaring fires, fearful noises, marine inundations, sea-destroyed villages – was written some two years *after* the 1883 eruption of Krakatoa. And since it is a much richer account than that written in 1869, to the sceptical eye it looks as though Ranggawarsita – having read all the newspapers and perhaps interviewed some residents of Banten (where most of the 1883 flood destruction took place) and spoken to friendly Dutch officials and perhaps to a few scientists too – took his first account of 1869 and fifteen years later, to put it bluntly, embellished it. He seems to have scattered some 1883 details, like glitter, on top of his rather bland descriptions of that earlier event.

And, by doing so, if that is what indeed he did, the poet suffers the inevitable fate of any writer of non-fiction who makes *anything* up: he finds that readers call into question *everything* he writes. His entire history is then suspected of being flawed – and readers look even at his first description of the explosion of 'Kapi' and the inundations and deaths that followed, and wonder not just when it happened, but if it happened at all.

Except, of course (and here I spring to Ranggawarsita's defence), at the time he wrote his first edition in 1869 he did not have any means of embellishing what he wrote. Yes, he might have seen accounts in the history books of the supposed eruption that took place in May 1680. But could he have made *all* of it up? Probably not. Most probably his writings for the first edition of the *Book of Kings* do come from his research into original sources. The trouble is – which sources? We know little of his historiography: we can only surmise that his description of an eruption in the Sunda Strait probably came from those ancient, peculiarly beautiful and very fragile Javanese manuscripts written on palm-leaves, and of which the *kraton* library at Solo had a very great number.

Matters here start to become somewhat vague. Of the 10,000 or so surviving palm-leaf texts – which are written in a variety of manuscript styles, including Balinese, Court Javanese and a curiously complex calligraphy called Mountain Script, with which Ranggawarsita (and a mere handful of others) was familiar – only a very small number actually relate the ancient history of Java. Most of them appear to stop (or start) in about the ninth century. Before that, very little of which we can be certain appears to be known about Java at all.

To give some of the flavour of this uncertainty: there are references in Ranggawarsita's work to a mysterious monarch called Jayabaya, who supposedly oversaw the writing of the accounts of the eruption that are to be found in some of the older palm-leaf texts. Jayabaya in turn is supposed to have been told about the eruption by a Hindu god named Naraddha, who descended from heaven and related fabulous stories that, he insisted to the king, should be inserted into all and any accounts of the history of Java.

So here we have it: an account that arrives from an ancient god, via an enigmatic tenth-century king who dictated material to scribes who wrote on leaves, and is then related through the good offices of a nineteenth-century court poet who, yes, could read those leaves but who was clearly also a man much taken to flights of fancy. Small wonder that the scientific community has received this basic story of Krakatoa's first recorded eruption with a healthy degree of scepticism.

Except for two things. First, the details are very good (even the relatively unadorned first account of 1869) and fairly convincing geologically. And second, there is a firm date given for the event: AD 416. Of that Ranggawarsita has no doubt: the Hindu god seemingly told Jayabaya that the event took place in the 338th year of the Shaka Calendar. This is a widely recognized Hindu dating system used only on these islands, which began in Western terms in the year AD 78, when Hinduism was supposedly brought south from the Champa Kingdom in what is today's Vietnam. To get the modern date of 416, one simply does the maths.

But there is not one other shred of independent contemporary evidence – not a line of dust in any of the ice-cores taken from either polar ice-cap, not a millimetre of shrinkage in the size of any tree ring* taken from any of the world's ancient forests – to suggest that there was a volcanic eruption anywhere in the world in the early part of the fifth century. The error rates from these techniques are in the range of plus or minus twenty-five years. So it seems clear from scientific evidence that no volcano of consequence erupted in the world during the first quarter of the fifth century; that much appears certain, the Shaka year, those glaring fires, the inundations of the sea and the explosion of the mountain Kapi notwithstanding. Without firm scientific evidence, and with the historical evidence little more than a vividly told tale from a Victorian poet–fantasist, one has to wonder seriously whether there was a fifth-century eruption at all.

The Confusions of AD 416 or AD 535

There is, however, quite abundant evidence that some kind of titanic event occurred about a century later. It can be seen from a very considerable body of tree-ring, ice-core and worldwide anecdotal evidence that a massive volcanic eruption most likely occurred somewhere in the region of Java or Sumatra around AD 535. Could this perhaps also be Krakatoa? Could perhaps the Shaka date in Ranggawarsita's history be an error – but all the other supposed observations, at least for his first account, be substantially correct?

* Volcanoes that eject immense amounts of dust into the atmosphere leave behind two kinds of easily recognizable signature. Slender bands of the deposited dust can be found trapped in ice-cores. And – because the dust causes a filtering of the sun and a lowering of worldwide ambient temperatures – there is also evidence that the growth of trees is at the same time briefly slowed. Tree rings appear much closer together in the cooler years, when there is slower growth. So the ring record provides a neat and easy way (providing always that a cut tree of suitable antiquity is at hand) of establishing the climatic record for hundreds of past years.

A slender and somewhat tenuous body of evidence suggests error to be the explanation. This evidence derives from the observation that volcanic eruptions, especially truly large ones that occur close to large places of habitation, trigger widespread social dislocation. People die in their hundreds, communications are severed, there is disease, ruin, a collapse of social order. And a barely recognized consequence of all this mayhem is that historical record-keeping suffers. It becomes patchy and incomplete. Historians, like everyone else, have little other than personal survival on their minds.

And the Javanese *Book of Kings* exhibits this patchiness, at just the right time. For all of the fifth century, the book contains its fairly routine and regular selection of entries – there appears to have been no interruption, no trauma, that ever caused a historian to stop writing about Javanese trivia for a protracted period during the hundred years between AD 400 and AD 500. That century on Java seems to have been blessed with an absence of awfulness. The year AD 416 appears with the account of the explosion itself, but, very pointedly, seems not to have been followed by years of disruption, with historians taking time off from their duties to attend to their own needs. There is just as much inconsequential detail in the Javanese palm-leaf history books for the ten-year period between 420 and 430 as there is for the period between 400 and 410.

But in the next century, the sixth, this is not the case at all. For the first thirty years of the sixth century, fully three quarters of the years have journal entries – the normal strike-rate, as it were. But for the eighteen years that follow the crucial year of AD 535, however, fewer than one fifth display journal entries. And then for the thirty years following that, the rate of mention of ordinary matters rises back to a little under three quarters the normal rate. So it looks very much as though *something* occurred in or around AD 535, something that sent the palm-leaf scribes of

Java into a tailspin, into a state of historical catalepsy, for almost the following two decades.

And what is more – there is confirming ice-core and tree-ring evidence aplenty from the world outside as well. Dating of both cores and trees is these days highly accurate, and it does now seem that between the years AD 510 and 560 some major event that sifted dust around the world and caused the sun to dim and arboreal growing conditions to slacken surely did happen (even if the error rate of twenty-five years is taken into consideration). There is also a Chinese record attesting to a huge detonation heard at around that time – an account that intriguingly adds, moreover, that the noise came *from the south* – to the south of China, in other words. And Krakatoa is of course due south of China.

It would be stretching matters to say that any of this evidence is wholly convincing: but it seems fair to say that of those two supposed early eruptions, only the later – that occurring in 535 – seems likely to have involved Krakatoa. The other record, if it is not simply a mistaken date, may have related to an eruption of any one of Java's other twenty active volcanoes – or it may simply be a mélange of myth, confusion, legend and embellishment, and may never have happened at all.

The Likely Eruption of AD 535

Assuming, then, that the first Krakatoa eruption did occur in 535, and not a century beforehand, it is fair to say from what little we know of the social conditions in the western Java of the time, that there were probably precious few people around to be aware of it. In particular there seems to have been no city worthy of the name within a hundred miles of the eruption. Chinese traders, ships' captains who made voyages along the northern and eastern

coasts of Java and Sumatra, appear to have left the most comprehensive written records of the region: a number of these speak of
a community of the time known as Si-tiao, which was most
probably on Java and which was possessed of 'fertile lands and
communities with streets'.

Another state, which in the annals of the Peking mandarinate
was called P'u-tei – probably in southern Sumatra – was populated
by a race said to be 'as black as lacquer'; its members liked to
row out from their settlements to sell chickens and fruit to the
emperor's passing sailing junks. There are also records of a rather
dyspeptic-sounding community called Holotan, who grumbled to
the Chinese that they were unceasingly subject to attacks by their
neighbours. And cannibals 'with tails' – probably early versions
of the ceremonial long headdresses still to be found in parts of
southern Borneo – also caught the attention of the Chinese court's
punctilious scribes.

But neither the Indian nor the Chinese traders who passed by
with their gold and jade and sandalwood and cloves noticed a
large city or any kind of sophisticated urban population in Java
or Sumatra. Fires might have lit the sky, and torrents of ash and
pumice rained down from the clouds, but the people of *Nusantara*
(the old Malay word meaning 'the islands between') who saw and
heard and were duly astonished, horrified or hurt, were villagers
only, artless country folk whose descriptions of those early and
startling events were inevitably vague and imaginative.

In 1999 a British television documentary, based on a remarkable book, *Catastrophe*, by a London-based author named David
Keys, suggested powerfully that the AD 535 eruption of Krakatoa
not only happened but was the primary cause of an extraordinary
number of seemingly unrelated yet world-changing events.

The climate changes triggered by the eruption – if that is what
it was – helped to bring about an astonishing series of utterly
apocalyptic events: among these, the television programme suggested, were occurrences of no less magnitude than the Fall of

the Roman Empire, the outbreak of the rat-borne Great Plague, the historyless miseries of the Dark Ages, the birth of Islam, the invasion of Europe by the barbarians, the collapse of Central America's Mayan civilization and the birth of at least four new Mediterranean states – the list goes on and on. And though the arguments promoting such ideas appear at times more than a little speculative, everything eventually distils into a single fact: something enormous did take place somewhere in the world in the first half of the sixth century AD, and it had a staggering effect on the world's climate. But what exactly *was* that something?

A volcano, by all accounts. Evidence used to suggest that nothing at all took place in AD 416 is the same evidence that indicates something very major indeed occurred 119 years later. Dust in the ice-cores, acid snows in Greenland and Antarctica, compellingly seductive data from thousands of tree-ring samples – all point to an event, somewhere, in the first half of the sixth century. And thanks initially to Ranggawarsita's writings, however unreliable, the finger points alluringly to Krakatoa as the site for whatever that event might have been.

Surprisingly, very few halfway reliable scientific tests have ever been undertaken to indicate the date of Krakatoa's previous eruptions. It somewhat defies belief that science has been generally content to allow historians to determine the story of Krakatoa's past, when rather more accurate methods – radiometric dating principally among them – could give the answers to a degree of accuracy that poets to the court of Solo unsurprisingly could never really match. The television programme-makers saw to it that this sorry state of affairs was remedied.

In 1999, as a response to the wide interest over the remarkable suggestions made in *Catastrophe*, the resident specialist on Krakatoa at the University of Rhode Island, Haraldur Sigurdsson, went on an expedition to Krakatoa* to use the magic of modern

* Financed by the British television company, Channel Four.

chemistry to try to find a definitive answer to the puzzle that
Ranggawarsita had set. He attempted this by taking samples of
charcoal from a number of various and evidently very ancient
lava flows that he found on Rakata, the surviving relic-mountain
of the 1883 eruption. He performed dating tests on the samples
using the well-known half-life of the carbon-14 isotope.

The results were, however, only moderately conclusive. The
event that had burned the charcoal had occurred, Professor
Sigurdsson was able to say, between AD 1 and AD 1200. There
had, in other words, been a very large volcanic eruption on
Krakatoa during the first 1,200 years of the Christian era – and
it may well have been a large enough event to trigger the climate
changes that would in turn cause the economic and social dislo-
cations (and the migration of plague-carrying rats) that would
cause the profound events that are the central thesis of *Catastrophe*.

But as to whether that single event can be pinned down to any
one year – and whether that year is likely to be AD 416 or AD 535,
there is no ready answer still. Perhaps only Ranggawarsita really
had any idea.

The Near-certain Eruption of AD 1680

Pure fancy was not so much of a factor 1,100 years later, however,
when Krakatoa may have lifted her skirts once again. *May have*,
though, has to be the operative phrase. We have already seen how
possibly vague and imaginatively drawn were the descriptions of
the supposed events of 416 and 535. There is no evidence at all
for any eruptions during the Buddhist Cailendra Dynasty. The
descriptions of whatever took place in 1680 do not exactly amount
to a paragon of scrupulous exactitude either.

As we have seen, there were just three European witnesses to
what might have occurred: the silver assayer named Johan
Vilhelm Vogel who first saw evidence of ruin on the island; the

writer named Elias Hesse who produced his all too vivid account of an event that, according to him, was still playing itself out more than a year later; and the unnamed captain of a Bengal trading vessel *Aardenburgh*.

The first two of these witnesses wrote accounts of a volcanic event that seem highly coloured, to say the least. And while the *Aardenburgh*'s master may well have spoken robustly of an eruption to attentive and well-lubricated audiences in Batavia's dockside bars, he seems to have written nothing in his log that was of sufficient interest to alert his masters in the Castle: the official records, comprehensive in all other respects, are silent. Something did definitely occur on Krakatoa, of that there is little doubt; but whatever it was, it was probably much less significant a happening than the eruption that seems to have taken place in the sixth century; not to mention what took place two centuries later, in the nineteenth century.

It did none the less take place within a respectable distance of a newly settled urban population. For Batavia, the primary Company town of the VOC, was in 1680 a full eight decades old, and it had attained some kind of settled maturity. It had a walled quarter and turreted administrative offices, a Chinatown and a collection of godowns, and any number of small terraced houses with streets and canals and taverns, forming a dreamy, steamy simulacrum of the VOC employees' much missed homes back in faraway Amsterdam or Leiden, Delft or Utrecht.

The Dutch who settled in seventeenth-century Batavia were not an especially content people, by all accounts. Their lives were a succession of uncomfortable trials. They were seldom fully well: they tended to succumb to a variety of tropical ills – malaria, cholera, dengue fever – and they were morbidly afraid of the air on which they suspected the responsible germs were borne. The foul smells from the coast,* brought in by the sea-breezes that

---

* The locals liked to use the beaches for their ablutions.

usually began to blow at breakfast-time, prompted everyone in the city to keep their doors and windows firmly shut until dusk; and then to shut them once more soon after, to keep out the evening mosquitoes. Everyone bathed in the city canals. 'The ladies unblushingly dived into these general public bathtubs,' wrote one Bernard Vlekke, 'a custom which was vainly forbidden ... because the canals were used as sewers and were therefore, *rather* filthy.'

And then there was the drinking and partying and the smoking, and the slightly desperate merriment of colonial life. No less an authority than Jan Pieterszoon Coen himself, the founder of it all, had decreed the beneficial effects of spirits: 'Our nation must drink or die', he is quoted as having once remarked – an epithet the Dutch distilling industry still likes to remember today. The average seventeenth-century Hollander in Batavia would take a glass of neat genever before his breakfast, and would then while away the day consuming glass after glass of arrack as he sat sweltering in his dark, airless house. And with small Dutch cigars costing no more than a few guilders for a box of a thousand, with big Havana cigars only a few guilders more, and a nut of dark shag big enough to fill a meerschaum bowl going for just a few pence, the Batavian air was always blue with tobacco smoke.

Down by the Jakarta waterfront at Sunda Kelapa there is still the slenderest of reminders of those times, barely preserved in a city that is eternally busy, endlessly and boisterously changing and (given its bewildering jumble of races and religions) all too often bickering with itself, sometimes very violently. Down where the oily waters of the dock slap against the splintered timber piers, the old Dutch spice godowns remain, huddled among the tenements of the fish market. There is a massively built ship-repair dock, with flagstone floors and teak beams, now turned into a restaurant that serves *rijsttafel* and ice-cold Bintang beer. There is a portion of the old city wall, with a round-topped lozenge of a sentry-box, badly in need of care and repair. And there is the Culemborg bastion, with a nineteenth-century watch-tower and customs office, Chinese characters carved into the floor and, it is said, a marker showing the hour meridian, the centre-point of Java Time (Bali being so far away east it is an hour later, Aceh in Sumatra, to the west, an hour before).

But the loveliest sight in Sunda Kelapa has nothing to do with the Dutch, the VOC or, seemingly, with Krakatoa at all. It is a far more elemental, far more timeless vision: the sight of the serried ranks of enormous and gaily painted wooden sailing ships – maybe fifty of them, on a busy day – that are to be found tied up alongside the long quay. They are a type of schooner known as *pinisi*, sailed by rough-and-ready Bugis from Sulawesi, or matelots from Kalimantan and the outer islands of the archipel-ago. They bring in wood – most often illegally cut from the great forests of Borneo and Sulawesi – and sell it in the Jakarta market before sailing home with televisions and washing machines and other necessities less easy to come by on the distant islands.

In one of the local waterfront bars I had fallen in with a forester who had been kind enough to explain to me, over a number of beers, the nature of the distribution of harvestable and protected hardwood trees throughout the archipelago.* Later in the after-noon, when it was still insufferably hot, he took me down to the cool of the docks, and (to illustrate a point he was making about the ruin of Indonesia's rain forests) we walked past the ranks of traders' boats – all moored on the slant, their enormous prows arching over the quayside, young men and pye-dogs sleeping in the welcome shadows they cast.

---

* The western trees – mainly dipterocarps, with winged sepals – are very different from the eucalypts and gum-trees that are found in the forests of the eastern islands. The former are distinctly Asian species, the latter Australian, separated by a Wallace Line of their own, echoing as one would expect the distribution of the islands' other living beings, such as the cassowaries, cockatoos, thrushes, kangaroos and apes.

The forester had mixed views about the traders who owned and sailed the ships. He admired them for their courage, their seamanship, their derring-do. He knew they travelled vast distances without proper navigational equipment; he liked their songs and poetry and wild romancing; he knew they would rarely permit a woman to sail on a vessel with them, that their seafaring tradition was everything. He marvelled at the physical strength of the sailors – was amazed still (though he had lived on Java for twenty years) at the way the minute, wiry and barefoot Bugis sailors would unload huge baulks of mahogany, pieces weighing twice as much as a man, and carry them down narrow and slippery gangplanks. But it was the timber they carried that vexed him: these seamen were unwittingly a part of the distribution chain that turned rare Javanese teak into baubles for Western living rooms, and they should, in his view, be stopped.

We went back to his flat, in a miniature skyscraper on the edge of the fish market. He lived on the twentieth floor, with his Chinese wife and three children. He had recently installed a steel front door, four inches thick, with bolts that made it look like the entrance to a bank vault. It was because of the anti-Chinese riots of 1998, he said – the scars and scorchmarks of which were still everywhere to be seen in Glodok, the Chinese area south of the docks. Mobs of Javanese had raided his apartment that terrible day, driven his wife and family into the street, stolen everything they owned. They had left his wife alone only because he was a Westerner, a foreigner.

But though this was all fascinating, and though his views on the rain forests and the Bugis traders were admirable, I found myself rather more enthralled by a picture that hung on his living-room wall. It was a fine eighteenth-century etching by the well-known Dutch cartographer Jan van Schley. It showed two well-laden Company ships, both heeling slightly before a good breeze, passing in front of an island with a pointed mountain. There was a row of trees a few feet up from the island's shore;

but otherwise the island was made up of naked rock. Flaming from its summit were great tongues of fire and a roiling, boiling mass of dark smoke that towered above the pair of galleons, and almost mingled with the clouds above. The picture was called simply *Het Brandende Eiland* – 'The Burning Island' – and it was a depiction, without a doubt, of the otherwise little-chronicled eruption that supposedly took place in 1680.

He had picked up the etching in an antique shop in Jogjakarta some years before. He knew that it looked somewhat fantastical and was more likely to be a figment of van Schley's normally restrained imagination than an accurate picture of a real happening. But it was a powerful image none the less – a reminder for his living-room wall of the awful power of the volcano near which they all then lived. And a more general and emblematic reminder, given his own domestic circumstances, of the highly precarious, often highly tenuous nature of life in the East Indies.

Before the Certain Eruption of AD 1883

Two centuries after the 1680 eruption that was pictured or imagined by van Schley, when Krakatoa did finally make up her mind to explode, and did so cataclysmically, the city of Batavia had become in outward appearance an entirely different place.

In the 1880s it was no longer simply a Company town, for a start. War with Britain a century beforehand had essentially done for it. Naval blockades during the war had starved the VOC of cash and had kept thousands of tons of Java's choicest exports marooned in the Batavia warehouses; and then the Treaty of Paris of 1782 that ended the fighting in 1784* broke the Dutch

---

* France and the newborn United States of America concluded their own peace with Britain; Holland, however, kept fighting for some while more, placing still heavier burdens on her faraway colonials.

Jan van Schley's early etching *Het Brandende Eiland*, showing two
caravels passing in front of what is presumed to be Krakatoa in full
eruption, in what is further presumed to be 1680.

trading monopoly in the region and placed huge financial burdens on the once grand, formerly secure Company. The Dutch share in the world spice trade promptly dwindled, the revenues from the newly imported plantation crops of coffee, tea and quinine were never sufficient to balance the VOC's enormous expenses, and after two centuries of operation the weary old Company had been declared bankrupt. Its commission to govern formally expired in 1799, and the Dutch government took charge of the East Indies as a purely colonial possession.

Six years later Holland was overrun by forces of the globally ambitious French emperor Napoleon I, who promptly installed his brother Louis on the Dutch throne. War with England then became, and remained for the next ten years, the dominant reality of all European life. It was a reality that spread east to the Indies too, and specifically to Batavia in her new role as the capital city of what was now called the Dutch East Indies. The British were on the prowl in the Eastern seas; the Napoleonic Wars that raged in Europe had a considerable effect, much of it still very apparent today, on the way that the city of Batavia and the government that was run from it were allowed to develop.

It was indeed a Napoleonic *maréchal*, one Herman Willem Daendels, who was to make the most evident changes, and who would determine the shape of the city that existed at the time of Krakatoa's grand ultimate explosion. His orders, which he issued promptly on his appointment to the job of governor-general in 1808, were simple: by any means possible and with no expense spared he was to render Batavia proof from any possible British military attack.

He did this by formally abandoning all the castles, warehouses and fortifications at the seaside, effectively closing down what was dismissively called *benedenstad*, the lower town, the old Batavia, and building an entirely new capital five miles inland, made secure by its geography from any possible sea-borne ambuscades.

Old Batavia, the now squalid, cramped and run-down creation of Jan Pieterszoon Coen, had by the eighteenth century become notorious across the Orient as a pox-ridden graveyard for its resident Europeans. The new Batavia to the south would truly be worthy, he decided, of its long-unrealized sobriquet: *The Queen of the East.* With this in mind he decided to call his new uptown suburb *Weltevreden,* or 'Well Contented', since that is what he fully expected its grateful Dutch residents to be.

He tore down Batavia Castle and built for himself a palace on a vast plain of neatly clipped lawns, where the governors-general of the East Indies would maintain their city headquarters for decades to come. And as he moved the epicentre of administration, so genteel society moved with him, such that by the middle of the nineteenth century a vacuum had been left in the old town, as the famous British colonizer Thomas Stamford Raffles* was to note in 1817:

Streets have been pulled down, canals half filled up, forts demolished and palaces levelled with the dust. The Stadhuis, where the supreme court of justice and magistracy still assemble, remains; merchants transact their business in town during the day, and its warehouses

---

* Although Raffles is best known for having essentially founded Singapore, he was also lieutenant-governor of the East Indies from 1811 to 1816, Java's brief British-ruled interregnum during the Napoleonic Wars. The Dutch have long since accepted with equanimity the five years of their territory's rule from British Calcutta: a portrait of Lord Minto – Raffles's superior – hangs today without remark among other Dutch governors-general in the Regents' Room of the old Dutch Colonial Office in The Hague. Lady Raffles is buried in a pretty Grecian tomb in the Botanical Gardens at Bogor, south of Jakarta. Her husband is memorialized in many ways: by having discovered and restored the marvellous Buddhist temple at Borobudur, in central Java; by having written a near-definitive *History of Java*; and by having named after him the planet's largest flower, *Rafflesia arnoldii,* which has blooms a yard wide, weighs as much as twenty-four pounds, and has a memorably horrible smell.

still contain the richest productions of the island, but few Europeans of respectability sleep within its limits.

By 1858 a passing Dutchman, A. W. P. Weitzel, was to amplify the theme:

After sundown Batavia is silent and empty; not only the offices and large warehouses but even the shops are closed; no carriage is heard any more and the few indigenous people who move along the streets make no noise at all on their bare feet; and if the police had not ordered them to carry torches, they would wander there as dark shadows.

And though the first *Thomas Cook* guide was written in 1903, twenty years after the eruption, it did manage to catch something of the atmosphere of the new city that Daendels had created out of the wreck of the old Company town, and that was well into its full flowering at the century's end:

Whilst Batavia proper — the lower town with its counting houses and shops, its native and Chinese populations, its canals and moats, its dust and dirt, and old-fashioned mansions — makes anything but a charming impression, the upper town, to which all Europeans return in the evening, reminds one of a gigantic park, in which villas are built in rows, and great trees shade the broad and gravelly paths, and spacious squares bring air and wind.

The years immediately before the eruption were stable, prosperous, expansive. Whatever setbacks the city had endured in the aftermath of the VOC's collapse at the end of the eighteenth century had been more than amply reversed in the cosmopolitan, buccaneering, free-marketeering years of the latter half of the nineteenth. The Suez Canal opened in 1869: an appetite for goods from the East — now far closer to European markets, with the short-cut through the desert and ever faster ships on routes — meant that new trading houses were springing up, and new markets for new tropical commodities and wares were emerging on all sides. The population of Batavia, like that of other favoured Eastern cities, began to grow, and fast: it jumped from half a million in 1866 to well over a million at the time of the eruption (merely 12,000 of those were Europeans, 80,000 Chinese, the rest all native East Indians understandably eager to take advantage of the growing wealth around them). As early as 1832, according to an account written by the renowned Dutch scholar of Javanese, Professor P. P. Roorda van Eysinga, there were widespread signs of an accelerating prosperity:

. . . hundreds of carriages of European officials and shop-people raising clouds of dust on the streets, while the Chinese, with their recognizable and unpleasant features, with their long pigtails and silk caps, are everywhere busy hammering, sawing, painting, sewing, building and so on. Rich Arabs and Chinese rode through the streets, half-clad Javanese carried heavy loads, shabby Eurasian clerks walked beneath their sunshades to their offices, old women sold cakes, an Indian sat calmly eating his rice on a banana leaf, and vegetable, milk and fruit sellers, butchers and hill-dwellers offering monkeys and birds all mingled together in the crowd.

This gathering crush of people and the ever accelerating bustle and pace of Batavian life had a further effect: just as in British India, so the wealthier and more influential of the European townspeople moved from the sweltering streets of the capital city up into the hills, to a cool and green town that the government promptly christened *Buitenzorg*, or 'Without a Care', the equivalent of the French *sans souci* (it has now reverted to the native name it had before, the decidedly less carefree-sounding Bogor).

Buitenzorg, just like its corresponding hill-stations at Simla and Murree and Ootacamund in India, had already become a fashionable place at the beginning of the century, its reputation firmly anchored once Daendels had decided, in 1808, to shift his personal headquarters to a great country house that had been built there by an eighteenth-century VOC commander. His officials

A Jakarta city scene, around 1865.

warned him against trying to make the journey: in the torrential
winter rains, they said, it would take thirty teams of horses to get
him there. 'I shall use thirty-one,' he snorted – and promptly
moved into what would be the principal palace for all the
governors-general that followed him, Raffles included.

The house survives today, essentially unchanged: a vast, one-
storeyed gleaming white palace, its immense airy rooms currently
filled with pictures of well-endowed and slightly clad young
women, the pictures and their subjects both equally assiduously
collected, it is said, by Sukarno,* who brought modern Indonesia

---

* Sukarno's private study is dominated by an immense oil painting of
happy-looking workers toiling in a Russian soviet. It was the gift of a
visiting politburo chief, and an indication of the clear left-wing leanings of
the man who was eventually to be replaced by General Suharto in an

to independence. The parklands around the *istana* are alive with thousands of roe-deer, imported by the Dutch a century ago to provide affordable and acceptable meat for the official banquets they so delighted in giving.

The modern world then came with an unexpected suddenness to the Dutch-created world of colonial Java.

On 24 May 1844 Samuel Morse transmitted the famous biblical message 'What hath God wrought!' from the Supreme Court in Washington to his colleague, Alfred Vail, forty miles away in Baltimore. Twelve years later, over almost exactly the same distance, the electric telegraph – which was to play such a crucial role in the spreading of the story of Krakatoa – was formally introduced to the Indies, with the connection of the great palace at Buitenzorg in the summer of 1856 to the colonial offices down in Batavia. From then on the pace of technological innovation in Java quickened. The island was connected internationally in 1859, acquiring an undersea line to Singapore (though this failed after a few days) and then, in 1870, links to both the Malay States and Australia. These proved to be totally stable: and so by the time of the Krakatoa eruption, the places where the explosion was seen and felt and heard and suffered were all connected, by the dots and dashes of Mr Morse's code, to the world beyond.

The eruption of Krakatoa was, indeed, the first true catastrophe in the world to take place after the establishment of a worldwide network of telegraph cables – a network that allowed news of disaster to be flashed around the planet in double-quick time. The implications of this rapid and near-ubiquitous spread of information were profound – and to such an extent that they deserve a separate chapter, which follows later.

Houses in Batavia were connected to one another by telephone from 1882; gossip could spread, as well as news and warning and

American-backed *coup d'état*, which led to the corruption and civil strife that disfigure Indonesia still.

invitations. There had been a gasworks in the city, and the luxury of piped gas for cooking and street lighting, since 1862 (the present gasworks still has one ancient gas-lit street lamp outside the office, which sputters to life from time to time). There was a tramway – drawn by horses from 1869 (with ten of the tiny Sumbawan tram-ponies dying every week) and then by noisy, dirty, ever chuffing steam engines that ran from 1882 onwards (the poor – meaning the Indonesians – were forced to ride in separate carriages from the Europeans). Railway trains were first brought to Batavia by the Dutch government in 1869, with the first line – up to Buitenzorg, naturally – completed in 1873.

And in 1870 that most potent symbol of European civility brought across to the Orient finally made it to Batavia: an ice-works was built. No longer did the genever-drinking Hollanders have to drum their fingers on the teakwood bars at the Harmonie or the Concordia Military Club, as they waited for the ice-chips from Boston, the vessels of what the Americans called *the frozen-water trade*, to appear on the horizon off Sunda Kelapa. Now they could have locally made ice delivered to their fretworked porte cochère doorsteps in Weltevreden every day, or sent to the *Indische* who worked behind the club bar. And they could be content in the knowledge that if the dinner party proved too boisterous or the numbers of guests in the club altogether too many, the host could simply send out for more ice and it would be there, available for delivery, fresh and dripping cold, every day of every following year. 'Everything in Batavia,' wrote a well-satisfied traveller named W. A. van Rees in 1881, 'is spacious, airy and elegant.'

Thus was Batavia quite comfortably arranged at the approach of the critical year of 1883. There was an air of calm contentment in the land (a long-drawn-out guerrilla war between the Dutch and Islamic-led forces in Aceh in northern Sumatra was proving costly for the Batavian government, but was otherwise of no great moment to the citizenry). The traders in Batavia were doing well. Just as in Kansas City, everything here was up to date: modern conveniences were being installed for the Europeans, and the huge numbers of *indigènes* flooding into the city each day were, if nothing else, testament to the capital's ever growing wealth.

The planters out in the countryside were rich as well, but their contentment was tinged by the perennial caution of the farmers, dependent on so many more factors than their own efforts. The newspapers of the day display an increasing concern in the 1880s, for example, that disease and blight might well ruin the crops; and so the Java planters began a programme of experiment and diversification – bringing in Robusta coffee plants from the Congo, for example, to ease the times when blight affected their Arabica or Liberia bushes.

Prospectors found tin, and began working it on the islands of Bangka and Billiton (with the brother of the then Dutch king, Willem III, the main promoter of the Billiton Tin Company). Wildcatters drilling shallow wells in Borneo found oil, though it would be some years before they thought it worth extracting, and many more years before the establishment of the huge combine that would one day become Royal Dutch Oil.

Plant importers, already delighted by the success of the cinchona trees that yielded as much as a seventh of their weight in pure quinine, brought in new rubber trees from Brazil (one of the ships carrying the precious seeds, bound for the Botanical Gardens in Buitenzorg, was passing through the Sunda Strait on the very day of the eruption).

Back in Holland, the moody and clumsily undiplomatic King Willem III was on the throne. In November 1880 he made a surprise appointment: Frederik 's Jacob, a 58-year-old former sailor, map-maker and sugar manufacturer who for the previous ten years had been director-general of the Dutch Railways, was to go to Batavia as governor-general. He took up his appointment the following April and conducted himself during his first years in office with an unassuming efficiency.

Frederik 's Jacob, governor-general of the East Indies in 1880.

There was a great deal of ceremonial about the tasks of a Dutch colonial governor-general – and it was not at all out of the ordinary to see Mr 's Jacob in an official uniform that was adorned (the better both to impress the natives, and to maintain the morale of the settlers) with yards of ornate gold brocade trim, silver and enamel stars, ribbons and garters of red, white and blue, knee-breeches and a tall felt hat with a feathered brim and a wild cockade. He wore it for the first official function of 1883, on 19 February, the formal celebration of the official birthday of his faraway Dutch king.

Although the birthday party in Batavia was a fine and formal affair, marred by nothing more untoward than a general eagerness for strong drink, nearly ninety miles away in a straight line to the west of the palace something was stirring, deep within one of the menacingly dark and forest-clad pinnacles at the northern end of the Sunda Strait. The island with its pointed mountain, first noticed and named almost exactly 300 years before, and which had been placid and beautiful for so very long, was now becoming restless again.

5

THE UNCHAINING OF
THE GATES OF HELL

And I thought: The world is our relentless adversary, rarely outwitted, never tiring.

— a Dutch pilot caught near Anjer, quoted in 'Krakatau', a short story by the novelist Jim Shepard, in his collection *Batting against Castro*, 1996

The rains are usually terrible in Java in the early part of the year, and the February of 1883 was no exception. There were floods in the lower-lying parts of old Batavia, and dozens of country roads were impassable. When the adjutants of the garrison artillery regiments inspected the city parade grounds on Waterlooplein on the afternoon of Sunday the 18th, they found the glutinous red mud too deep for their cannon-wheels. So they sent a message, via the aide-de-camp, to Governor-General 's Jacob up at his great white palace at Buitenzorg: the traditional military parade that had been planned for the following morning to offer loyal birthday greetings to his faraway imperial majesty King Willem III could not, it was greatly regretted, go ahead.

Some might have seen the cancellation as an omen. It was in any case not a happy time for the Dutch monarchy. The then head of the House of Orange – whose official titles included King of the Netherlands and Grand Duke of Luxembourg, and whose full and magisterial-sounding name was Willem Alexander Paul Frederik Lodewijk – belonged firmly to the glittering European aristocracy of a *belle époque*, an aristocracy that was only a very few years away from the corrosive effects of revolution and war, and neither wise enough nor prescient enough to realize it.

Willem, whose sixty-sixth birthday fell on 19 February, was a less than inspiring monarch. He had been on the throne for thirty-four years and was weary, moody, rigorously anti-Catholic and notoriously undiplomatic. He was also keenly frustrated by the limitations that had been imposed on the powers he had known as Crown Prince, which had been savagely cut back by the constitutional reforms initiated by his own father, Willem II.

But out in the distant colonies of the East, such regal maunderings were either unheard or ignored. Monday, the 19th of February, King's Day, was the culminating moment of a whole weekend of midwinter festivities. The party started on the Saturday, in the Willem III Grammar School, with a dance that the elite of the capital were expected to attend. The governor-general came down by special train from his mansion, made a speech welcoming everyone to the three-day saturnalia, inaugurated the dancing with a waltz with his wife, Leonie, admired the young girls' extravagantly full ball-gowns (waspishly noted by the columnist of the *Locomotive* as being fully a year behind the fashions of Paris), took part in the traditional eleven o'clock conga, and then took himself off home – leaving the party-goers to dance themselves into the kind of frenzy that was only permissible in a servant-rich colony with a long weekend of indolence and celebration stretching ahead.

It was a busy time for the governor-general. On the Sunday he

had church service to attend, alms to dispense, military parades
to bless – and then came unwelcome news about the weather and
the consequent cancellation of the following day's cavalry tattoo.
And on the next day, the Monday, 's Jacob had to get himself
gussied up in his finest raiment once again and travel down from
Buitenzorg to the sweltering and now rain-soaked capital for the
much more formal (but paradeless) day of festivities. Every Dutch
building was festooned with flags of red, white and blue, and
the ships in the harbour flew pennants and signal bunting. In
Waterlooplein, with its palaces and military barracks,* thousands
of soldiers – both the regular officers from Holland and levies
from the 'loyal races' throughout the islands – were arrayed in
tidy ranks for inspection.

The king's representative in the Indies, who, when he deigned
to come down to hot and steamy Batavia, held court at his
immense and newly completed white marble Doric-columned
palace on the Koningsplein – the King's Square – staged an official
morning audience that day. He ordered to be arrayed before him
his entire Council for the Indies, his senior civil servants, the
generals, the bishops, the foreign diplomats (including the British
consul-general, a Mr Cameron, and his American counterpart,
Oscar Hatfield) and the favoured elite of Batavia high society. He
announced, as was customary, an amnesty for a slew of prisoners.
He also told his sweltering audience that a dozen or so banned
persons – the concept of 'banning', so much a feature of later
apartheid rules in that other former Dutch possession in southern
Africa, was very much in force in the East Indies of the time –
were to be relieved of their ordeal, as a birthday bounty from the
representative of His Majesty.

The rest of the happy day was then devoted to games – which

* There was a tall monument to the victory at Waterloo (Willem's father
had been Dutch commander in the field) surmounted by a very small lion –
so small that it was regarded with amused contempt by most Batavians,
who thought it looked like a poodle.

included cricket, a sport that had infected the East Indies after a visit from the Singapore Cricket Club ten years before – or to parties at the two principal clubs, the Harmonie and the Concordia Military, or to a massive public display of fireworks. 'The Governor-General gave a gala dinner at the palace,' reported the next day's *Javasche Courant*, in the breathlessly sycophantic tones of the times. 'The palace was magnificently decorated and illuminated. All of the high authorities of the colony were invited, and they cheered with delight when the Governor-General raised his glass to the health of the King. Then there were wonderful fireworks on the Koningsplein, and thousands of people came out in the evening to enjoy the sight.'

Whether the worse than usual rains and the attendant cancellations were seen as any kind of augury or not, all seemed otherwise perfectly normal in a colony that this day of celebrations had already demonstrated was run with strict and meticulous order. The colonized people were at this time in their history by and large content, the merchants were prosperous, the big Javanese cities – Batavia, Surabaya, Bandung, Jogjakarta, Solo and Anjer among them – were generally peaceful and well mannered.

And yet, unknown to all but a few academics and seers, and to a few in those deeper recesses of Javanese and Sumatran *kratons* where the sultans lived and ruled, a multitude of strange and unrecognized forces were busying themselves – social, political, religious, economic forces that would erupt across the colony within just a very short while. The seeds of impending troubles – of risings, insurgencies, militancies that would in time mature to become generally anti-imperialist and specifically anti-Dutch – were just then starting to take root, were growing unseen, like mushrooms in the dark. We shall return to them later; for now they provide the faintest, barely audible *basso continuo* sounding beneath the more dramatic events that were to dominate the year.

Whatever might have then been going on beneath the outwardly content surface of East Indies society, it happened that at
this very same time quite another array of unseen forces, which
some historians would later link with the coming societal changes,
were also gathering. These, though, were physical forces, forces
related to the then unrecognized phenomena of tectonics and
subductions and fault-zones and sea-floor spreading, forces that
were regrouping after years of quiescence and that now – just as
invisible as the coming changes in politics and social life – had
begun to prepare for their awakening once more.

They were at work particularly beneath the surface of western
Java, readying themselves for a six-month period of violent and
nightmarish activity. They would first become apparent, and
violently so, just a scant ninety days after the smoke and flames
and thunder of the last fireworks of His Majesty's birthday party
had died away.

It began with a sudden trembling. At first it was slight, more of
a quivering of the air, a series of windy rumblings, of vague
flutterings of atmosphere that were barely to be noticed at all. In
normal times they would probably have passed without comment,
other than by some Dutch planter in a bar who might point with
amusement to the surface of his genever and get others to peer
down at how shaken and rippled it was. Seismic events, where
the rocks themselves moved, were a commonplace throughout
the islands. Earthquakes and eruptions seemed as everyday as
thunderstorms and plagues of mosquitoes.

But this one was a little different. For a start, the year had
already been curiously quiet across the entire colony. Between
January and May the Observatory at Batavia had logged only
fourteen earthquakes, and, of these, four were in eastern Java and
seven in Sumatra. The year was calm, people were lulled into a
kind of easy complacency.

And western Java was in any case a quietish corner of the

archipelago, seismically speaking. Everyone had heard the stories about ancient eruptions, true; and there were those who looked at maps and thought they had heard tell of when Java and Sumatra were one island that had broken apart during some terrific volcanic event, ages ago. But most believed that Krakatoa was long since extinct, inactive, peaceful and, most likely, dead. The Batavians who came out from town to swim on the clean white western beaches; the local bird-sellers who hawked pretty Anjer swallows to passengers on the ships setting off for the long sea passage back to Europe;* the bum-boat skippers who sold fruit and coral and curios to sea-borne passers-by: all thought of this corner of their islands as endlessly tranquil, a place far removed from the more violent activity that was so common near mountains like Bromo, or Merapi, or Merbapu.

But then the vibrations began. It was just after midnight, early on the morning of Thursday, 10 May, when the lighthouse keeper at what was then called First Point – the more southerly of a pair of lights on the enormous rocky headland at the south-eastern entrance to the Sunda Strait, known to approaching mariners as Java Head – felt what he knew only too well was a tremor in the air. The lighthouse suddenly seemed to shift on its foundations. The sea outside whitened, appeared to freeze briefly (as we now know it does above a depth charge), became uncannily smooth like a mirror, shivered slightly and then returned to its usual sickly swell.

It was really nothing much. There was no suggestion of where the vibration might have come from. The keeper checked his records: the last volcano to erupt anywhere near by was Lamongan, and that lay 600 miles to the east. Whatever had prompted this particular rumbling was probably closer than that. Though

---

* The birds, reported the *Illustrated London News* of the day, invariably died as soon as the ship encountered chilly weather: very few made it all the way to Europe.

it caused no obvious damage, it was strong enough, unusual enough in pattern and curious enough in location for the light-house keeper to log it, and to note in a report that he wrote during the following weekend and sent off to Batavia with his other weekly summaries.

Five days after the initial vibration the same happened again, except that this time it was stronger and more sustained, more widely felt. What had been felt in west Java was now felt on the other side of the Sunda Strait, in Sumatra. The Dutch *contrôleur* in the south Sumatran town of Ketimbang, Willem Beyerinck, was sufficiently roused by the thudding, rumbling bangs occurring beneath his feet on the night of 15 May to send a telegram, an official confidential message presenting all the facts to his superior, the Resident of Lampong. It took him five further days to pluck up the courage to send it: he had to make sure he was right. In the end he made the call: powerful tremors, he reported, were now being felt continuously up and down the Sumatran coast on the northern and western side of the Strait.

This was the first official word that something untoward was in the offing. And coming from a civil servant with the rank of controller, the news had considerable weight. Controllers in the colonial service of Holland were not a breed of men given to panic.*

---

* A *contrôleur* was one of the more junior grades in the Dutch colonial service, presiding over a subdivision of a Residency known as an *afdeling*, or department; but junior or no, a candidate had to spend four years at the College of Delft and pass with honours a rigorous examination that included the Javanese and Malay languages (both very similar, to be sure), French, German and English language and literature, Islamic law, algebra, geom-etry, trigonometry, geology (no doubt helpful for his present task), drawing, land surveying and levelling as well as a host of other easier dis-ciplines including, for some less explicable reason, the subtle mysteries of 'Italian book-keeping'. An official warning of troublesome seismic activity sent by a *contrôleur* would certainly cause senior members of the colonial administration to sit up and take notice.

The ships were the next to take note. The Sunda Strait –
seventeen miles across at its narrowest – was then, as today, a
frantically busy waterway. The number of vessels passing between Java and Sumatra on their way to and from Europe and
the Americas on the one hand, and China and the more distant
reaches of the East on the other, was prodigious in the 1880s.
There were at least ten ships in the vicinity when Krakatoa's first
eruption began: those definitely known to be near by included
the American brig *A. R. Thomas*; the British barque *Actaea*, commanded by a Captain Walker; the Dutch mail-packet *Zeeland*,
commanded by a Captain MacKenzie, on her way from Batavia
to the Indian Ocean and then by long sea to the Netherlands; the
Sunda, a steam ferry-boat skipping her way from Batavia to a
series of local ports; the *Archer*, an Australian passenger steamship
of the Queensland Royal Mail Line; the *Conrad*, a Dutch mailboat
heading northwards from Europe to Batavia; a Dutch barque, the
Haag, under the command of a Captain Ross; the German warship
Elisabeth, heading south from Singapore; and, more mundane than
romantic, the hoppers *Samarang* and *Bintaing*, both shuttling
between Java and Sumatra, performing harbour drudgery on
behalf of the Batavia Port Authority.

Each had a story to tell. The first to note something unusual
in the log was the *Elisabeth*, a German corvette returning home
to the motherland after two years in China and Japan, time spent
doing picket duty on the Imperial Navy's Far Eastern Station.*

---

* German commercial and military interests in the Far East were growing
fast in the late 1880s, not least because the Manchus in Peking's Forbidden City had been vastly impressed by the Prussian-led strengthening
of the Reich after 1871, and had asked the Germans to help modernize
their own armed forces. Matters were soon to turn sour, however; and
in 1898 Germany annexed for her own naval use – for vessels like the
Elisabeth – the port of Tsingtao on the Shandong peninsula. The influence
of the next fifteen years of German rule lingers still: German architecture
remains highly visible in the town today, and Tsingtao beer, one of China's

The ship had called briefly at Singapore and then, though it
bypassed Batavia, had stopped instead at Anjer to coal, take on
water and drop off a single passenger. The *Elisabeth* left the tiny
port's quayside on the morning of Sunday, 20 May. She turned
towards the south, trimmed her sails and set a course that would
take her down the Sunda Strait and out into the open ocean.

Her master, a Captain Hollmann, then became the first European to see the very beginning of the eruption of the mountain.
He was the first to write a report about what now seemed to be
behind all the rumbling and trembling that had been noticed
around the region since the lighthouse keeper's summary of the
curious vibrations that he had experienced earlier in the month.
It was 10.30 on the hot, cloudless summer morning. Captain
Hollmann was looking from his bridge directly across to starboard towards the 2,625-foot southern summit of Krakatoa,*
when suddenly something took place that he never imagined
possible. Without warning:

. . . we saw from the island a white cumulus cloud, rising fast. It rose
almost vertically until, after about half an hour, it had reached a height
of about 11,000 meters. Here it started to spread like an umbrella,
probably because it had reached the height of the anti-trade winds, so

---

better-known exports, was for years prepared under the supervision of a
Bavarian *Braumeister*.

* This summit, Rakata, lay at the southern end of Krakatoa and, since it
was by far the highest point, was the most visible feature of the thickly
forested, lozenge-shaped island, which measured about six miles along its
north–south axis, and was at its widest point in the south some two miles
across. The other high points, apparent only on a close inspection, were
Danan, a cratered peak in the middle of the island rising to 1,496 feet, and
Perboewatan, on the narrow northern end of the island, which was 399 feet
high. Two other islands are associated – Lang Island lying two miles to the
north-east, Verlaten a similar distance off to the west. Both, as suggested
before, are probably relics of an even greater super-Krakatoa of earlier
times.

that soon only a small part of blue sky was seen on the horizon. When at about 4.00 in the afternoon a light SSE breeze started, it brought a fine ash dust which increased strongly . . . until the entire ship was covered in all parts with a uniform fine grey dust layer.

Faced with the astonishing sight of a white cloud that was streaking up into the heavens, reaching what his navigating officer calculated was fully seven miles into the clear blue sky, the ship's marine chaplain, Father Heims, allowed himself a little more latitude than his superior in the Imperial Navy, and wrote:

. . . the crew had assembled on the upper deck in clean Sunday clothes, to be mustered in divisions. The commander had just looked at the parading crew and started to inspect his pretty clean ship, when a certain motion was noticed among the officers which were assembled on the upper deck and bridge in their Sunday clothes. Glasses and heads all turned towards the lonely countryside in which the shores of Sumatra and Java coincided with the small island of Krakatau: there, at least 17 nautical miles distant, an enormous shining wide vapour column rose extremely rapidly to half the horizon, and reached within a short time the colossal height not below 11,000 meters, contrasting in its light-coloured snow-like appearance with the clear blue sky. It was convoluted like a giant wide coral stock . . .

At this point the right reverend's prose turns rather more purple than he probably would on reflection have wished. He compares Krakatoa's rising plume of steam and smoke first to a giant cauliflower, then to a billy club, next to 'the convoluting steam column from the smoke stack of a gigantic standing steam locomotive' and finally to an odd confection that he christens 'three-dimensional steam balls'.

Mercifully, after only a few lines of such description, he abandons his quest for literary permanence, and returns to writing for his parishioners back home, who were no doubt eagerly awaiting his reappearance in the pulpit. In doing so, he provides

some highly useful evidence for those who would later study this
first phase of the eruption:

We did not hear any detonations. The veil over the sky was so dense
and uniform that the almost full moon was only barely visible during
the night . . . on the next morning . . . the ship, which was so clean
24 hours ago, looked very strange: it looked like a mill ship or, more
precisely, like a floating cement factory. On the outside everything –
ship's wall, torpedo pipes, the entire masts, etc. – was covered uni-
formly with a grey sticky dust . . . it had accumulated thick and heavy
on the sails; the steps of the crew sounded muffled . . . The people
enjoyed collecting the lava dust as polishing material, and it was not
very heavy work to collect the stuff in sacks and boxes.

  The sky above this ash rain disaster appeared like a large bell made
of rather dull milky glass in which the sun hung like a light blue lamp
. . . for another 75 German miles we had to sit in the evening with our
faces looking backwards as we sat together trying to get some air.
The distribution of the ash-fall would be over an area at least as large
as Germany . . .

One by one the other ships in the neighbourhood reported
their news. Some of the reports were made public within days or
weeks of the event; in later years the logs were found and published, or private letters surfaced from their amazed commanders
or crew, as well as messages from passengers who had been
aboard and knew that they had seen something strange and
wanted, earnestly, to tell of it.

  The British ship *Actaea*, for instance, which was sailing eighty
miles west of Krakatoa, noticed a 'peculiar green colour' in the
morning skies to the east-south-east; by mid-afternoon her sails
and rigging were covered in fine ash and dust; and when the sun
set it did so as 'a silver ball'.

  The hopper *Samarang*, en route to the port of Merak, felt a
sudden swell, massive enough to lift her and her screw clear out
of the water.

The *Zeeland*, sailing with her full complement of passengers and mail back towards Holland, passed within five miles of Krakatoa.* Her compass needle suddenly began to spin round and round, uselessly. When it settled it showed a deviation from normal of twelve degrees. Steam and debris then roared up from the most northerly of the three cones that could be seen on the island, and to the crew a deafening noise began to sound, seeming to combine the thunder of heavy artillery and rattle of continuous machine-gun fire.

Captain MacKenzie next saw to his astonishment a huge column of black cloud. Not white – despite what others had said he was sure it was, at this moment, black. It rose swiftly above the mountain, with lightning flashes deep within the clouds, and a continuous crackling sound. The sea all around the island was punctured by immense grey waterspouts rising into the air; it became so dark he had to reduce speed to five knots. There being no radio at the time, he frantically raised a string of coloured signal flags, alerting all who might be watching him. The Lloyd's agent at Anjer certainly was, for he noted in his log that MacKenzie was fast *standing into danger*, and others who came near him might suffer the same fate.

And then came the moment when a delft dinner plate fell off a dining-room table in the old part of Batavia and broke into a thousand pieces.

* To get into the Sunda Strait the *Zeeland*, like all other vessels passing along this great waterway connecting the Indian Ocean and the South China Sea, had perforce to skirt around another – non-eruptive – island that seemed almost to block the northern entrance to the channel. The island is known today as Pulau Sangiang. In the nineteenth century, however, at a time when so many of the coastal features sported English names – Pepper Bay, Welcome Bay, First Point, Java Head and Polish Hat are all along the Sunda Strait – this navigational nuisance of rock and forest was officially called, on the Admiralty charts, Thwart-the-Way Island.

The plate had belonged to Mrs van der Stok, a middle-aged Dutch lady who at the time of its breakage – shortly after ten minutes to eleven on the Sunday morning – was quite probably laying her table for family luncheon. It had been a part of her dowry on the day she had married Dr J. P. van der Stok – the distinguished scientist from Utrecht who had brought her out to Batavia some years before on his appointment as director of the colony's Magnetic and Meteorological Observatory. The couple lived in a single-storey house attached to the Observatory, and on that hot and cloudless Sunday morning both could not help but notice that something, somewhere, had gone badly awry.

First there was the plate, lying smashed on the marble floor of the dining room. Then in the living room Dr van der Stok himself, reading the Sunday edition of the Java *Bode* – the word means 'messenger' – heard all the windows and doors rattle and bang. From somewhere to the west came a low, rumbling sound, like that of distant artillery. He got out his pocket-watch and noted the time: 10.55 a.m.

He walked across to the Observatory, noticing immediately that the needles and pens suspended by their cocoon-threads on his magnetic declinometer were ticking and trembling violently – not in the usual side-to-side sweeps that one might expect from an earthquake, but in a series of buzzing up-and-down motions that did not register properly on the paper rolling from the drum. The more he thought about it, the more he realized something odd: the vibrations were not so much being felt through his feet, as if they had emanated from somewhere deep in the earth; they were in fact being felt *in the air*. True, there were ground tremors, and buildings were shaking – this was self-evident. But most of the shaking was coming through the very atmosphere itself. And vibration of this kind was the particular hallmark of an erupting volcano, not of the subterranean shaking of an earthquake.

Later he would see more commonplace left-to-right activity on his declinometer – but only when the ash had begun to drift down over the city that evening. Then he surmised quite rightly that the magnets were going wild simply because the falling ash was rich in iron, like a blizzard of tiny compasses.

For now, though, it was all vibration and rumbling and the occasional period of low and menacing thuds. Van der Stok knelt down and put his ear to the ground. Nothing. Nothing deep-seated. And what was more, these vibrations were continuing for long, long periods – an hour already, with no signs of abating. Earthquake vibrations last for matters of seconds only, a few minutes at the most – followed by periods of quiet, and then aftershocks, and then more movement and mayhem. This was very different.

And all of this made him now, at noon on that Sunday, quite certain that he knew what was happening. These particular kinds of vibrations were absolutely typical of those caused by a volcano. And so each time a fresh explosion of trembling started again, he noted the time in his official log-book. Had it been an earthquake, there would be less need to catalogue the aftershocks, the timings of which were in any case mathematically predictable. But this was evidence of a volcano, somewhere, and the measuring of its palpitations might give some clue as to its future behaviour.

All the while van der Stok was kept busy fending off inquiries from worried Batavians – men and women who flooded to his Observatory, even on this sunny Sunday, wanting to know *just what was happening?* This, most of them said, was like nothing they had ever known before. There had been a curious trajectory about each person's morning on that day. They had awakened to the unusual sounds, and they had been then merely puzzled. By the time they breakfasted, they had become concerned. The Christians among them had gone off to their churches, feeling moderately alarmed. After matins they had ventured back out on to the streets, by now in their droves, and they were, at least privately, in moods that were at first quite agitated and, as the thunder wore on, very apprehensive indeed.

The director noted with the dispassion of a trained observer a distinct racial difference in public attitudes to the events. The Dutch who called in to see him appeared to be outwardly calm, the men displaying either the equanimity of their long experience in the Orient, or the public stoicism, the stiff upper-lip, the code of *pas devant*, that they felt appropriate to their standing as proudly indifferent colonials. The native Javanese, on the other hand, seemed to be much more deeply concerned, with many frightened and, in more than a few cases, quite terror-struck.

To the Javanese and Sumatrans, and especially to the coastal people called the Sundanese – who were and still are a very distinct group well known for their mystical beliefs and deep piety – an event like this out in the Sunda Strait was heavy with suggestive power. In their view the eruptions showed that the spirit of the mountain, the widely feared Orang Alijeh, had for some reason been made angry, was now roaming abroad, breathing fire and smoke and displaying his displeasure. Such a happening could only bode ill for all. Most of the colonials officially and instinctively disapproved of the natives' superstitions, and van der Stok himself was icily dismissive. And yet some of the wiser old colonials did wonder about such things – at least, they would wonder after the terror was fully over, many months hence: *what had it really meant?*

For the moment, though, what was of more immediate concern was the need for a widespread battening down of the hatches, with the inhabitants of western Java and southern Sumatra waiting to see just what Nature – or the gods – had in mind to hurl down at them. For the next two days they had a great deal to keep them anxious.

The little south Sumatran town of Ketimbang is at the best of times a dreadfully vulnerable place: not only is it on a funnel-shaped bay, where the spring tides can rush in most dangerously; not only is it sited on mangrove swamps and mud-flats, ready to be inundated by every rising of the waters; but it also lies directly beneath a small volcano called Rajabasa – the mountain's flanks rise steeply to more than 4,000 feet immediately behind the cluster of coastal houses and their tiny fishing port. Willem Beyerinck, the colonial controller who had been one of the first to note the ominous initial rumblings five days before, was in time to be tested harshly by what happened. His wife maintained a close watch on the entire affair, from beginning to end, and kept a detailed journal. In May, or so it seemed from her detached and insouciant tone, the early stages of the eruption appeared to her more inconvenient than truly alarming.

When it all began on the Sunday morning she had been taking the air on her veranda, idly watching the ships that passed by up and down the ever crowded Strait. She would derive hours of pleasure from watching the long-distance boats fresh out from Batavia, their sails all slipped and bellying in the breeze as the craft began scudding their way towards Europe. There was always a great deal of shipping to see: the view from the controller's elegant little house was magnificent.

But then, without warning, she was jolted from her reverie: another hammer-blow, another set of violent tremors started up once more. 'We were much bothered,' she wrote. The vibrations were best seen in the water barrels kept stored in the bathroom, she said, since their surfaces rippled prettily with every detonation. She took up her diary, and began to make notes of yet another subterranean interruption.

She was writing all this in her journal when, quite unannounced, a *prahu* arrived and was hurriedly slithered up on to the mud, its long bamboo outrigger propping it to one side. Eight frightened-looking fishermen leaped from it, ran up the beach and made straight for Beyerinck's office. They jabbered excitedly, in a mixture of Sundanese and pidgin Dutch. They were from the island of Sebesi, they said, and they had all been together that morning – on Krakatoa.

They had gone there to gather wood for boat-building. They

had been felling trees and stacking cords, chatting contentedly among themselves, when suddenly they heard what they assumed was a burst of cannon-fire from a warship. It was probably, they thought, a Dutch man-o'-war exercising out in the Strait. At first they paid little attention, and carried on felling trees – until there was a second, terrifyingly loud report, which made them dash down to the beach to see what was going on.

As soon as they got there, they said, they saw the very beach itself split wide open, and jets of black ash and red-hot stones roared out into the air. They fled in terror, running for safety and then diving into the sea to swim out to where they had left the boat. The tide had risen dramatically, they said: just an hour beforehand they had been able to wade to the mooring-place.

The controller's wife, by all accounts a sceptical and somewhat hard-bitten lady, was in no mood to listen to these excitable natives. She told her husband, acidly, that it was simply impossible for *a beach to erupt*. He was ready to agree, to shoo the fishermen away. But then Beyerinck's superior suddenly arrived from his own headquarters further up Lampong Bay, in the little port-city of Telok Betong.

He was a Mr Altheer, then just a month away from the end of his five-year posting as Resident of Lampong, and he was keenly eager to do the right thing and leave with his reputation in good standing. He had just been telegraphed by the governor-general, he told his junior; he had been ordered to investigate a situation that could be heard by, and was now fast alarming, the entire Batavian citizenry. Whatever the risks, he and Beyerinck must leave for Krakatoa immediately.

And so the two men jumped into the official government launch that had brought the Resident down from Telok Betong, and they bumped out into the rough waters of the bay, turned due south and sped through what turned out to be, quite bizarrely, wave upon wave of floating pumice stone. They headed past the two islands of Sebuku and Sebesi that hid Krakatoa from their view, dodged masses of pumice and charred and floating trees, were drenched by massive sudden waves, enveloped in clouds of choking gas and a miasma of falling ash. It is twenty-four miles from Ketimbang to Krakatoa: it took the men four hours to bring the coastline of the island into some kind of view.

And though we do not know from their records whether the pair actually landed, we do know that they spotted exactly what it was that had so alarmed the fishermen before them: the northernmost beach of Krakatoa was indeed belching fire and smoke, and the smallest and most northerly of the three cones of the island, Perboewatan, was in the process of erupting, the roaring and belching and noise of its concussions getting stronger with every minute.

The two officials turned tail, their worries for their own safety finally taking precedence over Mr Altheer's concern for his colonial career. They sped back through an ever more dense coagulation of hot grey pumice, making their way through the fast-falling tropical night to the coast and the Ketimbang telegraph station. Shortly before midnight they sent a hurriedly composed message in Morse code, marked for the eyes of the governor-general only.

Within minutes came a reply: the Resident of Bantam, on the western side of Java across the Strait, reported seeing essentially the same thing: flames, belches of fire, rafts of floating rock, ash falls. And he had heard it too: the noise of what was undoubtedly an eruption, memorably terrible, and sounding to him like the crashing, screeching roar of a great ship's anchor chain that was being endlessly raised, its shackles banging hard and rustily against the vessel's sides.

More evidence had meanwhile been streaming in from all quarters. The northbound sailing vessel *Conrad*, enveloped in an inferno of choking ash and dust in which the ambient temperature was at least ten degrees higher than it had been elsewhere, had battled for well over five hours to pass through a near-impenetrable field of floating pumice, its grey masses packed tightly, like ice-floes. Forests on the flanks of Krakatoa were seen to be ablaze. The doctor on board the southbound *Sunda* saw bright-red clusters of fire, 'like sheaves of wheat', bursting from the column of smoke that poured from Perboewatan. He saw a new crater on the island's western side spurt a torrent of dark-red fire. Later that evening, when the *Sunda* was thirty miles away from the eruption and almost in the open ocean, the doctor asked a sailor to drop a bucket into the sea, and the man pulled back up only pumice, with barely any water at all.

Peculiar, ominous sounds had been heard up in Singapore, more than 500 miles to the north. An English plant-collector named Forbes, working more than 1,300 miles away in Timor, reported a sprinkling of ash around his grass hut. There were some fanciful reports as well: someone reported that all the chronometers in the government observatory at Surabaya in east Java, 500 miles away, had mysteriously jumped forward, and that the time ball by which ships in harbour might learn the hour had somehow stuck on its shaft. These later turned out to be nonsense.

On the other hand the usually circumspect Lloyd's agent – a man who in Anjer owned a small *pension*, the Anjer Hotel, down by the docks* – turned in what sounded like an entirely responsible report. He scribbled a hasty telegram to his head office in Batavia, for eventual transmission to the insurance exchange in London, with the first impression of what he was seeing: 'Krakatan [*sic*] casting forth fire, smoke and ash, accompanied by explosions and distant rumblings.' Only later in the day was he able to send a rather more discursive account.

---

* The agent was named Mr Schuit. But there is ample opportunity for confusion ahead, for in Anjer at the same time there happened to be a lighthouse keeper also called Mr Schuit, an unrelated widow-woman named Mrs Schuit and a newly appointed telegraph-master who was called Mr Schruit. Since all played major roles in the August cataclysm, it is as well to be forewarned.

So now, more than a week after the initial feeble quiverings had first been felt at the lighthouse, the cause and the source of it all had been seen, and in action. It was now well beyond any doubt that the long-dormant (but apparently not extinct) island of Krakatoa was in an entirely new phase of its geological development, active once again and fast starting to erupt. What would happen next, the scale of the catastrophe that would envelop the region in a little more than ten weeks' time, would positively beggar belief.

And yet two days later, after its alarming opening salvo, the island quietened down again. A thin plume of white smoke and steam still rose above the Perboewatan crater, hinting that something was continuing to roil beneath the surface. But outwardly, all looked tranquil once more. The low, triple-cratered island and its neighbours slumbered hotly, surrounded by a calm and deep-blue sea; and when viewed from the ports of west Java, they again became near-invisible, compared to the hazily violet and distantly looming silhouettes of the truly enormous volcanoes of Sumatra.

The two peaceful days went past, then three. After a fourth the governor-general decided that if all were really quiet, it might now be prudent to go and take a closer look at Krakatoa, both to see what had already transpired and, more importantly, to see if such an event looked likely to take place again.

The first-ever government inspector to visit the island had done so just three years before. He was a mining engineer from Doorn named Rogier Diederik Marius Verbeek, and he would make his name in later years with his monumental, 546-page study of the great eruption of '83. But in July 1880, when he first set foot on the 'geologically completely unknown terrain' of the island, he was himself quite unknown, a specialist only in the coal mines of east Borneo. He found himself near Krakatoa while on temporary

Rogier Verbeek.

attachment to Holland's splendidly named Imperial Beacons &
Coastal Lighting Service, which had a small ship named the
Egeron bound for an inspection of a lighthouse on a clifftop with
the rather less regal name of Flat Corner. 'On my return trip to
Batavia I was able to pay a short visit* to the islands in the Sunda
Strait,' of which Krakatoa was by far the most interesting.

He sketched the four islands of the group; he took a small boat
to the northern end, close to the soon-to-be-notorious 400-foot
peak of Perboewatan; he chipped away with his hammer at what
was evidently a recently made lava flow; he took samples of what
he later decided was a rather unusual dark andesitic obsidian – a

---

* Which he later said was for no more than 'a couple of hours'.

glassy,* evidently very rapidly melted-and-cooled rock that in this case had, most interestingly, a highly acidic character.

Its composition was in fact much more than simply interesting: it was highly suggestive of its having come from a melt of the half-oceanic, half-continental mix of materials that had been made deep inside what geology now knows to be a typical subduction zone. But Verbeek could not possibly have known this, nor could he have made any but the most primitive surmises about the rock's observed and rather curious acidity. The very concept of a subduction zone was wholly unknown back in the nineteenth century; along with the mysteries of sea-floor spreading and continental drift, these zones were only to be understood almost a century later.

And in any event Verbeek was not going to be allowed to make any further observations, since the crew of the *Egeron*'s pinnace were champing at the bit, eager to steam on home, and they kept blowing their siren to bid him stop hammering. He was frustrated too: it turned out to be far too difficult for him to pass along the Krakatoa shore through the dense jungle that stretched clear down to the sea. 'There was no time,' he admitted lamely, 'to collect any rock samples from the southern part . . . that is, of the peak.' But, he added drily, 'Little did I think that the places where I hammered rocks would disappear altogether three years later.'

Three years later Dr Verbeek very nearly missed what would be for him the culminating event of his geological career. He had left for Utrecht, to supervise the making of a geological map of south-western Sumatra, and only by the greatest good fortune did he come back to Java on leave in the summer of 1883. He actually completely missed the first part of the eruption, even so – his ship steamed past the fire-torn and half-ruined island in

---

* The Ancient Romans used shards of Vesuvius obsidian as razors, since the rock had the property of fracturing with extremely sharp edges.

July, six weeks after these first eruptions had begun. His absence forced Governor-General 's Jacob to choose in his place one of his deputies, an obscure mining engineer named A. L. Schuurman, to make the hazardous first journey across to Krakatoa. His mission was simple: to see what might be seen, and to make an official report on whether anything devastating was likely to happen again.

There was no problem in finding a suitable boat for Mr Schuurman. A combination of a widespread popular fascination with what had taken place and the eagerness of local shipowners to satisfy that fascination – the force of the market, in other words – were to supply him with exactly what he needed.

The British chaplain in Batavia, the Reverend Philip Neale, was to write later that since 'the spectacle was regarded by the Dutch as a curiosity . . . an agreeable excursion was made to the island by one of the mail steamers trading in the Java Sea'. The Netherlands Indies Steamship Company* was the first to recognize the tourist potential of the event, and came up in short order with an excursion vessel, the 1,239-ton *Gouverneur-Generaal Loudon.* On Saturday, 26 May, representatives from the Company tacked up notices in the Harmonie and Concordia Clubs advertising the delights of such an 'agreeable excursion' and announcing a competitive price of only twenty-five guilders. By

---

* The timetables of the various shipping lines that served the region make for delightful reading. The Netherlands Royal Mail Line, founded in 1870, 'maintains a regular fortnightly service between Europe and Java, leaving Amsterdam every alternate Saturday, calling at Southampton, Lisbon, Genoa, Port-Saïd, Suez, Colombo (occasionally), Sabang (Sumatra), Singapore and the beautiful island of Java as terminus. (Batavia, Samarang, Sourabaya, etc.) The best-equipped and most comfortable liners of today. Excellent cuisine. They carry the Royal Netherlands and Royal Italian mails to the Far East.' The single fare from Southampton's Extension Pier (leaving every other Tuesday at a time that connected with the London boat train from Waterloo) was £65.

Sunday morning they had closed their lists, such was the press of interest – and on Sunday evening the party set off. It was seventeen days after the first vibration, only a week after the first eruption. The *Loudon* was filled to its capacity of eighty-six passengers, and the government's Mr Schuurman was very much among them.

After steaming through the night towards a 'purple, fiery glow' that could be seen in the middle of Sunda Strait, the passengers watched as dawn finally broke.

The view of the island was fantastic: it was bare and dry, instead of rich with tropical forests, and smoke rose from it like smoke coming from ovens. Only the high peak [of Rakata] had some green left, but the flat northern slope [of Perboewatan] was covered with a dark grey ash layer, here and there showing a few bare tree stumps as meagre relics of the impenetrable forests which not too long ago covered the island. Horrible was the view of that sombre and empty landscape, which portrayed itself as a picture of total destruction rising from the sea, and from which, with incredible beauty and thundering power, rose a column of smoke. The cloud was only several dozens of meters wide at its foot, wheeling to a height of 1,000 to 1,200 meters while widening, then rising from there to 2,000 to 3,000 meters in height and in the meantime fading in colour, delivering its ash to the eastern wind which, falling as a dark fog, formed the background of the tableau.

The *Loudon*'s captain, T. H. Lindeman, kept well away from the island. But he loaned Schuurman a small boat, in which the engineer and a small party of curious daredevils approached the northern end of Krakatoa. The beach was covered with pumice; they struggled on shore through ash, into which they sank up to their calves.

Following the tracks of the most courageous, or perhaps the most stupid, we climbed inland with no further obstacle than the ashes which gave under our feet, the route being over a hill from where we could see, emerging from the ash, some broken tree trunks showing signs that their branches had been violently stripped off. The wood was dried, but nothing indicated that it had been alight, or smouldering. No leaf or branch could be found in the ash, and it is therefore likely that the deforestation must be attributed to a whirlwind . . .

The foolhardiness of the explorers knew no bounds. They climbed the crater, knowing how dangerous and unpredictable it had to be, and stared down in amazement into the deep, dish-shaped basin. Its bottom, Schuurman noted, was covered with a 'dull, shiny crust', which occasionally emitted a rosy glow, through which a powerful column of smoke escaped with what he then admitted was a truly frightening noise.

The clouds of smoke appeared to break through as with difficulty but with unmatched force, and they seemed to flee in numerous but closely linked, tremendous bubbles whose internal friction caused the turning and convoluting movement of the clouds in the lower part of the column of smoke . . . only at the edges of the point of eruption could the exhalation of steam from a number of cracks and gaps be observed.

The men stayed for most of the day, burning the soles of their shoes, coughing and spluttering in the clouds of ash, occasionally darting for shelter when the crater burped out a greater than usual bubble of smoke and sulphurous gas. And then, just after six o'clock, the tropical darkness began to fall (as Krakatoa is only six degrees south of the equator), and Captain Lindeman sounded the *Loudon*'s steam-horn to urge everyone to get off the island. One passenger, a Mr Hamburg, stayed a few moments longer to take photographs. Then everyone pulled out. 'We started our return trip to Batavia at 8 o'clock in the evening,' Schuurman noted at the end of his official report, 'thankful for the beauty and for a spectacle which made a deep impression on all, and an unforgettable one on most.'

For the next eight weeks, all seemed quiet – so quiet that, even though technically speaking the eruption was still going on, with smoke screeching from the Perboewatan crater and ash blowing high into the skies, 'visitors to Batavia, unless they had made inquiries, might have failed to hear of its existence at all'. The geologist H. O. Forbes, pleading for information about this unknown period of Krakatoa's life, added that many of the ships' reports that had come in from this time seemed to have been written 'either with the mind bewildered and confused by the terrifying incidents amid which the officers found themselves, or from the after-recollection of the events, of which under such circumstances the important dry facts of time, place and succession are liable to be unconsciously misstated'.

One seemingly reliable report that did come to light – though half a century later – was from a young Liverpool seaman named R. J. Dalby, who in June was aboard the barque *Hope*, six months out from South Wales bound for Saigon. While his vessel called in at Anjer for telegraphed orders – this was in the days before ships' radios, of course – Dalby was given shore leave, and he took a canoe across the Strait. The view on all sides, he remembered for a radio audience in 1937, was

. . . a real paradise, a profusion of vegetation rising from the seashore to the summit of hills several thousand feet high. I well remember one particular evening, just at the time when the land and sea breezes were at rest, the very atmosphere impressed one with a mystical awe. It was enhanced by the subtle scent of the spice trees, so plentiful on the island and, to crown it all, the sweet yet weird and melancholy chant of some natives, paddling their canoe close in to the dark shore. There were three of us in the boat, and we rested a long time trying to take in the strange grandeur of our surroundings; it was at this time that we noticed a long straight column of black smoke, going up from the peak of Krakatoa Island . . .

Was Dalby's recollection new evidence, perhaps, that by June the high peak of Rakata had now joined Perboewatan in erupting?

Certainly a second crater had opened up later on that month –
after a stiff wind had died down on 24 June, people on the Javan
coast could see quite clearly that two separate columns of smoke
were rising, and that the most northerly of the two was rising
majestically. The controller of Ketimbang, the doughty Mr
Beyerinck who had first paddled out to the island in May, went
back again in July and found two craters – but the more northerly
was not on Rakata, but at the foot of the insignificant peak in the
island's centre, Danan.

Dr Verbeek himself then saw Krakatoa, on 3 July, as he passed
by on his way back to Batavia from Europe. One must suppose
he knew nothing about what had just taken place: while Krakatoa
had been busily erupting, he had been sunning himself, somewhere between Gibraltar and Suez, aboard the eastbound packet
vessel *Prinses Marie*. The last time he had seen the island was in
1880: now, in the dark of the small hours,* he could see very little
more than a vague red glimmer on the vessel's port side.

And finally, on 11 August, a Dutch army captain named H. J. G.
Ferzenaar, who had been ordered to prepare a survey of the island
for the military topographic service, landed and spent two days
there. He went alone – the local governor ('unable to keep his
promise') refused to go, and all the other officials he approached
were too timid.

Ferzenaar found a bewildering variety of signs that the island
might be readying itself anew for something quite spectacular.
There were now at least three craters erupting – one, which he
thought looked especially potent, was on the southern side of the
mid-island peak, Danan. All told, he counted *fourteen* vents in the
rocky surface – fumaroles, one would call them now – from which

---

* That he was up and about at 3 a.m. suggests either that he had learned
enough about the May eruptions, presumably from his stops in various
ports like Port Said and Singapore, to be wanting to catch a glimpse, or
that he was a chronic insomniac.

The last map ever made of Krakatoa, sketched sixteen days before the
eruption by Captain H. J. G. Ferzenaar. All but the southernmost peak of
Rakata vanished in the cataclysm.

greyish or pink smoke was rising. Most of these vents were also
on this highly unstable-looking southern flank of Danan.

He paddled his *prahu* around the eastern coast of Krakatoa,
turned around the northern headland, passed on the outer side of
the small sliver of an island on the north-west side – and then
called it a day. Heavy smoke made visibility difficult; navigation,
especially in a vessel without power, was exceptionally trying.
He drew a map that showed as much detail as possible, including
the tiny spots and streaks of red from which the new eruptions
were beginning.

This small and handsome map would have to do: any proper
survey of the island had 'to wait until later, because measuring
there is still too dangerous; at least, I would not like to accept the
responsibility of sending a surveyor. A large portion could be
mapped from other islands, but I consider a survey on the island
itself inadvisable.'

His caution was well founded. Captain Ferzenaar was, as it
happened, the last human soul ever to set foot on Krakatoa. His
map represented the final time that anyone would be able to see

the entire fifteen square miles of tropical island – an island of people and forests and wild animals and visitors and history, which had existed in this place for at least the previous 60,000 years. The good captain sailed his tiny craft away from Krakatoa on the evening of 12 August. Two weeks and one day later most of the island that he had drawn suddenly exploded; its billions upon billions of tons turned into vapour and disappeared from the surface of the earth, for ever.

6

A LEAGUE FROM
THE LAST OF THE SUN

... it could not tell why the telegraph company caused it to be sent a full account of a flood in Shanghai, a massacre in Calcutta, a sailor fight in Bombay, hard frosts in Siberia, a missionary banquet in Madagascar, the price of kangaroo leather from Borneo and a lot of nice cheerful news from the Archipelagos – and not a line about the Muskegon fire.

– a contemporary account of the vexed mood of Michigan's *Alpena Evening Echo*, quoted as an example of information overload in *The Victorian Internet* by Tom Standage, 1998

The first that the outside, Western world knew of the extraordinary events that were starting to unfold in the distant and exotic East was a nineteen-word entry close to the bottom of the second column of page twelve of *The Times*, in London, on the morning of Thursday, 24 May 1883.

It appeared just below a story about a police raid on a suspected betting-ring in a pub in Newcastle-upon-Tyne, and just above an announcement by the London police that the number of paupers known to be in town ('exclusive of lunatics in asylums') was 52,032 indoors and 37,898 on the streets. There were advertisements in columns beside the entry: readers were invited to buy Negro Head Gin for thirteen shillings and sixpence a gallon, John Brinsmead's Pianos for thirty-five guineas, Moir's Mulligatawny Soup, Epps's Cocoa or, a brand still familiar today, Rose's Lime Juice Cordial.

Slipped in among the two gripping sagas and all the intimations of the prosperity and epicureanism of the Victorian readership, but with a journalistic economy that verged on the terse, was the following announcement:

Volcanic Eruption. Lloyd's Agent in Batavia under date of May 23rd, telegraphs: 'Strong Volcanic Eruption, Krakatowa Island, Sunda Straits.'

It was perhaps appropriate that the first news of the explosion of an island in the middle of the sea came through the agency, in both senses, of the Society of Lloyd's. This was an organization that by now was quite venerable, it having been more than two centuries since London merchants met in Lloyd's coffee-house to discuss the coverage of risks to their far-flung fleet of cargo ships and set up a mutual-aid arrangement to cover themselves in the event of any losses. Lloyd's had become formally incorporated by parliament in 1871, and was by the latter half of the century respected as the world's oldest and premier society of insurance underwriters for ships. In that capacity the body employed or retained scores of agents or sub-agents, as they were formally known, at almost every port and capital city in the world.

The Lloyd's agency system, which still exists, had been set up in 1811. In port-cities around the world, most often in the little streets close to the docks, there will still be an office with a brass plaque outside, or perhaps the enamelled crest with its cross-and-anchor badge and the words *Lloyd's Agent* picked out in scarlet. Filling the posts of agents of the Committee of Lloyd's has long been, from the Lloyd's point of view, quite simple: men have invariably been selected for being no more than 'resident and well-established at the place concerned, and of high commercial status and integrity'. From the applicants' point of view, it was less easy. The privilege of appointment was considerable: many applied, and only a few could be chosen.

The task of an agent was in good times one of great simplicity, in bad times one of formidable complexity. Agents were initially bound by their contract to do no more than 'to collect and to transmit to the Corporation information of likely interest to the Lloyd's Market, and insurers worldwide'. But in those times, more frequent then than now, when ships went down, or where there were collisions or strandings or piracy or arguments over cargo, it turned out they were also there to settle suits, to adjudicate disputes and to pay just claims on the policies of insurance that were underwritten by the syndicates of Lloyd's.

Although that first message about 'Krakatowa' reportedly came from the Lloyd's agent in Batavia, the colonial capital, it did so purely because of reasons of protocol. It was thought more appropriate to have the formal report of a major event like this come from the agent – in this case a Scotsman, a Mr McColl – who was based in the nation's heart, even if he were only transmitting second-hand information about an event he himself did not see. He may not have done; one of his deputies, however, most certainly did.

For Lloyd's, which had (and still has) a truly worldwide presence, also had as agent a man on the spot, someone with a bird's eye view of Krakatoa and all that was going on there – too much of a bird's eye view, as it would later turn out. He was the already encountered Mr Schuit, the Dutch owner of the sea-front Anjer Hotel that he had conveniently set down close to the docks in the small Javanese port of the same name.

The nature of Lloyd's business demanded that they have a presence in Anjer. Not only was it a bustling little coastal port in its own right, but it was the place where the northbound vessels, on passage for Batavia, would take on their pilot, and where southbound vessels would drop him. Anjer, principal pilot station of west Java, was the first port that newcomers would see in the island, their first landmark after passing the light on Java Head. It was a natural and necessary place for Lloyd's to have a man.

And Mr Schuit had been chosen to fulfil the task – for which Lloyd's paid him a modest retainer – because of his view. His inn possessed a large wooden veranda overlooking the sea, and he and his guests would come of an evening to sit in lounge chairs there. A remarkably lovely spectacle was spread out before them: the island-filled, mountain-ringed, sunset-spectacular Sunda Strait, with the seemingly endless passage of ships sailing (or steaming: this was 1883, after all) along it, on their various ways between the Indian Ocean and the South China Sea. This last was what convinced the Lloyd's Committee that Schuit was the ideal man for them in the town where they particularly needed to employ one of the best.

He was fascinated by the passing trade, and so were his guests. He bought and mounted a large brass telescope under his porch, so that he could identify the more distant vessels. With this he could see well enough to read the signal flags (there would be no marine radios for almost another thirty years) and could pass on messages to owners and agents as asked. He would look out especially for the distinctive arrangement of three flags that read 'ZD2' – this shorthand was known by all agents to mean 'Please Report My Passing to Lloyd's, London'.

He knew the Anjer harbour-master, who kept him fully up to date about all the vessels that docked to load or unload cargoes, or that simply stopped by to bunker, victual or de-rat. Schuit would thus send to London almost every day the names of ships that stopped, copies of the signals he had received, and statistics about the number of *quintals* of pepper, or *piculs* of coffee, *maunds* of this and *catties* of that, which had passed across the Anjer quays.

And as well as all the shipping and commercial information, he would also from time to time send to London entirely unrelated 'information of likely interest' – of which the entirely unexpected burst of activity on Krakatoa was certainly a prime example.

It was of interest to the underwriters back home not merely because of the fascination provided by the explosion of any big volcano – but because this particular volcano lay almost directly athwart the main navigational passage of the Strait, and so would be bound to interest any master whose vessel might soon be making passage in those waters.

In many ways the mechanics of Mr Schuit's job were, in the closing years of the nineteenth century, changing fast. The ships themselves were altering their appearance, drastically. Sail as a means of moving them across the oceans was steadily giving way to steam. Wooden hulls were being replaced by steel, copper nails by iron rivets. The Suez Canal had opened for business, making passages to and from Europe more rapid and less risky. There was a steady growth in traffic, with more cargoes as world trade increased, and with ships from more nations. Congestion in the shipping lanes reflected the ebb and flow of global business and global politics; and it also reflected (as with the warship *Elisabeth*, on her way home from a posting off China) the rise and fall of distant empires.

And the ways in which Mr Schuit and his like were transmitting their reports was changing too. For most of the previous seventy years he and his predecessors would have sent their signals to Lloyd's by hand of messenger, the packages of bundled slips going back to London on the very homebound ships about which men like Schuit were reporting. But now, ever since mid century, technology was beginning to make the lives of all kinds of far-flung intelligence-gatherers – Lloyd's agents, diplomats, traders and foreign correspondents among them – a good deal easier and much more efficient.

For the previous ten years Schuit had been sending all of his messages from Anjer – including the information about the first explosion of Krakatoa, which the still extant records show was transmitted at precisely 3.47 a.m. on 23 May – by way of two related and newly invented devices. The first was the electric telegraph, which, as we have already seen, came to the East Indies in 1856; the second was the submarine telegraph cable, which was to play a highly significant role in the unfolding of the Krakatoa story. This underwater cable arrived in Java after many fits and starts – the first one failed after sitting on the ocean bottom for only a month. But by 1870, thirteen years before Mr Schuit needed to get his story out to London as quickly as possible, the international cable connecting Batavia was working well, and his message was received only a short while after he sent it.

It took an event like Krakatoa's eruption – which astonished and mystified an entire educated world – to underline the real revolution that this new technology was visiting upon the planet. True, other events had already been recounted by means of the new machinery; and its utility – to commerce, diplomacy and news-gathering in particular – was in no doubt. But with the explosion of Krakatoa came a phenomenon that in time would come to be seen as more profound. This eruption was so enormous an event, and had so many worldwide implications and effects, that for humankind to be able to learn and know about it, in detail, within days or even hours of its very happening entirely changed the world's view of itself. It would not be stretching a point to suggest that *the Global Village* – the phrase is modern, and was coined by Marshall McLuhan in 1960, referring to the world-shrinking effects of television, even pre-satellite* – was

* The phrase was born in the foreword to a book called *Explorations in Communication*, published in 1960:

> *Post-literate man's electronic media contract the world to a village or tribe where everything happens to everyone at the same time: everyone knows about, and therefore participates in, everything that is happening the minute it happens. Television gives this quality of simultaneity to events in the global village.*

essentially born with the worldwide apprehension of, and fascination with, the events in Java that began in the summer of 1883.
And Agent Schuit's first telegram to London was one small
indication of that revolution's beginnings.

Although what *The Times* published was brief in the extreme,
what Agent Schuit actually wrote by hand was considerably
longer and more discursive, and started:

On Sunday morning last, from six to ten o'clock, there was a tremendous eruption, with continuous earthquakes and heavy rain of ashes.
On Sunday evening and Monday morning it was continued. The
eruption was distinctly seen here until nine o'clock this morning, and
smoke was seen until twelve o'clock; afterwards it cleared up a little,
and at this moment the air is clouded again. Capt. Ross reports from
Anjer that on May 22 he was sailing near Java's First Point and tried
to get Prinsen Island in sight, but found that it was surrounded by
clouds. Then he steered from Krakatan,* but found it to be the same

---

The telegraphic transmission of news about Krakatoa, disseminated simultaneously throughout the entire newspaper-reading world, had much the
same effect.

* The vexatious question of the proper spelling of the island arises here,
not surprisingly, given that within the space of a single day, because of the
telegraphic equivalent of Chinese whispers, the spelling changed from
Krakatau to *Krakatan* (probably a misreading of Agent Schuit's handwriting)
to the rather puzzlingly elaborate *Krakatowa*. By the next day, however,
25 May 1883, *The Times* had settled for *Krakatoa*, which is how the name of
the mountain has remained, in most of the English-speaking world, for most
of the following century, and since. An anniversary book published in 1983
tried gamely to turn its back on all but the supposedly proper spelling of
Krakatau; but the old wrong-headed one persists, despite all best efforts to do
away with it. Searching for the possible orthographic villains in the piece: the
Lloyd's men seem innocent; the telegraph operators may have made an honest
mistake; a *Times* subeditor working that night with the Lloyd's copy seems
to have made one executive decision on the first night – *Krakatowa* – and then
changed it the night after. All told, the newspapermen seem to have made the
greater error – but in doing so created a name that has stuck.

there. The captain observed that the lower island or mountain situated on the north side of Krakatan was totally surrounded by smoke, and from time to time flames arose with loud reports. Fire had broken out in several places, and it is very likely that the trees in the neighbourhood have caught fire. The mountain of Krakatan has been covered all over on the north side with ashes . . .

Schuit wrote this dispatch in English, since that was the language in which Lloyd's conducted its business, and he marked it to be sent to London and copied to the Lloyd's agent in Batavia. He was evidently a night owl, because it appears that he wrote his message – in longhand, and on the prescribed telegraph form – long after his dinner, and in fact very early in the morning on Wednesday, 23 May. He then took the completed sheets down to the small white stucco building that housed the continually open office of the Dutch East Indies Post and Telegraph Office and handed them to the clerk.

Since the message was marked URGENT, the duty officer sat down at his wood-and-brass Morse tapper and register, and, with the lightning speed (and near-total accuracy, aside from reading Schuit's handwritten *Krakatau* as *Krakatan*) for which good operators were renowned, dispatched the signal to his opposite number in Batavia. From the Batavia telegraph office,* at the corner of Post Weg and Kerk Weg (or what is now Cathedral Street), the message then underwent a form of mitosis, with one copy of the signal going to the Lloyd's office and agent just down the street in central Batavia, the other going straight on to London. The version sent on to London was dispatched from Batavia (or possibly originated at Anjer – of this we cannot be sure) at 3.47 a.m. on the Wednesday – in London, late on the evening of the Tuesday.

---

* The telegraph office was a pair of single-storeyed buildings that still stand and now form the core of a convent for Jakarta's Ursuline nuns.

The message took some long while to reach London – one reason why the first published report of the eruption appeared in *The Times* not of the Wednesday morning, as might be expected, but in the paper of Thursday, 24 May. It took its time to make its way from the East Indies capital to its British equivalent because of the mechanics of early-nineteenth-century communication: it began its long journey by first going north of Java up to Singapore, and doing so by way of the newly made and wholly revolutionary invention, the submarine telegraph cable.

There is a nice coincidence of geography and botany in the story of the building of submarine telegraph cables – a business that had only begun in 1850, when the first cable was laid between Dover and Calais. What allowed the industry to flourish – something that really only happened when cables ceased their infuriating habit of breaking in mid ocean, and they could then be relied upon to work and carry their signals without interruption – was the discovery of a handsome evergreen tree called *Isonandra gutta*, from which oozed a rubbery, workable and waterproof substance that was soon to be called gutta-percha.

A London firm called S. W. Silver & Company discovered that gutta-percha could be extruded like rubber, and could be made to cover copper wires that would then be proof against water. The firm's directors promptly changed the company name to the magnificently sonorous India Rubber, Gutta Percha & Telegraph Works Company – and under that rubric established factories that began to spin hundreds upon hundreds of miles of armoured, waterproof telegraph cables for ships to lay deep down on the ocean floor. ('The moment the electric telegraph was invented,' said a manual of the day, 'so gutta-percha, the very substance it demanded, was discovered.')

By 1865 the India Rubber, Gutta Percha & Telegraph Works Company was producing submarine cables as fast as the world was able to connect itself, and they were happily transmitting

The converted warship *Agamemnon* laying the first transatlantic telegraph
cable off the west coast of Ireland in 1857.

electronic messages hither and yon at great speed and with
near-total security. It was this guarantee of security and privacy
that was their real value: the disruption of wars that kept breaking out like wildfires all over Europe was making the cables
that passed overland risky means indeed of sending messages
anywhere.

And the coincidence? It so happened that the handsome evergreen tree with its rubbery sap was found in abundance in just
one corner of the planet: in Borneo, Sumatra and Java. Gutta-
percha, so critical for communication, became in the 1860s a
major East Indian export, just like pepper, quinine and coffee.
Though unseen in day-to-day life, it was an export that was to
have an enormous impact on the technological development of
the outside world. And further: though this substance that made
cables work so well just happened to be found in Java, it was
twenty years after the technology was first used that it was employed to connect Java with a rest of the world that was already

using it. The former may have been pure coincidence; the latter was pure irony.

Mr Schuit's signal thus passed along the 557-mile-long gutta-percha-covered cable that had been laid by the converted cargo ship *Hibernia* in 1870. A cable had first been laid along the route eleven years earlier, by the Dutch government – but the technology of 1859 was primitive, the demand slight, and when it broke, as it did after some four weeks, no one from the government bothered to order its repair.

On the second occasion the combination of commercial demand, market forces and new technology succeeded where the pioneering had failed: a brand-new private cable was laid on the orders of the British-Australian Telegraph Company, designed not so much to connect Java with the outside world, as to allow the vastly powerful Eastern Telegraph Company to connect its trans-India lines to the burgeoning populations in Australia and New Zealand.

And so the *Hibernia* laid the connecting cable to Batavia. Together with her sister-ship the *Edinburgh*, she then laid another from Banjoewangie in eastern Java to Port Darwin in northern Australia; engineers connected the two by a landline that ran the length of Java itself; and when finally in 1872 the Australian government completed its own landline across the continent, then London and Sydney could exchange messages with one another with consummate ease and near-total commercial security.

Mr Schuit's Morse coded message reached Singapore by way of the British-Australian Telegraph Company's gutta-percha-and-jute-twine-covered four-strand copper cable, the fastest and most secure thus far designed. The signal was then amplified and sent on its way towards London. It had two choices: it could either go, slowly and insecurely, via the long chain of landlines that had been established mid century, when telegraphy had first begun to expand; or it could go 'Via Eastern'. A customer could in those days specify on the telegram forms which cable should be used, and pay the costs which that particular cable company charged. Specify *Via Eastern*, and it made most of its long journey by sea. Leave the cable-routing box blank, and the message went the long and slow way and, for most of its length, by land.

But the land journey had a fine romance about it, even so. From Singapore it went up the Malay coast to Penang and then by a short sea journey to Madras. Thence ever westwards it progressed, by way of cities still known, or by towns obscure, long forgotten or with names no longer used.

The lines of creosoted pitch-pine telegraph poles took the cable to Bombay, then to a switching centre, from which it emerged as an armoured cable and dipped beneath the Arabian Sea to reach Karachi, then rose back on pole-supported lines to the village of Hermak in Baluchistan, to Kerman, Teheran and Tabriz in Persia, to Tiflis in Georgia, on to Sukhumi on the Black Sea coast, along the corniche to Kertsch* in the Crimea, to Odessa, up across steppes and coalfields to the Polish city of Berdichew (with a population of 52,000, which in those days before Hitler were almost all Jews), through Warsaw, Berlin and the North Sea port of Emden,† beneath the sea for one last time, before making landfall in East Anglia, and thence by telegraph pole for the final fifty miles to London. A telegram sent thus could take a week to reach its destination.

But if the operator marked the message *Via Eastern*, then it went swiftly and securely, beneath the sea. Thirty-five years before, the first insulated cable had been dropped from a ship called the

---

* Well fortified and 'known for its mud volcanoes', according to the 1882 *Lippincott Gazetteer*.

† The *Emden* was also, coincidentally, the name of the German surface raider that ransacked the cable station on Cocos Island, off southern Java, in 1916.

Princess Clementine moored in Folkestone Harbour and connected to a boat two miles away, with a message successfully sent between the two. Since that time the undersea cable had become fixed in the public consciousness. Alfred, Lord Tennyson had written a hymn to the romance of the idea of coded voices hurrying along the ocean floor; and so had Rudyard Kipling, whose brief poem 'The Deep-Sea Cables' remains among his best loved:

> The wrecks dissolve above us; their dust drops down from afar –
> Down to the dark, to the utter dark, where the blind white
>   sea-snakes are.
> There is no sound, no echo of sound, in the deserts of the deep,
> Or the great grey level plains of ooze where the shell-burred
>   cables creep.
>
> Here in the womb of the world – here on the tie-ribs of earth
>   Words, and the words of men, flicker and flutter and beat –
> Warning, sorrow, and gain, salutation and mirth –
>   For a Power troubles the Still that has neither voice nor feet.
>
> They have wakened the timeless Things; they have killed their
>   father Time;
>   Joining hands in the gloom, a league from the last of the sun.
> Hush! Men talk to-day o'er the waste of the ultimate slime,
>   And a new Word runs between: whispering, 'Let us be one!'

The undersea cable connecting Singapore with London, after passing first by land in those days to Penang, crossed the Bay of Bengal to Madras, hopscotched across India and then plunged into the Arabian Sea on the long passage from Bombay to Aden. It was then put ashore briefly at Port Sudan, nosed up to its receiving stations at Suez and Alexandria, crossed the southern Mediterranean to the island of Malta, travelled through the northern part of the Mediterranean to Gibraltar, between the Pillars of Hercules to Carcavelos on an Atlantic headland ten miles west of Lisbon, up to windswept Vigo on Spain's western

The worldwide network of telegraph connections used by Reuter's agency
for collecting and disseminating this most valuable commodity – news.

Galician coast, and finally it headed north, sheltered deep below
the storms of the Bay of Biscay and the Western Approaches, and
arrived at its landing place at Porthcurno, on the southern tip of
Cornwall, in England.

After this the messages did their final 200 miles by land, along
conventional wires that were carefully tended, since they carried

Samuel Morse.

the international and imperial traffic of the hallowed and respected Eastern Telegraph Company. The signals would arrive at the Receiving Room of what was called London Station around three hours after they had been sent from the Morse tapper in the faraway East. In the case of Schuit's Anjer message reporting the eruption of 'Krakatan', sent from Batavia at 3.47 a.m. local time on the Wednesday, the signals would have arrived at Lloyd's (subtracting the eight-hour time difference between London and Batavia, and adding the approximate three hours of transmission time) at about 10 p.m. on the night of Tuesday, 22 May. They had been marked *Urgent*; they were decoded from their Morse and sent immediately to the delivery address – the Foreign Intelligence Office at Lloyd's.

And then, as it turned out, to *The Times*. This paper, which was then quite intimately involved with the British establishment, had none the less a cosy arrangement with Lloyd's: any signal deemed to be of likely interest would be passed promptly across to the paper's foreign news editor. News of the eruption arrived too late to be of any use to that night's paper; but once Schuit's excited cable about explosions and ash falls and eruptions of fire had been read on the next day, Wednesday, 23 May, its worth as hot news was immediately apparent. The message was read in full by the duty editor; it was edited – heavily, since only seven words of it were actually published in the paper – and for some inexplicable reason the word *Krakatan* – itself an error, more probably the telegraph operator's than Schuit's – was changed, as mentioned, to the similarly eccentric *Krakatowa*.

The cable was received early enough to be published in all editions of the paper of Thursday, 24 May – including the Scottish edition, which was printed first, as well as the Final London Edition, which was printed last on the best-quality paper at around 3.30 a.m. and delivered to all the embassies and palaces and government offices of the capital.*

By mid morning all the loyal readers of what was then known as *The Thunderer*† came to learn of the event, and slowly but surely – since the volcano was to figure in the news dozens more times before the year was out – began to incorporate the name of this distant island, hitherto quite unknown, into their daily lexicon. And as it was incorporated into the lexicon, so it became, in short order, a prominent feature of received culture, all over the world.

Krakatoa achieved this happy status thanks in part to another of the great creations of the era: the news agency. Based in London, the first agency was founded by a German-Jewish businessman who, with great prescience, saw news and its fast delivery as a

* In 1917 *The Times* started producing a limited-run late edition on very high-quality paper that was christened the Library Edition. Five years later this was renamed the Royal Edition, and it was printed every day – except for a pause during the Second World War – until formally abandoned for budgetary reasons at the end of 1969.
† A *Times* columnist named Edward Sterling, known for his trenchant editorializing, wrote in 1829 that his paper had 'thundered out' in support of social and political reform – the phrase was widely noticed, and for at least the next century and a half the epithet stuck.

saleable commodity. He gave it the name to which his immigrant parents had changed theirs:* Reuter.

In 1815 it had taken the news of Napoleon's defeat at Waterloo four days to reach readers in London; when Napoleon died on the Atlantic island of St Helena six years later, most Britons remained in ignorance of the fact for the following two months. But twenty years later the telegraph had been invented, and by the 1840s its lines were spreading across Europe like the tentacles of kudzu; it was not long before entrepreneurs – like Julius Reuter, then a small-time newspaper publisher in Paris – decided that this new medium could allow news to be sped from place to place electrically and then sold to those in need of it, like any other commodity.

Speed – being first with the news, getting *the scoop*, beating the competition – was the most important thing to Julius Reuter. In those early days he was often too far ahead of the technology and had to come up with inventive solutions. To get news from Paris to Brussels before the telegraph link had been fully completed, for example, he used pigeons: the French news would be telegraphed to the border town of Aix-la-Chapelle; the messages would then be transcribed and taped to the legs of forty-five specially trained Reuter pigeons; two hours later the news would arrive in Brussels city-centre. It was a series of stunts like this – as well as his agency's reputation for factual reliability – that enabled Reuter to win contract after contract to supply news, from all the world and to all the world. From 8 October 1858, when his service properly began, the list of successes and scoops under the Reuter byline is legendary indeed.

Reuter was, for example, four days ahead of the London papers with his account of – important then, at least – the king of Sardinia's address to the opening of his parliament. He beat everyone with the news of the Austrian defeat at the battle of Solferino in 1859. By 1861 he had a hundred correspondents,

* From the surname Josaphat.

working worldwide. During the American Civil War – with the Atlantic still not connected by cable – he arranged for telegraphed news to be rowed out to boats at remote ports on the Americas' eastern shores, places like Halifax and St John's and Cape Race, and collected a week later by rowing boats sent out from Ireland. (When President Lincoln was shot on 14 April 1865, the news was carried aboard the SS *Nova Scotia*, taken off by whaling-boat when the liner closed on Londonderry and telegraphed to London by Reuter in time to be published in the subscribing newspapers of 26 April, twelve days after the event.)

By the time of Krakatoa's eruption, the entire East was fairly well connected with the newspaper-reading West, as Reuter had already so amply displayed by writing in timely fashion about the arrival of Admiral Perry and his American warships off Tokyo, and the subsequent restoration to the Chrysanthemum Throne of the Japanese Emperor in 1868. Timely – but not instantly, since Japan was not to be connected fully with the worldwide telegraph system until the Danes laid a cable between Tokyo and Shanghai in 1872, and connected the re-emergent state with the Great Northern Telegraph Company line that went between St Petersburg, Copenhagen and Paris, and on to London. From the time the Danes had completed this cable, all of the major Eastern cities – Shanghai and Peking, Manila and Tokyo, Saigon and Rangoon – were hooked into the system. They had become a part of the fast-growing network of international cables; and, because of this network, they had become beneficiaries of, as well as contributors to, the worldwide news-gathering operations of Reuter.

And Batavia was connected as well: it had a Reuter office and, in 1883, a stringer – a retained freelance who fed such news as he found into the agency wires. His name was W. Brewer, and he would turn out to be the point man who would send most of the properly factual reports of the eruption for distribution around the world.

In May, though, the first that Reuter heard of the eruption came not from their Mr Brewer but from London, and via the Lloyd's telegram. The agency got it right, but it got it late – a full day late. When the rest of the world was given the story under the Reuter byline, it was already 25 May. The largest Dutch newspaper of the day, the Rotterdam-based *Nieuwe Rotterdamsche Courant*, published it that Friday morning – having to be content with the undignified reality that a British newspaper had managed on the Thursday to scoop a Dutch paper with a story about an event in a Dutch colony.

Reuter, however, peddled its story hard. The paragraphs about the first eruptive event that had appeared in *The Times* of 25 May were fleshed out by Mr Brewer in Batavia, and could be found, translated into the vernacular where necessary, in that Friday's major newspapers in America and Southern Africa, in India and France and Germany.*

It was thanks to the combined agencies of all those involved – to Samuel Morse, to the directors of the India Rubber, Gutta Percha & Telegraph Works Company, to the Eastern Telegraph Company, to the Committee of Lloyd's, to Reuter and to the small network of eager correspondents in Anjer, Batavia and London – that this first remarkable story started to be told.

It was the first-ever story about a truly enormous natural event that was both *about* the world and was told *to* the world. Part of the planet's fabric had been ripped asunder: and part of that same planet, the part connected by cables and telegraphs and with access to newspapers, was now being informed of the event. And the very process of relating the dramatic happenings, especially in the weeks and months that followed, would enable all who heard and read and understood it to share in the cruel intimacy of the moment. Millions of people hitherto unknown to each other

* These subsequent items settled on Krakatoa as the volcano's name.

began to involve themselves, for the first time ever, in looking beyond their hitherto limited horizons of self; they started to inhabit a new and outward-gazing world that these story-telling agencies, and this event they were relating, were unwittingly helping to create.

The story of Krakatoa had a small beginning – seven newsworthy words, buried well down in the pages of a single London newspaper. As the summer of 1883 wore on, it was to become a very much greater story indeed. And when it was over, three months later, it was to have implications for society – for the laying of the foundations of McLuhan's Global Village – that have reverberated in a far more important way, and for far, far longer, than anyone at the time of the event could ever have supposed.

7

THE CURIOUS CASE OF
THE TERRIFIED ELEPHANT

Eau de Cologne: A perfumed spirit invented by an Italian chemist, Johann Maria Farina (1685–1766), who settled in Cologne in 1709. The usual recipe prescribes twelve drops of each of the essential oils, bergamot, citron, neroli, orange and rosemary, with one dram of Malabar cardamoms and a gallon of rectified spirits, which are distilled together.

– definition from *Brewer's Dictionary of
Phrase and Fable*, 1959

The final Monday of July 1883 was one of the last quiet days ever to be experienced on Krakatoa, an island that now had precisely four weeks remaining before it was blasted out of existence. It was also on that day, 30 July, that John and Anna Wilson's Great World Circus, long expected and universally welcomed, finally arrived in Batavia town.

They had been to Batavia many times before, the canny Scotswoman Miss Wilson well knowing they could be certain of a grand colonial crowd. On this particular occasion, the performers and their animals had sailed in on the liner from Singapore, and they promised their audiences the staging of amazements and delights in an atmosphere of more sumptuous comfort than could possibly be imagined.

Two years before, members of the audience had complained they were too crowded, and too hot. So for this visit Mrs Wilson had brought with her from New York a brand-new tent, a giant she had christened the Mammoth. As the guy-men hauled up the immense acreage of bleached canvas on the west side of the Koningsplein, so passers-by gasped at what they saw and heard. Room for 5,000 seats! the posters exclaimed. Real gas-lamp illuminations! blared the barker's horn. Unbelievable new attractions! proclaimed the newspaper advertisements including, the first time ever seen in the Orient, *Cannonball Holtum from Denmark, and His Incredible, Death-Defying Feats of Courage and Fearlessness.*

This time, the Batavians said to themselves as they handed over their one-guilder coins for tickets and watched the final preparations being made, Wilson's Great Circus truly was going to be the greatest that Java had ever seen.

The circus was to be – or so everyone thought at the time – the crowning glory of what had thus far turned out to be a delightful summer season. The volcanic grumblings and growlings over to the west in the Sunda Strait continued, true; but now that the initial surprise of the May eruption was over, the fact of all the fire and smoke and occasional tremblings of the earth had become part of the reality, an established routine. No one really gave it a thought – it meant no more than the occasional tremor might mean today to someone in Tokyo, or Los Angeles, or along the San Andreas Fault. Batavians made jokes about it all. It was not going to be allowed to cause any disruption of the gay social round – though one of the Batavia papers, the East Indies edition of the *Algemeen Dagblad,* did sound rather exasperated in June when it remarked sourly, 'What musical entertainment there is

WILSON'S
GREAT WORLD CIRCUS,
LAATSTE WEEK!
Heden Maandag 3 September,
GROOTE SCHITTERENDE VOORSTELLING,
ten behoeve van de
Slachtoffers van de jongste Catastrofe in Bantam.
OPTREDEN VAN MISS. FOGARDUS.
De beroemde Amerikaansche Duiven Koningin.
DE BEROEMDE FAMILIE NELSON.
Optreden van den heer O'BRIEN,
Optreden van de Dames ADèLE WILSON, SELMA TROOST, ROSA
LEE en BREDOW.
Het staat iederen bezoeker op alle rangen vrij te betalen zooveel hij wil.

De ondergeteekende neemt de vrijheid het liefdadige Bataviasche publiek beleefd uit te uoodigen de voorstelling ten behoeve van de slachtoffers in Bantam algemeen te willen bezoeken. Zij geeft de verzekering, dat de geheele opbrengst der voorstelling zal worden aangewend tot het genoemde liefdadige doel.

Hoogachtend,
ANNA WILSON,
Directrice.

(990)

This advertisement for Anna Wilson's Circus promises 'a great and brilliant performance on behalf of the victims of the recent Banten catastrophe'.

can hardly be enjoyed because of all the shaking noises of the doors and windows caused by Krakatau.'

None the less the social year that had begun so splendidly in February with the King's Day Dance at the grammar school – about which the papers still talked in the summer, so successful was it said to have been – rolled on, unstoppably. In mid May, for example, horse-racing was held up in the mountain cool of Buitenzorg, and a costume-ball in the stewards' hall on the Sunday of the two-day meeting – Governor-General 's Jacob naturally lending his august presence.

Then there was a *soirée dansante* held in the Batavia Plant and Animal Garden on 27 May. Usually this would be an uneventfully happy evening – but as it happened a small shadow was cast over it too. Not, however, by Krakatoa. Most of the guests had been hoping to see the Royal Bengal Tiger that, famously, had been presented to the garden earlier in the month by a German philanthropist named Mr Schröder. But the Garden announced that it had neither the space nor the wherewithal for housing this very large and fierce animal, and the curator ordered it to be put on the next boat to Melbourne – disappointing the dancers, who had hoped it might enliven their evening.

Any sense of chagrin that might have been felt by the dancers at the loss of their tiger was quite probably offset by another, much more practically consequential announcement that was also made in May. The 985-ton British steamship, *Fiado*, under contract to the Australian Frozen Meat Company, had, its owners announced to the papers, been fitted with up-to-date refrigeration equipment and would begin a regular service to Batavia and Singapore, bringing cargoes of frozen beef, lamb, pork and poultry.

The first such cargo arrived on 20 July. To judge from the newspapers of the day, which greeted the docking of the *Fiado* as they might the unexpected arrival of a monarch or a star, a wave of gastronomic ecstasy promptly swept the colony. The Australian meat, never seen before, turned out to be of extraordinary quality. 'Not even a large and well-bred Balinese ox could compete with this,' a local gourmand was quoted as saying. Meat was no longer a luxury; henceforward every European in the colony could eat as well in Java as they once had in Amsterdam. Perhaps, now, even better.

The epicentre of Batavian gaiety in that summer of 1883 was the newly renovated and extended Concordia Military Club, the indisputably grand white marble building at the southern side of Waterlooplein, directly across from where the governor-general had his palace.

That year the Concordia ranked marginally ahead of the Harmonie, which was admittedly the older of the city's two great social clubs and remains the better known today; even though

The grand ballroom of Jakarta's Concordia Military Club.

the Harmonie's building was torn down in the 1960s, like that of
the Concordia, the part of modern Jakarta in which it once stood
retains its name. At the time of the Krakatoa events the fabric of
the Harmonie was looking somewhat shabby, and the club was
suffering from a temporarily declining membership. Far better
balls and soirées were being held at the much swankier Concordia,
where, to the delight of most Europeans who were invited, they
were marked by a lavishness that often bordered on the decadent.

For example, there was a masked ball held at the Concordia on
Saturday, 28 July, just before the arrival of the circus. Three
hundred couples came, by horse-drawn carriage or in the back-to-
back conveyance known as a *dos-à-dos*. The gardens were illuminated with Chinese lanterns, there were obelisks lit with piped gas,
and a Turkish kiosk with a sky-blue cupola had been built for the
outdoor band.

And inside – under the ornate ceiling and gas-chandeliers, within walls groaning with portraits and mirrors and statuary, beside rare plants, flowers and soft-coloured veils of gauze, upon a floor of polished teak squares dusted with French chalk – they danced – *until the sun came up like thunder*, as in the East it was wont to do. The women, the finest of all Batavian high society, were seen to be wearing dresses that, to the more matronly onlookers and chaperones, were positively outrageous. So short! they chorused next day. So delightful! the men reminisced. 'If you want to enjoy the sight of beautiful pink satin shoes with fine ankles moving on the dance floor – go to the masked ball at the Concordia!'

The masks and costumes were as various as could be. One lady came dressed as a swallow, with a headdress and wings made of feathers from Anjer songbirds – birds that had lately been flying, in other words, in the turbulent volcanic airs of the Sunda Strait. Another, *Madame la Diable*, had black wings and gilded horns and a silk dress in black and red adorned with images of Lucifer. There was a Carmen, a Louis Quinze escorting an Italian farm-girl, buxom in gingham and Genoa lace. There was a toreador, a consistory of monks and a group of British sailors from a passing Royal Navy warship whom everyone thought were in fancy-dress, though they were simply in full fig, officially.

And as if this display were not enough – in the centre of the ballroom was a fountain gushing not water but pure *eau de Cologne*. This was by way of an experiment: a flower-vase was used as the centrepiece, and from deep in the lush enfoldments of its blooms gushed fountains of perfumed water that, when mingled with the scents of the assembled dancers, the cigar-smoke and the rich aromas of spices from the *rijsttafel*, made for *a symphony of olfactory delights* that . . . the newspapers, gushing too, found simply too overwhelmingly wonderful for words.

Then came August, and with it, at last, the circus. The company had come clear across the Pacific – one of their earlier perform-ances had been in a small town outside San Francisco – and were in the East determined to make the best impression. And so every imaginable act was on hand: tightrope-walkers, fire-eaters, a pigeon-charmer, an American who could somersault over eight horses, the Nelson Family of Acrobats, Hector and Faue the Lords of the Trapeze, Fräulein Jeanette and Her Amazing Bareback Riders, William Gregory the Gymnast King, the Well-Known Sweetheart from Earlier Years, Miss Selma Troost – with *Troost* being the Dutch word for 'consolation', a commodity that many lonely bachelors thousands of miles from home would no doubt readily welcome.

There were a hundred acts in all, and twenty Arabian horses on which the performers might show their paces. There were dozens of clowns; and on 22 August the Batavia Cricket Club staged a match against the Clowns' First Eleven, all of them wearing their circus costumes. The Cricket Club won, handsomely.

John Holtum, known around the world as the Cannonball King, was perhaps the stellar attraction. He was a 38-year-old Dane who had developed the skill of catching a cannonball fired at him from the far side of the circus ring. The first time he tried this, the ball, which weighed fifty pounds and at the time it struck him was moving at more than a hundred miles an hour, took off three of his fingers. He was not discouraged by this setback, however; nor was he put off when a rival in an Italian circus was sliced in two by a grenade he was attempting to deflect with what up to the moment of his demise was said to be a powerfully muscled chest.

Mr Holtum persisted; and by the time he arrived in Batavia that August he was the world's acknowledged leader in this limited field of endeavour. He liked to challenge men in the audience to catch cannonballs: 161 volunteers in Europe and America had already tried but failed, and the few who tried in Batavia failed as well, including the promisingly named Mr Thor, against whose fingertips the ball grazed, doing him no harm but losing him his wager. John Holtum also liked large men to try to pull him off balance with a rope – they always failed in that too. But when the great Dane pitted his resilience against four horses harnessed to a rope, they pulled in so confusing and angry a way that he fell over, and was pulled around the ring, in an undignified pother, showing himself not to be quite as invincible as he liked his audiences to suppose.

For every single night throughout the first four weeks of August, John and Anna Wilson's Great World Circus staged a performance – two on Saturdays. And, such were the limitations on social life for Batavia's Dutch lower ranks, as well as for those members of Javanese society as were permitted to attend, that the newspapers reported each and every performance, in full detail, and with a tone of breathless excitement as if such amazements had never been witnessed before. The results of the steeplechases were published; the names of all those who challenged John Holtum, and the outcomes; the number of runs scored and wickets taken in the cricket matches with the clowns; and, of course, the outbreaks of bad behaviour and curious mishaps that seemed to attend this circus, in just this particular month of 1883, like rarely before.

The bad behaviour broke out within the first week. Without the guiding influence of the circus owner, John Wilson – he was overseas, recruiting more performers – the competing rivalries of the various artistes apparently spilled over into violence. The circus members all stayed at the Hôtel des Indes, said to be the grandest hotel in the entire Dutch empire, and the fighting first broke out in the bar. They were drinking champagne, the newspapers said, and arguing volubly over who was the funnier clown or the most adroit performer on the trapeze, when one of them, scandalized by a wounding remark, hurled a glass at the other. From then a full-scale donnybrook broke out, with wine, beer, food and fists being thrown in wild abandon. Mrs Wilson was hit in the face; one of the performers had his cheek badly bitten; the athletes battled the gymnasts, the horsemen the jugglers; and in the end the police had to be called. It was a sorry affair, and all Batavians loved every minute of it.

The fighting in the Hôtel des Indes coincided with a sudden quickening of the eruptive mood across on Krakatoa. After Captain Ferzenaar's visit to the island, when he had recorded the three huge craters, the fourteen new steam vents and the vast clouds of boiling dust, ships passing along the Sunda Strait reported new and dangerous-looking activity. One master reported a 'vast eruptive column' on the 22nd. Another spoke of 'shakes and heavy blows' on the 25th. There were 'falls of ash' and 'a milk-white sea' and 'dull explosion'. Most ominously worrying of all – in Sumatra on the 26th, the last Sunday in August – a villager noticed 'hot ashes coming up through the crevices in the floor of his hut'. Whatever was happening deep below the ground was clearly beginning to overwhelm the capacity of the surface to keep it under control. Something, somewhere, had to give.

It is said that animals are presciently aware of impending seismic doom. Catfish jump out of the water. Bees mysteriously evacuate their hives. Hens stop laying for no apparent cause. Mice appear dazed and can be caught by hand. Deep-sea fish are found at the ocean surface. Hibernating snakes suddenly reappear from their lairs, frozen to death if they do so in a harsh winter. Dogs begin to howl for no obvious reason. (A retired United States Geological Survey scientist collected lost-pet advertisements in American newspapers and claimed to find a correlation, such that within two weeks of any rise in the number of missing animals, there was an earthquake near by.)

There is no firm scientific evidence that there is a connection, nor is there a true basis for a new pseudo-science called ethogeological prediction, which seeks to forecast earthquakes by observing carefully calibrated animal activity. Yet not a few geologists do feel it is at least reasonable to suppose that the infinitesimal subterranean shiftings and strainings that precede massive eruptions or earthquakes can be sensed by animals long before being experienced by man or his machines. But no one has yet measured the link, if indeed there is one.

But in Batavia in that August of 1883 there was one animal that, for some unexplained reason, did begin to behave in a most unusual fashion. It was a very small circus elephant, said by his keeper, a Miss Nanette Lochart, to be the smallest trained pachyderm in world history. He had been caught in Java, and she had trained him in a matter of weeks. The entire company adored him, and the Batavian public – especially the children, who got in for half-price, with their servants admitted free – were captivated by the sight of this miniature monster juggling balls with his three-foot trunk, or stepping gaily from tub to tub as he negotiated a little obstacle course.

But halfway through his stay, both the elephant and his keeper began to behave most eccentrically. Miss Lochart began to believe that the other artistes in the troupe, their dander up after they had started fighting with one another, might for some reason turn on the elephant and try to harm him. Perhaps, she thought, they might try to break into his pen and give him poison. Despite there being no evidence, she decided to take evasive action.

And so, midway through August, when the ash falls and thunderings and pillars of flame were just beginning to be noticed once again in Batavia, Miss Lochart moved her little elephant into her room in the Hôtel des Indes. He was, after all, her only worldly possession. She may have surmised that the hotel owner, a stern Frenchman named M. Louis Cressonnier, might take a dim view of an elephant in the hotel room, though no sign specifically forbade it. So she settled the animal down, said her goodnights, locked the door behind her and left for an evening of dining with friends.

The elephant, denied the company of his mistress, clearly unaccustomed to the luxury and comfort on offer in the East's premier hotel, and perhaps – just perhaps – sensitive to what was going on in the earth beneath his feet, promptly went berserk. He trampled through and across all the furniture in Miss Loch-art's room, smashing it to smithereens. He trumpeted. He roared. He stamped his not-yet-enormous feet so aggressively that other guests thought the entire hotel was about to fall down.

And in the end the Batavia constabulary were called. They found Miss Lochart; they demanded that she persuade her two-ton charge to leave the room without further ado; and M. Cressonnier further demanded that the entire troupe, and such animals that others among them might have sequestered in their chambers, leave the hotel forthwith and find other accommodation.

This they did. And no one thought any more about it.

Except that then shortly afterwards, on Monday, 27 August 1883, the mountain that had been grumbling and groaning for the previous ninety-nine days finally exploded itself into utter and complete oblivion.

For sixty million years the two tectonic plates that converge on Java had been grinding slowly and steadily towards each other, four inches every year. Now, on the very morning after the Great World Circus had given its best performance yet – with the artistes now all newly accommodated and the little errant elephant by all accounts behaving obediently and impeccably once again – the event that would be consequent upon all those years of subterranean shiftings and slidings was at last about to occur.

8

THE PAROXYSM, THE FLOOD
AND THE CRACK OF DOOM

And I thought: I would give all these people's lives, once more, to see something so beautiful again.

– Dutch pilot in Anjer, quoted in 'Krakatau', a short story by the novelist Jim Shepard, 1996

1. The Event

The death throes of Krakatoa lasted for exactly twenty hours and fifty-six minutes, culminating in the gigantic explosion that all observers now agree happened at two minutes past ten on the Monday morning, 27 August 1883. The observers, as is often the way of such things, agree on precious little else. Thousands of people, far and wide, suddenly became aware of the events in the Sunda Strait – but their accounts of it, like the accounts of any monstrous and traumatizing event, present today a morass of conflict and confusion.

The countdown to the final hours of the mountain's existence properly began at six minutes past one in the afternoon of the previous day, the Sunday. All across the colony, Dutchmen and Javanese alike were looking innocently forward to the long lazy stretch of the afternoon of a much needed day of rest.

The first indications that all was not right became apparent more or less simultaneously to a number of people near by. They were at the time almost all completing the last moments of their familiar Sunday ritual: pushing their chairs away from the luncheon-table, folding their napkins, draining the last dregs of the coffee, standing up and stretching their legs, picking up their cigars, dogs and wives for the Dutch tradition of the afternoon family walk.

In Anjer, from where most of those very early reports originated, the relaxed mood of the afternoon must have seemed peculiarly suited to the place. Anjer was a sedate, pretty little port-town, as pleasant a posting for a visiting Dutchman as it might be possible to find. It was situated in a shallow bowl in the volcanic coastal range, a place where the hills dipped steeply down to the sea and formed a cosily protective natural harbour. The beaches were wide and white, the fringing palm trees leaned into the trade winds, there were flowers and banyan trees and a paradise of birds, and everywhere a heavenly scent of spices.

The local people lived in kampongs of small thatched cottages, the colonials in neat white stucco houses with red roofs. The finer of these mansions – some, like that of the Assistant Resident,* sporting a Dutch flag flying from a staff in the middle of its magnificent lawns and a private dock with the official's impeccably maintained launch – could be seen to best advantage from out at sea, where they seemed separated from one another by acres of

---

* The Resident, who at the time of the eruption was a Mr van Spaan, administered the region from the headquarters of the Residency in Bantam, thirty miles away. Anjer town itself merited only an Assistant, a Mr Thomas Buijs, who died in the disaster.

deep-green jungle. There was usually a flag-signal flying from the pilot-station that spelt out: CALL HERE FOR MAIL; and the inbound ocean-going ships would indeed invariably call, giving with their presence an air of vibrancy to the town; and, because they were stopping for orders and not for stevedores, Anjer was free of the slums and squalor of a cargo port.

The Europeans, in their white tropical suits and topis, would leave their houses – servants had their Sundays off – and saunter on an afternoon along broad seafront avenues, under groves of tamarind trees. There would be crowds of local Javanese, children running everywhere, pye-dogs sleeping under upturned boxes, chickens, pigs, goats, creaking bullock-carts, insistent pavement salesmen – all of the carefree magic of an Eastern street, in other words, out for entertainment and fun on what seemed likely to be an easy, lazy summer Sunday.

Relations between colonizers and colonized in the East Indies were less than perfect – indeed much less than perfect, for the Dutch were not very kindly in the ways they wielded their imperial powers, and they are consequently remembered with much less affection today than are most of those other Europeans who ruled far-flung territories around the globe. Yet, by all accounts, on this particular Sunday any feelings of antipathy were soothed and muted by the holiday mood. People smiled at one another, Dutchman muttered cordial greetings to Javan, everyone saun-tered contentedly along in the broad heat of the early afternoon.

And then, without warning, from out to sea in the west – a sudden sound.

The first two accounts to be written were of a kind that was to be repeated, in essence, many dozens of times that day. 'We plainly heard,' wrote one, 'the rumbling of an earthquake in the distance.' 'We didn't take much notice at first,' wrote a second, 'until the reports got very loud.'

The newly appointed Anjer telegraph-master, Mr Schruit, was once again idling on the veranda of the Anjer Hotel, which was owned by his new friend, the confusingly named Mr Schuit, the local Lloyd's agent. It was clearly Schruit's preferred place to spend his Sunday mornings. He was a young man, and cut rather a lonely figure. His wife and children were still in Batavia, and, after weeks of searching, he had only now found them a suitable house in Anjer, and was at long last looking forward to a family reunion.

But until then, as for the past few months, his holiday Sundays were spent on the veranda, puffing on a cheroot, gazing out at the view. Three months earlier he had been there too, trying under Schuit's tutelage to decipher the flag message that was flying from the yards of the German warship *Elisabeth*, then sailing down the Strait – a message which almost certainly told of the first eruption. He did nothing about it then: he was new to the area, he was not on duty, and in any case the local Lloyd's agent had the matter in hand, was well able to read the *Elisabeth*'s flags, and was already sending his historic dispatch about what the telegraph operators would misread as 'Krakatan' spewing out its great clouds of smoke and ash.

But on this occasion Schruit was on duty, and much more observant than before. He remembered later seeing a fully rigged barque heading north, a billow of white sails gliding along the blue mirror of the sea. Then he spied the much less pretty steamer *Gouverneur-Generaal Loudon*, the locally familiar government-chartered vessel that had taken the eighty-six tourists to Krakatoa back in May, heading into Anjer port.

(On this occasion she was undertaking more mundane and customary tasks: first picking up a hundred coolies who had been hired to help build a local lighthouse and ferrying them across the Strait; then going on up the eastern Sumatran coast to the troublesome region of Aceh, of the north, and there delivering, among others, some 300 miscreants, all members of a chain gang destined to be put to work on a variety of government building sites.)

It was at the very moment when Schruit was watching the *Loudon* steaming towards the safety of port that there came the first roar of an explosion.

It was an extraordinary sound, he thought: far, far louder than anything he recalled from before. He looked sharply over to his left and saw, instantly, the unforgettable sight of a tremendous eruption. To judge from the billows of white smoke that were now tumbling up from the mountain – 'as if thousands of white balloons had been released from the crater' – it was a far, far larger eruption than anything he had witnessed when he was standing at this exact spot back in May.

Moreover, whatever was happening on the mountain was also having an immediate effect on the sea. It was rising and falling, strongly, irregularly, in bursts of sudden up-and-down movements of the sea-water that seemed immediately unnatural and sinister. It wasn't tide, or wave, or wash: it was some terrific disturbance, and the water was slopping up and down, dangerous and unpredictable.

He ran down to the beach, where he had spied his deputy telegraphist watching the eruption, transfixed. He said he too was utterly perplexed by the movement of the sea. Perhaps the tide was on the turn, he said. But, as he spoke, a furious rush of water roared towards them, sending them scurrying back up to the roadway. The two men ran to the small white stone building that was the Anjer telegraph office – and, as they did so, the enormous cloud from the volcano began to drift down on them. Within moments all Anjer was enveloped in dust and cloud and became strangely dark.

Some remember the cloud as black; others, like Schruit, are equally certain it was white. One of the pilots waiting for orders at the Anjer pilot-station, a Mr de Vries, swore it alternated in colour, from white (when presumably it was largely made up of steam) to black (when it was composed largely of eruptive smoke). But no matter: it was so thick and heavy that within moments an artificial night had descended on Anjer port, and the two men who groped their way to the cable office then found they had to light lanterns, in the middle of the afternoon, in order to be able to send their first message. They timed it at 2 p.m. Krakatoa, they tapped out in urgent Morse to their head office in Batavia, was beginning a major eruption. It was 'vomiting fire and smoke'. It was so dark in town that it was now no longer possible to see one's hand before one's eyes. What were the instructions?

Batavia replied, with equal urgency. Yes, they had already become aware that something was taking place. The governor-general himself, his sabbath ease disturbed, had been inquiring. People were milling about in the streets, worried. Chinese traders in particular seemed to have a peculiar sense of unease: the cable office reported hearing wailing. So it was important for Anjer to keep its telegraph station open and the information coming in, the operator tapped out. For the next six hours the operators did just that, giving the Dutch officials in Weltevreden (the name, 'Well Contented', must have prompted on this occasion a sardonic smile or two) a moment-by-moment chronicle, in the staccato language of the telegraph, of the unfolding events. 'Detonations increasing in loudness.' 'Hails of pumice.' 'Rain of coarse ash.' 'First flooding.' 'Vessels breaking loose in harbour.' 'Unusual darkness.' 'Gathering gloom.'

The Anjer harbour-master, who was by now aware that the crisis was frightening many of his friends and colleagues – 'the Day of Judgement has come' was a common belief – tried to collect as many of the local expatriates together as he could, to reassure them. How he imagined he might accomplish this is left unsaid. But he did manage to assemble a fair number of the colonial establishment – the Assistant Resident, the public works supervisor, the lighthouse keeper, the registrar, the town clerk, a local doctor and a prominent local widow – and tried to tell them that what they were witnessing would soon blow over, that it was, in his considered and experienced view, nothing to worry about. He could hardly have been more wrong.

At 2.45 p.m. the *Loudon*, all passengers aboard, set off for the forty-mile journey to the port of Telok Betong, at the head of Lampong Bay across in Sumatra. Her master, Captain Lindeman, steamed well to the east of the exploding island, trying as best he could to avoid the showers of rock and ash cascading down from the plumes of smoke. One British ship in the vicinity, the *Medea*, estimated that by mid-afternoon the column had risen to a height of seventeen miles, more than three times the height of Mount Everest; the *Medea*'s Captain Thomson said there were 'electrical displays' in the cloud, and explosions every few minutes were shaking his ship – even though he was at the time at anchor off Batavia, more than eighty miles to the east.

In the centre of the capital, meanwhile, people were very rapidly becoming aware that matters were getting out of hand. Two seasoned observers of Krakatoa's earlier throat-clearings – Dr J. P. van der Stok down at the Observatory in Batavia and the mining engineer Dr Rogier Verbeek up in the hills above town – had already telegraphed one another to find out what was going on. Van der Stok – the man whose wife had lost her delft dinner-plate in the May eruption and who himself had noted with great precision the time of the very beginning of the earlier events – once more swung into official Observatory mode, even though yet again this was a Sunday. He checked his watch at the very moment he heard the first loud rumblings, dashed from his house to the Observatory buildings and wrote the time down in the official log: 1.06 p.m. That time remains today, etched in official records, as the one known certain commencement of Krakatoa's final phase.

*

Confirmation of these figures then came from a totally unexpected source: the city's gasworks, to the south of Batavia old town. They proved, quite uncannily, to be of the greatest use to scientists who later studied the eruption. And they did so, quite simply, because of the way they had been built.

The most visible parts of any plant that produces gas from coke are the tall drum-shaped metal containers for the flammable gas – containers that are in essence telescopic, which 'float' on enormous ponds of water or mercury and which grow taller or shorter, higher or lower, depending on the amount of gas pumped from the works to be stored inside them. (Today's gasometers tend to stand tall against a city skyline in the morning, fall gradually over the day as the gas inside them is consumed, and then are replenished as more gas is manufactured overnight. In those cities like Batavia in the 1880s that had gas street lamps, the profile of variations in pressure, and thus the times of the varying heights of these gas containers, would necessarily be rather different. They would stand tall in the early evening and fall away during the dark, during the gas-illumined hours.)

What superintendents of gasworks have long known is that these storage containers – commonly, but in fact wrongly, called *gasometers* – also act as gigantic barometers. The pressure inside them, and in the lines leading from them, goes up and down by infinitesimal amounts according to the rise and fall of atmospheric pressure outside them. Normally one would never notice these small amounts of movement, since they would be superimposed on the much larger movements resulting from the consumption of gas. But an eagle-eyed superintendent, in charge of arranging the pressure in the gas lines according to demand, could indeed notice. Moreover, a paper register of the gasometer pressure is always produced (and was, for most of the time, in Batavia), which would show all the movements with great precision.

The pressure records are being taken constantly, but they can in fact record the minute fluctuations in the atmospheric pressure

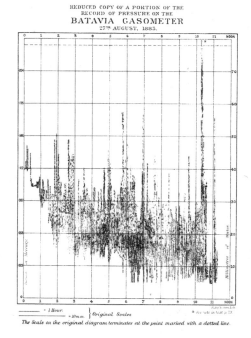

The invisible and inaudible pressure wave from Krakatoa's cataclysmic
final explosion, measured – until it blows off scale – at the Jakarta
Gasworks.

(and hence also the fluctuations caused by an event like Krakatoa)
only when the base pressure is low enough for the recording
meter to be affected by them. The gasworks superintendent would
increase this pressure each evening, when the street lights were
illuminated; he would keep it high until the middle of the evening;
and he would then lower it in hourly stages until dawn. So the
best recordings of changes in the atmospheric pressure would be
made during daylight hours, when the pressure in the gas lines
was kept low because of the low demand.

Which is exactly what happened – after a hiccup. For when the
very first explosions occurred at lunchtime on Sunday there is
no record, mysteriously. But then whatever problem existed

vanished, and the recording trace begins properly at 3.34 p.m. Batavia time (which, since this was still some while before the formal international establishment of time zones, was a little more than five minutes ahead of Krakatoa time).* From that moment on until dusk, and then throughout all of Monday morning after dawn, the Batavia gasworks pressure gauge provides an incredibly accurate, minute-by-minute record of the massive air-pressure waves that radiated out from the volcano, each and every time it erupted. The paroxysmal eruption itself at 10.02 on Monday morning blew right off the scale: it caused a pressure spike of more than *two and a half inches* of mercury, unheard of in any other circumstance.

By five o'clock on Sunday evening, when in normal circumstances ordinary civil twilight would be only an hour away, it was, in fact, nearly totally dark up and down the entire west Java coast, and was becoming similarly so in the capital. It was at this point that enormous chunks of pumice began to rain down from the sky.

There were three European ships inside the narrowest part of the Sunda Strait at the time – the *Loudon* with Captain Lindeman, which, because of the bucking sea, failed to reach Telok Betong and so anchored well out in Lampong Bay instead; the Danish salt-carrying barque *Marie*, which also rode out the enormous

---

* It was the International Meridian Conference held in Washington, DC, in 1884 that formally established the system of twenty-four time zones, each of which were essentially fifteen degrees wide (though which had deviations around countries, states and islands, where necessary, for neatness and convenience). The International Date Line was also set to run from pole to pole through the Pacific, though it had to be jiggled about because of various mid-Pacific islands that turned out not to exist. The whole notion of time zones was essentially the brainchild of a man named Charles Dowd, principal of a women's college in Saratoga Springs, New York, who wore his beard and hair in a design that perfectly emulated his hero, Abraham Lincoln.

and ever-growing waves in the same Sumatran bay; and the cargo-carrying barque *Charles Bal*, reaching the end of her long voyage from Belfast to Hong Kong. All three vessels were deluged with pumice: dangerous, heavy, sharp, fast-moving masses of rock, the larger pieces still warm to the touch.

The captain of the *Charles Bal*, W. J. Watson, found himself in a more perilous situation yet – somehow embayed, horribly pinioned in the sudden dark rain of rocks and compelled to beat around purposelessly, navigationally blinded. He was for a long while during the Sunday night just ten miles away from Krakatoa, closer to it than anyone else who survived. It enabled him to leave a record that was vivid in the extreme – except that chronologically (since it is thought that in the confusion he forgot to set his bridge chronometer to Batavia time) it was different by a single hour from everyone else's.

We first encounter Captain Watson* when he was beating northwards, with Java Head and First Point, Welcome Bay and Pepper Bay to his starboard, the great mountains of Sumatra to port, and the islands in the narrows of the Sunda Strait directly ahead. Then suddenly, at what he incorrectly records as 2.30 p.m. (it was in fact only 1.30 p.m.):

. . . we noticed some agitation about the point of Krakatoa, clouds or something being propelled from the northeast point with great velocity. At 3.30 we heard above us and about the island a strange sound as of a mighty crackling fire, or the discharge of heavy artillery at one or two seconds' interval.

At five the roaring noise continued and was increasing [wind moderate from the SSW, notes Captain Watson here, his mariners' routines never quite deserting him]; darkness spread over the sky,

* In an 1884 issue of the *Atlantic Monthly*, in a long interview conducted in San Francisco (to where the *Charles Bal* sailed after visiting Hong Kong) by the journalist E. W. Sturdy.

and a hail of pumice-stone fell on us, of which many pieces were of a considerable size and quite warm. We were obliged to cover up the skylights to save the glass, while our feet and our heads had to be protected with boots and sou'westers.

. . . we sailed on our course, until at 7 p.m. we got what we thought was a sight of Fourth Point light; then brought the ship to the wind, SW, as we could not see any distance, and knew not what might be in the Strait.

The night was a fearful one; the blinding fall of sand and stones, the intense blackness above and around us, broken only by the incessant glare of varied kinds of lightning, and the continued explosive roars of Krakatoa made our situation a truly awful one.

At 11 p.m. . . . the island became visible. Chains of fire appeared to ascend and descend between it and the sky, while on the SW end there seemed to be a continued roll of balls of white fire. The wind, though strong, was hot and choking, sulphurous, with a smell as of burning cinders, some of the pieces falling on us being like iron cinders. The lead came up from the bottom at thirty fathoms, quite warm.

From midnight to 4 a.m. of the 27th . . . the same impenetrable darkness continued, while the roaring of Krakatoa less continuous, but more explosive in sound; the sky one second intensely black, the next a blaze of light. The mast-head and yard-arms were studded with corposants* and a peculiar pink flame came from fleecy clouds which seemed to touch the mast-head and the yard-arms.

At 6 a.m., being able to make out the Java shore, set sail, and passed the Fourth Point lighthouse. At 8 a.m., hoisted our signal letter, but got no answer. At 8.30 passed Anjer with our name still hoisted, and

* This is the old name for those spheres of charged and luminous electrical clouds – known commonly to sailors as St Elmo's fire – frequently seen about the masts of sailing ships during storms. The word comes from *corpus sanctum*, 'holy body' – a reminder that in peril a sailor can do aught but put his trust in God.

close enough in to make out the houses, but could see no movement of any kind; in fact, through the whole Strait we did not see a single moving thing of any kind on sea or land.

At 10.15 a.m. we passed the Button Island, one half to three quarters of a mile off; the sea being like glass all around it, and the weather much finer looking, with no ash or cinders falling; wind light, at SE.

At 11.15 a.m. there was a fearful explosion in the direction of Krakatoa, then over 30 miles distant. We saw a wave rush right on to the Button Island, apparently sweeping entirely over the southern part . . .

. . . by 11.30 we were enclosed in a darkness that might almost be felt, and then commenced a downpour of mud, sand, and I know not what . . . we set two men on the lookout for'ard, the mate and the second mate on either quarter, and one man washing the mud from the binnacle glass. We had seen two vessels to the N and NW of us before the sky closed in, adding not a little to the anxiety of our position.

At noon the darkness was so intense that we had to grope our way about the decks, and although speaking to each other on the poop, yet we could not see each other. This horrible state and the downpour of mud and debris continued until 1.30 p.m., the roaring of the volcano and the lightning from the volcano being something fearful. By 2 p.m. we could see some of the yards aloft, and the fall of mud ceased; by 5 p.m. the horizon showed out to the northward and eastward, and we saw West Island bearing E by N, just visible. Up to midnight the sky hung dark and heavy, a little sand falling at times, and the roaring of the volcano very distinct, although we were fully 75 miles from Krakatoa. Such darkness and such a time in general few would conceive and many, I daresay, would disbelieve. The ship, from truck to water-line, was as if cemented: spars, sails, blocks and ropes were in a terrible mess; but thank God!, nobody hurt nor was the ship damaged. But think of Anjer, Merak and other little villages on the Java coast!

Other ships, more distant, experienced even more drama. The *Berbice*, a German paraffin-carrier bound from New York under the command of a Glaswegian, William Logan, found herself in a peculiarly exposed situation. When Logan saw the towering black clouds and lightning flashes ahead of him, from his position in the Strait's western approaches, he supposed it to be no more than a tropical storm. But as soon as flaming ashes began to fall on deck – a wooden deck that was only inches from his highly flammable cargo – he recognized what was going on, understood the perils of his position and promptly hove to in the lee of a protective island. He huddled there for the next two days – even though the island, by all accounts, afforded him precious little protection:

The lightning and thunder became worse and worse. Lightning flashes shot around the ship. Fireballs continually fell on deck and burst into sparks . . . The man at the rudder received heavy shocks on one arm. The copper sheathing of the rudder became glowing hot from the electric discharges.

The electricity in the air proved an even more serious problem, as Logan later recalled in an interview with an Australian newspaper:

Now and then when any sailor complained that he had been struck, I did my best to set his mind at ease, and endeavoured to talk the idea out of his head until I myself, holding fast to the rigging with one hand, and bending my head out of reach of a blinding ash shower which swept past my face, had to let go my hold, owing to a severe electric shock in the arm. I was unable to move the limb for several minutes afterwards.

Logan's crew were gripped with terror, volcanic dust covered the ship 'at least eight English thumbs deep', his masts and sails were alive with fire and sparks, his barometer fell impossibly low, all the ships' chronometers mysteriously stopped, and the world beyond him was concealed in a frequently impenetrable miasma of whirling dust and smoke. His account does, however, conceal one note of incongruous optimism.

As well as his thousands of gallons of paraffin, Captain Logan carried in his cabin a small package wrapped in brown paper and tied with string, addressed to the curator of the Botanical Gardens at Buitenzorg. Inside were five specimen seedlings of a variety of spurge found in the forests of the Amazon, known as *Hevea brasiliensis* – wild rubber. There had already been numberless plans to harvest rubber commercially from such trees where they grew wild in Brazil, but, for a variety of reasons,* all of the schemes failed: the *Berbice* was now bringing Amazonian plants to the Indies from which, it was hoped, plantation rubber could in due course be grown. The conditions of weather and soil made it likely that it would grow well in the East, the botanists predicted: dozens of related plants, like tapioca, castor bean and poinsettia already flourished there.

And this particular small story does have a happy ending. Despite the rigours of his passage through the Strait, Captain Logan, together with his ship, his cargo of paraffin and his infant rubber trees, all survived Krakatoa; and the parent-plants of what are now some of the most economically important rubber plantations in the world remain today in the Buitenzorg Botanical Garden, duly and safely delivered.

But otherwise the story of that long Sunday night makes for grisly reading. 'Everything became worse,' wrote an elderly Dutch pilot at Anjer. 'The reports were deafening, the natives cowered panic-stricken, a red fiery glare was visible above the burning mountain.'

---

* Not the least of which was an endemic South American leaf blight caused by *Michocyclus ulei*. The five plants sent on the *Berbice* were free of blight, and the plantations of South-East Asia have still not yet been infected, which many regard as akin to a miracle.

Hevea brasiliensis, Brazilian rubber.

At 6 p.m. the cable linking Anjer and Batavia finally broke – the line going dead at the very moment Telegraph-Master Schruit was telling government officials that yes, the eruption was continuing and indeed intensifying still. Schruit, tapping frantically at his Morse key, found he could not even make contact with the small town of Merak, seven miles up the coast. With his assistant telegraph operator in tow, he promptly dashed out into the gloom, ran through the old Dutch fort, fully intending to press on up the coast road to find and repair the rupture. He found it soon enough, just as he reached the drawbridge at the mouth of the harbour:

... there, a fearful sight met my eyes: a schooner and twenty-five or thirty *prahus* were being carried up and down between the drawbridge and the ordinary bridge as the water rose and fell, and nothing remained unbroken, including the telegraph wires which had been snapped by the schooner's mast.

But we felt no alarm as the water did not overflow its banks. Not entertaining any idea of danger, I sat down to table at about half-past 8. Of course I had made the necessary arrangements for beginning the repair of the broken line the first thing in the morning.

It was not to be. Anjer would not speak to Batavia again for the duration of this crisis – and Batavia would thus be wholly unaware of the terrible fate that would soon befall the town, and would befall all its neighbour villages up and down both the Java coast and across on the far side, in Sumatra.

The astronomical logs for 26 August note that civil twilight in Anjer port began that night at 6.22 p.m., half an hour after the sun had set, when artificial lights were first needed in the street; nautical twilight, the time when the horizon ceases to be the sharply delineated line that a navigator deems essential for working with his sextant, began at 6.47. Both periods would in normal circumstances endure for thirty minutes. This night there was no such thing. It had been dark in Anjer since mid-afternoon, and when the invisible sun did set, the darkness was Stygian indeed – the air a hot, ashy breath, filled with grit and sulphur, disorienting, confusing and poisonous.

By late evening it was the turn of the ocean to take over as the more terrifying manifestation of Krakatoa's gathering power. As the great volcanic engine pumped and stoked more and more explosive energy into the atmosphere, so the sea surrounding the dying mountain became progressively more and more disturbed – and communities that were already huddling, frightened, along the low coastline of the Strait began to experience ever greater waves, ever more dangerous seas.

The reports from after sunset speak continually of smashed boats and inundations of low-lying land, of ruined houses and of bystanders pulled off their feet into the raging waters. The first and most melancholy accounts were those later given to a number of newspapers in Java by the colonial *contrôleur* in the south Sumatran town of Ketimbang, Willem Beyerinck – the man who had given the first official news of the impending eruption back in mid May, when he telegraphed to the Resident of Lampong to say he had felt an outbreak of ominous tremors.

From that first Sunday afternoon, Mr and Mrs Beyerinck and

their three children were to endure a week of the most exquisite agony – much of which they remembered well; and by so doing they provided one of the more reliable chronicles of this very complicated series of events.

The Sunday had begun innocently enough, with the opening of a new village market. There was the ritual slaughter of a baby buffalo, the playing of a gamelan orchestra, perhaps a *wayang kulit* puppet show – the kind of ceremonial that the Beyerincks had seen countless times during their tour. But these were strange times. Krakatoa had begun to rumble again that afternoon, and it somehow cast a shadow over an opening that was not, in consequence, an entirely happy affair. There had been a local outbreak of cholera too – a housemaid had just died, and Mrs Beyerinck was worried about the health of her children. The children's *ayah* had seemed agitated for other reasons – complaining among other things that the birds that normally flocked around the family house had lately seemed restless, and that the auguries were not good. And Mrs Beyerinck, warily watching the smoke roiling about the summit of Rakata, was wise enough and prescient enough to accept that one ignored the superstitions of the local people at one's peril.

When they returned from the market, Mrs Beyerinck made what at the time seemed a strange request – that the family not go home, but make right away for a tiny village in the hills, where they rented a holiday cottage. Her husband, however, wouldn't at first hear of it. The locals, he said, would wreak havoc in Ketimbang town if he did so; and the wilder elements who had only lately been hired to pick the summer pepper harvest up in the highlands would soon hear that the Dutch *contrôleur* had run away, and would descend on the town in short order. No, he declared; the family would stay. Mrs Beyerinck went off to her room to sulk, only remembering later the distant tinklings of the gamelan and the rhythm of a great drum sounding what she thought was a threnody.

But then everything changed, very suddenly. Her husband sauntered down to the shore to see what effects the new eruption might be having – and came on a scene that astonished him. While in the distance the mountain was roaring and boiling from behind an immense pillar of clouds, here enormous waves were breaking on the beach, and the level of the sea was piling up, rising and falling alarmingly, crashing with a weird randomness against anything solid on the shore. There was no wind, no storm. But the surface of the sea had a terrible, writhing, coiling awfulness about it.

He could see the *Loudon*, with its cargo of Anjer coolies bound for the pepper fields of Telok Betong, beating up Lampong Bay towards him, then trying desperately to dock. It was being tossed every which way, one moment corkscrewing high on the crest of a huge mass of water, the next being twisted as if by an unseen hand and plunged deep down into a trough. The master then evidently lost his nerve and gave up the struggle, for, as Beyerinck watched in horror, the boat, now looking so vulnerable and fragile, suddenly turned away, presumably to try to ride out the fury in mid channel.

The *contrôleur* stared, now momentarily dumbstruck, as the thrashing waters rose higher and higher up the shore, soon reaching the outbuildings of his own Residency. Water began crashing against the stucco, breaking hard against what looked like increasingly insubstantial structures. It was this very sight that finally made up his mind for him. His earlier decision had been wrong, he told his servants: Mrs Beyerinck and the children should leave right away. Everyone should flee to their summer cottage up in the hills.

For a few moments, it seemed unlikely that they would make it. For at 8 p.m., as a hail of pumice began to rain down, the waves began their first orgy of destruction. They were eventually to reach well over a hundred feet in height, and right from the start even the precursors of the mighty waves, even the first tentacle-feelers of water, did the most amazing damage. In an instant Beyerinck's office suddenly came crashing down, along with a clutch of outbuildings. The family and their servants escaped drowning only by shinnying up coconut palms and waiting until the waters receded for a few moments' respite. Then they climbed back down, gathered up valuables, set the horses and their other animals loose and ran, as far as they could manage, inland.

Their flight was the stuff of the cinema epic. There was a dreadful roaring behind them as they stumbled, half blind, frightened, soaking wet, through miles of paddy, sinking into thick mud while trying desperately to outrun the ever pursuing monster. At one stage Mrs Beyerinck, by now covered with mud from head to toe, tried to shout, but her throat was horribly sore and she couldn't utter a sound. She felt her neck – it was thick with a collar of leeches. They ran on and on, getting lost, from time to time joining forces with other local people, who themselves were fleeing in great crowds from the thundering, roaring floods behind them. Pieces of pumice hurtled down from the sky, burning fiercely like jagged meteorites.

The family and such servants as had run with them reached the hilltop cottage at midnight. They broke out supplies, fed their terrified children, settled them to some kind of fitful sleep. The adults then knelt on the slatted floor and peered through the window towards the raging volcano, which they could see distinctly through the fog of falling rock. Outside the hut lay thousands of local people, all crying and wailing in desperation. Some of the more sober were praying to Allah for relief from the nightmare.

But it was not to end for some hours yet. One of Beyerinck's servants arrived just before dawn, saying that the entire Residency had been ripped from its foundations by a gigantic wave at about 2 a.m. All the signs suggested the waters were getting higher and higher, and the entire town of Ketimbang would likely go under. And indeed when the *contrôleur* sent scouts downhill at dawn to see the damage, it had been destroyed, totally. An enormous series of waves had flooded over every rooftop at about 6 a.m.: nothing was left standing.

Up at Telok Betong, where the Resident later said water had come within ten yards of his house, which was perched at the top of a hill 120 feet high, there was a mass of destruction. The harbour-master, waiting in vain for the *Loudon,* said he was swept off his feet eight times before he ran for his life. From up on the hills surrounding the town he watched as the Dutch Navy's well-armed paddle-steamer *Berouw* strained mightily at her mooring buoy. It looked to him as though not only might the chains give and the vessel founder, along with her crew of twenty-eight, but that the buoy might free itself too and be hurled about the harbour, destroying all other ships there – including the barque the *Marie,* which was waiting in the roads. Mass destruction seemed to be waiting in the wings.

And on the *Loudon* herself Captain Lindeman found himself dealing with the unimaginable waves, the close presence of land and a host of other ships near by (a perilous combination that sailors fear most in a storm, denying the vessel vitally necessary sea-room) – as well as a terrified crew. The locally hired men in particular were petrified by the eruption of St Elmo's fire in the riggings, and they left their posts in droves to try desperately to beat them out, to extinguish what was in fact inextinguishable. The phosphorescence was, they insisted, evidence of ghostly spirits: if these phenomena found their way below they would eat their way through the hull and the vessel would sink like a stone.

There was an almost endless succession of other, very similar reports. There were those from nine other nearby ships – like the magnificent American barque *W. H. Besse,* forty miles north of Krakatoa; the British vessels *Sir Robert Sale* and the *Norham Castle,* both of which were hove to off Sumatra; the Norwegian

The Royal Dutch Navy's armed paddle-steamer *Berouw* about to be picked up by one of the giant tsunamis generated by the eruption.

barque *Borjild*, eighty miles north-east of the volcano; the Welsh cargo vessel *Bay of Naples*, under way to Singapore and 120 miles south of Java Head; the Rotterdam Lloyd's steamship *Batavia*, well to the south-west of the entrance to the Strait; the steamer *Prins Frederik* which had passed Krakatoa on 25 August and was by the time of the explosion also well out into the Indian Ocean; the *Annerley*, southbound, and at the time of the eruption standing to the north of the Strait; and the British-flagged *Medea*, whose Captain Thomson had managed to measure with some accuracy the height of the volcanic cloud at the outset of the eruption, at seventeen miles.

There were all manner of curious survivals. One man had fallen asleep at home and awoke to find that the wave had lifted him and his bed to the top of a hill, and deposited him there in perfect safety. Another grabbed on to the corpse of a cow and floated to high ground. More bizarre still – and barely credible – was the man who reportedly found himself being swept inland next to a crocodile: he clambered on to its back and hung on for grim death with his thumbs dug deep into the creature's eye-sockets.

And there were in addition statements and newspaper interviews and private letters home from lighthouse keepers and Residents, Assistant Residents, *contrôleurs*, agents of Lloyd's, telegraph operators, harbour-masters and sharp-eyed civilians of all stripes, as well as an enterprising member of the Catholic clergy named Julian Tenison-Woods* who wrote an exceptionally long letter about the events to the *Sydney Morning Herald.* From this mass of information a broad summary can be distilled.

Krakatoa's final twenty hours and fifty-six minutes were marked by a number of phases. First, from early afternoon on Sunday until about 7 p.m. there was a series of explosions and eruptions of steadily increasing frequency and vigour. From early evening the ash falls and the deluge of pumice began. By 8 p.m. the water

---

* This was the kind of man whose like we do not see today. A London-born Passionist minister, amateur geologist and naturalist, he was compelled by ill-health to move abroad when he was in his twenties, and became an expert on the conchology and palaeontology of Tasmania during the time he worked as a travelling missionary for the Catholic archbishop of Sydney. He left the priesthood in 1883, when he was fifty-one, and travelled to Malaya, Singapore and the Dutch East Indies – where he became fascinated by the eruption of Krakatoa – and then on to the Philippines, China and Japan. He returned to Australia and died in Sydney six years later, in 1889 – 'a man of wide culture, a musician, an artist, and something of a poet', as well as a writer of hymns, the author of a book on the fishes of New South Wales, another on the history of Australia, and more than 150 other contributions to the scientific literature.

had become the next medium of transmission of the volcanic energy, and as night fell the temper of the sea in the Sunda Strait became one of unbridled ferocity.

Then, just before midnight, a series of air waves – fast-moving, low-frequency shocks sent out invisibly and inaudibly by the detonations – began arriving in Batavia. The time-ball on the astronomical clock down at Batavia's harbour stopped dead at eighteen seconds after 11.32 p.m. because of the ceaseless vibrations. Audible evidence of the explosions began to radiate outwards too, and there was a report from Singapore and Penang* that thudding sounds could be heard at about the same time. In Batavia a large number of people, kept awake by the explosions and for want of something better to do, were walking around the Koningsplein; they noticed that the gas lanterns suddenly dimmed at about 1.55 a.m. Along Rijswijk, the main shopping street, several shop windows suddenly and inexplicably shattered at about the same time.

Then at about 4 a.m. the nature of the explosions reportedly changed, very slightly, becoming less continuous but more explosive. Someone described the sounds as like a steam-engine, emitting full-throated *whoomphs* as it gathered speed. At about 4.56 a.m. an enormously powerful air wave was detected at the Batavia gasworks – suggesting, if travel time over the ninety miles to the volcano is allowed for, that something else had just happened deep within Krakatoa's heart. The culminating explosion – though no one on the ground at the time knew it – was soon about to happen.

There were four gigantic explosions still to come. The first was noted at 5.30 a.m. The Sumatran town of Ketimbang was then destroyed at 6.15 a.m., and Anjer, her Javan sister-port across the Strait – according to the few who survived to tell the

* These reports were also collected by Tenison-Woods, a reliable and properly disinterested observer.

tale – was inundated and wrecked very shortly thereafter. The second mighty explosion came at 6.44 a.m. – forty-one minutes after a dawn that, to those in all of western Java, never arrived that day. Ashes began to fall on Batavia at 7 a.m. – although Oscar Hatfield, the American consul in Batavia, reported seeing them falling in the consulate grounds two hours later.* At 8.20 a.m. a third, quite terrible explosion was felt in Batavia, and many of the buildings started to make what were described as 'crackling' noises. And then finally, at 10.02 a.m., came the culminating, terrifying majesty of it all.

Two minutes to go and, according to simultaneous reports: the sky was completely darkened in all of southern Sumatra; the *Loudon* was weathering heavy ash falls in Lampong Bay; the nearby *Marie* reported 'three heavy seas came after each other; at once a fearful detonation; sky in fire; damp'. The *Annerley* lit all her lights, noted that it was raining pumice stone, that the barometer was rising and falling half an inch a minute. In Batavia it became eerily dark again, and – most significantly – it started to get cold. From 10 a.m. the temperature began to fall – as many as fifteen degrees Fahrenheit over the coming four noontide hours.

Explosions like a battery of guns are heard across in Telok Betong. Lightning strikes the lighthouse at Vlakke Hoek in southern Sumatra. The lighthouse at Fourth Point, just to the south of Anjer, is hit by a vast wave and destroyed, ripped off at its base, leaving only an amputated stump of jagged masonry. An immense wave then leaves Krakatoa at almost exactly 10 a.m. – and then two minutes later, according to all the instruments that record it, came the fourth and greatest explosion of them all, a

---

* For some unexplained reason, Mr Hatfield left little by way of an interesting record of the Krakatoa events – and his report of the ash fall, which he timed much later than Tenison-Woods's very detailed and exact description ('pale yellow ... gloomy ... very dense'), suggests that certain of his consular faculties might have been wanting.

detonation that was heard thousands of miles away and that is still said to be the most violent explosion ever recorded and experienced by modern man. The cloud of gas and white-hot pumice and fire and smoke is believed to have risen – been hurled, more probably, blasted as though from a gigantic cannon – as many as twenty-four miles into the air.

'A fearful explosion.' 'A frightful sound.' Captain Sampson of the British vessel *Norham Castle* wrote simply in his official log: 'I am writing this blind in pitch darkness. We are under a continual rain of pumice-stone and dust. So violent are the explosions that the ear-drums of over half my crew have been shattered. My last thoughts are with my dear wife. *I am convinced that the Day of Judgement has come.*'

The British consul in Batavia at the time was one Alexander Patrick Cameron; and five days later he sat down in his study and had his confidential clerk write out, in the usual impeccable sweeps of fine Victorian copperplate, his summary of what he then knew of the disaster. The document remains today in the Public Record Office in London, largely unread and unconsulted because of a confusion that has led those who have chronicled the Krakatoa events to believe the British consul was in fact a man named Henry George Kennedy.

The error is understandable. Kennedy had in fact been consul in Sumatra, and was called in to replace Cameron when the latter asked for leave in November 1883. Kennedy wrote a summary of the terrible events for the Royal Society in September 1883. His name is known to what might be called the Krakatoa community today as a result, and most indexes of most books will have a reference or two to him. Alexander Cameron, on the other hand, remains forgotten and unsung. What he wrote, though, seems today a model of diplomatic felicity, as perfect a summary of the events as could be imagined, considering the awful circumstances of the moment.

British Consulate
Batavia 1st September 1883.

N° 15.

My Lord,

*Enclosed I have the honour
to hand Your Lordship a copy of my
telegram of yesterday giving notice of
the volcanic disturbances which have
lately taken place in the neighbourhood
of my Consular district.*

The spot where the subterranean

*Her Majesty's Principal Secretary,   forces
of State for Foreign Affairs
Whitehall
London*

The elegant copperplate and exquisitely courteous tone of Consul
Cameron's lengthy Krakatoa dispatch to Lord Granville, in London.

His report is dated Batavia, 1 September 1883, and is addressed
to Gladstone's foreign secretary, the Earl Granville:

My Lord:

Enclosed I have the honour to hand Your Lordship a copy of my
telegram of yesterday, giving notice of the volcanic disturbances which
have lately taken place in the neighbourhood of my Consular district.

The spot where the subterranean forces have found vent is the
island of Krakatau* lying in Longitude 105°27'E, Latitude 6°7'S, at

* Note that the consul spells the volcano's name correctly: as already
suggested, the misspelling Krakatoa seems more a consequence of the
carelessness of journalism than diplomacy. However, in the same paragraph
Cameron makes an error with his dates. *Even Homer nods.*

the southern entrance to the Straits of Sunda. This island was the scene of a volcanic eruption of less importance on the 20th May last which, although on that occasion an entirely new crater was formed, had no such disastrous results to life and property as have attended the explosions which commenced on the 27th inst.

The present outburst commenced on Sunday last, and on that night the inhabitants of nearly the whole of Java and Sumatra were alarmed by loud noises resembling the reports of heavy artillery, which continued throughout the night and at rarer intervals during Monday 28th inst. It soon became known that these noises were produced by a fresh eruption of Krakatau and since Monday intelligence has been slowly reaching Batavia from various quarters apprising us of the extent of damage done, and proving by the loss of life and property that this is one of the greatest calamities of this century.

The residencies of Bantam and Batavia were darkened throughout the early hours of last Monday by a thick cloud of grey ashes, the light diminishing gradually, as the cloud progressed from west to east, from twilight to almost total darkness at midday, and a continuous shower of ash fell during the forenoon giving the ground an appearance as if covered by snow. At about 11.30 a.m. at Batavia and at earlier periods of the day in the more immediate vicinity of Krakatau the sea suddenly rose, presumably owing to the subsidence of part of Krakatau and other islands or to a submarine upheaval, and a wave of considerable height advanced with great rapidity on the shores of western Java and southern Sumatra, causing greater or less damage according to its distance from the centre of disturbance. A second wave higher than the previous one followed the first at an interval of about an hour with even more serious results. It is now reported that part of Krakatau island, the island of Poeloe Temposa and other small islands in Sunda Straits have disappeared, and that a reef has been formed between Krakatau and Sibesie islands, the channel usually taken by steamers. Dwars-in-den-weg/Thwart-the-Way, an island at the northern entrance to the Straits, is reported

split into five pieces, while numerous small islands are said to have
been raised which had no existence previously.

These reports however still require verification and with a view to
ascertaining the extent and nature of the changes caused by the
volcanic action a Government survey-steamer has been dispatched to
the neighbourhood to take a new survey of the Straits.

The destruction caused by the waves on shore both to life and
property, although known from reports already to hand to be very
widespread, can hardly yet be estimated with any degree of certainty,
as owing to the action of the sea and the heavy rain of ashes, telegraph
and road communication has been either entirely interrupted or is
much delayed.

It appears beyond a doubt however that the whole of the south-
eastern coast of Sumatra must have suffered severely from the effects
of the sudden influx of the sea, and thousands of natives inhabiting
the villages on the coast must have almost certainly perished.

The west coast of Java from Merak to Tjeringin [has] been laid
waste. Anjer, the port where vessels bound for the Java and China
Seas call for orders and a thriving town of several thousand inhabitants
(natives), no longer exists, its former site now being a swamp.

The lighthouse at Anjer (Java's Fourth Point) has also been much
damaged.

Many Europeans, including numerous officials, and many thousands
of natives have been drowned, in the district of Tjeringin alone on the
southeast coast of Java it is reported that no less than ten thousand
persons have lost their lives. The result to agriculture in west Java
[is] not yet officially known. The fact however that owing to the
covering of ashes which spreads over the whole country, the cattle are
deprived of their ordinary nourishment, is in itself a very serious
consideration and measures have already been taken to supply the
afflicted districts with food for man and beast. It is to be feared that
the natives will be greatly impoverished by the damage done to fruit
and palm trees which form a source of wealth, while coffee and tea

gardens and standing crops of all descriptions must have suffered severely.

With a view to rendering safe the navigation of the Sunda Straits the Rear Admiral, Commander in Chief of the Netherlands Indian Navy, has stationed one man-of-war to cruise off the southern and another to cruise off the northern entrance to the Straits to warn vessels to proceed with caution.

In view of the quantity of shipping (principally British) which daily passes through Sunda Straits and the important nature of the circumstances above related I have thought it my duty to dispatch the telegrams mentioned in the accompanying memorandum, and trust my action will meet Your Lordship's approval.

I have the honour to be,

My Lord,

Your Lordship's Most obedient, Humble Servant,

A. P. Cameron

Her Britannic Majesty's Consul, Batavia

The island of Krakatoa, meanwhile, had in essence disappeared. Six cubic miles of rock had been blasted out of existence, had been turned into pumice and ash and uncountable billions of particles of dust. The rumblings and roarings continued for some while, then on Monday afternoon became ever fainter. By dawn on Tuesday they had stopped completely. That last great detonation at two minutes past ten on that Monday morning had blown the island apart, and sent most of it to kingdom come.

Now it was time for those who could, together with those whose duty it was, to venture out to see just what damage the eruption had caused.

Admiralty charts show the islands of Krakatoa before and after
the 1883 disaster.

2. The Effects

It was just before dawn on the Monday, and an elderly Dutch harbour-pilot, one of those stationed in Anjer to guide ships to and from the Batavia roads, was walking on the beach. He couldn't sleep; besides, staying inside was perilous, not least because the intermittent hails of pumice stones, many of them too hot to touch, threatened either to set ablaze the *atap* thatch with which his house was roofed, or to smash holes in it and wreak who knows what damage inside. Much the better, he thought, to watch the great events from the comparative safety of the shore.

There was not much visible through the gloom. The clocks said that the sun ought to be ready to rise; but the falling, swirling ash had effectively dimmed the view for more than a few yards in any direction. Krakatoa herself, thundering away angrily to the west, was quite invisible – except that there was a dark-orange glare to the ash clouds in the mountain's direction: it was like the view of a very distant furnace glimpsed, only half seen, through the dark clouds of its smoke.

But then, all of a sudden, the image shifted. Suddenly the old pilot, who had spent a lifetime guiding vessels through dangerous and unpredictable waters, became aware of something that was just barely visible, something that shouldn't have been there at all. He related to the Reverend Philip Neale, the British chaplain in Batavia who later in the year set about collecting the stories of eyewitnesses, exactly what it was:

Looking out to sea, I noticed a dark black object through the gloom, travelling towards the shore. At first sight it seemed like a low range of hills rising out of the water – but I knew there was nothing of the kind in that part of the Sunda Strait. A second glance – and a very hurried one at that – convinced me that it was a lofty ridge of water many feet high . . .

In the aftermath of Krakatoa's eruption, 165 villages were devastated, 36,417 people died, and uncountable thousands were injured – and almost all of them, villages and inhabitants, were victims not of the eruption directly but of the immense sea-waves* that were propelled outwards from the volcano by that last night of detonations.

It was in this one respect – the production of a number of massive and highly destructive sea-waves – that Krakatoa was then and remains today so very unlike almost all of the other of the world's great volcanic disasters. Its scale was phenomenal. The number it killed was unimaginably vast. But it was the way that it killed all those people that still sets Krakatoa apart.

Other volcanic eruptions around the world kill people in more direct and predictable ways – and they kill and injure, it should be remembered, a not insignificant number of people, since one in ten of the world's population is currently reckoned to live near volcanoes that are either active or have the potential to become so. So far as volcanoes are concerned, there are a great number of people – in the Philippines, in Mexico, on Java, in Italy even – who are currently living in harm's way.

The types of hazards to which such people are likely to fall prey, or to which their forebears fell victim in the past, are many and manifest. Erupted boulders and lumps of partly congealed lava – generally known by the term *tephra*, from the Greek word for ash – scream back down from the skies and flatten anything in their path. Perhaps a relatively small number of people, fewer than a thousand, died in this way from the Krakatoa eruption. All of them were in southern Sumatra, in the path of the prevailing

* The term *sea-wave*, or its Japanese equivalent, *tsunami*, is now generally preferred by the scientific community; *tidal wave*, a term that yet survives, is condemned as inaccurate, since the waves caused by earthquakes or volcanoes are in no sense tidal.

wind: the hot ash that burned them alive had sped westwards from Krakatoa on top of a cushion of superheated steam.

Most of the other means by which volcanoes kill their victims were not experienced here. In other eruptions lava flows surround and trap victims, and sear them to death. Earthquakes associated with volcanoes destroy buildings, and huge seismically caused cracks in the earth swallow people and the buildings in which they live. The terrifyingly fast-moving clouds of hot lava, ash pumice and incandescent volcanic gases, known to the French as *nuées ardentes* and to the rest of the world as *pyroclastic flows*, sweep people up and incinerate them in seconds – as with, for example, almost every one of the 28,000 inhabitants of St Pierre, in Martinique,* who in May 1902 had been persuaded to stay in town for a supposedly important election, but were burned and suffocated by the sudden pyroclastic flows coursing down from the eruption of Mount Pelée.

Clouds of sulphur-dioxide gas, usually released during eruptions, choke and poison their victims. Clouds of carbon dioxide suffocate them. Clouds of hydrochloric acid gnaw away at their lungs. The torrents of volcanic mud and water slurry that course down the sides of certain volcanoes and that have the Javanese name *lahars* (since there are so many such flows running down the sides of Javanese volcanoes – though not, as it happens, on Krakatoa) carry victims miles away, and drown and bury them.

* There were precious few survivors: the best known was a prisoner named Louis-Auguste Ciparis (or Sylbaris), who was in solitary confinement in an evidently well-insulated and nearly airtight cell. When found to be a survivor a miracle was promptly declared and he was set free. Barnum & Bailey had him perform in their travelling circus for some years before he got into trouble again and ended up in an American jail. He was fired from the circus when people lost interest, and died a pauper in Panama in 1955. His cell in St Pierre still stands as a tourist attraction; visitors are taken there in a bus called the Ciparis Express.

Sometimes secondary events can prove fatal. In 1985 a small eruption of a Colombian volcano called Nevado del Ruiz melted a glacier near the summit: the resulting river coursed down a valley that was quite unused to such huge flows, and the mud sea that was eventually created drowned an entire village below, killing 23,000 people. There are still more obscure risks: for example, volcanoes that erupt beneath glaciers – which tend not to have too many people living near them – produce sudden floods of melting ice, which have recently been given the exotic Icelandic name *jökulhlaups*. These can also prove fatal.

However, of all the victims whose deaths can be attributed directly to volcanic activity during the last 250 years, fully a quarter are now believed to have died – drowned or smashed to pieces – as a result of the gigantic waves that were created by the eruptions. The entire Minoan civilization on Crete was supposedly wiped out in 1648 BC when volcanic tephra from the eruption of Santorini – or, much more probably, the tsunamis thrown up by the eruption – destroyed the palaces at Knossos. More than 10,000 people died in 1782 in the waves that were created by an avalanche of volcanic debris that hurtled into the sea from Japan's Mount Unzen. In 1815 a similar number of Javanese died when Tambora exploded, sending pyroclastic flows raging into the ocean, with tsunamis radiating out in all directions and inundating the coast.

Careful study of the records for the last two and a half centuries has come up with a total of some ninety tsunamis for which volcanoes alone can be held responsible – and the greatest of these by far was the 1883 eruption of Krakatoa. About 35,500 men, women and children died as victims of the two gigantic waves that accompanied or were caused by the death throes of this island-mountain, and they account for more than half of all those in the world who are known ever to have died from waves caused by an erupting volcano. So this should be remembered well: it was neither fire nor gas nor flowing lava that killed most of the victims of Krakatoa. All but the thousand who were burned in Sumatra by the immolating heat of newly made ash and pumice and scalding gases died by the primary agency of water.

During the eruptive days back in late May the state of the sea was certainly noticed, but was never once reported to be the cause of any undue alarm. The hopper *Samarang* noticed a swell powerful enough to lift her screw out of the water; the lighthouse keeper saw the surface of the Strait turn suddenly white; the rudder of the *Bintaing*, another small hopper, swung around and hit her own hull with a mighty clang when a freak wave caught her. But that was about all: the eruption in its opening stages was about ash falls and noise and that seven-mile-high column of coiling smoke. The ocean seemed to prefer not to become involved.

But three months later matters were very different. The way that Krakatoa's immense outpouring of thermal energy was converted into mechanical energy – for this conversion is what essentially determines both the immensity and the enormity of any volcanic eruption – was altered. The noise was there, on an extraordinary scale. The expulsion of material high into the sky went on, both in gigantic amounts and for a very long time. But most of the mechanical energy went into the enormously difficult task of moving the ocean – movement that, once started and given additional shoves from behind, can become one of the most powerful natural forces imaginable.

In August the state of the sea was something noticed by all. Right from the beginning, when Telegraph-Master Schruit took his lunch and strolled out on to the hotel veranda to first see the column of smoke, it was the strangely erratic motion of the sea that most alarmed him. On the far side of the Strait, in Ketimbang, Monsieur *Contrôleur* Beyerinck too was astonished by the punishment his town's little dock was having to take from the curiously restless waters. The ships out in the Strait – the *Loudon*, the

A classic wall-of-water tsunami generated by only
the most moderate of earthquakes on Krakatoa.

Marie, the *Charles Bal* – all reported on the state of the sea. For
them it was not so serious, as waves at sea are less dangerous to
a ship than waves close to land. The electricity in the air and the
rain of flaming rocks from the sky were quite dangerous enough.

As darkness fell, so the sea became ever more furious. At 7 p.m.
on the Sunday, Beyerinck saw small boats being tossed about. At
the same time on the Javan side, Schruit found that his telegraph
cable had been snapped by the mast of a schooner tossing on the
waves. Between 7 p.m. and 9 p.m. several houses close to the
seafront in the small town of Tyringin, well to the south of Anjer,
were reported destroyed and swept away.

At about 7.30 p.m. a quarry near Merak, where dozens of
Chinese labourers were hewing out stone* for the new Batavia
docks, was then inundated, and the camp where the workers slept
was washed away: they may have been the first casualties of what

---

* It seems now a measure of the Chinese labourer's legendary tolerance for
appalling working conditions that so many were still hewing stone in
Merak, despite the terrifying nearby concussions, to say nothing of the
flames and the clouds of ash.

was to be a long and mortally expensive night. But now there was a lull: though a village five miles out of Anjer was reported to be submerged at 10 p.m., by midnight the sea was glass-smooth once again; and at 1 a.m. on the Monday morning Schruit, still trying feverishly to repair his severed cable (he eventually failed), noticed only small oscillations in the surface of the sea close to where the Anjer canal debouched into it.

Then at 1.30 a.m. one almighty wave is reported to have rushed up the long funnel of Lampong Bay to Telok Betong, where it ripped through and ruined several houses. Although it was clearly highly destructive, and though the time of its occurrence seems to be accurate, having been cross-checked with other witnesses (not least the servants of Beyerinck, sheltering with his family in their hilltop cottage), this one wave appears to be something of an aberration – far larger than its predecessors but unrelated to any particular event at the volcano. It was indicative, however, of what was to come.

The greatest and most terrifying volumes of water began moving in concert with Krakatoa's four culminating explosions – the first eruptive paroxysm being timed, as we have seen, at 5.30 a.m. It was as though then something deep within the mountain had begun a series of low-frequency pulsations, the sea moving back and forth in time with each pulse, and the amplitude of these movements becoming greater and greater, the *volume*, as it were, of the waves becoming stronger and stronger with each sequence of pulses. The four major tsunamis that were caused by, or were coincident with, these giant volcanic explosions then hit the shores like planet-sized wrecking balls, the effects all unimaginably and fatally destructive.

The destructive capacity of a great wave can be calculated, with difficulty, from a mess of competing and combining features, including the configuration of the shoreline, the funnelling effect of cliffs and headlands, and the depth of the coastal waters. It seems from the various eyewitness reports that what was most impressive about the waves that struck the shores of Java and Sumatra that morning was their sheer size – the high and un-stoppable moving walls, the majestic volume of hundreds of billions of tons of roiling, thundering, foaming green water.

The last four great explosions of Krakatoa's life took place at 5.30 a.m., 6.44 a.m., 8.20 a.m. and, finally and most terrifically of all, at 10.02 a.m. – all of these well-chronicled moments being recorded in Krakatoa Time, which (because each local Dutch administrator still set his official watch according to when the sun rose and set and reached its noontime peak *in his own district*) was in those days 5 minutes and 42 seconds behind what the capital's civil servants regarded as Batavia Standard Time. The energy that was released in these eruptions was transformed into a variety of violent effects. There were massive expulsions of rock and ash and gas. There were torrents of heat, searing and welding together everything around them. There were sounds – bangs, cracks, thunderous roars, shattering low- and high-frequency noises – that were so loud they could be heard thousands of miles away. Seismic shocks were triggered that caused buildings 500 miles away to rock on their foundations.

And the eruptions also produced two kinds of shock waves. One was a wave that passed invisibly through the air, a sudden burst of pressure that bounced around the world, and was recorded as doing so, moreover, a remarkable *seven* times. These air waves – which recorded as pressure spikes at the Batavia gasworks, ninety miles to the east – radiated outwards from Krakatoa very fast, at what was an easily calculated velocity of about 675 mph. They were recorded as reaching Batavia at 5.43 a.m., 6.57 a.m. and (there seems, curiously, to be no firm record of any air wave resulting from the third explosion) at 10.15 a.m. respectively, Batavia Standard Time. (These events took place before the invention of time zones, either in the East Indies or anywhere else in the world. This, taken together with the dubious accuracy of many of the mechanical clocks of the day, the absence of the coordinating abilities of radio, which had of course not quite yet been invented, and the wide range of anecdotal reports from frequently panicky eyewitnesses, makes it tricky, though not entirely impossible, to construct a firm chronology of what took place in the aftermath of the eruptions.)

The other shocks, considerably more complex in the way they moved, of much shorter duration but of equally extraordinary geographical spread, involved the disruption of the surrounding sea-water. Sea-borne waves in general move much more slowly: in the relatively shallow waters of the Sunda Strait probably at an average speed of about 60 mph.* However the Krakatoa tsunamis were forged, it would take one of them about thirty minutes from the moment of eruption to travel to the closest point on the mainland.† And it would be thirty-seven minutes before the wave was close enough to the town of Anjer for the people there to see it, to recognize just what it was that was

---

* The speed of a tsunami is directly proportional to the square root of the depth of sea through which it travels. In mid ocean, where the depths are measured in thousands or tens of thousands of feet, it can move at speeds of up to 500 mph; where the water is 900 feet deep it will slow to 115 mph. In the Sunda Strait, where the water depth varies from about 500 feet in mid channel to twenty feet and less at the edges, the speed of travel appears to have averaged about 60 mph. When a fast-moving deep-sea wave encounters the shore, it changes shape drastically: out in mid ocean it will be fast moving but only a few feet high; as it reaches shore it will slow down, pile up on top of itself and very swiftly become enormous. A wave generated by Krakatoa might have started out with a height of ten feet and a speed of 100 mph; when it got to Telok Betong, or Anjer, or Merak, it may then have slowed to only 20 mph – but it could have been as tall as a ten-storey building, with frightening consequences for anything or anyone in its path.

† The nearest land is Point Tikus in southern Sumatra, on the west side of Lampong Bay – but happily it is in the shelter of a small island, which would slow the wave's momentum.

bearing down on them and to start – a fairly, but not entirely futile, gesture – to try to outrun it.

It would take a further fifteen minutes for a great wave like this to seek out and destroy the quarries in Merak in the north, and drown all the Chinese workers there (as it did). It would take seven minutes fewer to flatten and wipe out all of Tyringin in the south (as it did also). And it would be one hour and one minute* before the same wave, slowing itself down but building itself up all the while, would reach all the way up to the head of Lampong Bay and, as it was equally sure to do, wreak havoc in the attractive little south Sumatran town of Telok Betong.

The coastlines of Sumatra and Java are, like any coastlines, made hugely complex by all the inlets and island-shadowed estuaries, bays and peninsulas, rocks and reefs. The way that an inrushing wave behaves as it courses towards the shore is only vaguely understood – making it somewhat challenging to try to work out from the survivors' tales which wave actually struck and destroyed each affected town, village, kampong and home on the edges of the two great East Indian islands.

Which wave was it that killed the vast majority of those 36,000 who were lost?

Was it 'the low range of hills rising out of the sea' that was seen, chillingly, by that elderly Dutch pilot in Anjer at dawn? 'The sight of those receding waters haunts me still,' he was to write later, since for him this *was* the killer wave, without doubt. 'As I clung to the palm tree . . . there floated past the dead bodies

---

* The accuracy of these figures comes from the Royal Society report, which calculates the speed of the onrushing waves as the square root of the product of gravity and the water depth, $V = \sqrt{gh}$. The Dutch mining engineer Verbeek came up with slightly different figures and used a more complicated equation to find V, the wave speed: $V = \sqrt{g/2h(h + \epsilon)(2h + \epsilon)}$, where g is gravity, h the water depth and ϵ the height of the wave crest above normal.

of many a friend and neighbour. Only a mere handful of the population escaped. Houses and trees were completely destroyed, and scarcely a trace remains of where the once busy, thriving town originally stood.'

Or was it the climax of all that terrible agitation of the sea that compelled Mrs Beyerinck across in Ketimbang to demand that her husband and family flee for the hills and the safety of high ground? Was it the 'giant black wall of water' that roared into Telok Betong at 7.45 a.m., picked up the gunboat *Berouw* as though it were a child's bathroom toy and dropped it in the middle of the Chinese quarter of town? The same wave that stranded the government's revenue cutter, and smashed all the local *prahus* and scattered the fragments of their hulls about like so much confetti?

Could it have been one of the 'four waves' supposedly seen that morning by an engineer named R. A. van Sandick? He was a passenger aboard the *Gouverneur-Generaal Loudon* – the steamer which, it will be remembered, was unable to dock at any of the quays in Lampong Bay because of the raging surf. The waves, which came in at tremendous speed sometime between 7.30 and 8.30 a.m.

... destroyed all of Telok Betong before our eyes. The light tower could be seen to tumble; the houses disappeared; the steamer *Berouw* was lifted and got stuck, apparently at the height of the cocoanut trees; and everything had become sea in front of our eyes, where a few minutes before Telok Betong beach had been. The impressiveness of this scene is difficult to describe. The unexpectedness of what is seen and the tremendous dimensions of the destruction, in front of one's eyes, make it difficult to describe what has been viewed. The best comparison is a sudden change of scenery, which in a fairy tale occurs by a fairy's magic wand, but on a colossal scale and with the conscious knowledge that it is reality and that thousands of people have perished

The tide-meter at Jakarta registers a sudden swell at 12.36 p.m., two and
a half hours after the eruption – showing how relatively slowly tides
move, compared to the fast-spreading barometric pressure wave recorded
at the gasworks.

in an indivisible moment, that destruction without equal has been
wrought . . .

Or was it perhaps the wave that struck Merak at 9 a.m. – the
wave that drowned all but two of the town's 2,700 inhabitants?
An accountant named Pechler who somehow survived by running
before it, climbing further and further uphill until he was beyond
range, certainly would imagine this tsunami to be immeasurably
vast: it destroyed stone buildings that stood on top of a hill later
measured at 115 feet high; it drowned all thirteen Europeans
who lived there and who had had good reason to feel secure,
surrounded as they were by walls of heavy masonry on the summit
of a good high hill. But the wave displayed all the insouciance of
its great power; and at the time it roared over, submerged and
then wrecked these mansions it was towering above them by a
good twenty feet – meaning that whether what Pechler saw was
the wave or not, it was at least 135 feet high, formidable in its
terror. It drowned everyone in the town below, and when the
waters receded almost everything in the town was either smashed
beyond recognition or swept clear away.

Or yet again, might the great wave have been the one that was
recorded when Merak was savaged once more, at 10.30 a.m.? A

Dutch *contrôleur* named Abell, on the road to Batavia with his *wedono** to report to his superiors details of tragic happenings yet further down the coast, looked around to see 'a colossal wave' roaring up the shore. It was, he said later, taller than the tallest palm tree he could see – a wall of water that no one caught by it could possibly have survived, something so dreadful it was quite beyond nightmares. Might this have been the one?

The answer on this occasion is probably yes. In fact, almost without a doubt, however compelling and awful the accounts of eyewitnesses to the other tsunamis of that dreadful morning may be, this last was indeed the one, the real killer wave. It happened at what seems to have been the correct time – with a travel speed of 60 mph, its arrival at Merak at 10.30 would put its time of origin at Krakatoa at almost exactly ten o'clock, which is the moment of the culminating, self-destroying explosion.

Most crucially, this one wave is recorded as having hit with extraordinary destructive power, a short while either before or later than the Merak 10.30 a.m. arrival, at all of the population centres of the west Java and south Sumatra coast. 'An immense wave inundated the whole of the foreshores of Java and Sumatra bordering the Strait of Sunda,' reported a contemporary study, 'and carried away the remaining portions of the towns of Tjiringin, Merak and Telok Betong, as well as many other hamlets and villages near the shore.'

Its arrival was also recorded on the well-armoured tide-meter in Batavian Harbour – at 12.36 p.m. A wave so powerful as to give an almighty jolt to that tide-recorder would have to have

---

* A *wedono* was an indigenous colonial official of almost the same rank as the European *contrôleur*, who acted as his district officer. Dual administrative rule was a permanent feature of Dutch colonialism – a native official called a regent supposedly worked alongside the Dutch Resident, for example – and, provided both sides acknowledged where the power truly lay, the system generally worked well.

been enormous indeed. It would also have had, if travelling at
60 mph, to have begun its journey some two and a half hours
beforehand. This means, in other words, that it would have
originated at a few minutes past ten in the morning. Undoubtedly,
from all the evidence, this too was Krakatoa's most colossal
wave, the biggest consequence of the biggest and final explosion.
It was a wave so enormous and so powerful that it turned out to
be the grimmest of grim reapers, the terrible climax to a long
and deadly day.

'Everyone was frozen with horror,' wrote the Resident of
Lampong, Mr Altheer, of the moment when he heard the
explosion, just after ten on that Monday morning. He well knew,
from what had already happened disastrously three or four
times before during the previous twenty hours, just what to
expect: another tidal wave, probably much larger than before
since this was so great an explosion, would now come racing
out from the island, and it would arrive within minutes. That
is, of course, had there been an island: Altheer had no means
of knowing that Krakatoa was no more, having just been blown
to oblivion.

In the event the wave reached Telok Betong at 11.03. One
anonymous European, writing some days later in a Batavia newspaper, was down on the town's shore, helping the local people
who had already had their houses wrecked by the morning's
earlier onslaughts from the sea. He was just lifting a huge wooden
beam from on top of a trapped man, when he heard a scream. He
looked up and saw a tall front of water rearing up and rushing
towards him at a barely believable speed. There was a thunderous
noise as it hit the beach and began rushing, crashing upwards
through the town.

At this point the man's specific recollections become confused,
his sudden panicked flight jumbling all conscious experience
together into one amorphous mass. He is not alone in his con-

fusion. The event must have been unforgettably dreadful, but in its details liable to the highly selective amnesia of those caught up by it.

Each of those snared by the Telok Betong wave speaks of running, wildly, panicked, trying madly to stay ahead of the wave, following natives running wildly too; and, in the particular case of the anonymous European writing in the *Java Bode*, of running behind a woman who stumbled and dropped her baby and could not abandon it and so was swept away, of running behind another woman who was – somewhat incredibly, it must be said – in the very process of delivery as she raced on, screaming and bloody, of seeing a man desperately trying to avoid the wall of water by climbing up as high as possible, by running up every slope that he found, of snatching hurried looks behind him to see, horrible in its immensity, the ever pursuing wall, which from time to time smashed against some obstacle and broke, disintegrating into huge and dirty grey piles of spray and wreckage-filled foam, but then regrouping and following him always with a roaring relentlessness, with an unstoppable energy, with a dogged and seemingly murderous resolution such that he could only continue to run, despite being so leaden-legged and air-starved and exhausted, run ever onwards, always impelled by the frenzied gale that howled ahead of the wave, and by the certain knowledge that if he stopped or took a wrong turn that set him downhill rather than up he would be brought down drowned and his body crushed and hurled against the broken walls and jagged edges of spars and smashed glass and masonry that was rising up all around him.

Any doubts about the power of this single awful wave would be dispelled later by the discovery of a single compelling piece of evidence: the position of the Dutch steam gunship, the *Berouw*. The brief fame of this doughty little craft – four guns, a draught of six feet, a thirty-horsepower reciprocating steam engine, paddle-wheels and a crew of four European officers and twenty-

The *Berouw*, well and truly stranded – but very little damaged – a mile and a half up the Koeripan River. Hunks of rusting iron remained in the jungle until the 1980s.

four native ratings – provides a singular measure of the ocean's ferocity.

The captain of the *Berouw* had been the first to warn the mate of the *Loudon* that too strong a sea was running for him to risk a landing. That was at about 6 p.m. on the Sunday. The Telok Betong harbour-master then spotted her in difficulties about five hours later, in the middle of the night – she was well lit, and her plight was clearly visible through the gloom. Exceptionally strong waves were breaking about her, and the official feared that not only might she break her mooring lines, but that the heavy chains holding down the two-ton conical steel mooring buoy to which she was attached might snap as well.

Then early next morning, disaster struck. There were two

eyewitnesses: both the anonymous European in Telok Betong and the *Loudon* passenger R. A. van Sandick saw her lifted up on high by one of the 7.45 a.m. waves, then saw the mooring springs part one by one. The ship broke free of her buoy and was transported high on the crest of the mighty wall of green water. She was swept westwards for a quarter of a mile until, as the wave broke, she was crashed down precipitously on the shore, at the mouth of the Koeripan River.

It is thought that this fearful crash – in which the vessel remained upright – killed all of the crew. But it was not the end of the ship's own nightmare. When the great wave of 11.03 a.m. hit, the ship was picked up once again and carried westward a further two miles. She was driven all the way up the Koeripan River valley, along which the tsunami sped, and crashed down when the wave was spent, about sixty feet above the level of the sea from which she had been plucked. She lay askew across the river, forming a bridge. She was upright once again, a macabre tomb for the twenty-eight members of the crew.

She was found and inspected the following month by the crew of a rescue ship: 'she lies almost completely intact, only the front of the ship is twisted a little to port, the back of the ship a little to starboard. The engine room is full of mud and ash. The engines themselves were not damaged very much, but the flywheels were bent by the repeated shocks. It might be possible to float her once again.'

But whether possible to float her or no, no one ever seemed interested in trying to slide her back all that way to sea. This was no *Fitzcarraldo*. And so the *Berouw* remained where she was thrown, lying athwart the river for the better part of the next century, picked apart by scavengers over the years, like a carcass, or rotting quietly in the steam and sun.

The hulk was more or less intact when it was visited in 1939: it was rusting and swathed in vines, and had become home to a colony of monkeys. Pieces of her were last seen in the 1980s.

Nowadays she is all gone. The Koeripan River trickles uninterrupted past where she lay, and the only memorial is her great mooring buoy, sitting on a plinth at the site where it was washed up, two miles from where it had last floated, and fifty feet higher than the level of the sea. The name *Berouw* is the Dutch word for 'remorse'.

The devastation in Sumatra was fully matched by that across the Strait in Java. The tales from the survivors are every bit as memorable and dismaying. In the main towns – Anjer especially – the ruination was near total. There were only momentary lapses into levity: a telegram received in Batavia reported tersely *Fish dizzy and Caught with Glee by Natives*. For the rest, all was melancholy. And for the most melancholy memorial of all, a symbol on the scale of the *Berouw* over on the far side, one need only look at the great granite lighthouse on what was called Java's Fourth Point, a little way to the south of Anjer.

It survived the first onslaught, as had the gunship; it survived the wave that drove the *Berouw* up on to the beach; but when the wave that hit Telok Betong at 11.03 struck Anjer – about fifteen minutes earlier, since Anjer is closer to the volcano – it picked up an immense piece of coral rock, weighing perhaps six hundred tons, and dashed it against the column. Despite its iron cage of reinforcing ribs, the light crashed down, extinguishing one of the most important navigation beacons of the entire Sunda Strait. And although his wife and child were drowned, the keeper himself survived. With the phlegmatic way of both the well-trained lighthouse keeper and the fatalistic acceptance of a true Javanese, he returned to his duties as soon as was physically possible, and had a temporary light erected, and lit, within a matter of hours.

The stone stump of his lighthouse can still be seen, standing like an old and rotten tooth, rising no more than ten feet above the ever grinding waves of today's more peaceful sea. A replacement, built by the Dutch government three years after the eruption, is close beside it – except that it has been placed a prudent distance, probably about a hundred feet, back from the shore. And it has been constructed entirely of iron, just in case.

The stump of the Fourth Point light remains. And the carcass of the paddle-steamer gunship high in the river valley. But that is about all. The town of Anjer did not survive. Nor did Ketimbang. Nor Telok Betong. Nor Merak. Nor Tyringin. The Anjer Hotel, from whose veranda the first signs had been spotted weeks before, was no more than foundations and twisted banyan roots. The massive Dutch fort walls, which had survived the depredations of centuries, were cracked and tumbled into no more than a shapeless mass of weathered stone. Railway tracks were twisted and scattered across the ground like so many yards of iron ribbon. Iron gearwheels, shards of broken iron and fractured lumps of machinery seemed to be everywhere. Giant boulders sat in entirely improbable places, picked up and smashed down as though they had been pebbles. Thousands upon thousands of houses and settlements up and down the coasts of Java and Sumatra were ruined, flattened, everyone in or near them crushed or drowned or never to be found again.

And what also did not remain was the volcano that had caused it all. To everyone's astonishment, it was seen, once the dust had cleared and the gloom had been swept from the sky, to have totally vanished. Krakatoa, after the final majestic concatenation of seismic and tectonic climaxes that occurred just after ten on the Monday morning, had simply and finally exploded herself out of existence.

Lloyd's agent in Batavia, the Scotsman Mr McColl, was able to send the following message within the week to his colleagues back in London, as concise a summary of the reality as that from his diplomatic colleague Consul Cameron down the road, and only a little less elegant:

We shall probably not be in possession of full particulars for some days yet, as telegraph lines are damaged and roads destroyed, but so far we can give the following particulars. The island of Krakatoa, the summit of which peak was 2,600 feet above water level, has totally disappeared beneath the sea, and the neighbouring island of Dwaisin-deweg* is split in five parts. Sixteen new volcanic islands have been formed between Krakatoa and Sibesie,✝ and the sea bottom in the Straits of Sunda has completely changed. In fact the Admiral Commanding-in-Chief has issued a circular stating that till new soundings have been taken the navigation of the Straits of Sunda is likely to be extremely dangerous. Anjer and lighthouse and the other lights of southwest Java have all been destroyed. The subsidences and upheavals we have alluded to caused a large wave about 100 feet in height to sweep down on the southwest coast of Java and south of Sumatra. This was swept in for a great distance, thereby doing great injury both to life and property. We are here only twelve miles away from one of the points on which the wave spent its fury. The whole coastline to the southwest has changed its configuration. The inhabitants of the island of Onrust were only saved from the flood which swept over the island by taking refuge on board two steamers. At Merak government establishment the inhabitants took refuge on a knoll, fifty feet high, but were all swept off and drowned, with the exception of one European and two Malays, who were saved. Mauk and Kramat, on the west side of Batavia roads, have been laid waste, and about 300 lives lost. In Tjeringin only one house has been left standing. Both the native and European officials have perished. A rain of mud also fell at the above place, which is situated opposite to where Krakatoa once lay.

---

* This is the skerry that British Admiralty charts were wont to call Thwart-the-Way. Mr McColl, just like Consul Cameron, was wrong to suggest it had split: it retains its insular integrity to this day, sitting smugly as a large navigational hazard at the northern entrance to the Strait.
✝ This also turned out to be untrue.

Anjer seems to have been completely destroyed. Lloyd's sub-agent there wires from Serang: 'All gone. Plenty lives lost.'

3. The Experiences

Not much of great excitement seems ever to have happened on the island of Rodriguez, which in the late nineteenth century was one of Britain's more remotely idyllic tropical possessions. According to the 1881 census some 5,000 people lived there, contentedly farming the forty square miles of agreeable farmland and happily fishing the 200 miles of sandy coastline (the relic of an old volcano itself) that had been set down in a lonely corner of the western Indian Ocean. Mauritius, the notional mother-ship of which Rodriguez was then and still remains a dependency, lies 350 miles away to the west. There is 'a regular steamer service' today, and an occasional plane; in the latter part of the nineteenth century there were infrequent supply calls by a chartered sailing ship. A telegraph cable connecting the capital village of Port Mathurin with the capital of Mauritius, Port Louis, was not built until the beginning of the twentieth century.

The people of Rodriguez, who were Creole speaking and (according to a short book written in 1923 by a civil servant who claimed 'no pretence of fine writing') possessed of 'a deep brown velvety skin ... hair of a very deep black, woolly and curly ... protruding thick red lips ... and magnificent snow-white teeth', were descendants of slaves imported by the French to cultivate their sugar plantations. They had been left behind when the French were thrown out by the British at the end of the Napoleonic Wars.

Their lives were run under the genial superintendency of four British imperial administrators, a quartet who might well have found their way into a Gilbert and Sullivan operetta – a magistrate, a medical officer, a chief of police and a 'First Class' priest (the last paid an annual government stipend of a thousand Mauritian rupees to remind the woolly-haired local people that God was, most naturally, an Englishman and, in this corner of the world, a Catholic Englishman to boot).

Placidly unexciting though Rodriguez may have been through its three centuries of inhabited existence, it did make an appearance in the history books, courtesy of the volcano in the far-off East Indies. In August 1883 the chief of police on Rodriguez was a man named James Wallis, and in his official report of the dependency for the month he noted:

On Sunday the 26th the weather was stormy, with heavy rain and squalls; the wind was from SE, blowing with a force of 7 to 10, Beaufort scale. Several times during the night (26th–27th) reports were heard coming from the eastward, like the distant roar of heavy guns. These reports continued at intervals of between three and four hours, until 3 p.m. on the 27th, and the last two were heard in the directions of Oyster Bay and Port Mathurie [sic].

This was not the roar of heavy guns, however. It was the sound of Krakatoa – busily destroying itself fully 2,968 miles away to the east. By hearing it that night and day, and by noting it down as any good public servant should, Chief Wallis was unknowingly making for himself two quite separate entries in the record books of the future. For Rodriguez Island was the place furthest from Krakatoa where its eruptions could be clearly heard. And the 2,968-mile span that separates Krakatoa and Rodriguez remains to this day the most prodigious distance recorded between the place where unamplified and electrically unenhanced natural sound was heard, and the place where that same sound originated.

A popular Victorian science writer, Eugene Murray Aaron,* explained to his readers why this figure of 2,968 miles should amaze them one and all:

---

* He was also a world expert on the poisonous bites of the tarantula.

If a man were to meet a resident of Philadelphia and tell him that he had heard an explosion in Trenton [NJ], thirty miles away, he might be believed, although there would be some doubt as to his powers of imagination. If however he should make the same assertion of an explosion in Wheeling, West Virginia, three hundred miles away, all doubts of his accuracy would vanish. But if, with every sign of sincerity and a desire to be believed, he should earnestly insist upon his having heard an explosion in San Francisco, three thousand miles away, he would receive a pitying smile, and his listener would silently walk away.

Yet just this last marvelous thing was true of those . . . on the island of Rodriguez . . .

It was heard in a score of other equally exotic places besides. No sound was heard in Rodriguez or anywhere else before Sunday, the 26th, nor any after the night of the 27th. And there is general agreement (although among the usual welter of confusions, not the least of them caused by the same lack of time zones that frustrates attempts to make a chronology of the eruption and the sea-waves) that the loudest sounds occurred everywhere in the middle of the day on the Monday, suggesting that they originated on Java some short while before noon.

So, for example, the detonations were clearly heard in early afternoon, local time, on what is now the notorious British-owned American base-island of Diego Garcia.* In those days it was also a Mauritian dependency, where local farmers pressed palm oil and made copra, and where there was a coaling station for steamers

---

* Diego Garcia has an exceptionally unhappy recent history. To help the US create what is presently its most strategically important overseas base, the British in 1970 leased the Americans the islands, assuring the Pentagon they were uninhabited – when officials in Whitehall knew this to be palpably untrue. The 2,000 islanders were forcibly removed to Mauritius, to make way for the base. In 2001 the High Court in London ruled their exile illegal and suggested they be allowed to reclaim their former lands.

crossing the Indian Ocean. The plantation supervisors plainly heard the explosion while they were taking their lunch. 'Nous avons cru tellement à l'appel d'un navire en détresse,' they later reported ('We thought it was a ship in distress firing its guns').

There were scores of broadly similar reports. The explosions were heard in Saigon and Bangkok, Manila and Perth, and at a lonely cable station south of Darwin called Daly Waters.* From Port Blair, the capital of the Indian prison-islands of the Andamans, came news that someone heard a sound 'as of a distant signal-gun'. No fewer than eighteen different sets of witnesses in what was then Ceylon came forward with stories ('Captain Walker and Mr Fielder were puzzled at various times . . . by hearing noises as if blasting was going on', 'Sounds as of firing of cannon at Trincomalee', 'Mr Christie of the Public Works department . . . presumed some man-of-war was practising with her big guns, out of sight of land, as he could see no ships').

His Highness the raja of Salwatty Island, in New Guinea, said he had heard strange sounds and demanded of a local doctor why the white men were firing their cannons. Stockmen driving cattle across the Hammersley Range† in western Australia heard what they thought was artillery fire to the north-west. In Aceh, at the northern tip of Sumatra, the location then (as still now) of a fierce pro-independence rebellion, the Dutch garrison commander assumed a local fort had been blown up by insurgents, and ordered all his men to battle stations. The Honourable Foley Vereker, who, despite belonging to one of Ireland's leading military families, had been cast out to the remoter colonies as commander

* Daly Waters, with a current population of about thirty-five, once had Australia's first international airfield, since Qantas used it as a refuelling stop. The telegraph cable from Singapore and Batavia once terminated here, and a pony express would, until 1872, take messages further south across the desert to where the cable to Sydney began once again.
† The Hammersleys are now the site of one of the world's largest iron-ore mines, at Mount Newman.

of HMS *Magpie*, off Banquey Island, near Borneo, recorded in his log how he and his crew all heard the sound. And close by them, those Dayak islanders who had recently murdered a local official named Francis Witti (and, according to lore, had eaten his torso and limbs and had shrunk his head as a keepsake) heard the extraordinary sound too, assumed it to be the authorities coming to get them and fled deep into the jungle.

Ships were launched from scores of places by eager would-be rescuers and salvors, convinced there was an unseen vessel in trouble. A pair of fast ships set out from Macassar,* for instance, because they assumed another was in dire straits; two more set out from Singapore; a government boat went out to search off Timor; and when the sounds continued in Port Blair, the British authorities on the Andamans sent out a lifeboat too. In Singapore it became impossible, on one set of telephone lines, to hear yourself speak, since 'a perfect roar, as of a waterfall, was heard, and by shouting at the top of one's voice the clerk at the other end heard the voice, but not a single sentence was understood. The same noise . . . was noticed on every line here.'

There was one aberrant report – from a man named Foley on Cayman Brac, now a small nodule of highly expensive Caribbean real estate, but then a forlorn sliver of a tropical sandspit, a day's sailing south of Cuba. Mr Foley insisted that he heard the banging cannonades, and that they happened in rapid succession on the Sunday. But there is neither corroboration nor a common-sense explanation. There was no eruption anywhere in the Caribbean at the time (it would be another nineteen years before Mount Pelée exploded with classically Plinian intensity); and though freak atmospheric phenomena might be able to explain away this report of the explosion being heard *twelve thousand* miles away,

---

* From whence came the eponymous sweet-smelling hair-oil, the bane of countless English chair backs and the cause of the creation of the protective lace furniture shroud called, somewhat unoriginally, an *antimacassar*.

the fact that Mr Foley also claimed to have heard it twelve hours *before* Krakatoa exploded suggests his memory, or hearing, was indeed at fault.

Yet there were some oddities about the dissemination of the sounds – not the least being that a great number of people in Batavia, Buitenzorg and west Java generally heard nothing. Others simply felt strangely deaf, or heard a curious buzzing in their ears, or else were aware of wild swings in the pressure all about them, as if they had been caught in some silent atmospheric hypertension. Experts in the field have taken many a stab at explaining why this might be. Some point out that the behaviour of sound waves in the upper and lower atmospheres is very different, and that in the speeding up and slowing down that any wave experiences on passing through them there may be a focus-like phenomenon brought into play that would make one locality receive a lot of sound, another very little. Others, less sophisticated, explain it by reminding us how snowfall muffles sound – and that ash falls, which covered Batavia and its suburbs at the time, are likely to do much the same.

None the less, the overall conclusion remains inescapable, both to historical anecdote and to science: the sound that was generated by the explosion of Krakatoa was enormous, almost certainly the greatest sound ever experienced by man on the face of the earth. No man-made explosion, certainly, can begin to rival the sound of Krakatoa – not even those made at the height of the Cold War's atomic testing years. Those other volcanoes that have exploded catastrophically in the years since decibel-meters were invented – Mount St Helens, Pinatubo, Unzen, Mayon – have not come close: no one suggests that the explosion of Mount St Helens in May 1980 was heard much beyond the very mountain ranges in which it was sited.

Dr Verbeek, with the modest assurance of one who had seen and heard and experienced the vastness of the eruption, stated in his report of 1885 that 'the exceptionally loud noises require our attention . . . the large explosions that in loudness have far exceeded all known noises. At no earlier event was a noise heard over such a large part of the earth's surface.' Under the impact of Krakatoa's explosion, 13 per cent of the earth's surface vibrated audibly, and millions who lived there heard it, and when told what it was were amazed.

The inaudible waves, it was soon discovered, had ventured even further afield. The thousands of Europeans and Americans who noticed and recorded them – without in most cases ever realizing just what they were – did so, all around the world, at more or less the same time. The fact that they did so at all points up, quite unexpectedly, one of the newly formed habits of middle-class Victorian society – a set of habits that never anticipated such a catastrophe as Krakatoa, but none the less in due course took full advantage of its effects.

The new-fangled habits of the late nineteenth century included, among the time's multitudes of other scientific advances, the development of increasingly precise means for forecasting the weather. And while cost and complication limited popular access to most other sciences, it did become rapidly possible – and indeed rather popular – for people to buy and use scientific instruments to help them understand the daily fluctuations in their climate. Consequently, as Victorian homes, clubs and hotels filled up their halls and vestibules with the ever newer and more handsome barometers, recording thermometers, sun-gauges and rain-gauges, so the middle classes became an unwitting army of amateur meteorologists, faithfully tapping the glass each day the better to predict whether it would be Fine or Stormy, Changeable or Fair.

The most costly and sophisticated of these instruments was the recording barograph. Because of its price, it was reserved most commonly for the mantelshelf in the club, rather than for the hall at home. The task of this small machine is to record, with an ink trace on a sheet of graph paper secured around the circumference of a clockwork-driven drum, the slight hourly variations in atmospheric pressure over the week that it takes for the drum to rotate a single time.

A well-made barograph is a joy to behold – an elegant confection of brass and steel, mahogany and glass, its mechanicals visible inside its crystal case, its clockwork heart ticking away happily as it takes the pulse of the day. And the ink trace – flowing gently up and down, sometimes more steeply downwards if bad weather is on the way, arching up again if the storm passes over at speed – has a seductively sinuous beauty to it also: the records of the passing week's atmospheric alterations are stored in a small drawer under the instrument, to be studied later, whenever the weather becomes the subject for reminiscence or chatter.

One very noticeable aspect of a barograph's recorded trace is, however, just how smoothly the weather changes. The line invariably curves up or down slowly, steadily. It does not jump erratically, like a seismic record during an earthquake or a lie detector revealing a falsehood. Atmospheric pressure changes with measured deliberation – a feature that the curves on a barograph reflect, with their steady and considered moves across and along the ever unrolling snake of recording paper.

As scores of people around the world came to change their paper for the week that ended on Sunday, 2 September 1883, and as they smoothed the records out to place them away in the drawer, they all, almost simultaneously, noticed something. On the trace for the Monday of the week just gone, the 27th of August, there was a sudden and unanticipated jerk. A hiccup. A notch, an interruption – an altogether most puzzling thing.

The pen that had been so smoothly and seamlessly noting the pressure on the instrument's vacuum chamber had suddenly been flicked up, and then equally violently snapped down again. When looked at more closely, the oscillation was even more peculiar than that: first there was a sudden recorded rise in pressure, then two or three minor oscillations, then a very deep depression, followed by a less steep rise, then more small oscillations, and then finally, after an interruption that lasted for the better part of two hours, back to the smooth and gently changing trace of normal times. In summary, it seemed as though, and for some inexplicable reason, there had been the quite impossible occurrence of *an earthquake in the air.*

It took only a matter of hours of excited discussion between observatories and weather-fascinated members of the lay public to draw the inescapable conclusion. This, faraway though it may have been, was all Krakatoa's doing.

As soon as news of the extraordinary degree of the eruption had become widely known, it remained a simple matter to check the times of the strange two-hour-long blips on the barograph traces, to make an allowance for the probable approximate-speed-of-sound rate of travel of the shock wave, and to figure in the time difference between Krakatoa and the various club mantelshelves around the world. And lo! they all matched. The eruption that had sent out flame and ash and tidal waves and an incredible explosive sound had also sent an invisible, inaudible shock wave that passed cleanly through the atmosphere, and had been recorded, quite unexpectedly, on scores of machines designed for the much more prosaic task of suggesting to middle-class Victorian gentlemen in Birmingham and Boston and beyond whether they should take their umbrellas to luncheon.

Except that it was, as is much that relates to Krakatoa's eruption, much more complicated than it seemed at first sight. When the traces were examined more closely and compared with other barograph traces from more distant cities around Europe and then around the world, it appeared that the shock wave from Krakatoa's final cataclysmic explosion had travelled around the earth not once but seven times.

The barographs, barometers and weather stations all recorded the signature two-hour wave, with the amplitude of the oscillations diminishing at each pass; it had apparently reverberated, flown back and forth and around the planet in a manner that seemed quite out of proportion to the magnitude of the original event itself.

All this provoked much fluttering in the scientific dovecotes. Every weather expert in the world suddenly wanted to know what was going on – why a pressure wave like this would behave in this peculiar way. In scientific London the degree of interest was particularly intense – and it prompted what was an entirely unanticipated response: that, despite Krakatoa being on Dutch sovereign territory, it would be best if it were to be left to a distinguished *and entirely British* body to investigate its eruption.

The high-handedness, seen from today's perspective, quite boggles the mind. Perhaps it was the vast reach of British influence of the day that made this seem desirable to some; perhaps, more specifically, it was the existence of all those records from all those British-owned and British-designed barographs (for all of those instruments, in places as far-flung as Melbourne and Mauritius and Bombay, turned out to have been manufactured in England) that provoked this entirely unwarranted – but it has to be said, quite unresented – example of British imperial busybodyness.

The timetable went like this. The explosion occurred in late August. In early September the British barograph paper records – initially from the leather-bound and entirely masculine fastnesses of London clubland, but later from weather observatories at Greenwich, Kew, Stonyhurst, Glasgow, Aberdeen, Oxford and Falmouth – were changed, and the blips noticed. Suspecting that something of absorbing scientific interest was afoot, a senior British government official named Robert Scott – the secretary to the Meteorological Council – promptly sent telegrams to his colleagues in observatories around Europe, asking if they would examine their traces too.

And back came the reports, from Vienna and Berlin, Leipzig, Magdeburg, Rome, Paris, Brussels, Coimbra, Lisbon, Modena and Palermo and other places besides, confirming in all respects what Scott suspected: that a wave of sudden pressure had swept around and around the planet from its birthplace in the Sunda Strait; that the passage of the wave had been a remarkable event; and that, moreover, it had lasted, echoing around the globe for no fewer than fifteen days following the eruption.

Scott found this quite extraordinary, and told his superior, an old India hand and engineer named General Richard Strachey. In December – only four months after the eruption, and so with unusual dispatch – the pair presented a brief paper to the Royal Society, that most estimable and ancient of British scientific institutions. It was entitled 'Notes on a Series of Barometrical Disturbances which Passed over Europe between the 27th and 31st of August 1883'. It caused an immediate sensation.

And it did so because here was one of the first provable instances in which a natural event occurring in one corner of the planet had effects that spread over the entire world (or what would be the entire world, if further records could be sought from the Americas and Asia and elsewhere, for they would show the same evidence). Here was the event that presaged all the debates that continue to this day: about global warming, greenhouse gases, acid rain, ecological interdependence. Few in Victorian times had begun to think truly globally – even though exploration was proceeding apace, the previously unknown interiors of continents were being opened for inspection, and the developing telegraph system, allowing people to communicate globally, was having its effects. Krakatoa, however, began to change all that.

The world was now suddenly seen to be much more than an immense collection of unrelated peoples and isolated happenings:

it was, rather, an almost infinitely large association of intercon-
nected individuals and perpetually intersecting events. Krakatoa,
an event that intersected so much and affected so many, seemed
all of a sudden to be an example of this newly recognized phenomenon. And so it was up to a British scientific society – most
decidedly a British one, given the imperial mood of the day, like
it or not – to investigate it.

A decision to do just this was taken in January, following the
reading of two more short papers presented to the Royal Society,
both describing the scene on the ground in and around the Sunda
Strait. The first paper was by the British consul in Batavia – now
a Mr Kennedy from Sumatra, since Consul Cameron had fallen
ill – and the other by the socially well-connected Captain Vereker
of HMS *Magpie*, who reported from Borneo. Both papers amply
confirmed the view in London that this extraordinary event off
Java had been so huge and so *world-affecting* that a body had to
be set up right away to investigate it. And so on 12 February
1884 an advertisement, in the form of a 'Letter to the Editor', was
placed in *The Times*:

THE KRAKATOA ERUPTION

Sir – The Council of the Royal Society has appointed a committee for
the purpose of collecting the various accounts of the volcanic eruption
at Krakatoa, and attendant phenomena, in such form as shall best
provide for their preservation and promote their usefulness. The
committee invite the communication of authenticated facts respecting
the fall of pumice and dust, the position and extent of floating pumice,
the date of exceptional quantities of pumice reaching various shores,
observations of unusual disturbances of barometric pressure and of
sea level, the presence of sulphurous vapours, the distances at which
the explosions were heard, and exceptional effects of light and colour
in the atmosphere. The committee will be glad to receive also copies
of published papers, articles and letters bearing upon the subject.
Correspondents are asked to be very particular in giving the date, exact

time (stating whether Greenwich or local), and position whence all recorded facts were observed. The greatest practicable precision in all these respects is essential. All communications are to be addressed to –

Your obedient servant,

G. J. Symons, Chairman, Krakatoa Committee*

Royal Society, Burlington House

It took five years for what at first might have seemed a some-what pumice-obsessed Committee to study all of the complex and new types of information that flowed from the event. Their final report, issued in 1888, had 494 pages of text, as well as countless drawings, graphs and exquisite coloured prints. It stood as a lasting masterpiece of determined study, elegantly composed style and splendid Victorian *brio* – and it collated, among other things, all of the pressure-wave observations that had led to the establishment of the Committee in the first place.

And what was found out about them was simple but remarkably beautiful: that the shock waves from Krakatoa had radiated across the world like ripples on the surface of a pond – the surface of a vast and slightly flattened sphere in the case of the earth, of course, rather than the merely circular surface one would find on a pond. They had radiated outwards at a speed approximating that of audible sound: between 674 and 726 miles per hour.

The waves had travelled outwards, expanding their width until they were halfway to their goal and then contracting again until they reached their precise antipode – which, in the case of Krakatoa at 6°06'S, 105°25'E, is a point (at 6°06'N, 105°25'W) in the Pacific Ocean off Botoga, Colombia. Then, having taken

* The thirteen-member committee was esteemed in the extreme: among the members was the hydrographer of the navy, the great geologists Archibald Geikie and Thomas Bonney, the physicist who discovered fluor-escence, Sir George Stokes, and the aforementioned General Richard Strachey, who was such a towering figure of Indian engineering that he had a bridge over the River Jumna named after him.

The sound of the great explosion could be heard as far off as Rodriguez
Island, nearly 3,000 miles from its origin. Records suggest that people
living within the shaded area were well able to hear the rumbling and
banging, most thinking it the noise of a naval bombardment.

nineteen hours to reach this nameless and watery antipode, they
headed off back again and returned to Krakatoa (with the passage
noted on all the barographs in between, at a bewildering variety
of places that included St Petersburg, Toronto, the Antarctic
island of South Georgia and a village that is now a pretty New
York suburb called Hastings-on-Hudson).

Every time the wave was noticed, it was found that the time of
its passing agreed with the eruption time that had been marked

by observers back in the Sunda Strait. The wave's passage above the Greenwich Observatory, for example, was recorded on all the barographs' registers – with the sharp upward tic of pressure, the minor ruffles on the record, the sudden downward blip, further ripples, the slow upwards rise to the resumption of normal state – at 1.23 p.m. on the Monday. Krakatoa Time was seven hours ahead of London – meaning that at 10.02 a.m., the local time when the volcano exploded, it was 3.02 a.m. in Greenwich. Subtracting that from the time that the Observatory barographs recorded the blip gives a figure for the wave's travel time of ten hours, twenty-one minutes – the precise figure that could be calculated for inaudible shock waves moving across the 7,220 miles of a Great Circle separating London from Krakatoa.

The Greenwich Observatory corroborated the figures for the first pass – and for the six further passes of the shock as it moved back and forth across the capital before it had weakened to the point where it could no longer be detected. And as it did so, two things became even more clear: that the eruption time was exactly right, 10.02 a.m., and that the world now knew a great deal more about the transmission of atmospheric shock waves than ever before. Meteorology in general profited mightily from the findings; and in the mid twentieth century, when large atmospheric explosive tests were conducted during the Cold War, the way in which shock waves were propagated through the atmosphere was well understood also. The Krakatoa Committee had, even if only in these respects, fully justified its existence.

The tsunamis that killed so many on the shores of Java and Sumatra crossed the world as well. It could be seen from the beginning that up close to the volcano the waves were enormous, and killed thousands. That they then became ever smaller in proportion to their distance from Krakatoa was to be expected. But the discovery that they were in fact so deeply powerful, and radiated away from the volcano so aggressively that they could still be detected in the sea as far away as the English Channel, was the cause of general astonishment.

The first to receive firm news of the appearance of some faraway Krakatoa-induced waves was Charles Darwin's son George, shortly after he was elected (by the narrowest of votes) the professor of astronomy at Cambridge.* His friend Major A. W. Baird, who had the post of chief of the Tidal Survey of India, wrote to him in Cambridge to say that 'the wave caused by the volcanic eruption at Java is distinctly traceable on all the tidal diagrams hitherto received, and I am informed of a great tidal disturbance at Aden on August 27; but the daily reports are always meagre in information. Kurrachee and Bombay also show the disturbance, and as far as I have examined the wave reached halfway up to Calcutta on the Hooghly.'

This last – the news that waters had rushed up the Hooghly River almost to the city that was then the capital of British India – did it. The Royal Society promptly asked for an immediate report. Major Baird swiftly obliged with a six-page summary of his Survey stations' reports from across that immense swathe of imperial territory that stretched between Aden and Rangoon. And the Krakatoa Committee, recognizing a significance that went beyond the simple threat to Calcutta, immediately commissioned a senior Royal Navy captain to investigate the phenomenon, worldwide.

Records from tide-gauges at ports all across the world were speedily gathered in. An early analysis showed a fascinating, but not entirely unanticipated, trend: almost all of the stations that recorded sudden and unexpected waves that could be positively

---

* Sir George Darwin's contribution to science was mostly theories that were later to be disproven. Most egregiously he calculated mathematically that the moon was created by being torn away from the cooling earth – an idea now universally discredited. He also wrote papers on contemporary fashion, and claimed never to do more than three hours' work a day.

linked to the eruption (by their timing and their type) lay to the west and south of the island.

Almost all: not Batavia herself, which lies eighty-three miles away to the east as the crow flies, and considerably further so far as a tidal wave might pass. Despite where she lay, the capital city did indeed witness what even the Royal Society saw fit to call 'a wall of water', when the wave hit her gauge at 12.36 p.m. on the Monday afternoon – two hours and thirty-four minutes after the explosion. According to the Reverend Neale, the water rushed into the Batavian canal system, rising suddenly by several feet, forcing hundreds of merchants and residents to flee for their lives.

The day – unusually cold, half dark and drab, the air still filled with grey, gritty ash that got in the hair and the eyes and the teeth – had begun, surprisingly, with a fair sense of stoic normality. The steam-trams were filled with people setting off for work, the markets were thronged, the private horse-drawn carriages were trotting around the Koningsplein, their occupants talking excitedly about the events of the night before, confident that the worst was over. Then came the arrival of what was swiftly understood to be the huge relic of the great tsunami – the remains of a wave that somewhere had been much, much worse – and it made all these good burghers of Batavia realize, very suddenly, that in fact the worst was still to come.

The maximum height of this bore (the needle on the Batavia tide-meter shot up vertically, clear off the scale) was at least seven feet and six inches – a fraction of the height of the devastating waves that destroyed Anjer and Telok Betong maybe, but an impressive enough display. The waters promptly fell back again, to ten feet *below* normal sea-level, and then rose back up again, then sloshed back down – oscillating a total of fourteen times over the next twenty-eight and a half hours, the height of the successive waves diminishing all the while. Finally, after what was no more than a three-inch ripple hit the Batavia tide-meter at 5.05 on the afternoon of the next day, the Tuesday, they vanished clear away.

But Batavia alone in the area experienced the great wave. Almost no other places to the north and east of the volcano experienced anything at all – Singapore's tide-meters registered nothing, nor was there any discernible blip in the records of Hong Kong, Yokohama or Shanghai; and even at Surabaya, at the eastern end of Java, the disturbance that was picked up on the port's three tide-gauges was only ten inches, 'too insignificant to be otherwise noticed'. There is a very simple reason for the lack of any dramatic effects on this side of the volcano, as a glance at the map will show.

To the east of Krakatoa the two sides of the Sunda Strait pinch inwards like the jaws of a nutcracker. There are islands blocking the way too – Thwart-the-Way Island being one such, notorious in its nuisance value – and before a wave has any chance of touching Batavia port herself it reaches long fingers of shallows and sandbanks and further inlets and reefs, all of them conspiring to slow down and frustrate the eastward movement of any wave. Nothing would stand in the way of a sound wave or a shock wave; but, faced with the dissipating influence of the shoals and headlands, a water wave would essentially not move eastwards at all, as the recorders everywhere confirm.

However, to the west of Krakatoa, barring the presence of a small headland called Vlakke Hoek in southern Sumatra that acts as a small chicane on a westbound wave's right-hand side, there is only the wide-open sea of the Indian Ocean. Any tsunami moving out from the eruption in this direction would be free to go wheresoever it wished, without maritime hindrance or interruption. And in August 1883 the great ten o'clock wave did indeed fan out westward entirely untrammelled, and managed to go just about anywhere and everywhere it wanted. Two types of wave were detected: what were called long waves, which reverberated back and forth at periods of as much as two hours;

and the short waves, which were steeper and with a much less regular and more frequent repeat.

The old Dutch port of Galle, close to the southern tip of the island of Ceylon, is where the arrival of these short waves – or more precisely, a sequence of fourteen waves, each separated by just a few minutes – was first noticed. The *Ceylon Observer* correspondent filed on 27 August that

. . . an extraordinary occurrence was witnessed at the wharf at about 1.30 p.m. today. The sea receded as far as the landing stage on the jetty. The boats and canoes moored along the shore were left high and dry for about three minutes. A great number of prawns and fishes were taken up by the coolies and stragglers about the place before the water returned.

A woman was killed at the port of Panama – still in Ceylon, not on the isthmus – when she was swept from the harbour bar by an immense influx of water. Both the Panama harbour-master and the local ruler, the splendidly titled Ratamahatmaya, said later that ships had suddenly sunk downwards and were then drawn backwards to be left stuck in the drying mud, their anchors exposed – and just as suddenly were borne up by an inrushing surge of water. The local streams, with hitherto sweet water, all promptly turned salty for at least a mile and a half upriver. The woman who died, from the injuries she sustained in falling while she was carrying a sheaf of paddy from the fields, is thought to have been the most distant casualty of the eruption that took place nearly 2,000 miles away.

At Hambantota, further south still, Ceylon government officials estimated the height of the wave to be twelve feet, and said that, like at Panama, its currents were irresistible, taking small craft back out to sea, and then sweeping them back and dashing them to pieces on shore. But however violent, there were no casualties here; nor were there any further afield.

The long waves tended to be the ones that were recorded by the

Tiny oscillations in the tides were noticed nearly 11,000 miles away from Krakatoa, such as here at Socoa, a small port near the French resort of Biarritz.

automatic tide-gauges around the world, and it is these that make up the bulk of the formal record; the short waves tended to be more the stuff of anecdote, and, because they oscillated so swiftly, rarely made an appearance on the recorders. By the time the long waves reached India they were diminishing, fast – fourteen inches high in Madras, a series of ten or so six-inchers at Calcutta, a foot high in Karachi, half that in Aden. They spread south-westwards towards the African coast as well: they broke a hawser of a boat moored in Port Louis, Mauritius; and in the rarely visited Indian Ocean reef harbour known as Cargados Carajos the captain of the *Evelina* reported huge, smooth oscillations in the sea, breaking only when they came into contact with coral heads. Already the wave was 2,662 miles from its point of origin, and racing steadily along at a calculated 370 miles each hour.

A four-foot-high wave was noticed at Port Elizabeth, on the bleak and generally unlit east coast of South Africa,* and undulations were picked up at Cape Town. A visiting German South Polar expedition (which failed to reach its goal) on the island of South Georgia saw the icebergs and brash in the harbour of the whaling station at Grytviken lifted fifteen inches in a series of a dozen recorded and remarkable swells.

And so the waters progressed ever outwards – with numerous waves of different types and styles, heights and frequencies, and deriving from what oceanographers now reckon were a number of different causes too. Eventually they ran out of steam and reached as far as they could go, in the further recesses of north-western Europe. By the time they reached the North Atlantic, and then the Bay of Biscay, the oscillations were small indeed – such that the tide-diagrams had to be photographed and blown up in order to be able to measure the fluctuations in the record.

But they are there all right, tiny but still distinct. In Socoa, a tiny French harbour near the more celebrated resort of Biarritz, and 10,729 sea-miles from Krakatoa, there were seven undulations, each of them three inches high – barely enough to be noticed by promenaders on the beach, though I like to fancy pomaded young men and their lady friends skipping amusingly out of the way when the unusual small swells suddenly threatened their boots and their turn-ups. Further north at Rochefort, a

---

* That this particular wave was so unusually large is hardly surprising: the coastline between Durban and Port Elizabeth is notorious for giant waves, caused when northbound Antarctic storm systems slam into the south-westerly-flowing Agulhas Current, concentrating the confused water into shallows above a peculiarly narrow continental shelf. It is one of the most hazardous coastlines in the world – and the arrival in 1883 of a four-foot Krakatoa-induced tidal wave would have only served to remind local mariners about sorrows, single spies and battalions.

town on the Charente a little north of the Gironde and Bordeaux, the magnifying power of the estuary pushed the waves up to five inches high – they had sped there from the volcano at a calculated (and now slightly faster) rate of 414 miles per hour, barely slowing as they did so.

And finally, turning the corner into the English Channel, the slightest trace only is noticeable. There is a ripple recorded at Cherbourg, another at Le Havre and an irregular but discernible series of undulations at Devonport, close to where all Royal Navy cadets are now trained to be officers. But closer in – at Portland, Plymouth and Dover, nothing. Maybe there is just the vaguest sign of it on the gauge on the inner side of the Portland breakwater – though the Royal Society report admits, 'the indications of disturbance are not very conclusive, as no regularity of period is traceable in the small indentations which do appear'.

I confess I would have derived no small pleasure from discovering that on the Tuesday morning, when waves were seen in France and in the West Country, the tide-gauge in Dover port also suddenly startled its keeper, with a splash, or a slop, or a curious and inexplicable swell. But there was to be no such luck. With Dover being no less than 11,800 sea-miles from the Sunda Strait, and lying at the distant end of a channel in which the water shallows to a few hundred feet and less, which would kill or dampen the kind of long waves that were produced by the eruption, it is perhaps not surprising to learn that the gauges here showed no deflection at all. The air wave may have found its way to Greenwich, seven times; but the sea-wave was brought up short, 500 miles from home, and never arrived near the British capital, even once.

Yet other, quite different effects of the eruption were before long visible in London, New York and other northern capitals, and many of them were aesthetically and dramatically quite memorable. Art was born out of the after-effects of this volcano – art that was then quite unexpected. Though not so popular today, it is not entirely forgotten. For the millions of tons of dust that were hurled into the upper air in the East Indies disseminated themselves around the world for many years and caused all manner of extraordinary phenomena – not the least of which were sunsets. These were seen all over the world decked out in the most lurid rainbow of colours, and they attracted the interest of a great number of suddenly excited painters.*

One of the more prominent of these was Frederic Edwin Church, a member of what came to be known as the Hudson River School of American nineteenth-century landscape painters. He turned out to be precisely the kind of artist who would benefit from the atmospheric consequences of Krakatoa.

Frederic Church specialized in highly dramatic landscapes and highly coloured skyscapes – he had a predilection for the grand (his gigantic *Niagara* presents an astonishing image of the raw power of falling water) and the excessively radiant (his *Twilight in the Wilderness* has an unforgettable richness about its evening colour). Both of these artistic preferences came together in December 1883 when Church – supposedly well aware of the remarkable effects of Krakatoa's spreading trail of dust on the world's sunsets – travelled north from his ornate Moorish castle in the riverside town of Hudson, to the very tip of upstate New York, on the Canadian border. There he would try to capture an image of what he suspected would be an especially livid northern twilight.

He chose Chaumont Bay, at the very eastern end of Lake

---

* It has long been supposed, but never proven, that J. M. W. Turner, whose impressions of sunsets made him an international institution, was painting evening skies coloured by the aftermath of the 1815 eruption of Tambora. The link between Krakatoa and the sunsets of the late 1880s is well established; the similar effects of Tambora can only be surmised, with Turner's paintings usually offered as evidence.

Ontario. The early-winter ice would be piling up in the westerly winds; there would be newly undraped trees on the wispy penin-sulas; and above all there would be the vast expanse of the lake into which the setting sun would appear to sink. He chose to render the image in watercolour. The resulting picture – not surprisingly called *Sunset over the Ice on Chaumont Bay, Lake Ontario* – has a range of colours in the sky, a gently intermingling play of pinks and mauves and orange and salmon and purple that is quite astonishing, and unusual, and suggestive of *something* happening, something inexplicable, high in the evening atmos-phere. It is the only major painting to be created in the immediate aftermath of Krakatoa: and even if Church had not set out with the deliberate intention of making post-eruptive art, the piece stands now as vivid documentary testimony to the giant volcano's effects.*

Lesser artists had a field-day. The most notable was William Ascroft, who lived beside the River Thames in Chelsea. Early in September, two weeks after the eruption, he noticed that London was suddenly being gifted with a series of memorable setting suns and, more interesting, unusually strong afterglows. He painted them at a furious rate – creating a total of no fewer than 533 watercolours over the months of his fascination.

On especially gorgeous evenings he might make several paint-ings, one every few minutes, creating as he did so a kind of time-lapse image of the entire process. On 26 November, for example, he painted the aftermath of the sun's disappearance once every ten minutes between 4.10 p.m. and 5.15 p.m., catching a sequence of fiery purples and oranges with all the fleet-footed accuracy of a film camera. He wrote lengthy notes and analyses of what he saw – 'Blood Afterglows' and 'Amber Afterglows' among them – and examples of the beaming coronas that often surrounded the

* It is privately owned by a collector in Philadelphia.

setting sun itself and which were named, after the Hawaiian naturalist* who first spotted them, 'Bishop's Rings'. All 500 of his paintings later went on show at an exhibition in a museum in South Kensington. They remain today inside what is now the Natural History Museum, locked away and half forgotten.

Dust of all grades and compositions was thrown into the air by the eruption. Much of it, too heavy to be kept on high for long, fell down as drifting veils of grey, and was widely reported as having done so. Ships at sea experienced dust falls for a fortnight after the eruption: the *Brani* and the *British Empire* came under a slow rain of a white ash that one master said 'looked like Portland cement', when they were sailing in the Indian Ocean within a 2,000-mile range of the volcano; the *Scotia* experienced falling dust until 8 September, when she was off the Horn of Africa, 3,700 miles away.

But the lighter material, the finest particles of all, were thrown up right through the troposphere until, almost defying the pull of gravity, they were caught up for months in the lower reaches of the stratosphere† itself. Modern estimates suggest the Krakatoa eruption hurled material at least 120,000 feet into the air – some say 160,000 feet, or thirty miles. Tests have since shown that up so high, material can hover in a kind of weightless stasis.

A dust particle with a diameter of a micron – whether it is an

---

* This was the Reverend Sereno Bishop, who while sporting a name well known in Hawaii where he worked as a missionary, was not related to the founder of Honolulu's famous Bishop Museum.
† The stratosphere, a band of near-vacuum that lies between about eleven and thirty miles above the earth's surface, differs from the lower band of the troposphere in one important way: while the temperature declines steadily with height in the troposphere (as any climber or flier well knows), it does not do so in the lower reaches of the stratosphere. And in its upper few miles the temperature, so long as the sunlight is not cut off by the earth's shadow, actually begins to climb.

aerosol droplet or a tiny fragment of volcanic silicate mineral makes no difference – has recently been shown to take many weeks to descend vertically through just half a mile of stratosphere. A particle of half a micron in diameter will take many months to fall, so slight is the tug of gravity upon it. Yet horizontal movement was apparently no problem for the Krakatoa material. The strong globe-encircling winds spread them far and wide. And the rains that would tend to flush out those particles that might have been tempted to stay in the lower reaches were of course non-existent up high.

And so they stayed, undisturbed, for very long periods. And by refracting and filtering and in a myriad other ways altering so vividly the colours of the sunlight that passed by them, and by staining the crepuscular skies with vermilions and passion-fruits and carmines and royal mauves, so they ensured more potently than any other effect that Krakatoa would soon become the most famous volcano in world history.

Krakatoa killed more people than any other eruption, and for that it remains notorious: but it became much more widely known to hundreds of millions of people around the world for a more benign and beautiful reason, one that all could readily see for themselves each time they looked westwards at eventide.

The poets were inspired in much the same way as the painters. Tennyson is widely believed to have been thinking of Krakatoa when in his almost wholly forgotten epic poem *St Telemachus*, published nine years after the eruption, he wondered out loud:

> Had the fierce ashes of some fiery peak
> Been hurl'd so high they ranged about the globe?
> For day by day, thro' many a blood-red eve, . . .
> The wrathful sunset glared . . .

The Royal Society's Krakatoa Committee, displaying the almost obsessive need for the complete and the comprehensive that was so much a signature of Victorian studies like this, invited responses from the general public. They received wagon-loads of material,* and painstakingly catalogued every single report of every atmospheric phenomenon, no matter how trivial, of which they were made aware. Two thirds of the Society's eventual 494-page report is devoted to 'the unusual optical phenomena of the atmosphere, 1883–1886, including twilight effects, coronal appearances, sky haze, coloured suns, moons &c'.

Forty-eight further pages give the details of the 800 places where unusual phenomena had been seen, organized into chronological order. The list actually starts some months *before* the cataclysm, presumably to give an observational base-line from which the deviations that follow can be measured. So the first report comes from a town called Graaff-Reinet, in the centre of the South African tablelands, beginning during the southern winter – with someone noticing the presence of 'fine sunsets, gradually increasing from February to June'. The very first eruption of the final paroxysmal cycle, it will be recalled, took place towards the end of May.

And thereafter came a cascade of responses from people who had seen or had been told about the Royal Society's announcements in the newspapers. A seemingly endless string of reports is included, from a bewildering variety of places and people and ships and lighthouses – all with news of strange phenomena, most of them seen in the skies. A blue moon was spotted by a Mr Haughton in Kokkulai, Ceylon. The lighthouse keeper at the Chinese city then called Chefoo – now Yantai – saw a pale-red glow, like fire, in the west. There was a blue sun seen by a Dr Earl Flint in Rivas, Nicaragua. Captain Faircloth of the Caribbean Signal Service saw 'a lurid glare' emanating from the sun setting

---

* When a centenary study of the eruption was published in Washington by the Smithsonian Institution in 1983, members of the public were similarly asked to send in reports of anything to do with the eruption. The editors received not a single response.

over Nassau in the Bahamas. The scientific journal *Nature* — which collected dozens of such reports in tandem with the Society – had first a report of a green sun seen in Colombo, and then a letter from a Reverend W. R. Manley, a missionary in Ongole, south India, who saw 'splendid twilight glows . . . deep red more than one hour after sunset'.

And Gerard Manley Hopkins, the Victorian poet and Jesuit priest, then teaching classics at Stonyhurst College, wrote a lengthy essay for *Nature*, outlining in detail what he had seen – in a style unusual for the normally arid magazine, but easily recognizable to those who know their *Wreck of the Deutschland*:

. . . the glowing vapour above this was as yet colourless; then this took a beautiful olive or celadon green; not so vivid as the previous day's, and delicately fluted; the green belt was broader than the orange, and pressed down on and contracted it. Above the green in turn appeared a red glow, broader and burlier in make; it was softly brindled, and in the ribs or bars the colour was rosier, in the channels where the sky shone through it was a mallow colour . . .

There were four main kinds of phenomena, all amply evident from these pages and pages of reports. There were the sunsets themselves; there were the vivid and highly unusual colorations of the moon (often blue,* sometimes green), the occasional colorations of the sun and, very rarely, of some of the larger planets; the whitish solar coronas that were frequently seen just before sunset; and the monstrously flaming afterglows.

The afterglows in fact turned out generally to be a more dominant and widely noticed feature than the actual sunsets themselves. They are brilliantly hot-looking glows that appear from time to time some way up in the sky above where the sun has set some minutes before. The geometry of their origin is well

---

* Though the phrase 'blue moon' dates back to the sixteenth century at least, and has no connection.

known – having been studied assiduously after the eruption. They are caused when the rays of the sun, at an ever increasing distance from the observer, pass tangentially to an optically unusual layer in the atmosphere. In the case of the afterglow sightings that were made after Krakatoa, the optically unusual layer was the drift of ash – the ash particles absorbing and reflecting and causing a fiery reddening of the red light that is the last to be bent from the source, before, thanks to the disappearance of the sun and all of its light now coming from well below the horizon, they eventually vanish altogether.

A pattern also emerged swiftly from the Royal Society's massive catalogue of observations. There could be no doubt that the immense cloud of stratospheric ash that spread out from Krakatoa wound itself around the planet in a westerly direction – as one might expect, with the world turning eastwards underneath it – and spread both northwards and southwards as it did so. At first, in other words, the blue suns and moons and the fiery afterglows and the Bishop's Rings and the extraordinary sunsets appeared in the low latitudes, close to the latitude of the volcano: during all of September in places no further north than Honolulu, no further south than Santiago in Chile.

But then the cloud spread itself further afield. By the beginning of October the phenomena were seen in the Gulf of Mexico, then Nashville, Buenos Aires, the Canary Islands, Shanghai. By now, six weeks after the eruption, the particles were refracting and reflecting and dissipating and dispersing light over fully sixty-two degrees of latitude and had spread, quite literally, half a world away from their birthplace.

And so the trend continued: by late October the amazing sunsets were causing bystanders to gasp and write poetry, to send letters to newspaper editors, and to paint vivid pictures in places like Tasmania, South Africa and the southern cities of Chile. After which the cloud of volcanic aerosols, still wafting and widening north and south, performed a strange shiver and apparently began to move backwards and outwards at the same time, so that sometime around 23 November, after touching western Canada and California, it became apparent not in Alaska, the Aleutians or Hawaii but in England, Denmark, Turkey, Russia and (coming from the west) Siberia.

Examination of all of the northern hemisphere records – including the 500 sunsets of the Chelsea artist Mr Ascroft, who started to paint in earnest in November what he saw each evening on the Thames – appears to show that countries lying to the east were to be affected later. It looks, in other words, as though the cloud that had in its early days been sliding ever westwards was now moving in the opposite direction, as though it were trying to describe a long and lazy spiral across the surface of the earth.

(Close study of these upper-air movements later turned out to be quite crucial for modern meteorology. Analysis of the effects of the Krakatoa eruption – which still continues today, particularly at universities in Hawaii, Rhode Island, Oxford, Auckland and Melbourne – has informed very many areas of science, but in particular has quite revolutionized the business of weather-forecasting, helping to nudge it from its earlier and rather dubious standing as a mere drawing-room fancy into something that approaches the modern science of today. Each time, for instance, that one sees a map of the unfolding patterns of the jetstream, it is well worth remembering that it was the study of the stratospheric movement of the Krakatoa aerosols that led to the understanding of this particular weather-making phenomenon. Reverend Bishop in Hawaii seems to have been the first to notice, and called the initial spread of ash the Equatorial Smoke Stream.)

The eruption particles continued to move 'at about 73 mph' – such again was the scientists' exactitude – until, by the end of the year, they settled wherever they were and stayed, moving downwards under gravity's pull with an infinite slowness. And so they seemed to hover permanently in the sky and, though having effects not quite as radiantly beautiful as in those first months, gave the greatest of pleasure to all below who saw them, for the next two or three years. Mr Ascroft chronicled the entire long life of these sunsets from his Chelsea studio: they did not, he wrote, 'entirely fade from view until the early part of 1886'.

And the spectacle was only the half of it. The cloud reached the environs of New York in December. In the city itself they saw one thing. 'The entire island seemed ablaze,' said the *World*.* 'Great tongues of flame shot up from across the water, reddening the southwestern sky and tinting the Jersey shore with delicate shell colors.' *The Times*, then a less restrained newspaper than today, was only marginally more circumspect: 'The clouds gradually deepened to a bloody red hue, and a sanguinary flush was on the sea; the brilliant colours finally faded to a soft roseate [Peter Mark Roget's *Thesaurus* had been available since 1852], then into pale pink, and finally died away upon the darkening horizon.'

Out in the countryside, the results were very different, and the florid sunsets caused no end of confusion. In Poughkeepsie, seventy miles north along the Hudson valley, the *Daily Eagle* noted with wry pleasure on Wednesday, 28 November, Thanksgiving eve, that:

Po'keepsie firemen have always been noted for their zeal and promptitude in going to fires, and their efficiency in putting them out, but the effort last night was a little too much for them. The light of an immense conflagration was visible, the bells pealed out vehemently and the boys ran vigorously down Market to Montgomery, down Montgomery to Riverview Academy they rushed – and when that point was reached it became evident that the fire was on the other side of the river, and a few moments of cooler reflection convinced them it was too far to reach, although it could probably last until they got there. Still, there was no means of transport available, and no likelihood of water. The fire being located 91,000,000 miles off, it would have

* Of baseball's *World* Series fame.

taken the boys somewhere in the neighborhood of seven or eight million years to get there, let them run their best, and their terms would have expired before getting back. The sun is rather a large customer to tackle in the ways of fire, it beats a barn to death. We think the boys did well not to run out of hose.

Various causes are assigned for the peculiar light in the sky, the main one being the reflection of the rays of the declining sun upon the haze in the horizon. For several days past also there has been a peculiar state of atmosphere, which may or may not have something to do with it.

The no doubt embarrassed 'boys' who were duped so nicely by the sunset belonged to the town's Hose Company No. 6 (of seven), better known as the Young America Hose Company, and they were based close enough to the river to be invariably the first called out to deal with a fire in the western end of town. A few days later, trying to assuage their pain, a meteorologist wrote helpfully to a neighbour paper, the *Rochester Democrat and Chronicle*, to say that the same confusing light had been experienced at his end of the state as well; and in his opinion whatever it was that had prompted the volunteers down in Poughkeepsie to dash off on their horse-drawn pumping engines was caused by 'a stratum of decomposed vapours in the upper atmosphere'.

The Poughkeepsie *Sunday Courier* went further, suggesting with some prescience that 'the apparent reflection of a large conflagration, which called out our fire department' was caused by the sun's rays bending through 'extremely small water droplets . . . perhaps mixed with dust and smoke, sifting out the blue and yellow rays'. But another correspondent, probably taking down the office copy of *Old Moore*, offered only that the light show, all *lumière* and no *son*, was simply an augury of fine, anticyclonic weather in the days to come. Given the coming coldness of the season – made much worse by the dust – he could hardly have been more wrong.

Certainly the month of November 1883 was a time of unforgettable light shows throughout the northern world. In addition to
the fire-spotters believing they had seen a blaze in the western
suburbs of Poughkeepsie, there were reports that the fire-engines
from New Haven, Connecticut, had been sent out too, for much the
same reason. There was for a while a curious, half-panicked mood
about people who had to see these ghastly skies night after night:
to some they seemed almost apocalyptic, often unnerving; and it
was only when they were explained away as being caused by dust
from a distant volcano that people began to relax, and to bask in
the simple sight of a terrible beauty they would long remember.
But it was not to be a permanent fixture, there or anywhere.

And then there was the matter of temperature. Batavians noticed
the chill immediately. At dawn on the very Monday morning of
the eruption – though it was less a dawn, more a vague lightening
of the drab ash-filled gloom – it was colder than records had
shown for years – 65°, fifteen Fahrenheit degrees lower than
normal. People were seen shivering in the streets – though
perhaps as much from fear as from a need to keep warm. Dense
clouds hung in the air for days afterwards, enveloping the city
and an area perhaps 150 miles in diameter in a grey shroud
through which the sun's rays could not penetrate.

Logic would suggest that a veil of dust particles spreading
around the world would in time produce much the same effect,
with those places that languished under the sunset-inspiring dust
clouds feeling chillier than normal – though on a lesser scale than
places near by. And to an extent they did. Oddly, the Royal
Society, so assiduous in cataloguing the sound and light shows
put out by Krakatoa, never bothered to consider the idea that the
world might be cooled down by all the particles in the upper
air. The Society's editors present a catalogue of the world's
barometric pressures but none of the world's ambient temperatures. Those studies had to wait until much, much later – a

rather puzzling omission, considering the time's enthusiasm for climate-related studies, and one never satisfactorily explained.

And when these studies of temperature came – the first carried out in 1913, the second in 1982 – both found that as expected there had indeed been a worldwide drop in temperature. It had amounted on average to about one Fahrenheit degree and it had occurred, according to all the surviving records, at a time that appeared to be coincident with the eruption of Krakatoa. What has not been established, and what still concerns the scientific community, is which came first: did the eruption lower the world's temperature? Or did a lowering of the world temperature because of some other reason perhaps – unthinkable though it seems – somehow prompt the crust to undergo stress and strain and crack, and a rash of volcanoes to explode?

There is no doubt that there is a correlation, a definite link. Benjamin Franklin* was the first to notice it, and told an audience at the Manchester Literary and Philosophical Society that the 'dry fogs' that had seemed to cool the European summer of 1783 and made the ensuing winter exceptionally bitter were almost certainly the work of dust in the air. He had examined the volcanic records and found a fissure volcano called Lakagígar, or Hekla, in Iceland that had erupted earlier in the year (curiously, exactly a century before Krakatoa). It had produced great clouds of dust, for week after week, which tumbled up high into the atmosphere. This, he declared, must surely be the culprit.†

The infamous eruption in 1815 of Tambora, on the Indonesian island of Sumbawa, 700 miles east of Krakatoa, ejected twice the volume of material into the atmosphere (eleven cubic miles of

* He was at the time – 1784 – the first American ambassador to France.
† Gilbert White's *Natural History and Antiquities of Selborne*, an essential bedtime companion for many an English reader, mentions the weather during the summer of 1783 as being unusually cold, with his Hampshire village experiencing 'thick ice on 5th May'.

rock, ash and dust, compared with Krakatoa's six). The devastation it caused locally was profound – supposedly 50,000 dead, an entire language (Tambora) extinguished, an entire island rendered uninhabitable for years. But its climatic effects were astounding too. For it lowered the world's temperature by almost one Centigrade degree, on average: for every day when the normal temperature might be 33 °F, just above freezing, the temperature in the year after Tambora would be 31°, and ice would have formed on every pond and, more fatally, in every newborn crop, flower and hatching egg.

So in New England the farmers claimed that 1816 was 'the year without summer'. There were frosts as far south as New Jersey in late May, in upper New England in June and July, and the growing season was slashed from the usual 160 days to seventy. Soup kitchens opened in Manhattan. Livestock had to be fed on fish carried over from the Atlantic seaports – 1816 is also still remembered as 'the mackerel year'. There were crop failures – 'the last great subsistence crisis of the Western world' – and, as a result, there was emigration to the western states. No small number of today's Californians can rightly lay responsibility for their being Californians squarely at the door of the proximate cause of that year's ruinous cold – Tambora, a volcano unknown to most of them, and 10,000 miles away. (Although there was migration into California from Europe, in Newfoundland the reverse took place: migrants were sent back east across the ocean, because there was not enough for them to eat.)

And yet back in Europe it was quite as bad. The weather for 1816 is the worst recorded, with low temperatures stretching as far south as Tunisia. French grapes could not be harvested until November. The German wheat crop failed entirely, and prices for flour had doubled in a year. In some places there were reports of famine, and in others there were riots and mass migrations. The diaries and newspapers of the day present a litany of miseries. It is said that Byron composed his most miserable poem,

'Darkness' – *Morn came and went – and came, and brought no day –*
under the influence of that dismal year; and Mary Shelley may
have composed *Frankenstein* while gripped by a similarly
unseasonable melancholy.

Nowadays sophisticated instruments and the measurements
they take have usurped the role of anecdote and diary. Ice-cores
show minute layers of ash, or increases in sulphuric acid, as
indicators of eruptive material in the atmosphere. And there is
stunting of tree rings – the creation of a 'frost ring' in trees
that have suffered through an exceptionally cold winter. The
examinations of deep ice-cores, and of such trees as were living
in the nineteenth century, have confirmed what the stories had
long suggested: that eruptions of any of the world's larger volcanoes tend to coincide with periods of a cooling of the earth, some
of the periods longer and with a very much lowered temperature,
others shorter and with less of a fall in the mercury (the precise
decisive factors are still not quite agreed). Tambora's eruption of
clouds of ash coincided with a cooling of the world in 1815; and
so, in 1883, did the appearance of the clouds of ash from Krakatoa.

The most tragic of cargoes to move out from the volcano happened
also to be the slowest. The audible sounds and the unhearable shock
waves may have sped away at more than 700 mph, and the dust
may have wandered across the globe at more than seventy. The
immense rafts of floating pumice that drifted away from where
they splashed into the seas around Krakatoa made it as far as the
south-east coast of Africa – but they did not make landfall for more
than a year, travelling half a mile each hour, at best.

And when they did arrive, and were found washed up on the
shores, they were discovered in some horrifying cases to have
transported skeletons along with them, bringing as passengers
the unidentifiable remains of some of the unfortunate thousands
of Javanese and Sumatrans, Dutchmen and Chinese, who had
perished.

Pumice is one of the better known by-products of vulcanism. The most widely used products are, of course, volcanically produced rocks, used for building stone. These range in type from the dark basalts and gabbros, such as were used for making the spires of Cologne Cathedral, to the paler andesitic rocks, as are to be found in the temple lanterns all around Kyoto. Volcanic soils, especially a group called andosols, are uncommonly rich in minerals, and, in the attractive phrasing of the *Encyclopedia of Volcanoes*, 'have nourished many ancient civilizations'. And scores of the most ordinary, everyday items have incorporated volcanic products – particularly a highly absorbent mineral derived from weather ash called bentonite – in their manufacture: batteries, surfboards, refrigerators and air conditioners generally make use of ash invisibly, while the cheap building material known as breeze block makes no secret of its origins: crushed-up coke, cinders, furnace clinker and, in places where it is readily available, finely ground pumice and volcanic ash.

Pumice resides also in many an old-fashioned bathroom, sitting beside the loofah and the scrubbing brush. It is pleasantly abrasive and, because of the high proportion of gas bubbles that are caught in it before it solidifies in flight, it is of such low density that it floats quite readily. Makers of distressed denim fabrics also like to use it in their giant washing machines, where it brushes softly against the cloth, whitening and ageing it in a way that finds favour with youngsters.

But these more benign uses of pumice tend to shroud the awful truth about the immense tonnage of it that was released by Krakatoa. The headmistress of a mission school in Zanzibar,* off the east coast of Africa, wrote to the Royal Society in response to the appeal, to report that

---

* Zanzibar, a British Crown protectorate, became the empire's leading producer of cloves, after seeds were brought from the Spice Islands of the Dutch East Indies in 1818.

. . . about the third week in July 1884, the boys . . . were much amused by finding on the beach stones which would float, evidently pumice-stone. The lady who was with them . . . also noticed that there were a quantity of human skulls and bones 'all along the beach at high water-mark'; these were quite clean and had no flesh remaining on them, and were found at intervals of a few yards, two or three lying close together.

The closer to the volcano, the thicker the rafts of pumice, of course. On the west coast of the island of Kosrae, in what is now Pacific Micronesia, huge plates of pumice sixteen inches thick were hauled from the beach early in 1884: they were covered with barnacles, and many were accompanied by the roots of huge trees, with extra pumice lumps caught up in their roots, helping them stay afloat. These trees, torn up and floated 3,000 miles to the east, were presumably parts of Krakatoa's old forests – the same forests that had been noted and painted by Captain Cook's home-bound expedition in 1780, and those that the Sundanese boat-builders had been cutting when they were forced to flee for their lives from the first eruptions of May.

The crews of ships moving through fields of pumice – such as those 'acres in extent' that were encountered by one vessel coming into the Sunda Strait from Australia in January – were struck by the peculiar sound of the bow slicing through the rock. There was no real noise, 'just a soft sort of crushing sound'. And all the passing ships did their best to avoid desecrating the terrible cargo the pumice rafts all too often carried. A crewman on the vessel *Samoa*, which was heading south-westwards, off into the Indian Ocean, wrote of the nightmarish unreality of such encounters:

For two days after passing Anjer we passed through masses of dead bodies, hundreds and hundreds of them striking the ships on both sides – groups of 50 and 100 all packed together, most of them naked. We passed a great deal of wreckage, but of course we cannot tell if any vessels were lost. We also passed bedding chests and a number of

Rafts of pumice, many laden with the remains of victims,
drifted as far away as Zanzibar.

white bodies, all dressed like sailors, with sheath knives on them. For
ten days, we went through fields of pumice stone.

What the seamen witnessed on the *Samoa*, and on the *Bothwell
Castle*, and on the *Loudon* and the *Berbice* and the *Charles Bal* and
the *Kedirie* and a score of other ships beside that scoured the
Sunda Strait during those weeks in late August, September and
October does not bear too much repeating, so awful is what they
have to say. Most reports were much more dreadful than the
following account, which was published in a letter to *The Times*,
from a correspondent writing from Batavia in October:

The British ship *Bay of Naples* had called at these islands and had
reported that on the same day, when 120 miles from Java's First Point,
during the volcanic disturbances, she encountered carcasses of animals
including even those of tigers, and about 150 human corpses, of which
40 were those of Europeans, besides enormous trunks of trees borne
along by the current.

Yet it is what they did *not* see that remains, to take the longer
view, of greater significance. For what they did not see was this:
the half-mile-high pointed peak of Krakatoa. They did not see it
smouldering menacingly in the aftermath of what it had done, as
most volcanoes are prone to do.

Usually – whether named Vesuvius, or St Helens, or Pinatubo,
or Unzen or Etna – a volcano explodes, and in so doing causes

manifold devastation and death. Then it simply stands there, raging and smoking ever less fiercely, presiding with a titanic smugness over the ruin it has so lately made. But, uniquely in much of volcanic history, Krakatoa did no such thing.

For Krakatoa had gone. Six cubic miles of rock of her, most of the island's great bulk, had just vanished, either blown into the sky or collapsed into the sea, and with the most thunderous roar and the greatest loss of life ever recorded in certain history.

For so long before that Krakatoa had been an island of no consequence. It had been little more than a genial, easily recognized sailors' companion spotted off the bow of an approaching ship, a sea-mark that would always help guide any navigator who was feeling his way up or down this most vital waterway between Java and Sumatra. It was that old 'island with a pointed mountain', and nothing more.

Now in the middle of the summer of 1883 it had suddenly and without much warning gone totally berserk, sent the sea berserk as well and then had, essentially, vanished. Not vanished in name, perhaps; not vanished from memory either; and recently, and in much the same form, it has been reborn (as we shall see). But in August 1883 this inconsequential little island went mad and disappeared. The reasons just why this happened – as it did, and when it did – have occupied the minds of a great community of geologists around the world for all the long years since.

4. The Explanations

Why did Krakatoa happen? Why, indeed and more generally, do volcanoes do what they do? Why does the *terra firma* upon which we so confidently and innocently secure all our lives, sometimes and so capriciously tear itself open and cause such fearful destruction as it does so?

To those caught up in such a moment of appalling terror, such as the thousands whose lives were wrecked in 1883, it all must seem a most monstrous injustice, a terrible cheek perpetrated by the earth and its presiding deities. Krakatoa is a stark reminder of the truth of Will Durant's famous aphorism 'Civilization exists by geologic consent, subject to change without notice.' Yet geology, which is an unemotional and rational science, allows us to step back from our shock and dismay at such events, to accept a longer view – and to be awed by something rather different: that despite her seemingly cruel caprices, this planet in fact enjoys by and large an extraordinarily fortunate situation.

The simple, very obvious features of the earth – its location in space, its size, the processes that led to its creation, processes that include the very volcanic events that took all the lives west of Java – happen to have been suited perfectly, when taking the long view, to the sustenance and maintenance of organic life.

To victims of a volcanic eruption like this, of course, the very reverse must seem true. But consider location, for instance. Planet earth is sited just close enough to the star around which it orbits to derive only benefits from the latter's infernal solar heat. It is neither so close as to risk the boiling of its oceans and the loss of its water into outer space by photo-dissociation in the upper atmosphere, nor so far away that all its present liquid water remains uselessly and inconsumably frozen.

The size of the earth is spot on too. Thanks to its moderate size its gravitational pull is just right. It is strong enough to overcome in particular the escape velocities of the molecules both of water and carbon dioxide, which means that we have a sheltering canopy – a benevolently situated *greenhouse*, even though this is a word with more negative associations today – that first allowed life's building blocks to be assembled, and then ensured that the fragile living entities so made could be cosseted against the perilous radiations from outer space.

And then there are the volcanoes – just the right number, of just the right size, for our own good. The deep heat reservoir inside the earth is not so hot, for instance, as to cause ceaseless and unbearable volcanic activity on the surface. The amount of heat and thermal decay within the earth happens to be just perfect for allowing convection currents to form and to turn over and over in the earth's mantle, and for the solid continents that lie above them to slide about according to the complicated and beautiful mechanisms of plate tectonics.

Plate movement and convection and the volcanic activity that is their constant handmaid may not seem, to the victims of eruptions and tidal waves, to be in any way benign, or to be good for the planet as a whole. And yet, taking the long view once again, they most certainly are: the water, carbon dioxide, carbon and sulphur that are so central to the making and maintenance of organic life are all being constantly recycled by the world's volcanoes – which were also the probable origins of the earth's atmosphere in the very first place. It is not merely that volcanoes bring fertile volcanic soils or useful minerals to the surface; what is more crucial is their role in the process of bringing from the secret storehouses of the inner earth the elements that allow the outer earth, the biosphere and the lithosphere, to be so vibrantly alive.

Almost all our neighbour planets are, so far as is known, volcanically lifeless. They are also, on all the available evidence, more or less biologically lifeless – and that is quite probably at least in part because they *are* so volcanically dead. Only Io, one of Jupiter's many moons, seems to sport a significant number of volcanoes: spectacular sulphur-rich fountains of magma have been seen spouting on its surface. But there is no suggestion of plates or of any movement of the solid crust, either on Io or on any planet or moon known to exist between Mars and Pluto. The vigorous business of plate movement apparently does not occur on planets that are hotter than our own; nor does it on those that are much more frozen and more deeply dead.

But it is the movement of the plates, and the internal storms that rage below and cause them to slip beneath or alongside one another or tear themselves apart along their suture-lines, that is the driving force behind our earth's highly unusual degree of vulcanism. Plate movement, as well as shaping the planet's topography, also creates most of the very vulcanism that is central to its life. Plate tectonics, in other words, is the key to it all – and any examination of just why Krakatoa happened as it did, and how it did, must inevitably now refer to this newly minted catalogue of knowledge about the workings of the earth.

It was of course not always so. In the distant past, whenever the earth behaved with terrible and unanticipated violence, mankind could do little more than wonder, horror-struck, at the sheer effrontery of it. In very early times this wonderment was answered, inevitably, mainly by religion and the making of myths. Volcanoes were hills occupied by temperamental gods: they could be appeased by frequent sacrifice. The appeasing flesh could be that of a young human (a small child thrown every twenty-five years into the crater of a particular Nicaraguan volcano, for instance, would guarantee its quietude) or an animal (Javanese today toss chickens into the crater of Mount Bromo – superstition plays an important role in East Indian attitudes towards their volcanoes still).

The ancient Greeks and Romans then hammered some kind of order into their beliefs, as might be expected: the idea of the existence of Hades, the nature of such gods as Pluto and Vulcan, the character of Titanic monsters like the fearsome, wild-eyed and flaming-tongued Typhon were all connected with the wayward behaviour of an earth that all then knew had a terrible and dangerously hot interior. It was no coincidence that the gateway to Hades – believed by the Ancients to be in the earth's centre – was the Romans' most notorious local volcano, Mount Etna, with its gas-belching vents known as *solfataras*, and the phrase 'sailing to Sicily' was for a while a euphemism for entering the fiery furnaces of the Devil's domain.

The seers of the classical world were on rather shakier ground when it came to deciding just why, other than for divine reasons, there was just so much heat inside the earth. The Greeks – the philosophers Anaxagoras and Aristotle in particular – favoured the human analogy of *trapped wind*, with the friction of the escaping wind causing the generation of heat, a sort of volcanic vindaloo. The Romans, on the other hand, and among them most notably Lucius Seneca, favoured the notion that the heat came from the combustion of a vast inner-earth storehouse of sulphur – and in some Roman poetry of the time this idea extended to the burning of deeply buried reservoirs of alum, coal and tar.

This idea, that volcanoes were the consequence of the steady burning of a finite store of earthly combustibles, exerted a grip on the scientific mind for centuries. Then, as chemistry developed as a science, so its innumerable secrets offered themselves as the favoured sources for all the necessary heat, and were widely accepted as doing so. During the seventeenth and eighteenth centuries a great many seers – Isaac Newton among them – believed that so-called exothermic chemical reactions were the answer. By 1807, when the Geological Society of London, the world's oldest such body, was founded, the oxidation of newly discovered alkaline metals, such as sodium and potassium, was thought to be an answer.

Even as late as the 1920s there were two now notoriously blinkered scientists who clung to what might seem today quite fatuous chemical theories. One of them, Arthur Louis Day, proposed in 1925 that volcanic heat was due to a series of complex chemical reactions between gases, and he won support from the redoubtable and influential Sir Harold Jeffreys,* while at the same

* Sir Harold was one of the last hold-outs against the theory of continental drift, writing into the late 1950s that the earth's crust was simply too rigid to permit it. He was widely regarded as a brilliant figure – an expert on the monsoon, and on the physics of cyclones – but was a memorably bad lecturer, devoting much time to the dynamics of boiling porridge and confiding its secrets not to his Cambridge classes, but to passers-by outside

time dismissing vulcanism generally as a phenomenon that was merely 'local and occasional, not perpetual and worldwide'.

However, in tandem with all those chemists and physicists who for so long had such an influence on geophysical thinking, there were also other natural philosophers – René Descartes most notable among them – who started out on what would prove to be the right track. In the mid seventeenth century Descartes – better known for his *cogito, ergo sum*, and for his legacy of Cartesian coordinates – came up with a quite revolutionary idea: that the earth originated by way of gravitational attraction and gaseous condensation, that heat was an essential primordial component of this process, and that its slow decay resulted in the earth having three internal concentric parts: a highly dense and incandescent liquid core, a half-cooled plastic central region, and a cold, solid and comparatively light crust. Moreover, there was ample primordial heat left over from the creation process to power all known volcanoes for a very, very long time.

The subsequent advent of the science of field geology, the furious debates that went on between Neptunists, who believed all rocks to have precipitated from a primeval ocean, and Plutonists, who saw countless of them as having their origins in melting and magma, belongs to another story, temptingly diverting though the various interlocking sagas may be. In essence, though, the mystery that occupied most minds for most of the late nineteenth and early twentieth centuries was simply *why rocks melt* – what combination of physics and chemistry, of depth, of heat and of the presence or absence of water in the mix of minerals would lead a rock to become plastic and mobile and molten, and then to emerge on the surface and cool and harden and solidify back into rock once again.

The chemist and the chemistry that sought to answer questions

---

the open window to whom he customarily spoke. Like George Darwin, mentioned earlier, he also held the Plumian Chair in Astronomy.

about the make-up of the earth in earlier times had been overtaken
by the physics and the physicists seeking to do much the same in
recent years; and though the physics answered much of the detail
involved, many of the fundamental questions remained doggedly,
in essence, unresolved.

Or at least they did until that memorable July day in 1965
when, as I have explained in an earlier chapter, the soft-spoken
and self-effacing Canadian geologist J. Tuzo Wilson managed to
combine both the chemistry and the physics of the earth into
one, inaugurating the science of plate tectonics. In doing so he
launched a brand-new and all-encompassing global theory that
would offer the answer to almost everything volcanic that had
ever been wondered at.

Uniquely in the solar system this planet sports a crust that
is, by virtue of this process, being constantly destroyed and
regenerated – an ever mobile chemical factory where materials
that exist in solid, liquid and gaseous states are being recycled
endlessly. They are burst out from the middle of oceanic plates
by a process, newly understood, that allows upwelling materials
to melt *without heat being added to them* – to melt simply because
the pressure on them is relieved by their being convected upwards
and outwards towards the atmosphere.* There are volcanoes
here in these mid-crustal ridges, big but not especially explosive
volcanoes, mountains that ooze basalt, like those in Hawaii and
Iceland, the Azores and the rift valleys of East Africa.† They are

---

* This is a complex subject, well beyond the scope of this story: since it
involves phrases and concepts such as enthalpy, adiabatics, isobaric entropy
and mole fractions, this is perhaps just as well. However, it is vitally
important to a proper understanding of plate tectonics, and I have included
references to useful books on the topic in the 'Recommendations for Further
Reading'.

† Mount Nyiragongo, in the East African Rift, is one of the more malign of
the volcanoes to be found at a place where plates are pulling apart from
one another. The lava flows are immense and unpredictable (though the

the stuff of research and fascination in their own right. But they are the distaff side of the volcano of this account, the Alpha to Krakatoa's Omega, the mid-plate reciprocal to all that goes on at the plates' edges, *the other side of the story.*

For the materials that rise up in the middle, along with whatever they sweep before them on their way, are in due course swept down again at the peripheries of plates. They are swept down by the process that is most crucial of all, which, though an essential part of earthly regeneration, also leads directly to the making of highly explosive, dramatic and deadly arc volcanoes like Krakatoa. Colloquially the phenomenon that exists at these plate edges is known among geophysicists and vulcanologists as *the subduction factory* – and Krakatoa stands front and centre in one of the largest and most complicated of these extraordinary, world-shaping entities.

The factories and the subduction zones that underpin them are essentially coextensive. It probably bears repeating that each of the zones is where one of the world's many heavy oceanic plates slowly collides with one of the many lighter and thicker continental plates and slides, buckling as it does so, underneath. The zones are very long, and very thin. If unravelled they would extend for about 19,000 miles. But they are rarely more than sixty miles wide. The total area of the subducting world's assembly-lines amounts thus to about a million square miles – about the size of Greenland, or the American Confederate South, or Argentina.

And enclosed within the zones, and formed, allowed to grow, and then destroyed or mutated or otherwise dramatically affected by the processes going on inside them, are about 1,400 of the

---

calamitous eruption of 2002 happened to have been predicted, accurately, by an unpaid and heroic Congolese vulcanologist named Dieudonné Wafula, whose reports were widely ignored), and its gas emissions kill people and wildlife, including large numbers of elephants, who are suffocated and then covered with a thin coat of lava.

world's 1,500 historically active land volcanoes. Of all visible volcanoes, 94 per cent, in other words, stand within subduction zones. A mere handful of countries – Indonesia, Japan, America, Russia, Chile, the Philippines, New Guinea, New Zealand, Nicaragua chief among them, *and in that order*, play host to most of them: these nine countries are home to more than nine out of every ten volcanoes that are liable to erupt today or have done so in recent history.

The most readily recognizable subduction zones are those that enfold the Pacific Ocean. As a reasonably familiar example, consider that which runs along the western edge of South America, and which has created the chain we know as the Andes.* This is where the heavy basaltic Nazca Plate collides with the lighter granitic-and-sedimentary-rock South American Plate. (It does so simply because it is at the same time splitting itself away from its neighbour, the Pacific Plate, along what is called the East Pacific Rise – close to where the Isla de Pascua, Easter Island, is hoisted above the ocean surface.)

The subduction factory that results is a classic of its kind, creating dozens of volcanoes running from the Andean peaks of Ruiz and Galeras in the north, in Colombia, via Chacana, Cotopaxi and Sangay in Ecuador, Huaynaputina† in Peru, Lascar in Chile, Llaima and Villarica on the frontier between Argentina and Chile, and, at the southern tip of the continent, Monte Burney and Cerro Hudson, this last volcano erupting massively in 1991. All told there are sixty-seven volcanoes that have been manufactured by the processes of this one subduction zone – and since there are

* From which comes the word *andesite*, one of the more common indicator-rocks found in a typical subduction-zone volcano.
† Despite its generally unfamiliar name, this rather small Peruvian volcano had one of the biggest eruptions in world history, in February 1600 – creating a 'spike' in Greenland ice-cores rarely equalled, even by Tambora and Krakatoa.

4,000 miles separating northern Colombia from southern Chile, and since there is a sort of serrated regularity to the Andes, that means there is more or less one volcano piercing the sky every sixty miles.

Much the same number of volcanoes, with similar intervals between them, is to be found at the other subduction factories around the Pacific – in Alaska and the Aleutian Islands, in the Kamchatka Peninsula, in Japan and the Kurile Islands; and an even greater number is to be found in the most volcanic part of the world, the great subduction zone that stretches 3,000 miles from the northern tip of Sumatra to what is called the Bird's Head on the north-western tip (the West Irian side) of the island of New Guinea.

In this immense factory, there are at least eighty-seven volcanoes that make up much of the archipelago that politics has lately chosen to call Indonesia and the Philippines. Indonesia itself has and has had more volcanoes and more volcanic activity than any other political entity on the earth, in all recorded history. It is a country that is defined by its place at the heart of a subduction zone and is essentially made up of volcanoes and precious little else. On the island of Java alone today there are twenty-one volcanoes that remain fully active. Their eruptions are invariably spectacular and terribly dangerous. And because a very great many people live and work near the volcanoes (not least because the volcanic soil, thanks to the recycling mentioned earlier, is nutritious and ideally suited for farming), they are the cause of a dismaying number of deaths.

The earth fashioned three of the five greatest volcanoes of historic time in this one gigantic factory. The largest the world has ever known was made there: Mount Toba, which erupted 74,000 years ago in what is now northern Sumatra. It had a Volcanic Explosivity Index, or VEI, of 8 – the highest on a scale that is now universally used to classify all eruptions (save for those which merely ooze lava, without exploding). Toba's *humongous*

EURASIAN

NORTH AMERICAN

JUAN DE FUCA

PHILIPPINE

PACIFIC

AUSTRALIAN

⌁ PLATE BOUNDARY

△ VOLCANO

The world and its pattern of tectonic plates. Where oceanic and
continental plates meet, there is volcanic and seismic activity in great –
and often terrible – abundance.

explosion – the curious adjective is now officially used to describe giant volcanoes, the equivalent of the cyclonic sea-state that is these days termed *phenomenal* – left behind an immense lake, fifty miles long and fifteen wide, with the sheer caldera cliffs rising 800 feet straight out of the water. The eruption left layers of dust eighteen inches thick on the ocean floor 1,500 miles away, and must have placed a severe crimp on the development of such Ur-humans as were struggling for existence in those times: it must have lowered the ambient temperature by many degrees, and made even more harsh a climate that was already in the midst of changing into yet another Ice Age.

The eruption of Tambora in 1815, in this same subduction zone, is reckoned the second greatest in history, with an Explosivity Index of 7. (This index, which was first created at the Smithsonian Institution in Washington, is based on two features: the amount of material that is ejected in an explosion, and the height to which it is hurled through the atmosphere. These two factors are clearly observable in modern eruptions; they are also deducible from the records of the past. Even though there were no literate eyewitnesses to Toba, and very few to Tambora – which has to be the principal reason neither has lingered in the public consciousness, while Krakatoa clearly has – the total mass that was ejected from each eruption can be calculated with some precision from an examination of the local geological record, and the distribution of the ash falls far away on the seabed can suggest with fair accuracy the heights to which the columns rose into the sky.)

Third in the list is Taupo in New Zealand, which erupted in AD 180, hugely; and fourth is Novarupta in Alaska – better known as Katmai, on the landward end of the Aleutian chain – which did so in 1912. This last was the largest recent eruption on the North American mainland, but, because of its remoteness, it was little noticed except by what – in terms of calderas and domes and frozen lakes – it left behind.

And then, fifth in the list of all volcanoes known, with a VEI of 6.5, with more than six cubic miles of rock and ash and pumice and dust hurled dozens of miles into the lower stratosphere, with sounds heard 3,000 miles away, with tidal waves of enormous force and height, with shock waves that ran four times to the far side of the world and almost three times back, and with more people killed and more livelihoods ruined than by any other eruption in world history, comes Krakatoa.

Seven weeks after the eruption, when the dust had cleared, the Netherlands government ordered Dr Verbeek and his colleagues to investigate exactly what had happened. The team of four took off in the government hopper-barge the *Kedirie*, on 11 October, and spent the following two weeks examining every possible aspect of the now seemingly dead remnants of the mountain. The orgy of self-destruction was more than amply evident. It was, Verbeek wrote later, 'the most interesting eruption witnessed by the human race until now'. But very little of the original mountain was left to see.

The southern quarter of the island remained but was sliced open, as if with a vertical carving-knife – so that the original peak of Rakata looked, from the south, almost the same, but with everything to its north missing. The exposed northern face of Rakata was almost perfectly vertical, and in cross-section, when viewed from the north, quite perfectly triangular; it was pierced with vertical lines and radiating systems of lava-filled dikes and sills and plugs of newly formed rock, all covered with several feet of grey pumice dust, so that it looked from afar exactly as it was – a perfect cross-section, as one might see in a teaching-chart, of a one-time volcano that had been blasted in half and into oblivion.

But at least the summit of Rakata was, more or less, still there. The two northern peaks of Krakatoa, the summits known as Danan and Perboewatan, were, to the expedition's awestruck fascination, no longer anywhere to be seen. Nor was the little skerry of andesite known (because of its shape) as the Polish Hat: it had quite vanished, presumably vaporized in that one paroxysmal instant.

The very opposite had happened to the two small islands, Lang and Verlaten, which had once enfolded Krakatoa like a pair of parentheses. Rather than vanishing into thin air, these two now appeared to be very much larger than they had before. Their beaches, it turned out, had since the eruption become choked and swollen with enormous amounts of stranded pumice. Larger they may have been – but the essential difference about their appearance as maritime parentheses was that now they were enfolding and bracketing *nothing* – between them was just a huge expanse of empty, lifeless sea, with the immense broken fang of Rakata peak rising alone straight out of the ocean as a reminder of what had once been there.

The sea to the immediate north of the cliff was very deep – nearly a thousand feet. Clearly an enormous new caldera had been created – almost the entire volcano had collapsed into an immense void below, and the cliff of Rakata, neatly bisected where it had been shorn off, was all that remained to the south of the collapse. Off to the north-east two entirely new little islands had risen from the waves, and were christened Steers and Calmeyer Islands; because they were composed of little more than stranded rafts of soft pumice they were eroded back to sea-level in very short order; on today's charts there are just warnings of 'patches of discoloured water', fifteen feet deep, suggesting where they used to be.

Back in 1885, when Verbeek wrote his official report, there were only the vaguest explanations of just why all of this might have happened. It was easy enough to describe what had happened – the science of descriptive vulcanology was in any case well advanced, and had been for many years. But when the vulcanologists of the day came to explain the reasons for the violent behaviour of their charges – as true for every volcano in the world as it was for Krakatoa – there was very little understanding of the processes of the world to offer them a basis for coming up with a theory.

After all, only a few decades before, many believed that basalt and flows of lava were simply precipitates from the sea. Until 1857 many geologists thought that volcanoes were caused by the bulging upwards of horizontal flows of lava – and not that they had been built vertically by the discharge of their own products. And at the time of Krakatoa's eruption Alfred Wegener – who first came up with the idea of continental drift, which was to lead to the theory of plate tectonics, and who might well have set the bewildered community of vulcanologists off in the right direction – was only three years old.

And so while in all the official reports and learned papers about the event there was plenty of description of the ruin and dismay that Krakatoa had caused, and though there was much speculation about why the volcano exploded with the violence it displayed, there was next to nothing by way of sensible wondering about the larger mechanisms that triggered it.

This was true for Verbeek in his report, for instance. He spent countless pages describing in detail clogged pipes, steam vents and collapses of central parts of the main volcano. What he concluded did display a remarkable prescience: he said that a good deal of the vanished volcano had foundered into the sea, and had not been blasted into the atmosphere. He suggested that the Plinian violence of the explosion was a result of sea-water mixing suddenly with the magma, and flashing over, turning into super-heated steam, in a gigantic and uncontrollable explosion that is these days given the somewhat less than attractive name of a *phreatomagmatic* eruption. But he never tried to step back and wonder why Krakatoa was where it was, and why it did what it did in the first place.

The same was true also for John Judd, president of the Geological Society of London and author in 1881 of a then classic work, *Volcanoes*. He too wrote eloquently of the way in which hot magma and sea-water mixed, and of how pumice was created by a lowering of the magma's melting point by the addition of water — but, once again, he missed the central point. He never even tried to grapple with the central issue: why Krakatoa?

The last popular book on the subject* was written in 1964. Even then, still lacking any solid theory that might account for the world's inner processes, the author could only really describe what a volcano was ('a hole in the ground through which hot gas, molten material and fragmentary products rise to the surface'), say where volcanoes were to be found and name the kinds of material that came from them. And when he arrived at the specific case of Krakatoa, which was described over many pages and with a quite magical literary skill, the author turned desperate. The book begins to speak in terms of 'The Demon' going in to 'press the attack', his 'searching fingers boring into the defences', and the 'pent-up energies of time' and 'primeval forces' readying themselves to do battle. One can hardly blame him. Neither he nor anyone else had an inkling of what really caused Krakatoa. And that was hardly his fault: he was simply a very few years too early.

But once plate tectonic theory was in place, all that changed. Nowadays there is a ready explanation for what happened and why. Essentially the same explanation accounts for the eruption of Toba at the north-western end of the subduction zone, and for Tambora's at its eastern end, and for those of all the other volcanoes in between.

Krakatoa erupted because of what happens when two plates collide — specifically, because of what happens when the north-bound Australian Oceanic Plate collides, as it has been doing for

---

* *Krakatoa*, by Rupert Furneaux, had the unfortunate distinction of being published in 1965, almost on the eve of the announcement of the discovery of plate tectonics.

many millions of years past and as it continues to do today, with that part of the Asian Plate that, for the sake of simplicity, we will call by the name it enjoys today, Sumatra.

The oceanic plate is cold and made of the heavier, darker, less acidic suite of rocks that underlie all oceans, so as it hits it begins to sink below the warmer and lighter rocks of which Sumatra and all other continents are made. As it sinks it takes with it, downwards, the small wedge-shaped sliver of continental rock that it either scratched or smeared off the Sumatran edge; it also takes along with it some of the sands and clays that had accumulated on the Sumatran coast, the water that was trapped chemically in these, and a fair amount of atmospheric air and sea-water besides. This entire geological cocktail – an amalgam of cold and heavy basalt from the plate; granite-like rocks from the Sumatran crust; sands, clays, limestones and vast quantities of air and water – then plummets. And, as it does so, everything suddenly changes.

Water is the crucial ingredient in this process. Not only does it lubricate the motion of the plates and help the subduction continue, but, even in very tiny amounts, its presence lowers the temperature at which the rocks of the mantle will begin to melt. And since the water also lowers the density of the wedge-shaped mélange that is being swept and smeared downwards too, the molten rock that is being created below it finds that the rocks above it have suddenly become (thanks to the water) less dense, less rigid, less strong. They have become, in other words, a perfect exit route for the partly melted rock below, enabling it to rush upwards, to melt even further because of the decompression mentioned earlier. Then, with the dissolved carbon dioxide and water vapour suddenly turning back into gas and frothing out of solution, the whole mass rushes up and out as a torrent of phenomenal explosivity into the unsuspecting open air: as a gigantic and classical subduction-zone volcano.

That is why Krakatoa exploded. As to why it exploded so

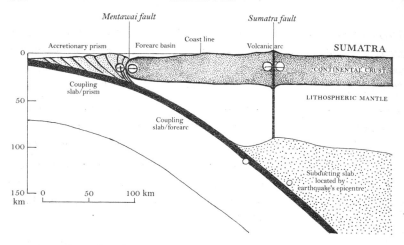

A cross-section showing the basic elements of an oceanic plate –
upwelling new material from the centre, spreading outwards and then sliding beneath the lighter continental plate it then encounters. Volcanoes
and earthquakes are an inevitable feature of this last process of *subduction.*

powerfully and so very noisily – this entirely different debate
continues apace today.

There are some clues. The geography of the islands indicates, for
example, that there was once an ancient super-Krakatoa, and that
at some unspecified time in the past it exploded and collapsed
into itself, leaving behind a caldera; the parenthesis-islands of
Lang and Verlaten were clearly the caldera walls, the cliffs at the
edge of the old volcano. The volcano that succeeded this then had
three distinct peaks – Rakata, Danan and Perboewatan. Each was
an exit passage for a gigantic magma chamber that clearly existed
deep below the region.

So there can be little doubt from this simple evidence alone
that the 1883 Krakatoa existed above a large chamber of magma,
and that with the three exit-pipes above it weakening its roof, it
had a propensity, in times of violent stress, to collapse. The
question that has occupied the minds of many specialists in recent
years is this: was it the fact that sea-water managed to get into

this chamber at the moment of collapse that was the primary cause of the deafening explosion and the tidal waves? Or was it simply one contributory factor, with some other process also at work to make things even more dramatic?

A series of experiments performed in pressure vessels in a laboratory in Australia has suggested that other factors were indeed at work – but that they were complex and subtle. They suggest that a pulse of fresh basalt from deeper in the earth may have been unexpectedly injected into the base of the magma chamber; that this new pulse heated the existing magma above it, causing a violent convection current and the sudden frothing of even more gas – and the sudden breach of the chamber roof. This idea of magma mixing has lately taken hold: processes going on even more deeply within the subduction zone may perhaps have contributed to the might of the Krakatoa event.

And then, finally, there is the overall siting of Krakatoa, halfway between Java and Sumatra. It lies directly above what might be called a hinge point around which the two islands are slowly swinging, the Strait ever widening, the islands turning like the pages of a northward-closing book – Sumatra moving to the north-east, Java to the north, Krakatoa in the middle.

There is certainly a complex network of faults in the Sunda Strait. Their existence is one of the reasons why there is a strait there, an absence of island mass, in the first place. Slowly, very slowly, science is trying to make some sense out of the complexity of it all. Geophysicists in Troy, New York, have spent recent years placing a rash of Global Positioning System receivers on the nearby islands, and have found that all manner of tiny move-ments are taking place – that the main subduction continues to creep away, as it has done for millions of years, but that tiny little sideways jogs are taking place too, small weakenings, creations of a blizzard of tiny faults that make the region into the most remarkable of geological laboratories – a fascinating study, even if Krakatoa had never existed.

The basic tectonic structure of the region: the Australian Plate is moving
north to collide with the Asian Plate, while all manner of stresses and
faults build up along the collision zones by Java and Sumatra.

But it does exist, and will play its tricks on the world once
again, and before very much longer. The processes that led to the
events of August 1883 are unstoppable. There is a subduction
factory of monumental proportions to the south and east of
Sumatra. It is uniquely sited around and beneath the small island
that lies on the hinge-point between Sumatra and Java. The island
is surrounded by the volatile waters of the sea, water that causes
mayhem if it gets within a mile of boiling magma. The island itself
is surrounded by countless small faults and zones of weakness, as
well as by a raft of components of basic rock – acidic rock,
sedimentary rock – that is twisting and turning every which way
under a barrage of stresses and strains that exist more notably
here than anywhere else on earth. Small wonder, indeed, that
there is only one Krakatoa. The place where it blew itself apart
is so geologically dangerous that one can almost imagine there
being room for a dozen more.

*

They counted their dead, and they buried them where they could, which was usually where they found them. The Dutch officials reacted with commendable speed, burying bodies at the rate of several hundred a day, drenching the swamps with carbolic acid, pulling down wreckage, setting cleansing fires. The king back in Holland opened a fund. Dutch mothers sent blankets, tents, food. A flotilla of ships travelled east, to see what could be done. The Great World Circus staged benefit performances in Batavia, before packing up and going home, taking their distressed little elephant with them. The process of rebuilding began, with the Fourth Point lighthouse at Anjer, remade with iron plates, hurried back into operation to ensure the safety of the commercial shipping lanes, a symbolic beginning of the rebirth. The cable lines to and from west Java and south Sumatra were repaired. The aid workers came into town. The charities set up shop. The scientists fanned out to investigate, to report, to recommend.

But in time they all went home again, to deal with other problems and to answer fresher questions. They left the coastal people of Java and Sumatra, and those island shore-dwellers known as the Bantenese, among their patched-up ruins, and in time they forgot all about them. They did not stop to wonder where these people might eventually look for sustenance and succour.

Perhaps they should have done. For it turned out that not a few of these unhappy, dispossessed and traumatized people eventually looked to the west, to Mecca, and to the benevolent power of their Islamic religion to answer their needs. This was a political and religious consequence of the disaster – a consequence entirely unanticipated by the ruling Dutch colonists – that was to have the most profound and longest-lasting fallout, for the Indies, for Europe, and beyond.

9

REBELLION OF A RUINED PEOPLE

The leaders formed an élite group, which developed and transmitted the time-honoured prophecies or vision of history concerning the coming of the righteous king – the Mahdi.

– from *The Peasants' Revolt of Banten* in 1888
by Sartono Kartodirdjo, 1966

The central market in Serang, an unremarkable crossroads town a few miles inland from the little pepper port of Banten, sells everything and attracts everyone. On Tuesday 2 October 1883 – five weeks after the eruption, while the dead of Java and Sumatra were still being buried and the ruins of the towns and villages on the coast were still being cleared – a Dutch fusilier stopped by to purchase his weekly supply of tobacco.

In normal circumstances it would count for nothing that this man was a part of the ruling foreign enginework of the Indies: the merchants of Serang were ecumenical in their pursuit of trade, and the tobacco-seller, like everyone else, would happily accept the custom of anyone – brown, yellow or, as in this case, a white European from the curiously privileged group who ruled over them.

But these were not normal circumstances. All of a sudden there seemed to be a curious feeling of tension in the air. The Dutch had been aware of it for some days now – a kind of muted resentment, a vague hostility that made people look away, or mutter among themselves in hushed tones whenever a Dutch official happened by. Perhaps they were imagining things. After all, the Krakatoa relief operations – all organized by the Dutch – were now in full swing, Dutch money was pouring into the area, shelters were being built, roads cleared, businesses reopened. The Dutch governor-general himself, aboard the steam-yacht *The King of the Netherlands*, had paid an official visit.

The local people had every reason, one would have thought, to be grateful for the colonists' help in speeding along their programme of rescue and rebuilding. It wasn't the fault of the Dutch that the tragedy had happened: but, without a murmur of complaint, the Dutch were quite generously helping the people who were worst affected. True, the relief efforts organized from Rotterdam and Amsterdam were more concerned with ensuring that Dutch-owned businesses were able to stagger back on to their feet; but if the native people derived benefit as a result – well, that was in part what colonialism was all about, surely? And they thus had ample reason to look kindly on their faraway benefactors, *n'est-ce pas?*

But then here in Serang, the unimaginable happened. It was while the young soldier was in the process of handing over a fistful of guilders for a package of fine-cured and locally grown tobacco with which to pack his meerschaum, that a bearded man, dressed entirely in white and armed with a curved dagger, suddenly threw himself on the soldier and began to stab him repeatedly in the back.

The astonished fusilier, gravely wounded, managed to stagger into a nearby Chinese shop. The attacker, his task completed to his satisfaction, ran away and was soon lost in the throng. The market was thrown into chaos. Nothing like this had happened before. Troops from the garrison – one of the five in Java's First Military Region, and one of the smaller – immediately flooded into the area, and promptly arrested a number of known malcontents. But none could be proven to have been the attacker: the would-be assassin seemed to have got away with it.

Then much the same thing happened again six weeks later. Another young man, also dressed ostentatiously in white robes, somehow managed to infiltrate the garrison headquarters itself, and when he was challenged brandished a long knife and slightly wounded a locally raised sentry named Umar Djaman. The attacker was this time captured and interrogated: military investigators, bewildered by the man's confusing answers to their questions, suggested in their report that the motive for his assault was an inexplicable case of 'extreme religious zeal'.

To the local military commander the attacks were unprecedented, and sinister. True, there had only been two of them, and they might well have been perpetrated by the same deranged man (though the assailant held in custody in November refused to confirm that he had also carried out the October incident). But two attacks or not, it seemed to the puzzled soldiery, and to those already aware of the sullen mood, that there had been a mysterious outbreak of a weirdly fanatical anger, and that it was for some reason directed specifically against the Dutch masters. It would be prudent, the soldiers suggested to their political superiors, that the authorities from henceforth be permanently on their guard.

They were right to be careful. The events in Serang that autumn turned out to be the beginning of a long and exceptionally violent period in western Java – a period that culminated in a memorably dangerous and politically ominous rebellion that erupted five years later, in 1888. The Banten Peasants' Revolt, as the episode is now generally known, is thought by many today to be a turning point in the region's colonial history – one of the milestones on the road leading to the eventual expulsion of the Europeans in 1949, and the creation of modern independent Indonesia. There had been many small rebellions in Java over the years; but what happened in Banten had a significance that transcended many of the other outbreaks of violence and hostility.

For what took place among the population of the north-western tip of Java between 1883 and 1888 was not, however, of political significance alone. The time also had great religious significance, since it marked a period when Islam had become fully entwined with the local political developments of the day and – so many scholars now accept – had also begun actually to dictate at least some of the major political developments of the period. It was not the first time, of course. In India, the Mughal rulers had become amply caught up in the politics of the subcontinent; and in Spain, ever since the Arab governor of Tangier had invaded via Gibraltar in AD 711, Arabs were to run large tracts of the peninsula for much of the next four centuries. Islam had wielded enormous power in southern Europe too.

In the East Indies, matters proceeded rather differently. A close look at these five years, particularly among the unusually pious people of Banten, shows clearly the beginning of militant and anti-Western Islamic movements – movements spawned in Java, but that have since become an important feature of the *realpolitik* of the modern world. An examination of the events that began with this pair of attacks on the colonial military in the autumn of 1883 suggests that the driving force behind most of the subsequent violence in west Java – prefigured by the bearded men in white, acting out of their 'extreme religious zeal' – was without a doubt fundamentalist, militant, anti-colonial, anti-infidel Islam.

Many reasons have been put forward to account for the late nineteenth century's upsurge in anti-Dutch feeling in the region – and for the parallel upsurge in Islamic zealotry in the East Indies. Poverty, alleged colonial tyranny, corruption, the unbearable heaviness of the imperial yoke – all of these factors, here in the Indies as in a score of other territories similarly burdened by the authority of outsiders – bore down on the local people and, as their education and awareness of the world increased, began to make them restless. Sporadic revolts, irritatingly persistent outbreaks in other regions of Dutch East India – in Aceh and Macassar and the Moluccas particularly – all appear to have been driven by what historians would later accept was a growing mood of restlessness – just as anti-colonial movements were developing at much the same time in India* and Malaya, and elsewhere.

In Java and Sumatra, however, there was one additional factor that seemed to have played a role in fomenting a mood of general popular unease – and that, surprisingly, was the devastating eruption of the huge volcano. The geological processes that destroyed Krakatoa, in other words, appear to have played no small part in creating the political mood of the moment. That the volcano and the economic and social dislocation it caused had an effect of some sort seems now undeniable; but whether its impact was limited and peripheral, or whether it can be linked to the development of movements that in turn led to the eventual seeing-off of the Dutch, is a matter of some debate.

The immense geophysical turbulence of the East Indies – with twenty-one active volcanoes and ten active solfataras on the island of Java alone – has long played an important part in mystical belief. Each volcano has a god – Krakatoa's being the widely feared Orang Alijeh – and he readily displays his anger with earthly conditions by spewing forth fire and gas and lava. But more: the Javanese in particular take a global view of their

---

* The Indian Mutiny – or the First War of Indian Independence, as it is called retrospectively in the subcontinent – took place in 1857 and, though eventually quelled, was a sure indication that the writing was on the wall for the British in India, as well, in time, as for the rule of foreign settlers elsewhere around the world.

vulcanicity, believing that their island is where the earth and heaven have been arranged closest to one another, and where transmissions between one sphere and the other are more common and more intimate than anywhere else on the planet.

So, on Java, volcanic eruptions are much more than simple expressions of dismay by distempered deities. They are astral messages sent directly down to the earth, and of an importance that would be ignored only at man's peril. Given such a system of beliefs, it might perhaps not be wholly unreasonable to suppose that Krakatoa's almighty act of self-immolation in August 1883 was seen locally as possessing the most profound of inner meanings.

So did the eruption somehow act as a political catalyst? Did it, for reasons rooted deep in this Javanese mysticism, drive a wedge between the terrified and dispossessed people and the paternalistic Dutch authorities? Did it then nudge them towards the comforting stability of Islam? And did Islam's subsequent defiant stance against colonialism then somehow offer such succour and comfort to those who were dispossessed and terrified that they wholeheartedly accepted the invitation to follow its precepts and demands, however extreme they might be?

And still further: did Islam come to act as a banner under which these people might turn against the Dutchmen whom they could now, all of a sudden and with the clarity of a new perspective, see not as their benevolent leaders and well-intentioned mentors but, as so many imperial agents are eventually viewed, as their oppressors? And if Krakatoa played a part in this chain of events, then can the eruption of Krakatoa come to be seen in a sense as an unwitting, readily adopted *political* event in and of itself – an event with effects that would resonate in the East Indies for many years to come?

At the time of the eruption, the Dutch in the East Indies were showing signs of momentarily losing their grip. The imperial purpose, quite coincidentally, seemed to be faltering. The old self-confidence of the Hollanders had taken a beating, and a mood of reform and change was in the air.

The cause of their discomfiture, though they might be loath to admit it, had been the publication in Amsterdam twenty years earlier of the book that had sent a shudder through the conscience of an entire Dutch people, and forced them to wonder just why they were running, in so questionable a way, a colony so far from home. The short novel that had had this extraordinary effect, Netherlands-wide, was written by a man who briefly hid behind the pseudonym Multatuli, and it was called *Max Havelaar.*

The author was in fact a young colonial official named Eduard Douwes Dekker (Multatuli, a somewhat self-pitying by-name, is Javanese for 'I have endured much'). In 1855, as the protégé of the governor-general of the day, he was appointed Assistant Resident of a small west Javan regency called Lebak, which is coincidentally not far from the garrison town of Serang. He arrived there under the impression that he was on a secret mission to correct a slew of injustices that he knew had been visited on the local people – but over the three months he remained in the post he managed, by a relentless campaign of whistle-blowing, to ruffle the feathers of the entire Dutch administration. After uncovering tales not just of mismanagement and inadvertent cruelty, but of murder and corruption on a far greater scale than he had imagined, he resigned, returned to Holland and eventually wrote the book that was to become one of the great landmarks of recent Dutch literature.

It was published in 1860, to the shock, astonishment and dismay of an entire country, which learned for the first time the details of the manner in which their officials were running their most distant and wealthiest possession. The book was a savage indictment of the colonial attitudes of the Dutch – and in particular of that astonishingly exploitative Dutch invention known as the *Kultuurstelsel,* the Cultivation System, which was introduced in 1830 and which compelled all villages to set aside one fifth of

their crops for the government in order to pay the cripplingly
high land taxes. All villagers were held collectively responsible
for the tax payment, and to ensure that responsibility was met
no one could travel beyond his or her village without official
permission – which was seldom given.

The system made the Dutch rulers fabulously rich; but upon
its exposure in *Max Havelaar* one critic wrote that he had now
seen demonstrated 'that almost nothing of the great revenues
from the island was devoted to the education or benefit of the
natives; that no mission or evangelical work was undertaken, or
even allowed, by this foremost Protestant people of Europe; and
that next to nothing in the way of public works or permanent
improvements resulted to the advantage of those who toiled for
the alien, absentee landlord, the country being drained of its
wealth for the benefits of a distant monarch'.

The Dutch – government and planter alike, for *Max Havelaar*
focused much of its attention on corruption within the coffee
plantations – were condemned as 'synonyms for all of rapacity,
tyranny, extortion and cruelty'. Dekker cheekily dedicated his
book to King Willem III – 'as Emperor of the glorious realm . . .
that coils yonder round the Equator like a girdle of emerald, and
where millions of subjects are being maltreated and exploited in
your name'. For doing so, and for daring to write so intemperate
an exposé and to lay it before a smug, insouciant Dutch public,
he was vilified, attacked and forced into the same kind of exile (he
died in Germany) that was suffered by the similarly evangelizing
Dutchman, Vincent van Gogh.

But reform of the kind that Dekker was demanding did eventually come about. *Max Havelaar* was debated in the Dutch parliament. The iniquities of the *Kultuurstelsel*, so vividly described in
the novel, were slowly recognized, and through the years following the sensation it was gradually abolished.* Pepper was freed

* A mere coincidence, the government insisted.

MAX HAVELAAR,

of de

KOFFIJ-VEILINGEN

der

NEDERLANDSCHE HANDEL-MAATSCHAPPIJ,

door

MULTATULI

EERSTE DEEL

AMSTERDAM,
J. DE RUYTER.
1860.

The title page of *Max Havelaar*, published in 1860.

from its strictures in 1862, two years after the book's publication; clove and nutmeg were taken off the list in 1863, tea, cinnamon, cochineal and indigo in 1865, tobacco in 1866. And eventually a wholly new approach to the governance of the colony took root. By the end of the century the East Indies were ruled under the principles of a brand-new and so-called Ethical Policy. The Dutch now started to take sedulous care of their subject peoples. Under the new scheme they employed officials not simply to repress and squeeze profits from the territory, as in the past, but to take charge of public health, to improve education and to offer agricultural help, the better to advance the condition of the people.

This reform – too little, too late, and not enough to still the nationalist mood – was perhaps Eduard Dekker's greatest legacy. But it was not to be in place until the beginning of the twentieth

century. At the time of the Krakatoa eruption – and at the time
of the events that led to the Banten rebellion – most of the old
colonial attitudes and most of the old colonial establishment still
held sway. Matters were beginning to change and to improve;
but they had not yet fully done so, and the unreformed state of
the colony left ample room for those who were determined to
agitate against the Dutch and their unrequested mastery to make
such mayhem as they could. Among those most eager to lead the
agitation, and to make the most mayhem, especially in Banten
and the ultra-religious west of Java, were the more conservatively
minded Muslims.

One hundred and seventy million Indonesians are currently
members, notionally or devotedly, of the Islamic faith. It is the
most populous Muslim country in the world, and the greatest of
all success stories – if numbers are the best indicator of success –
in fourteen centuries of Islamic proselytizing. All of its people are
either converts or descendants of converts: it is easy to forget
that the world's greatest Muslim populations – in Iran, Malaysia,
India, Pakistan, Bangladesh and Indonesia – all belong to a
faith that is quintessentially and inescapably Arab. Indonesia was
converted by Arabs, and it looks to Arabia and Arabians still for
spiritual guidance and direction.

Islam, it should not be forgotten, is at its heart an imperial
religion, and Arabism is perhaps the greatest of all contemporary
imperial movements – one of the many reasons for its current
collision with the West, which of course has its own competing,
profit-driven imperial agenda. The collisions between Arab-
inspired Islam and its agents, and the money-driven, trade-
driven West and hers, have been many and various: those that
occurred in the East Indies in the latter part of the nineteenth
century are now, when seen from today's perspective, classics of
the kind.

Islam first came to the East Indies in the thirteenth century, and ironically (considering the present schism between East and West, between spirituality and materialism, between God and Mammon) it came with Arab traders who were in search of business there. There is a grave of a sultan in north Sumatra that dates from 1211. There is another, at Gresik in east Java, which sports designs indicating that it was carved by masons from India in 1419. A late-fifteenth-century mosque in Demak, on the north coast of Java about 300 miles east of Batavia, was clearly the result of architectural compromises between Javanese and Arab builders. It had a holiness to it that the local mullahs regarded as both profound and ineffable, and they declared that to visit it seven times – though there is no spiritual explanation for the number – had the spiritual worth of the single haj pilgrimage to Mecca.

In Banten itself Islam became properly established at the beginning of the sixteenth century, a little later than in much of the rest of Java, and considerably later than in north Sumatra. It caught hold immediately, spread with extraordinary speed, and before long became a model to which Arabs and hajis alike could point with pride. Among the Bantenese and their coastal compatriots the Sundanese, the religion achieved a degree of penetration that was almost unrivalled in the archipelago. The west Javanese soon had a reputation for being more assiduous, more spiritual and more fundamentalist than almost any others. It was difficult for a traveller to pass between Batavia and the coast without seeing scores of mosques, and without hearing the five-times-daily cry of the muezzin, calling the willing faithful, here in their millions, to prayer.

Yet, it is important to remember that East Indian Islam was always of a much milder stripe than that practised in the Middle East and Africa. The lingering influence of Hinduism, in particular, led to a significant local dilution of Islam's rigours. Regional superstitions, pockets of animist belief and a whole host of religious oddities washed over the mullahs' teachings – with the result that the Islam that developed in Java, especially, turned out to be highly syncretic, a maze of compromises that drew influences not merely from Mecca but from a patchwork of other beliefs as well.

In spite of this rather off-centre aspect of Javanese Islam, a central feature of life on the island, and in particular of the lives of most Banten Muslims, remained the pilgrimage to Mecca. Although all good Muslims everywhere were required to take part in the haj, figures compiled by the Dutch government suggest that more Bantenese and Sundanese went to perform the obligations of orthodoxy than any other group in Java. And the figures were all the while rising steadily: in 1850 just 1,600 undertook the haj; by 1870 it was 2,600; and in the 1880s an average of 4,600 took off on boats to Arabia.*

The Dutch authorities were understandably wary of the practice, and they could have used the harsher regulations of the Cultivation System – to curb the travel of suspect individuals, for instance – to prevent it. But they soon realized that to forbid a custom of pilgrimage that was centuries old would have been fatally imprudent: all they could do was to try to make sure the pilgrims were persuaded to keep their potentially corrosive sojourn in Arabia as short as possible, and to monitor the behaviour of them all just as soon as they came home.

What bothered the Dutch was that the longer the pilgrims stayed away, the more 'Arabized' they were on return, the more they held the Dutch infidels in contempt, the more they tended to take part in violent acts against the colonial power. 'Mecca was nothing but a hotbed of religious fanaticism,' wrote Snouck

---

* Three times during the 1880s there was what was called a *Haj Akbar*, a 'Great Haj', when the ceremonies on Mecca's Plain of Arafat happened to take place on a Friday. Such a haj occurred in 1880: no fewer than 9,544 Javan and Sumatran pilgrims took part that year, with Banten supplying by far the greatest proportion.

Hurgronje, the leading Dutch scholar on Islamic matters of the time, 'where people were inculcated with hostile feelings against Christian overlords in their homeland.'

(The history of militant Islam is long and extremely complex, and well beyond the scope of this chapter's account of the political effects of Krakatoa's eruption. Yet it is perhaps worth mentioning that the rise in extreme anti-Western Islamic feeling in some corners of the world – like the Dutch East Indies – came about when it did and as it did because elsewhere in the Muslim world, in the late nineteenth century, Islam was coming under an increasing threat from Western imperialism. In North Africa and the Middle East, for example, European powers – the French and the British most notably – were seizing territory or assuming influence on all sides, to the dismay of the mullahs and the mosque.

The mullahs in Mecca, not unreasonably, saw those pilgrims who were coming from the East – from lands that were already under the unwelcome control of Dutch infidels themselves – as having a use. They could perhaps be messengers, men who could return to their homes to spread the Word, try to reassert Islamic purity and authority, and somehow eventually – as their supreme goal – wrest the archipelago from the menace of the unbelievers' control. The fact that the Krakatoa tragedy took place just when these developments were beginning to unfold is one of those historical coincidences too attractive to ignore.)

It is usually the case with the upsurge of any political or religious movement that one figure, a charismatic leader, or a demagogue, or both, becomes the identifiable personality of the movement. Such was very much the case in west Java, with the steady rise to prominence of a Java-born mystic named Haji Abdul Karim. Abdul Karim, whose teachings played no small role in the Banten rebellion, was from the middle of the 1870s the leader of a powerful local Sufi movement, which he and a corps of acolytes managed from his headquarters in Banten town.

Abdul Karim had started his Islamic education early. He had been to Mecca when he was a mere child; by his teenage years he spoke and read Arabic fluently, he had a scholarly knowledge of Islamic theology. He returned to his birthplace in his late twenties, and, as his mentor back in Mecca suggested, set himself up as a seer and messenger of Allah – a role that endeared him mightily to the Javanese masses. He had been in trouble with the Dutch authorities for violating passport regulations, and so was already regarded as a scourge of the infidels, a thorn in the imperial flank.

By the late 1870s his home had become a place of pilgrimage: tens of thousands of fanatic Bantenese and Sundanese would come each day for a laying-on of hands, or a few words from this remarkable man. He was showered with alms. The Dutch Resident – suspicious no doubt, but well aware of the power of the man – paid an official visit. At first the message that this *wali Allah* offered to his growing army of followers was simply one of the need for piety, orthodoxy and asceticism.

But as the number of his disciples grew, so his message dramatically changed – though whether it did so at the behest of Mecca or on Abdul Karim's own initiative is not clear. His revised version was considerably more alarmist, and for the ruling Dutch it was deeply ominous. For Abdul Karim began to predict what other devout Islamic seers were busily preaching, much to the worry of authorities in other regions of the world* – that the Mahdi, the messianic figure who would come to save the world from godlessness in its last days, was shortly to appear.

And in this pronouncement appears at last the key, the single link of chain that connects two apparently unconnectable features: on the one hand a volcanic eruption and on the other a movement

---

* Most notably in the Sudan, where between 1880 and 1885 a number of insurrectionary leaders described themselves as Mahdis, and caused enormous political and social unrest.

A Javanese imam who had performed the same pilgrimage to Mecca as the
rebel leader Haji Abdul Karim.

for political change. The prediction made by this charismatic
Islamic mystic and ardently accepted by tens of thousands of his
followers, *that the Mahdi was about to come,* turns out to be intimately connected to the eruption of 1883. And it is so connected
because the version of Islamic teaching that deals with the Mahdi
and his Holy War against the infidel holds that the arrival of the
Mahdi is always accompanied by a series of definite signs. *There
would be diseases of cattle. There would be floods. There would be
blood-coloured rain. And volcanoes would erupt, and people would die.*
　And it so happened that each and every one of these predictions
had occurred in Banten *in precisely the manner that Haji Abdul
Karim had forecast.* Cattle were dying on all sides because of an
uncontrollable outbreak of murrain, the foulest of all bovine

plagues. The west Javan coastal villages from Merak south to Labuan had been devastated by tsunamis. The rain was still tinted brown with the ash that swirled ceaselessly in the skies over Java. The island of Krakatoa had blown herself to pieces. And 36,000 people had died in the tidal waves from the ash flows and the gas flows that had resulted.

What clearer signs could any devout believer possibly demand as an indication that the Day of Judgement was at hand, the Mahdi was on the way and the Holy War against the infidel was about to begin? Small wonder, some might say, that two of the foot-soldiers in the coming war, dressed in martyrs' white, pressed their attack against the unbelievers, just weeks after the eruption was done. The fact that Abdul Karim had himself long since returned to Mecca* to assume a senior post in the Sufi hierarchy there made no difference: his teachings had been heard, his disciplines were in place, and a network of his so-called *tarekat*, the brotherhood he had established to carry on his work, was functioning like a well-oiled piece of machinery.

One of those who would be bold enough to link the two events, to put Krakatoa at the head of a long chain of happenings that culminated in the 1888 rebellion, was by chance one of the eruption's eyewitnesses. He was called R. A. van Sandick. A technical-school teacher from Deventer in central Holland, he had been hired by the colonial government for his knowledge of hydraulics. He just happened to be aboard the official vessel the *Gouverneur-Generaal Loudon* when Krakatoa exploded.

He watched with horror as the events unfolded; he plunged promptly into the relief effort, learning as he did so as much as he could about the social conditions of west Java, and how they had been changed by the tragedy. In 1892 he wrote a short, seven-chaptered book, *Leed en Lief in Banten* (*Sorrow and Love in*

---

* He left in 1876, given the kind of send-off one might expect for a pope or a saint.

Banten), which was the first to offer details of Abdul Karim's predictions. The following translation may be a little shaky, but the message in the relevant chapter is abundantly clear:

The mullahs and teachers of religion in the *pesantren,** who were stirring up the people in Banten, took the opportunity given by the enormous and deep-felt impression left by the Krakatoa eruption, to expand their influence. Was it not, they said, the revenge of Allah, not only against the unbelieving dogs, but also against those Bantenese people who were serving these *kafirs,* these infidels? There was no doubt: the disaster of Krakatoa was a sign of God, the great omen of which the holy Abdul Karim had spoken. Had he not predicted heavy earthquakes, and the end of the world? And see, the sun was darkened for hours, and now after the eruption the sun shone as a red or sometimes as a grey or blue ball on a grey firmament. Was this not strange, these nameless colours shining these days at twilight?

Did not God create the tidal waves that rose 30 metres above normal sea-level? And did he not speak in a thunder, as a result of which the whole of Banten shook in deepest darkness? And, ask the fishermen of the Sunda Strait – has not the bottom of the sea been raised by a God? Has not three-quarters of the island of Krakatoa disappeared? Are you blind to all these deeds brought about by God? Be humble for the Almighty! Pay for your sins! Can you still doubt, said the mullahs, now that you know that Abdul Karim has predicted all this?

A somewhat more sinister development was the discovery that autumn of a number of documents and letters, written in Arabic,

---

* The *pesantren* were Islamic boarding-schools or seminaries that still exist in large numbers across modern Indonesia. They exerted a powerful influence on the attempt to spread Muslim orthodoxy and dogma in the nineteenth-century East Indies, and have considerable social force still. That Indonesian Islam is so mild remains irksome to the *pesantren* leaders: their eventual hope is to bring the stray sheep of Java and Sumatra fully back into the Muslim fold.

which were circulating in the towns of Banten. The Dutch Colonial Police who managed to intercept specimens said immediately that they were attempts by foreigners to foment trouble in the wake of the eruption. And though most of the letters in fact seem to deal with the immense social problems caused not by Krakatoa but by the cattle-plague, suggesting it had been the work of a wrathful Allah demonstrating his displeasure with the Dutch infidels and their local stooges, the letters' interest today turns more on their origin than on their content.

Most of the letters appear to have come, via messengers, from Arabia itself. And though the entire peninsula was then under the rule of the Ottoman Turks, it was still the fountainhead of Islamic orthodoxy. Fundamentalism prevailed most especially on that particularly devout desert southern tract of the peninsula known as the Hadhramaut, now part of the eastern side of Yemen.

The fact that nineteenth-century Java was being whipped into a fury in part by Yemeni fundamentalists – acting directly (it is said, though not proven, that Arab mullahs were in Banten soon after the eruption), or indirectly (the letters and distributed propaganda documents), or through their proxies (of whom Abdul Karim was the most prominent of scores of Arab-educated hajis) – is oddly mimicked by similar events that appear to be taking place around the world today. The spiritual vigour behind today's Islamic militancy comes in large measure from the mosques of the Hadhramaut; and there are figures abroad today, Saudis and Yemenis both, who are every bit as defiantly anti-Western as was the East Indies' Haji Abdul Karim more than a century ago. The historical parallels are intriguing, and with implications that will keep scholars busy, no doubt, for many years.

The first two strikes on the soldiery of the Serang garrison turned out to be part of what would become a much larger plot. The planning was meticulous and took years – though the first suggestions of rebellion were made just after the eruption in 1883, the outbreak itself did not occur until five years later, July 1888. In all cases the leaders and instigators were hajis – the rebellion was Islamic-inspired, Islamic-led. Teams of forty were selected. Oaths were demanded and offered, with all the participants solemnly agreeing, in writing, to perform the killing. Fighters were chosen, schooled in the techniques of *pentjak* – an East Indies version of fencing – and heavily armed with newly made swords and lances and the viciously sharp curved daggers called *goloks*, all of them made by sympathetic metal-workers in Batavia. White robes and white rag-turbans were made and collected for the warriors. Lists of targets – all of them European, all of them *kafirs* – were selected. Rumours were circulated that a Holy War was at hand, creating frightened apprehension among the Europeans, a mood of eager anticipation among the natives in their kampongs. Come the morning of Monday, 9 July 1888, and the stage was properly and fully set.

The first attack was made at a village called Sanedja, which today is a suburb of the industrial town of Cilegon.* Long before dawn teams of partisans cut the telegraph wires, blocked the escape roads, then at first light swarmed into the compounds of the various Europeans – the Assistant Resident, the salt-sales manager, the collector, the junior controller – and hacked them and their families down wherever they were found. There was nothing pretty about the assault, and little that was noble: the first family to fall victim was that of a clerk named Dumas: while he managed at first to escape through a window, his *amah* – whom the assailants mistook for his wife – was attacked with lances. The Dumas baby was sliced to pieces in her arms, and when the servant was later found she was alive but terribly lacerated, still cradling the dead infant. Dumas himself was later discovered sheltering with a Chinese: he was dragged outside and shot.

The prison was attacked and broken open, the inmates freed.

* The site today of the enormous Krakatoa Iron & Steel Works.

The Assistant Resident, a man named Johan Hendrik Gubbels, was chased from one end of town to the other: his young daughter Elly was stoned to death, her head crushed with a boulder. Her sister Dora was hacked down and killed by men who, as the morning wore on, were increasingly frenzied, seemingly enjoying what was fast becoming an orgy of bloodletting. Gubbels himself was eventually found and stabbed to death. His body was dragged out into the open air for the rebels to see – and they howled their approval.

There were occasional acts of unexpected mercy. Mrs Dumas, for example, was found and – somewhat improbably – released after she had signed a paper saying she agreed to be converted to Islam. But otherwise the killing and sacking went on and on for hour after hour – until late in the day there arrived a full battalion of Dutch infantry and a squadron of cavalrymen. The infantrymen were armed with a new and quite terrifying weapon, just arrived from Holland: the repeating rifle. It was this weapon, above all else, that finished this fierce but, in the end, very brief rebellion.

The white-robed rebels believed, as Holy Warriors in any conflict are wont to do, that their piety would surely protect them against the Dutch bullets. But it did not. They died under the hail of Netherlands lead just as surely as would any godless infidel. And the Dutch military were quite evidently in the mood for killing that afternoon: when they opened fire with bullet after bullet, they did not intend to take prisoners. Thirty of the rebels were killed and thirteen more were wounded, out of a total of perhaps a couple of hundred. When the identities of the casualties were checked days later, almost all of them were found to be hajis, men who had waged war in the name of Allah the Merciful, as the legacy of their long-absent spiritual leader, Haji Abdul Karim.

The hajis' twenty-four victims were Hollanders and their Javan employees – *kafirs* too, in the eyes of the dagger-wielding fighters. There were civil servants, merchants, prison-warders, wives, daughters. They were regarded by the Muslims as the initial victims of what would be an eventual *perang sabil*, a Holy War, in which all trace of infidel behaviour and attitude – and people – would be rubbed out.

But, of course, no such thing happened. The rebellion had been crushed; an inquiry was staged; the Dutch slowly instituted reforms; taxation was eased; strictures on travel were relaxed; a new mood of tolerance and ethical standards took root. In the kampongs, talk of the Mahdi's coming evaporated, as did the fanatical mood for war. An accommodation – uneasy at first but more comfortable as the years progressed – was eventually reached between the competing requirements of the Muslim and the Christian faiths. The Peasants' Revolt of Banten faded in popular memory.

From today's perspective the rebellion is regarded very much as a way-station on the route to eventual Indonesian independence, the beginning of the end for this alien peculiarity of Dutch rule so very far from home. The Islam that had driven the Bantenese to fight so brutally in 1888 became, in time, more of an organizational structure for the coming revolution, and less the banner under which the revolutionaries might fight. But the Indonesia that was born in 1949 was a Muslim state, and it remains one today – with Islam in Java and Sumatra in a much more aggressive mood than it has been for a long, long time.

When the Muslims first turned aggressive, with the attacks on the soldiers in the late autumn of 1883, Krakatoa had just erupted, and the ruin and devastation that was its legacy made a wretched contribution to the miserable lives of millions of people around the Sunda Strait. Their misery was swiftly exploited – cynically, some might say – by the calculating Islamic leaders of the day. The melancholy condition of the Javanese and Sumatran peasantry was exploited by a corps of mullahs and scholars who had come back from their pilgrimages to Mecca and the Hadhramaut, eager to recruit like-minded East Indians to help wage an essential first strike against the godless Western infidels and *kafirs* who were posing such a threat to the purity of Islam.

To that degree, the eruption of Krakatoa did indeed help to ignite a political and religious movement that flared briefly and violently in Java, and that left an indelible mark on the polity of the East Indies. Had anyone been in prescient mood, the Banten rebellion might also have struck a tocsin note – a warning of similar events that could well occur very many years later.

The bombings that took so many lives on the island of Bali in the autumn of 2002, for example, seem a haunting echo of those happenings in north-western Java more than a hundred years before.

10

THE RISING OF THE SON

And then,
the most humble of plants,
a moss.

And then,
one morning,
the first sound of an insect,
so dry
you would think it
still mineral.

And then,
hope.

– Max Gérard, 1968

It would be a bold local fisherman indeed who, any time after the summer of 1883, would dare steer his craft between the cliffs and islets and shallows that form the outer shell of old Krakatoa, and drop nets into the waters directly above where the volcano had once stood.

The sea in these parts by now had a fearsome reputation. For a long while after the cataclysm the Sunda Strait was a place that terrified mariners, and those who had to pass through it did so as quickly as they might. The idea of lingering to catch fish was quite out of the question: merely to peer down into the seas and wonder what might be going on deep below would give most passers-by the shudders.

The danger of a further catastrophe remained for a long while uppermost in the minds of everyone who had survived the first. For months no one would venture near the charred ruins of the remaining islands; only those who went out on the scientific expeditions dared, and they were reckoned to be foolhardy in the extreme.

But economic necessity is a hard taskmaster; and by the time six months had passed, the fear and the apprehension dissipated, as they always do. The various Javanese gods had been placated (with flowers and sweetmeats and offerings) and their anger assuaged (in part by the attacks on the Dutch soldiery). Slowly, one by one at first, and later in companionable little fleets, the *prahus* and the smacks were out bobbing among the Krakatoa reefs again, looking for fish. This time they may have been dodging the occasional clumps of pumice and stranding on the odd unanticipated shoals, but their doughty and long-experienced captains soon took to behaving as though nothing much had ever really happened.

And such remained the case, the fishing improving, the waters placid and unremarkable and comfortingly deep, the volcanic dangers steadily receding in the public memory – until one day, after almost exactly forty-four years had passed. Then, on the evening of 29 June 1927, a group of fishermen who were hauling up their nets after a day spent innocently trawling for wrasse and sweetlips, and trolling by line for grouper and skipjack, witnessed something entirely unexpected and wholly extraordinary.

With a great roiling and rumbling sound, a clump of enormous gas bubbles suddenly broke the surface of the sea. The bubbles seemed to be all around, to be rising in strange and random combinations to port, to starboard, ahead, abaft.* It was very confusing, and very frightening. Exactly where under the sea these bubbles – which exploded in clouds of spray and ash and foul-smelling sulphurous gas – were coming from, and whether they were coming from one point or from many, was difficult to say. The panicky sailors, caught in the midst of them, seemed to think they were concentrated a point more or less above where Danan, the middle of the three former Krakatoa peaks, had once been.

As a sea-mark, a point of reference, there had long been near the centre of the caldera a curious clump of needles of light-coloured rock that mariners (and the hastily printed new navigation charts) named Bootsmans Rots – Bo'sun's Rock. These guano-stained pillars, nearly vertical sheets of andesite that are, with the peak of Rakata, the only real relics of the old Krakatoa, rise fifteen feet out of the ocean directly above the old central peak of Danan – like 'a gigantic club which Krakatoa lifts defiantly out of the sea', as one early visitor had it. Around the islets the waters, alive with scores of sharks, are 600 feet deep at least: the pillars rise from some unfathomable depths, and most fishermen still regard them today as they did back in the twenties, as a warning to *keep back*, a reminder that the volcano, if not all

---

* A concentration of escaping gas from the seabed can, in certain circumstances, create a zone of negative buoyancy, where passing ships are at risk of sinking. This happened in the 1970s when a seabed gas well in the North Sea fractured, and an inverted cone of small bubbles rose from it to form, at the surface, half a square mile that was more gas than water, and not at all buoyant. Moreover, the escaping gas was highly flammable, which nicely doubled the hazard.

fully there in person, was still there in spirit, at the very least.* And as if to underline the warning on this evening in June, the eruption of bubbles appeared to be coming almost from directly beneath the pillars, perhaps just a little to the north-west of them, and thus a little to the west of the old crater. Moving through the bubbles the fishermen felt the water quickly grow warm† – and there came a point where steam could be seen rising from where the bubbling had become most fierce. As the men paddled and sailed away as fast as they could, and as night began to fall, so they saw a diffuse red glow settle on the water, as if the bubbles were somehow mingled with fire.

Dr Verbeek, who had been the first to step on to the remains of the ruined mountain back in October 1883, and who had compiled his masterly study of the eruption two years later, would have known well what was happening. He died in 1926, but in 1885 he had written, with astonishing foresight:

. . . in any renewed activity of the volcano it is to be expected that islands will arise in the middle of the sea basin that is surrounded by Rakata Peak, Sertung and Panjang, just as the Kaimeni arose in the Santorini Group, and just as formerly the craters Danan and Perboewatan themselves formed in the sea within the ancient crater walls.

* It will be recalled that the 1883 eruption threw up a pair of low spits to the north of the ruins, which were called Steers and Calmeyer Islands. The breakers had eroded Calmeyer back down to sea-level at the time of a visit in May 1884, and Steers lingered only until the end of the same year. At the time of the renewed volcanic activity in the twenties all that remained of them was a pair of oddly shaped and navigationally inconvenient shallows.
† The crater lake in the caldera of the notoriously destructive Mount Pinatubo in the Philippines has a similar hot spot above a vent; steam hangs above the lake at this point, and up close the water hisses with bubbles and is hot to the touch. I once paddled a plastic canoe into the hot zone, and it began to melt, sagging alarmingly under my weight.

The bubbles were the first indication at the surface that a new volcano, lurking somewhere deep on the bed of this bathymetrically uncharted corner of the sea, was trying to build itself up. It came as something of a surprise, despite Verbeek's prognosis: when a survey was made in 1919 a shoe-shaped ridge was found to have developed to the north-west of Bo'sun's Rock, but there was no evidence that it was part of a developing volcano.

But swiftly, in the aftermath of the random eruptions of bubbles and clouds of steam of June 1927, a distinct line of froth and bubbles and plumes of steam started to develop in the water – such that by the end of the year scientists were able to map a quarter-mile course through the water that appeared to mirror a rent in the seabed's surface, a thousand feet below.

The tenor of the activity then changed. The bubbles became more fierce, large fountains began to play from the surface of the sea, black froth, steam, spurts of ash and bombs of pumice began to surge from between the waves. Cones of water sixty feet high shot into the air, with rays of black magmatic material, like needles of jet, rising fifty feet further above the water-cones. As the eruptions became ever stronger, so domes of water, half a mile across, rose out of the sea, and the mixture of volcanic material within them gave a curious flecked appearance, with mottled layers of black and white and grey, so very different from the vivid blue seas all around.

And then, most bizarre of all, flames started guttering on the surface of the water, and then shooting out in huge yellow jets and sheets of fire: observers had the impression that the water itself was now ablaze, or had been covered with flaming oil, as if the scene were the aftermath of some terrible maritime tragedy.

Finally, on 26 January 1928, the volume of bubbles and flame transmuted into ash and solid rock, and broke surface: a thin curve of brand-new land appeared for the first time above the sea. This new land grew, black and sickle-like, for several days, until it formed a humped and scimitar-shaped island. It looked like a

A current official depiction of what the Hydrographer of the Royal Navy
styles *Anakrakata* – the island of Anak Krakatoa, growing steadily at a
rate of five inches every week.

sand dune 500 feet long and ten feet high, with a concave steeper
side on its south-western edge and a rage of smoke and explosions
discharging from its base. A Russian geophysicist named

W. A. Petroeschevsky was on hand to see* the birth of this new piece of the world's real estate, and he gave it the name its successor still has today: *Anak Krakatoa* – the 'son of Krakatoa'.

The mortality rate for new marine volcanoes is very high, and this one son did not survive for long: after a week the relentless power of the surf wore it away, and all that was visible in mid February was a patch of muddy-coloured water, occasionally pierced by a funnel cloud of smoke, steam, ash and, every so often, small ragged pellets of hot and plastic lava. Then, some months later, a new island appeared once again. This time eruptions from two separate points created a pair of cones that rose 700 feet above the sea and were joined to one another by a slender spit of land: but then the volcanic activity died away, the waves attacked and chewed away, and this new confection, after all too brief a life, slipped back beneath the surface.

Corrosive encounters between this matched pair of seemingly equally relentless and powerful forces – the volcano and the ocean – went on for the better part of the next three years. On some occasions the process of volcanic creation won the day, and land was produced that survived for a while. Sometimes the equally awesome power of the rainy-season seas and tides and currents made maritime mincemeat of it all, and reduced it to a pile of submarine grit.

The number of explosions was prodigious: during the twenty-four hours from noon on 3 February 1928, no fewer than 11,791 separate detonations were counted; on 25 June, an even more remarkable 14,269 – ten eruptions every minute of the day and night. The second of the islands stayed where it was long enough for scientists who were in Batavia attending the Fourth Pacific Science Congress in May 1928 to arrange an excursion there and do some real-time fieldwork: they were vexed when it slid back

---

* He later built a concrete and corrugated iron bunker on Panjang Island, to the north-east, from which to view the new activity.

Anak Krakatoa – the highly eruptive 'child of Krakatoa' – shown in 1979,
nearly half a century after its explosive birth from below the sea.

beneath the sea again, destroyed by the relentless power of the waves.

Sometimes it was not just the waves that did the destroying: the newly appearing volcanoes occasionally self-destructed, blowing themselves to pieces, as happened with the third of the Anak Krakatoas in early August 1930. But gradually, and as a tacit reminder of the gigantic and unopposable forces of the subduction zone that was working away beneath it, the volcanic forces began to gain ground, and the island they were trying to create began to achieve a certain permanence.

On 11 August 1930 the submarine vents made their fourth concerted attempt to sculpt a lasting memorial on the surface. They put up a ring-shaped island that had the appearance of a large black doughnut – and it stayed put for two days. On its second day of existence a monumentally large phreatomagmatic eruption – the kind that results from the mixing of hot lava and hot gas with cold sea-water – tore upwards into the sky, reaching a height of almost a mile, and then dumped an enormous quantity of volcanic detritus back on top of the fragile wisps of island below.

Those that witnessed the explosions noticed a feature that would soon be regarded as typical of this kind of eruption – the so-called 'cock's tail' jets. The upward jets of the explosions are black with the material they carry, but they have outer edges that are rich with condensing steam, and so are starkly white. The whole phenomenon looks much like the tail of the more dramatic kind of male chicken.

And the dumping of an enormous volume of new material, all at once, seems to have done the trick. It allowed the island a degree of permanence that enabled it to stabilize and consolidate itself. Ever since then, the rate at which fresh ash and rock accumulate on the surface of the new island has managed to exceed the rate at which the island's edges are eroded away by the ceaselessly ruinous action of the sea.

The moment that Krakatoa's son was fully born it could be assured of the continued existence that it enjoys today. On the charts of the region the hydrographers of the various navies, recognizing the new status, steadily changed the colour of the island's outline from stippled blue, signifying *new, temporary and uncertain*, to the unbroken black that means *established, permanent and fixed*. It has been designated so ever since: Anak Krakatoa (or Anakrakata, as the Royal Navy's latest chart of the region now calls it) has been from August 1930 onwards as permanent a feature of the East Indies as Java and Sumatra have long been or, to be more realistic, has been as permanent as the islands of the Krakatoa complex that came before it.

It has, however, been an extraordinarily active volcano, growing rapidly and unstoppably ever since its birth. The observatory set up on Panjang Island by Petroeschevsky proved invaluable for the steady monitoring of its progress – as it grew from the twenty-foot-high weakling, half a mile long, that started life in

1930, to the 500-feet-tall peak, a mile long and half a mile wide, that it had become in 1950, to the 1,500-foot-high double-cratered monster of an island that it is today.

Its growth in size – from nothing – has been matched precisely by the growth – also from nothing – of its population of plants and animals.

For when Anak Krakatoa rose from the sea it was in all probability totally empty,* devoid of life and, in essence, quite sterile. Both its surface and its interior were, it was thought, far too hot to permit the existence of almost any kind of living thing; and the island was far too new to have any history, to possess any former biology or botany that might have the potential to generate a resurgence of life. The mountain was, to the fascination of biologists from around the world, a *tabula rasa*, ready to have the polychrome marvels of life painted upon it, layer upon layer, year upon year. It was a Garden of Eden, yet a Garden without plants, without animals and without mankind – and with a whole world of scientists waiting to see what might grow there, and what might not.

But of course what remained of old Krakatoa was a clean slate too, the island remnants most probably all burned and sterilized by the flames of 1883. These two locations – the ruined remnant of old Krakatoa, and the newborn innocent of Anak Krakatoa – have thus become sites of huge international interest, where answers are still being sought to two fascinating questions. On the ruins of old Krakatoa – *how did and how does life recover?* And on the virgin-island that was later created in the midst of those same ruins – *how did and how does life start?* What were the differences, if any, between *life returning* and *life beginning?*

---

* The question of whether *all* life was totally destroyed, and whether the remnants of Krakatoa were totally sterile, remains open. Certainly all initial science undertaken on the islands assumed that life had been wiped out. But in later years this view was challenged, and severely.

Of course these two questions could not at first be either asked or answered at the same time: biologists had forty-four years with only one site in front of them that they were able to study. In those early days there could thus be no kind of comparison. Ever since 1930 the three-island remnants of greater Krakatoa (if the scorched masses of Verlaten and Lang islands – Sertung and Panjang respectively – are to be counted, in ecological terms, as relics of the old volcano) and the brand-new single island of Anak Krakatoa have been standing there, beside one another, inviting inspection and comparison. Biologists from then onwards have been able to examine each, and try to work out if the mechanics of life-recovering-from-ruin (on the old islands) and life-starting-from-scratch (on their new neighbour) operated in the same way, in similar ways, or in altogether different fashions.

It is a study that continues today. More than a century after the creation in the Sunda Strait of what has turned out to be the extraordinarily useful biological laboratory of the new Krakatoa community, not all the answers are in, by a long chalk.

In considering the recovery of Krakatoa itself – which was all that could initially be considered – nineteenth-century scientists had one significant problem: because they could not be entirely certain what kinds of life had existed on the island before the eruption, they could not say in what direction the island was likely to attempt to recover – what state it might be under pressure to return *to*.

Clearly it had once been richly endowed: John Webber's famous sketch,* drawn when Captain Cook's expedition made its melancholy† pause there in 1780, shows palms and ferns in gloriously

---

* Less famed for its artistic quality than for the fact that it is the only known drawing depicting Krakatoa's pre-eruption botany.
† The expedition was in cheerless mood ever since Cook himself had been killed, in Hawaii, some months before.

feral abundance. Present-day botanists have pored over the picture to try to ascertain the various species Webber depicted: there is a type of grass that returned to the island in 1920, a palm-tree called *Licuala spinosa* that came back in 1982, and a fern that was first seen again in 1987.

Following the *Resolution*'s sojourn, there had been some cultivation on the northern flank of the island, with a scattering of people (once even a small prison), and with goats, a vegetable garden and trees grown for firewood. The very few scientists who had landed on Krakatoa during the seventeenth, eighteenth and early nineteenth centuries had collected specimens of grasses, pepper plants, orchids and mahogany trees, as well as an unusual kind of parasitic mistletoe. One Dutch biologist went there looking for snails and found five types.

But no one had ever tried to produce a definitive systematic list of the entire populations that existed before the eruption: all that could be said with certainty was that Krakatoa had been covered with a snail-rich, orchid-rich, pepper-infested and grass-floored tropical rain forest, more or less similar to that found in today's Sumatra.

Despite this irksome lack of knowledge about what had gone before, the biologists from around the world who headed off in the direction of Sunda Strait knew that what awaited them in the aftermath of the eruption could well be fascinating. It would, one of those heading to the island wrote, 'be very interesting to follow step-by-step the progress of the development of new life on this land now dead but which, in a few years, thanks to the intense heat of the sun and the abundance of equatorial rains, will surely have been recovered in its green mantle'.

The scientists fanned out with dispatch – and with care. Just like investigators who take elaborate precautions not to contaminate the scene of a disaster or a crime, so most of the biologists who came to Krakatoa did their best not to sully, with such usual contaminants as bacteria or seeds or rats or measles, the rare post-eruptive purity of the islands. It was a purity that remained untouched for some considerable while.

Rogier Verbeek was the first on to the island, in October, a scant six weeks after the eruption. And he was too early: when he first clambered on to the dusty shore, at a time when the islands' floors were still almost too hot to touch and mud flows were still pouring from the lava cliffs, he could see no living thing, nor any evidence that anything alive might be lurking near by. From a personal point of view it was a shame: given his heroic dedication to the story of the eruption, it might have seemed appropriate for him to be the first to find clear evidence of new life.

In fact it was a Belgian biologist named Edmond Cotteau who spotted the first stirrings, when he visited with a French government-sponsored expedition six months later, in May 1884. The leader of the expedition had reported finding much the same lifeless devastation as seen by Verbeek: 'the magnificent vegetation which had been so often admired there remains nothing but a chaos of enormous trunks, whitened and desiccated, among the surrounding desolation'. It was dangerous too: Rakata's main cliff was eroding fast, and rocks were rolling down its sides in a ceaseless tumble, making an unending noise 'like the rattling of distant musketry'.

It took the men a frustratingly long time to find a sheltered beach out of range of the fusillades of bouncing boulders. But then Cotteau, who had walked southward from the eventual first landing site on the north-west corner of Rakata, and who had managed to get all the way around the point to what is now called Handl's Bay, suddenly spotted something.

It was nestled between two rocks, on an otherwise arid and seemingly death-filled spit of grey and dusty land. This was the very first living thing that could with certainty be said to have appeared after the catastrophe: and it was, Cotteau wrote with measured excitement, *a microscopic spider*. He looked hard for

Nephila maculata, a ballooning spider.

another, but could find only this single specimen. Yet significantly, and with a nice symbolism, 'This strange pioneer of the renovation was busy spinning its web!' The lonely little spider was hoping, in other words, that it would eventually be lucky enough to catch a fly.

The arachnid's optimism was admirable, considering the trauma that must have otherwise unsettled him. Yet as it happened (though whether it happened for this one animal we cannot say), it was an optimism that was not at all misplaced. For within months an abundance of life – and that almost certainly included at least the modest sufficiency of flies required to satisfy a small army of spiders – began to return to the islands, in earnest.

This first spider's appearance on the island – and then the appearance of many of the life forms that subsequently resettled Rakata – in time triggered a question that has continued to vex the biological community for the many years since. Was there a chance that some of the animals and plants that first appeared did already in fact still exist on Krakatoa, as survivors? Or had life on what remained of Krakatoa been utterly extirpated – had it really been blasted and bombed and withered by the searing heat, and then buried under a hundred feet of ash?

Life returns to the Krakatoa beaches: a coconut husk, a morsel of random
flotsam, sprouts a shoot, ready to become island vegetation.

If this last was the more likely explanation, then all of the new
life that went into the repopulating of the islands must have
arrived on their shores and crags from across the intervening
stretches of sea. And if this was the case – if all the newly
established forms of life were newcomers, in other words – how,
exactly, had they come?

Had this one spider been lurking in a crevice and, though
perhaps badly singed, been sufficiently *compos mentis* to spin his
web for M. Cotteau? Or had a passing seabird, the spider lodged
in one of his claws, landed on the otherwise uninhabited island,
and left the insect behind when it flapped off into the air again?
Had the spider floated in on a coconut husk, clinging grimly to
the mesh of hairs until all the bobbing stopped? Or had it been
borne in on the air, wafted on the breezes?

Today it seems most likely that wafting was the means by
which this one baby spider reached the sea-red shoreline of
Rakata. It is well known now that some spiders and other wingless
creatures have a propensity for 'ballooning' – extending a strand
of thread of silk from their bodies and allowing the wind currents
to catch it and bear it and each of the creatures off to an unknown
destination. Ballooning spiders can travel effortlessly for scores

of miles: the sea crossing to Rakata from either Java or Sumatra would take no more than a trivial few hours. And in drifting and wafting on the breezes, this creature becomes a member of what has recently – and delightfully – been named the *aeolian plankton*, windborne kin to the microscopic drifters of the sea.*

Once properly under way the rush of life returning to the islands was impressive in both its speed and abundance. Crews of passing ships first thought they saw patches of green about a year after the eruption. In June 1886 an expedition spent four days on Rakata, and found they were right: they counted no fewer than fifteen flowering plants and shrubs – mostly beach plants, sug- gesting that these at least had arrived by sea – two mosses and eleven ferns. The visitors also found a gelatinous layer of blue-green algae in a moist film on top of the volcanic ash: this layer – wherever it might have come from – probably helped spores to germinate, it was later thought, and provided some kind of support for young and feeble rootlets.

Clearly something had helped – because by the time a new set of visitors arrived the following year there had been a positive orgy of rampant growth. There were now dense fields of grasses, so tall that a man could hide himself. The variety of grasses included Java's well-known alang-alang, which is always the first to grow (conveniently) after a forest fire and (rather less so) after a farmer has cleared a field for planting. There were tufts of wild sugar-cane poking out of the ash piles, many more ferns than the eleven that had been counted the previous year, scores of types of sand-binding creepers, hibiscus plants, self-fertilizing orchids, a very recognizable red-leaved coastal tree known as the Indian

---

* Southern Californians became briefly alarmed in the early autumn of 2002 when clouds of ballooning spiders wafted onshore from the Pacific. After the terrorist attacks of the year before, puzzling phenomena like this became suddenly invested with sinister overtones.

Almond, three varieties of fig trees and a pine-like tree that the
Australians named (for its resemblance to the lush plumage of
their native cassowary bird) the casuarina.

By 1906 the forests were thickening, the trees maturing, the
climb to the 2,000-foot summit becoming ever more difficult as
proper forests began to cloak the mountainside. Parties of visitors
now had to hack their way in, getting attacked en route by red
and black ants and carpenter bees, being surrounded by swarms
of colourful butterflies, slipping on large earthworms, taking
pleasure in seeing kingfishers, nightjars, green pigeons, wood
swallows, bulbuls and orioles. Some visitors had reported seeing
a large monitor lizard, and said that coconut palms had returned
and were lining Rakata's southern shore.

Ever since then the island has become entirely overgrown.
Casuarina trees on the coast stand well over a hundred feet tall.
The mixed forests inland are alive with birds (among which are,
prettily, the Zebra Dove, the Pied Imperial Pigeon, the Greater
Coucal, the White-bellied Fish-eagle, the Brahminy Kite, the
Orange-bellied Flower-pecker, the Pied Triller, the Mangrove
Whistler and the Magpie Robin), together with beetles and centi-
pedes, geckos, dragonflies, grasshoppers and tree-dwelling snails,
a pompilid wasp that is designed solely to hunt and kill spiders
(to the consternation of the descendants of M. Cotteau's first find)
and a large snake that was initially identified as a boa-constrictor
but that later turned out to be the species of the somewhat more
congenial reticulated python.*

And civilian mankind's arrival, which was not always as carefully choreographed as the visits of those early biologists, resulted
in the introduction of less comely animals. In 1917 a German
named Johann Handl, to take one of the stranger examples,
arrived on the southern end of Rakata with his family and

---

* More than twenty-four feet long, and a very powerful swimmer, easily
able to reach the island from the mainland.

servants, and announced that he was settling on the old volcano as a pumice collector. He built himself a small house on Rakata during (and presumably to get away from) the Great War; he planted a garden and lived comfortably in this somewhat unusual hideaway for the following four years. But it turned out that he had, presumably inadvertently, brought along with him in his boat a breeding pair of most unwelcome guests. A substantial population of *Rattus rattus*, the black rat, is now happily established on the island, and makes mayhem among the nests of most of Rakata's coastal birds.

And as the years wore on, so the numbers and types of plants and animals on the Krakatoan remnants waxed and waned, and in time created for themselves (by the way of what outsiders call *the law of the jungle*) some kind of biological equilibrium – a state that is never perfectly reached, a kind of biological *nirvana*, endlessly sought in every kind of complex community, yet rarely entirely attained.

Herr Handl's garden, once abandoned, filled quickly with ten kinds of weed. In the early 1920s a number of newly discovered large bees, velvet ants,* fungus gnats, scoliid wasps, mosquitoes, crane flies, swallowtail butterflies, fruit bats and woodpeckers were found. In fact Rakata was shown, forty years after the eruption, to be home to fully 621 species of animal. And by 1931 there were fully one hundred species of spider, according to a British spider expert called Mr Bristowe – the number and variety of everything having swelled almost exponentially.

Assuming for the moment that most of what exists today on the three islands of Rakata, Panjang and Sertung was brought in from across the sea (and was not born out of hidden survivors of the islands' original population) – how did it all arrive?

That first spider, as mentioned, very probably was of the

* These are in fact a kind of wasp.

ballooning variety. Other creatures and plants invaded by quite different means – all of them, when taken together, offering a powerful demonstration of the insistence of life to burst forth wherever it can, all showing the unquenchable nature of the fire in what the more romantic of today's biologists like to call 'the crucible of life'.

The first samples of colonizing greenery, for instance, the creeping beach plants and shrubs and the small coastal forests, came by sea, rafted across on driftwood and pumice and other debris,* or hitch-hiking in with birds that feed on fruit and then excrete the seeds. The pioneering plants found in the inland areas were almost certainly created from wind-borne or bird-borne spores or seeds – and they had to be tough enough to survive with very little water and in the full glare of the sun. (Both they and their sea-borne coastal cousins would have an additional advantage if they were hermaphroditic, and could get along in an environment somewhat wanting for sexual partners.) The presence of the thin veneer of blue-green algae helped – and it may well have been the key to getting the inland plant populations properly under way. The figs, especially, were typical of what could be brought in by this method – their presence in abundance being evidence of the way the fig tree, once settled, then manages to propagate itself.

As the spread of those first plants increased, and as new ones were introduced and started to compete and then struggle for existence and room – as the botanical ecology of the island began to change, in other words – so the zoological ecology changed too. As the coastal grassland began to give way to casuarina forests, as the woods on the mountain's upper slopes began to get darker and wetter and danker, so the populations of animals

---

* There is an early sepia photograph of a coconut's half-shell lying on an ash beach, with a stalk sprouting a leaf and rising from its upper side, a pale root feeling its way into what passes for earth (see illustration on p. 358).

altered. The butterflies and beetles and open-country birds and reptiles that were the first to colonize the island, and that positively liked its dryness, started to be replaced by forest animals, geckos and skinks, bats and birds – the hobby, the barn owl and the hawk-eagle – that favour shade and like to live in a warm world dripping with moisture.

The overall result, a century and more after the eruption, is the existence today of a group of islands that have a markedly different biological and botanical make-up from the two great landmasses that lie fifteen miles to the north (Sumatra) and the east (Java).

One example will suffice: on the Javanese and Sumatran mainland there are twenty-four species of termite. Six of these live in hardwood trees, seven live in the dead trunks of living trees, six in wet softwood and five make their nests in the soil. On Rakata Island, though, there are a total of only eight types of termite. Not one of them lives in the soil; only one likes to inhabit the dead parts of living trees, just two like softwood and by far the greatest number – five species – prefer to live out their days in hardwood trees alone. Just why this marked difference might be is still a topic for much reflection. Perhaps Rakata's soil is still too newly volcanic, or the dead wood is perhaps just not dead enough. Perhaps the environment is fresher, more raw – there must be some good reason why termites do not much care for the island that once blew itself to pieces, and why they like the islands that have gone untouched for thousands of years.

Because of unanswered questions just like these, Krakatoa has remained for many decades the focus of intense studies worldwide, a fascination for a score or more of the world's leading botanists, and the target of expeditions and field-trips by the dozen. And yet, though the mechanics of the repopulation of the islands are now reasonably well established, the principal question that we set aside earlier remains sturdily only half answered: was the first population entirely fresh and new? Did it arrive on the devastated islands by sea and by air, coming from the volcanically wounded but far from biologically sterile outside? Or was it not really new at all? Did it start off with seeds or with living animals that somehow managed to survive the original inferno?

The controversy became so established a part of botanical lore that it long had a name: *the Krakatoa Problem.* Its central question – survivors or outsiders? – dogged entire generations of scientists, and was the trigger over the years for some bitter, angry, re-criminatory and downright invective. Most of the ugly words swirled around the person of a forthright and feisty Dutchman named Cornelis Andries Backer, who held the delightfully titled post of 'Botanist with Special Responsibility for the Flora of Java' at the Buitenzorg Botanical Gardens; he first visited the islands in 1906.

Backer looked sceptically at the notion that all Krakatoan life had been destroyed, a theory agreed by almost the entire botanical establishment of the day, and proclaimed it to be near-total nonsense. He looked in particular, for example, at sweeping state-ments like that written by his superior, the Botanical Gardens' director, Melchior Treub, who had led the major post-eruption expeditions to Krakatoa and had written:

. . . at the time of the eruption the trees felled or smashed by violent outbursts must have been half-carbonized, in view of the extremely high temperatures that certainly prevailed over the whole island. After that, Krakatoa had been covered, from the summit right down to sea-level, in a layer of burning ash and pumice. This layer had a thickness varying between one and sixty meters. In those conditions it is clear that no vestige of the flora would have been able to exist after the cataclysm. The most persistent seed and the most protected rhizome must have perished . . .

Backer weighed into them with the kind of rhetoric hitherto unheard of in the genteel world of Edwardian botany. In 1929 he wrote and self-published a 300-page monograph that denounced the 'hasty' and 'careless' botanical work that had gone before, which, he insisted, resulted in the lazy, easy conclusions that all Krakatoan life had been wiped out.*

He had a venomous disregard for those who had carried out the early studies. Treub, he declared, was a prime example, a man who 'was no florist, and whose knowledge of tropical plants was very limited'. Treub's expedition to Krakatoa had been 'much too short', the data acquired 'very incomplete', and his trip so shoddy an exercise that it was not worth calling it a scientific exploration at all but rather 'a mere excursion of persons interested in the problem but not seriously devoted to trying to solve it'.

Other botanists went later to catalogue the growth of new plants. Backer accused them of 'misspending their money', acting under 'childish delusions', indulging in 'vague speculations' and making a series of expeditions that was 'a complete failure'.

The tone of his remarks set off a firestorm of criticism from scientists around the world. But the underlying points he made were all seen to be valid: the principal one being that no one, he said, had ever spent enough time or carried out a systematic enough survey to be totally sure that nothing had survived the original cataclysm. It was easy to take a look at the island and surmise that nothing could have lived through the fire; but it had since become well known that some kinds of seed not only survive fire but actually need high temperatures of this magnitude to germinate properly. Was it not in fact highly likely that such seeds had existed, and survived, on Krakatoa?

The ash layers on the upper slopes of Rakata were thin, and

* Backer had himself been at first easily and lazily convinced of the likelihood of total annihilation of all life. But then came evidence to the contrary – most notably, twenty-two years after the eruption, the discovery of a cycad, a plant that looks like a cross between a palm and a fern, which seemed much too large for something that had grown entirely from scratch. The idea that this might have been a survivor of the blasts set Backer thinking – and it ended up completely changing his mind.

would have been washed away by heavy rains. What if some roots and rhizomes that had been lurking beneath the earth's surface had lived – surely they would begin to sprout once tropic warmth and moisture and sunshine flooded their now ash-free setting?

Then again – the first expeditions had all noted (but had never properly investigated) the presence of greenery in the deeply scored valleys that lay between Rakata's summit ridges. Why had this greenery, whatever it was, never colonized the two lower islands, Sertung and Panjang? Why had these islands been given their vegetative resurrection much later than the upper slopes of Rakata? If airborne and seaborne immigrants were the source of this life, then all three islands should be gifted with new life at the same time. But they weren't. The upper slopes of Rakata got it first.

The answer to this and a number of similar unconsidered conundrums, Backer suggested, was that Rakata's colonization probably came *from within* – that surviving plants on the island's upper slopes had created the new life there; this was an upper-slope phenomenon that was entirely lacking on the islands Sertung and Panjang, which were lower in altitude.

It all made excellent sense – but it was a theory that was now, thanks to the sloppy fieldwork and hastily written conclusions of the first years after the eruption, quite impossible to prove. And that was the shame of it: no one could henceforth *ever* be sure what had happened on Krakatoa's relic islets. Bad science, in short, had left mankind puzzled, a raft of questions unanswered, and the Krakatoa Problem essentially unsolved and, very likely, for ever insoluble.*

*

* Although modern ecologists are still fascinated by and so still debate the question, a consensus appears lately to have emerged: that while perhaps some species *did* survive the cataclysm, rendering the Krakatoa relics less than totally sterile, there probably was not enough relic life to 'mess up' nature's experiment – conducted in full view of a fascinated world – in what was effectively true primary colonization and then the steady succession of the plants and animals that did that colonizing.

The same was not the case, however, over on Anak Krakatoa. For this was an island that was wholly new, and one whose newness precluded any possibility of there being survivors at all. Survivors *of what*, one might well ask.* And science was not about to make the same mistake that Backer accused it of making with Krakatoa. A later director of the Botanical Gardens, Karel Dammerman,† whose 1948 study of the islands became revered as the biological equal to Verbeek's famous geological study, said that in Anak Krakatoa

. . . we have an island originally entirely devoid of animal and vegetable life, with even a completely sterile soil. It is therefore of the utmost importance that the flora and fauna of this island should be constantly examined, and at regular intervals, and it is greatly to be hoped that this unique opportunity *will not be neglected, as it was in the case of Krakatoa itself. [My italics.]*

The first creatures to appear and to be noted on any of the four Anak Krakatoas (the first three islands were eroded to nothing by the waves: it was the second of these that was visited by scientists) were insects – first a very desiccated black cricket and

---

* It is perhaps not too far-fetched to suppose that one primitive life form could have survived the birth of Anak Krakatoa, and that is the kind of heat-loving bacteria that clusters around the hydrothermal deep-ocean sulphurous vents known as black smokers. These creatures, which are magnificently known as chemolithoautotrophic hyperthermophilic archaebacteria, are thought to be similar to the first life forms that were ever on this planet, which lived in the ancient seas of three and four billion years ago. None is known to have been found so far on Anak Krakatoa; and this part of the Sunda Strait remains too dangerous and unstable for the kind of submarine investigation that would be necessary to prove their existence clustered around old Krakatoa's still-active vents, if there are any.

† Dammerman's modesty and reticence are memorialized in a mollusc that he discovered, which is named *Thiara carolitaciturni* – one of the rare examples of a nomenclature honouring a *persona* rather than a person.

next a female brown ant, both of which were already known to exist on Rakata, two miles distant. But their existence was cut short by the vanishing of their home; and the third Krakatoa did not survive long enough or peacefully enough for anyone to venture out to survey it.

But once the fourth edition of the island appeared in August 1930, and once it seemed to be enjoying some permanency, the scientists came out in their droves. One of the first was William Syer Bristowe, the English arachnologist who had enumerated the wild profusion of spider species on Rakata.* He was sailed over to the ashy shores of Anak, and in short order discovered a beetle, a mosquito, some ants – and three species of spider.

Plants came next: fifteen months after the emergence of the fourth Anak Krakatoa the northern coast of the island was littered with floating tree stumps, bamboo stems, roots and decaying fruit – eighteen seeds were discovered, and of these ten had already taken root. Another visit added four more plant species to the list, all of them already well bedded-in, together with moths, fungus and a number of migratory birds, mainly sand-plovers. All seemed set fair for an explosion of new life – when the volcano at the edge of the new island unexpectedly and catastrophically erupted once more, and all life appeared to have been snuffed out.

This was to happen three more times. Not until after a spasm of truly devastating eruptions in 1953 did some kind of volcanic stability return to the troubled young island – and yet then, and very unfortunately, it turned out to be a quarter of a century more before scientists returned in any significant numbers to the region.

For some curious reason, scientists stayed away from the new island. Perhaps biologists were just too fearful of the region's unpredictable vulcanicity; or perhaps they were afraid of the

---

* Bristowe is perhaps the most famous figure in the spider world, known for calculating that the weight of insects devoured by British spiders in an average year exceeds the total weight of all British people combined.

political troubles of the Indonesia of the time; or perhaps there were more mundane reasons, such as cuts in departmental budgets or the reordering of academic priorities. Dammerman's plea of 1948, that the world keep a very close watch on the island, was widely ignored – with the result that considerably less is known today about the resettlement of the island than should be known.

Krakatoa had itself suffered from bad and lazy science at the beginning of its post-eruptive phase. Now Anak Krakatoa was suffering from twenty-five further years of insouciance and benign neglect. It was left until the 1980s for research work on both mountains to begin again in earnest. It continues to this day – with every botanist and zoologist suddenly realizing that in order to learn as much as possible about these uniquely interesting and remarkably contrasting biological situations, there is much catching up to do.

The geological make-up of the island has changed in recent years, and in the 1960s lava flows – which were hitherto unknown in the Krakatoa region – began to cascade from the crater and flow down to the sea. More than half of today's island is currently covered by congealed black lava – meaning that large areas of Anak Krakatoa previously vegetated are now barren once again. Students of island biology find this irksome, to say the least.

Ian Thornton, an Australian biologist with a long-standing fascination for Anak Krakatoa, devised a simple experiment to see how rapidly insect life flooded into one of these seemingly barren lava flows. He placed plastic containers filled with sea-water on top of the flows – and waited to see how many airborne arthropods* they might catch. In ten days he found seventy-two species, including wasps, earwigs, moths and beetles: the aeolian tide of life appears to be quite as unstoppable as King Canute once found the sea to be.

---

* The *Arthropoda* is a vast division of the animal kingdom, and includes both spiders and insects.

A thick coastal casuarina forest on Sertung island, with Anak Krakatoa
and Rakata in the background.

About 150 species of plant now inhabit the island: there are
casuarina forests on the low and soft-soiled north-eastern shore;
so-called wild sugar-cane, the aptly named *Saccharum spontaneum*,
bursts out of the hot and ashy slopes; delicate ferns are growing
in the shaded parts of some of the jagged lava cliffs.

Once the plants were there, providing seeds and fruit and shade
and moisture, and once the insect colonies that were first to be
established had grown more varied and abundant, so the birds
arrived and settled. The first to do so had to be ground-nesters
(there being in the early years an inconvenient absence of trees)
– birds like the savannah nightjar, the collared kingfisher (which
can build its nest in the sides of gullies) and the white-breasted
waterhen, which can settle in the mesh of salt-grasses at the
margin of the sea.

Then, when the casuarinas were tall enough to allow nesting,
in came the fruit-eating and insectivorous birds like the bulbul

and the crow. And as the forests thickened, some amphibians that had somehow found their way across the sea began to slink in and make their nests – monitor lizards, paradise tree snakes. And, inevitably, rats.

Next a generation of fig trees started to flourish – and fruit-eating and fig-eating pigeons and doves arrived to feed on them. They began to jostle for space and, in doing so, began to drive out some of the lesser first arrivals, among which were the ground-nesting birds whom the jungle law dictated had now probably outstayed their welcome. Raptors then took over from the doves. In time the peregrine falcon arrived, established himself as Anak Krakatoa's avian monarch and, together with the barn owls, began to feed sturdily on the rats.

Thus, steadily and slowly, the population strengthened, evolving in appearance and flavour from being just the result of casual happenstance, becoming the ever more determined and rugged collection of island species that it remains today. And yet: nature proposes, but fate disposes. All of this happy development has been interrupted again and again – in the seventies and the nineties – by the mountain blowing its top.

Today the population that has consolidated itself is distinctly different from that on the relics of old Krakatoa, as well as from that on Java or Sumatra. But the degree to which the animals and plants are actually going to be permitted to sustain themselves is far from clear: the ash and the lava that falls nearly continuously now is wreaking havoc with what could otherwise be a vastly theatrical biological experiment, laid on for the world to see. What could be grand theatre turns out, all too often, to be just a tease.

The Great Chain of Being, an idea that has been in existence since the time of Aristotle, connects every living thing into one vast and seamless hierarchy – a system in which the Almighty, with Man just below, stands at the apex. If one wishes to look at illustrations of the processes that lie at the lower end of this grand and somewhat fanciful scale, one need only look at the creation of life that can be seen on Anak Krakatoa and at the re-creation of past life that can be seen on the relics of old Krakatoa. In both places the processes are in fact remarkably similar, though varied in detail.

Both processes seem to have begun with the making of films of bacteria, which clung to the beds of volcanic ash and coated the ragged, burned ruins of once-hot rock. Matters got properly under way with, on the one hand, the arrival of fungi and simple grasses, and with, on the other, the addition of spiders and crickets and beetles. Things continued with the establishment of ferns and orchids and more general plants, a mix of botanies into which were eased the herbivorous birds and a scattering of small animals; then came the fruit and fruit-eating insects and the perching, nesting birds – and finally the larger animals with teeth and snapping jaws that would, in time, prey on all of these.

The list is seamless, the Great Chain set down for all to see. Bacteria. Plant. Insect. Fruit. Herbivore. Carnivore. It is the classic development of life – a development a little more complicated on old Krakatoa perhaps, because of what lived there before and may have survived – but in all other senses, and assuredly so on Anak Krakatoa, entirely classic.

To the outside world the eruption of 1883 may have spelled death and devastation. To the world of biology and botany, however, the subsequent energetic happenings on islands in the Sunda Strait represent nothing more or less than a freeze-frame picture of the future of life itself – a demonstration of the utterly confident way that the world, however badly it has been wounded, picks itself up, continues to unfold its magic and its marvels, and sets itself back on its endless trail of evolutionary progress yet again. The crucible of life turns out to be the most difficult of vessels to break: not even the world's most dangerous volcano could do it truly irreparable damage.

EPILOGUE
THE PLACE THE WORLD EXPLODED

The cars that sweep swiftly southwards along what passes for west Java's corniche have to be prepared for all manner of delay and interruption – lumbering bullock-carts, stalled lorries, lurching cyclists drunk on palm wine, sprawling street fairs, impromptu political demonstrations, undisciplined scatterings of chickens and goats and cattle, and on every corner of the roadway small children, children everywhere. It is frustrating driving; by the time the cars reach the outskirts of the small town of Carita, few on board will be in any mood to notice a small, undistinguished and yellowing wooden structure that is set well back from the road at the north end of town, on the brow of a low hill above a tapioca plantation.

Most probably those passing, especially if they are from afar – and Carita is these days a seaside holiday destination, so the coast road is frequently crowded with prosperous Indonesian families trying to escape the oppressive heat and crush of Jakarta – will be looking to their right, and not to where the building stands on their left. For on the right-hand side, the west, the view is quite soothingly magical – especially so at about six each evening, when the sun is setting over the distant blue hills of Sumatra.

Just as in an old Chinese watercolour, so the shades of evening

blue seem to merge in an infinite series of layers: the deep aqua-
marine of the sea in the foreground, the bold azure of the darkening twilight sky, the pale powder blue of the Sumatran mountains
behind, and in between them the scattering of islands of the
Krakatoa archipelago. Edged in pastel blues that are dark or light
according to their distance, the islands change with the shadows
that they cast upon one another, or as the smoke that is usually
rising from the peak in the centre of the group drifts and curls
above and around about them.

And yes, you find yourself saying to yourself in an almost
incredulous whisper, *this is where it all happened.* This is Krakatoa,
the place with a name now firmly annealed into the language,
welded into the world's public consciousness, a name that has
become a byword for nature's most fearsome potential for
destruction.

The steep, sharp, instantly recognizable peak on the left-hand
side of the little cluster of islands is Rakata, the dead relic, the
ruined husk of the great eruption. The low and less distinguished
islands of Panjang and Sertung hug the horizon, the wrecked
parentheses of the ancient caldera. Sometimes, in certain lights,
they can be tricky to distinguish against the pale backcloth of
Sumatra: their distances seem compressed, so that from the Java
shore they look as though they are a single uninterrupted island,
even though they are in fact two, and one is a good deal closer to
shore than the other.

And rising from the mid-point of the pair, in fact almost exactly
in the middle of the neat little archipelago, is a peak that, though
lower than Rakata, has at this distance and from this angle the
shape of a perfectly formed cone – with a plume of smoke sometimes rising slowly above it and, on the line where mountain-top
and smoke cloud meet, a sinister, beautiful, ominous-looking
orange glow of fire. This is the centrepiece of the tableau, both
in fact and in fable: this is the dangerously fast-growing
adolescent child of the cataclysm, Anak Krakatoa.

The beauty and strange menace of the scene is memorable: small wonder that passing southbound motorists are enraptured, and look steadily across the sea to their right. The yellow-painted buildings above the tapioca trees on the left hold no attraction at all, and they are generally ignored, passed by and, if glimpsed at all, instantly forgotten.

Perhaps they should not be. For the buildings are the field station of the Krakatoa Volcanic Observatory, and in one of the simply furnished rooms within the small cluster of structures there is a device – its electronics a little long in the tooth these days, but its metal casing, dials and instrumentation cleaned and oiled and cared for still – that measures as exactly as it is possible to measure what is going on beneath the earth below Krakatoa. This is the machine that will warn the region, the country and the world, one hopes, in the unlikely event that things begin to go awry.

The device, which many years ago was gifted by the Americans, is designed to alert all those in Indonesia whose task it is to watch out for signs of trouble – the civil defence agencies, the army, local hospitals, managers of food depots and blanket stores, and everyone who lives in those low-lying coastal areas that might be inundated by tides – if another catastrophic eruption is imminent.

The technology is simple enough. Some years ago a group of geologists from the Geological Survey of Indonesia and the US Geological Survey installed an array of seismic sensors on Anak Krakatoa, scattering some into clefts in the lava surface and settling others into holes drilled some few feet into the slopes of the mountain. The sensors were connected to a coder and to a radio transmitter built into a tough aluminium box. This box was then buried in a trench dug on the eastward-facing, Java-facing slope of the island, a couple of hundred feet above the sea and in line-of-sight with the Observatory that was at the same time being built north of Carita.

A solar panel on a mast above the buried box assured an uninterrupted source of power, and therefore a seamless flow of signals – such that night or day, every day of every year, what was happening seismically on this most potentially violent centre of the Krakatoa complex would be sent instantly across the Strait, to be picked up by the cluster of radio aerials that rises above the yellow-painted, rarely noticed and insignificant little Observatory.

The rules laid down by the Volcanological Survey of Indonesia require that there will always be at least one observer on duty inside the building. When I stopped by, the point-man was a thin, tired-looking and rather nervous forty-year-old named *mas* Sikin,* who lived in a nearby village. When we met he was halfway through his week-long shift, keeping the world's most notorious volcano under close invigilation – a duty for which he was paid the equivalent of fifty dollars a month, together with a substantial ration of rice.

He occupied two of the Observatory's rooms – the others were assigned to the Survey's chief, whose office was eighty miles away in Bandung and who stopped by only in the event of an emergency. In one of Sikin's pair of rooms there was just a cot and a hand-basin. In the other, under a formal portrait of the current Indo-nesian president, Megawati Sukarnoputri, on a trestle table beneath which were four large twelve-volt car batteries, was the monitoring machine itself, a black-and-silver chrome box with a metal plate identifying it as a radio-seismograph, made by a venerable American earthquake-measuring company known as Kinematics, Inc.

There is a needle, a large revolving drum and a sheet of paper.

---

* It is often the case, as here, that Indonesians have just one name. The prefix *mas* is simply an honorific, akin to 'brother', and is a way of describing and addressing one who is younger than oneself. Had Sikin been much older, he would have been deserving of the title *bapak*, or its more widely diminutive *pak*, meaning 'father'.

On this paper, which is changed every twelve hours, is a series of traces done in purple ink, recording second by second the activity across, upon and deep beneath the island. Today's trace indicated only the merest of trembles; the night before the needle had waved unsteadily for a few hours in the middle of the night; and the week before – Sikin took the trace down from a cardboard folder on a shelf above the recorder – the lines were crazed, as though someone had shaken the inked needle in a sudden fit of anger. The lines were blurred and entwined together, because the needle had been vibrating and waving back and forth both at a great frequency and with considerable amplitude: that week Anak Krakatoa had clearly undergone a spasm of some sort.

Not enough of one, however, for Sikin to have called out his superiors in Survey headquarters in Bandung. A routine eruption, of which last week's had been a classic of the kind, was nothing to get excited about: Anak Krakatoa is like a great safety-valve, blowing off steam and a good deal else besides on a regular basis, never holding itself back and distorting itself dangerously, with an enormous relieving eruption as the culminating climax. Generally speaking it is the active volcanoes that do not erupt that are the dangerous ones: inside them, energy is being stored up, little by little, until the stresses become too great and there is a catastrophe. On Anak Krakatoa there is continual release – which may look dramatic and may on occasion make for trouble and cause casualties, but which suggests that, in the short term at least, the danger is predictable and any crisis manageable. So long as the volcano is watched, current belief has it, the neighbourhood is safe.

A routine eruption is invariably visible from shore some minutes before it is detected by the seismometers and is then written on to the seismograph drum. That recent bad day's eruption – it was a Sunday afternoon, Sikin remembered, and he was standing at the Observatory door puffing on his clove-flavoured *kretek* cigarette – began with a sudden whoosh of dust and smoke that could be seen pouring from a vent just behind the obvious main summit of Anak.

He said that he watched for a moment only, counting the seconds by snapping his fingers. He walked back to the Kinematics machine and, sure enough, ten seconds after the first sight of the smoke, after ten snaps of his fingers, the needle began to move.

There was at first a great swing, several inches to one side, after which it slammed back to the other side so fiercely it might look to a stranger as though the needle would break. Then it moved back again, and again and again, the trace writing on top of itself, but with movements that were now diminishing somewhat as the drum unrolled, so that the record began to look like an arrowhead, tapering towards a point. It was a familiar pattern, remembered distantly from old newspaper pictures or images on museum walls at places that had suffered badly from seismic shocks, places like Skopje and Anchorage and Istanbul, or the volcanoes of Mount St Helens or Unzen.

Sikin was still clicking his fingers while he watched the machine's passionless unrolling – until another five seconds had passed, when he went over to the open doorway and cocked his ear. Sure enough, right on cue, there came from across the Strait a rumble, like distant thunder, or the shaking of a theatrical thunder-sheet. And then silence.

Below him, behind the tapioca plants, he could see that the masts of the *prahus* in the river had begun to swing back and forth as the craft shook at their moorings. The sea surface had the sudden look of hammered pewter – until the swell took over, the breeze ruffled away any pattern that might have been briefly imposed upon it, and everything returned to normal. Across on the mountain the smoke had lifted away from the summit, which was now quite clear; the billow of black had risen well into the sky and was being borne away southwards in the streaming winds. Otherwise the sky was cloudless.

Soon there was just a single ragged blot floating in the air, together with the traces written on the paper drum, to stand as a record of how Anak Krakatoa had once again reminded the surrounding world that it was still very much alive. And only the paper would survive. In six months' time a car would arrive to take it and all the rest away, to be stored in a damp basement in Bandung.

It is not entirely clear whether one is formally allowed to visit Krakatoa. The archipelago is a part of a national park,* is a protected treasure, can be dangerous on occasion and in theory is officially off-limits to those without government sanction. The bureaucrats safely in their offices in Jakarta fret over the scrapes that visitors might get into. People have been killed or injured on the island, hit by flying lava bombs. The Sunda Strait suffers from notoriously fickle winds and seas, is crowded with fast-moving cargo ships and has deep waters that are alive with hungry sharks. The local vessels commonly used for the crossing break down with depressing regularity: few Americans will forget the fate of the 27-year-old Californian women Rickey Berkowitz and Judy Schwartz, who, trying to cross to Krakatoa in 1985, found themselves drifting in a leaky open boat for three weeks, surviving on a diet of peanuts, rainwater and Crest toothpaste.

In Bandung I had been handed a piece of paper dripping with official permit-stamps and signatures, and told that *just this once*, an exception to the rule, I might be allowed to go to Krakatoa on my own. But in Carita it was perfectly evident that no one gave

* The Krakatoa archipelago is a detached part of the Ujung Kulon National Park, most of which includes the peninsula in Java to the south of the islands and known as Java Head. The one-horned Javan rhinoceros is plentiful in the park. One of the long-term benefits of the 1883 eruption has been the reluctance of a superstitious people to live and settle in large numbers anywhere near the volcano – a reluctance that has protected a very rare species from what would otherwise have been, in the face of population pressure, almost certain extinction.

a thought about ever getting permission, and that whether it was allowed or not, going across to Krakatoa was simply, like so much in the East, a matter of nothing more than supply and demand. If you wanted to go, then, for a price, go you most assuredly could and would.

And so, early one morning on a Carita beach that was already swarming with boys selling shells, sarongs, fried squid, coconuts and kites, and with cheerful young women offering very un-Islamic-sounding full-body massages and broad winks that promised even more delights, I found myself among groups of young men who pestered me slyly, as though in a Saharan souk, hissing theatrically *You like go Krakatau?* Consequently, within an hour or so, after I had looked critically at the small armada of boats on offer, I had selected a sleek yellow wooden *pinisi*, a fishing craft with a reliable-looking 70-horsepower Evinrude engine, had found a guide with the improbable name of Boing, and had waded out into the surf and clambered aboard.

The skipper first made a drama of unfurling his national flag and tying it with twine to the jackstaff. It turned out that just by chance, we were sailing on 17 August, which was the anniversary of Sukarno's famous proclamation of independence in 1945.* With a mischievous grin, the captain then pulled up a case of Bintang beer from the cool waters down in the bilges, tossed a couple of cans each to his two shipmates and to Boing and to me, waved a salute to something that sounded like the glories of Indonesian freedom and the likely continuation of good post-colonial living, burped, hiccuped, gunned his engine noisily, bounced his boat through the green heaps of surf and finally sped off unsteadily into the open waters of the Strait and towards the hazy western horizon.

Early on this hazy morning, it wasn't possible to see the

* The formal end of Dutch rule came four years later, just after Christmas 1949. The August date is none the less the preferred time for celebration.

archipelago from sea-level – until we had been cruising steadily for about half an hour. I spent those first minutes gazing up at a frigate bird high above us, flicking its scissor-like tails to change direction. There were dolphins too, playing under the bow; and flying fish launching themselves like small missiles, darting across the troughs between adjacent swells.

And then the skipper nudged me out of my reverie. 'Rakata!' he cried – and sure enough, rising through the haze directly ahead of us, was the perfect pyramid-shape of the last relic piece of old Krakatoa. To its right, as I squinted into the distance, I could soon make out the smaller cone of Anak Krakatoa, a puff of white smoke rising above it, and a slash of white running across the face of the mountain, a lava flow that had so far escaped weathering by the elements. The skipper indicated that it was as well that the smoke rising above the volcano was white. If it turned grey – if it were filled with debris, in other words – then it would be time to think about leaving. Fast.

Between our position now and the islands ahead were the main north- and southbound shipping lanes of the Sunda Strait, and for a half hour negotiating them seemed to occupy the skipper's mind more keenly than the colour of Krakatoa's smoke. For the lanes were very busy, and when you are in a small craft, down at sea-level, the immense speed of the onrushing cargo ships is almost impossible to calculate.

There was, for example, the northbound container vessel that, when we first saw her, was a mere speck on the port horizon. Within five minutes, however, this speck had become a massive ship whose hullside proclaimed that she belonged to COSCO, the China Overseas Shipping Company. She was bearing down on us with an awful speed. We cut our engine and let her pass us, and when she did so she must have been no more than 500 yards ahead. The nub of her bulbous bow elbowed the waves aside, setting us rocking alarmingly as we sat, hove to, and watched her immense bulk slide cinematically in front of us.

And then she was past, safely. Her enormous screw thrashed wildly in front of the huge rudder; and as she drew away to our starboard we could see her name written in Chinese, and her port of registry: Shanghai. She was on her way home, probably back from a voyage to ports in Africa and the east coast of South America. There was no indication that she ever saw us; such crew as were on the bridge were most likely standing on her own port side, gazing from their vantage point across at the volcanoes.

Once she was safely gone, we sliced and bumped across her mile-wide wake, dodged another couple of smaller southbound ships and edged in towards the lumpy, confused-looking waters of the volcanic caldera itself. The boat began to lurch alarmingly again, as though we were passing through a line of rapids. The skipper grinned. He knew how strange a phenomenon this was. The submerged lip of the old caldera, it seemed, was somehow playing havoc with the tides and currents, tripping up the streams, creating a ring of intersecting overfalls that broke all around us in ragged rings of white and green.

We edged closer, coming to within half a mile of Rakata's huge vertical cliff, which was blindingly lit by the midday sun. Seen from this distance and angle, it displayed a textbook cross-section of a wrecked volcano: before us was the dark central vertical spire of the old core, and its sheared-off surface pierced by dozens of veins of long-frozen pipes of lava, the whole cone capped high up in the sky by a ragged crown of trees.

And then we were through the broken waters and into the belly of the thing, the omphalos of the Oriental world, a place where the waters were unimaginably deep once more; and down in their depths, unimaginable things were happening. Within the caldera, Rakata was large enough to shut out some of the northbound swells and to divert the currents, and so once we were inside the submerged walls and in Rakata's lee the sea suddenly became calmer, more congenial. The boat stopped its corkscrewing and resumed a more steadily upright putter to shore.

We set a course first towards the strange tilted aggregation of guano-covered pillars called Bo'sun's Rock, around which the waves gnawed hungrily. We turned slightly to port just as we seemed ready to touch it, and left it to our starboard; then we headed to the south side of Anak Krakatoa itself. The plan was to circumnavigate the island before landing on the beach on the east side. The skipper was showing off now, and liked to hug the shore for my benefit: the island, the child of Krakatoa, now an enormous black bulk a few feet off to our right, smoked contentedly and calmly; and the smoke, we all noted, remained steadily white.

Most of the western and northern shores of the island consisted of dark-grey lava flows – and the one paler flow, newer than the rest, that I had seen from afar. They were all horrible gnarly things, mostly quite unweathered, with rocky tentacles that probed into the sea, where the waves washed around and sucked hungrily underneath them. The land above the flows was spiky and crammed with razor-sharp cliffs of frozen basalt. Once in a while I could see a single red flower, sunning itself from within a cleft; and seabirds would perch on the highest points, surveying the world around them. But otherwise the flows were lifeless and harsh, the raw front edge of the volcanic process, all solidified into hundreds of yards of dead, unyielding and ugly black rock. The crater itself was invisible from here; the smoke column, though, wafted ever upwards.

Once we were around the eastern side, however, the island took on a completely different aspect. The slope down from the now-visible summit became much less pronounced, and instead of lava there was ash and, in places closer to the beach, ashy soil. It had been transmuted into soil because, fringing the eastern and northern flanks of the island, there was now a long copse of trees – and over time (though not very much time, since the island had only been born in 1930) they had died and fallen over and decayed, their corpses mingling with the ash to produce, to judge from the gorgeous fecundity of the growth all around, a wonderfully humus-rich substrate.

From this vantage point, indeed, Anak Krakatoa looked like a perfectly normal tropical island, with no suggestion that it was one of the youngest islands in the world.* And it was towards its fringing woodlands that the skipper directed his boat. We dropped anchor fifty feet from shore and splashed through the shallows, then up on to the scalding beach. There was a path through the casuarina trees: we walked in as quickly as we could – the sand was far too hot (whether from the pitiless sun or the volcanic origins of the sand, I could not be sure) to allow any dawdling – and set up camp in a grove, where we would build a fire and take our lunch.

It looked for all the world as though we were in a tropical forest. The vegetation was thick and dripping with moisture. Butterflies swirled in the thermals. Birds called from high up in the canopy; and one of the boat's crew showed me the nest of what he said was an owl. There were the footprints of rats and geckos; the fine pumice sand was alive with ghost crabs, which skittered delicately along on tiptoe, as if keeping away from the heat; and along one patch of sand close to where we were eating

---

* In size and shape Anak Krakatoa looks much like one of its immediate successors, the island of Surtsey, off the south coast of Iceland. It was created in 1963, now has grazing animals and, perhaps in time, will have a human population too. There are even newer islands, however, all of them volcanoes: an island appeared near Iwo Jima in 1986, and the Japanese christened it Fukoto Kuokanaba; an islet near the Metis Shoal in Tonga's Vava'u Group appeared in 1995 and was named in honour of the then much favoured rugby international Jonah Lomu; and in 2000 an undersea volcano named Kavachi erupted in the Solomons – this may yet consolidate as the world's youngest island.

Aerial photographs show the uncanny similarity between Anak Krakatoa, below, and its sub-Arctic cousin Surtsey, off Iceland. Geologically and tectonically, however, the islands and the volcanoes that created them could not be more different.

there were the tracks of some much larger animal, about which the crewmen only grinned, ominously.

After eating grilled fish and rice and drinking the remains of the Bintang, Boing and I set off uphill. The crewmen had in any case fallen asleep in the shade – making us promise beforehand that we would return two hours before nightfall, or risk being run down by a freighter if we tried to cross the Sunda Strait after dark. It should in any case take no more than an hour to get to the summit: Anak Krakatoa was only 1,500 feet high.

But of course climbing a third of a mile up a high hill made only of newly fallen ash is a far from easy occupation. First, there was the simple matter of getting out of the coastal forest – a hundred feet of thick, lush vegetation through which we had to hack our way until it ended abruptly, with a patch of low grasses and a sudden blaze of brilliant sunlight as we emerged right on to the naked flank of the volcano. Not only was it unbelievably hot here – and this was the kind of heat that drills painfully up through the soles of even the best insulated shoes – but the ash that rose up steadily ahead slipped and slid, and opened up into scores of small chasms and runnels and rills, such that for every five steps upwards, I fell backwards four.

We passed the aluminium box with its radio aerial, pointing directly at the faraway and, at this time, invisible coast of Java: Sikin would be there, I fancied, watching the paper roll steadily out from the Kinematics drum with nary a vibration coming from his charge. The island was quiet this day and, judging from the column of pure white smoke that coiled up from the summit ahead, was likely to remain so for a while.

But it had evidently not been so quiet very recently. As we climbed higher, we saw hundreds of rocks on all sides that had clearly whistled down from on high after a furious eruption and crashed into the sides of the hill. Craters had formed in the ash around where the rocks had fallen, just as though bombs or artillery shells had exploded: the craters gave the surface the curious appearance of the landscape of Ypres or Passchendaele, only here it was dry, not muddy, and sloping, not flat.

Some of the lava bombs had been huge, some as large as a motorbus – and whenever we edged past one of those, with Boing laughing in the way that only Javanese can laugh, with their fatalistic attitude to all happenings good and bad, I confess that I looked up in the sky, moderately apprehensive. If Anak Krakatoa decided on a tectonic whim to hurl one of those into the sky, then gravity would ensure that life for those below would become very short and concentrated indeed.

Up we trudged; until we reached a point where the last grasses – tall clumps of the so-called wild sugar-cane, *Saccharum spontaneum* – petered out, and the landscape became nothing more than ash, bomb crater, smoke and the ever widening panorama of the sky. The skyline itself was quite near, and when after ten minutes more or so I breasted the ridge – panting, perspiring, glad it was all over – I was actually surprised at how easy it had all been.

I stood tall on top of a truck-sized lava bomb, and took in the immense view. I gazed down at our island, at the curved cusp of the grove of trees by the beach below, at the black-sand shore and at our yellow *pinisi*, tiny and fragile, swinging on her anchor. I gazed down at the lava flows, great black frozen rivers of coiled and frozen magma that had not so long ago been pouring down into the boiling ocean. I looked over at the jagged outcrop of Bo'sun's Rock, welling out of its private froth of surf, and over to the low island of Panjang to the east, and the immense half-conical wall of Rakata directly ahead.

And then I tried to look across at where the archipelago's other island of Sertung should lie – only at this point I was suddenly confronted by an immense wall of sloping grey ash that rose high, high above me. What foolishness! I suddenly realized. What a mistake to have made! The relief I might have briefly felt at supposedly reaching the summit of Krakatoa's child vanished in an instant: it turned out that I was not even halfway up the mountain. Where I stood was no more than a false crater, the mere relict rim of a much earlier eruption. Anak Krakatoa's widely feared active crater, the summit of the volcano and the site from behind which the eruptive smoke was even now billowing, was yet another long, long slog away.

There was nothing for it. Boing and I manfully slogged away upwards once more, as we were duty bound to do, slipping and sliding ourselves painfully up and up, in the fierce heat and dazzling sunshine, ever wary of what mischief the mountain might be planning. The sky widened further and further; the sea below became a dazzling, gleaming sheet of steel; the temperature rose in an almost terrifying way that seemed to have no relation to the tropical sun. After thirty wearying minutes more, we stepped over a rock edged with a crust of yellow-stained sulphur crystals, and across the teeth of a ridge – below, spread ahead like some infernal dish of hell, was the crater itself.

The white smoke had by now enveloped us: it was hot water vapour, mixed with the curiously attractive smell of sulphur dioxide and dust. The surface I could see ahead was a fragile-looking crust, newly baked and broken in places, with plopping gobbets of hot mud spurting into the air and hissing, machine-like jets of gas roaring and whistling up into the cloud. From afar, the volcano had appeared quiet; but from up here, on the very lip of its mouth, at the working end of the heir-apparent to the greatest volcano the modern world has experienced, it seemed anything but.

The mechanics of the making of the world were all in evidence, just a few feet ahead of where I stood. All this talk of subduction zones, of the collisions between two of the world's immense tectonic plates, of the unfolding of the ring of fire – it all came down to this. Here, in this hot, crystalline, yellow-grey, wheezing, whistling, mud-boiling cauldron, was where the consequences of subduction were being played out.

The power of the process was all too apparent here also, in the strangely compelling symphony of grindings and snortings and sulphurous snarlings, in all the rushings of yellow and green gases, and in the snapping and straining of the rocks and crystals and crusts. This was a place that was filled with nameless and unfathomable activities, and it had a terrible, fascinating menace. It was a place that was all too evidently primed, ready at an instant to explode again – and, in exploding, to do goodness knows how much harm to the goodness knows how many souls waiting unwittingly down below.

After a while the sulphur began to catch in my throat, and Boing started to become anxious that we might in any case be staying too long. And so we trudged downhill for the last time, soon glissading through clouds of ash, passing at a run the Observatory radio transmitter and the clumps of sugar-cane, before meeting the fringe of the woods and diving thankfully through the final few hundred feet into the comparative cool of the shade of the seaside casuarina trees.

The crew had gone out to ready their boat for the journey back to Java, and Boing swam over to talk to them. I was peckish, and pulled out from my haversack a squashed chicken sandwich, made for me in the hotel before we left. I sat on the trunk of a fallen tree in the quiet, reflecting on the afternoon, and on the awesome, epicentral, deeply symbolic place above that I had been fortunate enough to see.

And then I heard a rustling, crackling sound in the woods, a strange unearthly noise that made the hairs rise suddenly all along the nape of my neck.

I stopped eating, and looked around. There was no other sound – not even from the boatmen, who were by now probably well out of earshot. The rustling continued, and it got louder – until, suddenly breaking out of the cover of the jungle, emerged the head and then the body of a six-foot long lizard, waddling slowly and steadily towards me, its jaws wide open.

Varanus salvator, the five-banded swimming monitor lizard, now an all too common inhabitant of the ruined islands.

It was a horrible, strange, weirdly shaped creature – a long fat brown body with what looked like a thick seam of flesh running the length of its midsection. As it walked, its tail thrashed from side to side, and from its small flat-topped head came a tongue, a foot or more long, that flickered in and out menacingly.

The beast as a whole did look menacing, and very dangerous indeed. Deep down I knew that it was probably quite harmless, and that it was in all likelihood simply a specimen of the great five-banded monitor, the wonderful swimming lizard known to the Javanese as the *biawak* and to science as *Varanus salvator*. But that deeper realization came only later in the day; at the precise moment on that August afternoon when it emerged from the trees, while I was sitting alone in the jungle on the side of a hot and very active volcano, the animal looked like nothing so much as a fully fledged dragon, and I was more than a little alarmed by his arrival on the scene.

So I threw him my sandwich. He took one disdainful look at it, gazed up briefly at me – and then grabbed the Carita Beach Hotel kitchen's doubtless carefully prepared confection of chicken and white bread between his wicked-looking teeth, and skittered off back into the darkness of the jungle, his armour-plated tail thrashing its valediction.

I got up cautiously from my tree and, with as much dispatch as was consonant with the dignity of the occasion, walked down to the shore and on to the sand. I hurried through the cooling waves, out to where the yellow fishing boat was waiting. I decided not to say what I had seen.

The crew were impatient for home, and we set off eastwards at such a speed that before long the cone of Anak Krakatoa and the relic ruins of the world's greatest volcano were all sliding down astern of us, and merging with the horizon and the setting sun. And as we sailed on into the gathering dark, so the twinkling lights of the west of Java were coming up fast over the bow.

RECOMMENDATIONS FOR
(AND IN ONE CASE, AGAINST)
FURTHER READING AND VIEWING

'Wake up, wake up; you've got to get in the shade!'
I shook my head and opened my eyes again. There was a
man kneeling over me. He wasn't a native, and didn't suggest
an explorer or a traveller. He was wearing a correctly tailored
white morning suit, with pinstripe pants, white ascot tie, and
a white cork bowler.
'Am I dead?' I asked. 'Is this heaven?'
'No, my good man,' he answered. 'This isn't heaven. This
is the Pacific island of Krakatoa.'

– from *The Twenty-One Balloons*,
by William Pène du Bois, 1947

Just after 8.32 on the crystal-clear Sunday morning of 18 May
1980, the long-awaited, universally expected eruption of Mount
St Helens, in the south-western corner of Washington State, blew
away the entire northern face of what was then America's most
notorious volcano. The event turned out to be a classic of the
volcanic art, camera-ready for the textbook: an ash cloud rising
sixteen miles into the sky, and visible 200 miles away; the mountain's summit suddenly reduced in height by 1,300 feet; scores of

square miles of countryside burned and devastated; 22,000 further square miles blanketed with debris; billions of trees swept flat; and fifty-seven people killed, most of them suffocated by clouds of boiling grit.

And yet, though the eruption of Mount St Helens – which was televised, filmed, photographed and chronicled in more loving detail than any other eruption in history – was to become briefly so very famous, it never even came close to dislodging Krakatoa from its position as the most notorious volcano of all time. For some curious reason – and part of that reason quite probably no more than the euphonious nature of the volcano's given name – the saga of Krakatoa has remained firmly and immovably welded into the popular mind.

The principal elements of the story of its great eruption of 27 August 1883 – the immense sound of the detonation, the unprecedented tidal waves, the death-rafts of drifting pumice, the livid sunsets – all still play their part in the world's collective consciousness. They remain annealed into the popular mind in a way that the spectacular eruptions of the planet's other truly great volcanoes, like Etna, Santorini, Tambora and St Pierre – and even the Vesuvius of Pliny and Pompeii – have still never quite managed to match.

Krakatoa – the name. That may well account for it. But there are other reasons too – among them the timely appearance of two items of popular culture relating to the event. One is a slim volume of a children's book, published to near-universal praise in 1947; the other, a Hollywood film released twenty years later to near-universal scorn. More than any other external factor, these two creations quite probably account in large measure for the extraordinary durability of the Krakatoa story.

The children's story was *The Twenty-One Balloons* by William Pène du Bois: it won America's renowned Newbery Medal in 1948, and has never been out of print since. It tells the story of a maths teacher from San Francisco named William Waterman Sherman who flies in a balloon westwards across the Pacific, crash-landing (after seagulls pecked holes in the silk fabric) on what turns out to be 'the Pacific island of Krakatoa'. Here the impeccably dressed locals are all fabulously rich, since the volcano in the island's centre sits directly on top of an immense diamond mine.

The resulting story is all about the Professor's adventures among the remarkable people of a utopia, which, because of the eruption of 1883, swiftly becomes a dangerous dystopia. All have to flee in a specially built balloon-lifted platform. The book – 180 pages, endearingly illustrated by its thirty-year-old author – is enchanting; most intelligent children will have read it, and they will in consequence know Krakatoa as, at the very least, a place both dangerous and beautiful, and wondrously exotic.

Children who were born in time to read the first editions of *The Twenty-One Balloons* would have been in their early thirties in the year 1969. They would thus have been a precise demographic target for one of Hollywood's archetypal B-movie directors, the otherwise little-known Bernard Kowalski, who in that year made the universally known, much derided, utterly improbable, irredeemably mediocre and magisterially mistitled epic *Krakatoa, East of Java.**

The ensemble cast – Maximilian Schell, Diane Baker, Rossano Brazzi, Brian Keith and Sal Mineo among them – might possibly

---

* Mr Kowalski directed some fourteen films and countless episodes of popular American television shows. Prior to *Krakatoa, East of Java* he made *Bucket of Blood, Screaming Skull* and *Attack of the Giant Leeches*; four years after *Krakatoa* he directed an epic, which presumably involved the activities of dangerous snakes, called *Sssssss*. The director is, however, not entirely responsible for siting the volcano at the wrong end of Java: his film was based on a book of the same name by an even more obscure writer named M. Avallone: it is to others we should look for matters of geographical exactitude.

have saved a stronger script or storyline. But the sheer lunacy of the plot, which involved sunken treasure, wayward hot-air balloons, long-legged and half-naked female Japanese pearl-divers, escaped prisoners and a series of very obvious polystyrene models of a volcano, inevitably forced whatever grand vision Kowalski might have had to disintegrate into farce.

Despite the lavish technological promise offered by both Cinerama and Technicolor, the film performed very badly at the time, remains generally a cinematic joke today, and is thought of as merely a less costly precursor of such titanic disasters as *Ishtar*, *Waterworld* and *Heaven's Gate*. *Krakatoa, East of Java* can be seen very late at night on some obscure American television channels; by contrast in Britain, where for some reason the film still enjoys the status of a minor cult classic – a fondness for kitsch, some say – it was part of the expensive and much touted television schedules as recently as Christmas 2001.

In the late 1980s Lorne and Lawrence Blair, two seemingly indefatigable and irrepressibly enthusiastic British explorers,* produced a series of extraordinary television documentaries about the island of Indonesia called *Ring of Fire*. In the way of such things, the television company then produced a book (*Ring of Fire: An Indonesian Odyssey*, London, Inner Traditions International, 1991), which is copiously illustrated and informative. One of the films, cheekily titled *East of Krakatoa*, has two minutes of memorable footage of the early eruptions of Anak Krakatoa in the thirties.

In 1999 Channel Four showed an ambitious two-part television series based on David Keys's remarkable book *Catastrophe: An Investigation into the Origins of the Modern World* (London, Century, 1999), which, as Chapter Four indicates, speculates that an early eruption of Krakatoa may have thrown the entire known world of the time into profound disarray. The idea has supporters and

---

* One of the pair wore a monocle, which made them highly caricaturable.

detractors in equal measure: it ought to be read, sceptically, for a good analysis of the possible early history of the volcano.

There have been surprisingly few books about the volcano's 1883 eruption in recent years, other than an immense number of specialist and technical volumes. One of the few is *Krakatoa* by Rupert Furneaux (London, Secker & Warburg) – but it was published in 1965, an unfortunate two years before the establishment of the theory of plate tectonics arrived to answer all questions about why volcanoes erupt, and so the book has a necessarily limited value. It is, however, a stirring tale, and exceedingly well told, and I made liberal use of some of the eyewitness descriptions that Furneaux so assiduously dug out of various Dutch and maritime archives of the day. Ian Thornton's *Krakatau: The Destruction and Reassembly of an Island Ecosystem* (Cambridge, MA, Harvard University Press, 1996) is thoroughly up to date and much more readable than its title suggests; but, on the other hand, it concentrates heavily on the biogeography of the island, which those hoping for the more general story may lament.

The enormous and well-nigh definitive *Krakatau 1883: The Volcanic Eruption and Its Effects* by the distinguished vulcanologists Tom Simkin and Richard S. Fiske (Washington, DC, Smithsonian Institution Press, 1983) is required reading for anyone with a serious interest in the event and its aftermath: my own copy is thumbed to the point of near destruction. It has scores of illustrations, diagrams, tables and a vast bibliography, all of immense use to someone like me. But it is at heart a scientific book, and its appeal will tend to be limited to the specialist: the fact that no one ever answered the authors' appeal for yet more eyewitness descriptions suggests either that there are no more to be had (which is not true: at least two entirely fresh accounts appeared while I was doing my own research) or the audience for the book was limited to scientists and somehow missed the kind of people who hoard old letters and journals from long-dead relatives who once travelled Out East.

The Royal Society's famous report, *The Eruption of Krakatoa and Subsequent Phenomena* (London, Trübner & Co., 1888), can still be found, expensively, in antiquarian bookshops; as can the heroic *Krakatau* by R. D. M. Verbeek (Batavia, Government Printing Office, 1886), with copies available – at a price – in either Dutch or French. Simkin and Fiske very obligingly translated much of Verbeek's work into English (for the first time) in their own 1983 volume. Serious students of the volcano should make all possible attempts to read at least some of this marvellously enthusiastic work, in whatever language available.

Finally, in the must-read category: anyone with the available funds should buy for their shelves the massive, astonishingly detailed and beautifully written *Encyclopedia of Volcanoes* (San Diego, Academic Press, 2000), not least because it is edited by the Icelandic vulcanologist and world-renowned Krakatoa enthusiast, Haraldur Sigurdsson, presently a professor at the University of Rhode Island.

Other books I found useful and interesting included:

Abeyasekere, Susan, *Jakarta: A History* (Singapore, Oxford University Press, 1987)

Angelino, A. D. A. de Kat, *Colonial Policy. Volume 2: The Dutch East Indies* (The Hague, Martinus Nijhoff, 1931)

Armstrong, Karen, *Islam: A Short History* (London, Weidenfeld & Nicolson, 2000)

— *Muhammad* (London, Gollancz, 1991)

Bangs, Richard, and Kallen, Christian, *Islands of Fire, Islands of Spice* (San Francisco, Sierra Club Books, 1988)

Barty-King, Hugh, *Girdle Round the Earth: The Story of Cable & Wireless and Its Predecessors to Mark the Group's Jubilee* (London, Heinemann, 1979)

Berger, Meyer, *The Story of the New York Times 1851–1951* (New York, Simon & Schuster, 1951)

Bertuchi, A. J., *The Island of Rodriguez, a British Colony in the Mascarenhas Group* (London, John Murray, 1923)

Blue, Gregory, *Colonialism and the Modern World: Selected Studies* (Armonk, NY: M. E. Sharpe, Inc., 2002)

Blussé, Leonard, *Strange Company: Chinese Settlers, Mestizo Women and the Dutch in VOC Batavia* (Dordrecht, Foris Publications, 1988)

Bruce, Victoria, *No Apparent Danger: The True Story of Volcanic Disaster at Galeras and Nevado del Ruiz* (New York, Harper-Collins, 2001)

Cardini, Franco, *Europe and Islam* (Oxford, Blackwell, 2001)

Carson, Rob, *Mount St Helens: The Eruption and Recovery of a Volcano* (Seattle, Sasquatch Books, 1990)

Clarke, Arthur C., *Voice across the Sea* (London, Frederick Muller Ltd, 1958)

Colijn, H., *Neerlands Indie Land en Volk* (Amsterdam, Elsevier, 1912)

Conrad, Joseph, *An Outcast of the Islands* (London, T. Fisher Unwin, 1896)

Couperus, Louis, *The Hidden Force* (Amherst, MA, University of Massachusetts Press, 1985)

Cribb, Robert, *Historical Atlas of Indonesia* (London, Curzon Press, 2000)

Daum, P. A., *Ups and Downs of Life in the Indies* (Singapore, Periplus, 1999)

Daws, Gavin, and Fujita, Marty, *Archipelago: The Islands of Indonesia* (Berkeley, University of California Press, 1999)

Decker, Robert, and Decker, Barbara, *Volcanoes* (New York, W. H. Freeman, 1979)

De Vries, H. M. (ed.), *The Importance of Java Seen from the Air* (Batavia, H. M. De Vries, 1928)

Fairchild, David, *Garden Islands of the Great East* (New York, Scribner, 1943)

Forster, Harold, *Flowering Lotus: A View of Java in the 1950s* (London, Longman, Green & Co., 1958)

Friederich, Walter L., *Fire in the Sea. The Santorini Volcano: Natural History and the Legend of Atlantis* (Cambridge, Cambridge University Press, 2000)

Geertz, Clifford, *The Religion of Java* (New York, The Free Press, 1960)

Gilbert, J. S., and Sparks, R. S. J., *The Physics of Explosive Volcanic Eruptions* (London, Geological Society of London, 1998)

Haigh, K. R., *Cableships and Submarine Cables* (London, Adlard Coles, 1968)

Hall, R., and Blundell, D. J. (eds.), *Tectonic Evolution of Southeast Asia* (London, Geological Society of London, 1996)

Hamilton, Warren, *Tectonics of the Indonesian Region* (Washington, DC, US Geological Survey, 1979)

Helsdingen, W. H. van, and Hoogenberk, Dr H., *Mission Interrupted: The Dutch in the East Indies and Their Work in the Twentieth Century* (Amsterdam, Elsevier, 1945)

Heuken, Adolf, SJ, *Historical Sites of Jakarta* (Jakarta, Cipta Loka Caraka, 2000)

Hicks, Geoff, and Campbell, Hamish, *Awesome Forces: The Natural Hazards that Threaten New Zealand* (Wellington, NZ, Te Papa Press, 1998)

Hillen, Ernest, *The Way of a Boy: A Memoir of Java* (London, Viking, 1993)

Hobhouse, Henry, *Seeds of Change: Five Plants that Transformed Mankind* (London, Sidgwick & Jackson, 1985)

Huntington, Samuel P., *The Clash of Civilizations and the Remaking of the World Order* (London, Simon & Schuster, 1997)

Johnson, George (ed.), *The All Red Line: The Annals and Aims of the Pacific Cable Project* (Ottawa, James Hope & Sons, 1903)

Kartodirdjo, Sartono, *The Peasants' Revolt of Banten in 1888* (The Hague, Martinus Nijhoff, 1966)

Keay, John, *Empire's End: A History of the Far East from High Colonialism to Hong Kong* (New York, Scribner, 1997)

Kemp, P. H. van der, *De Administratie der Geldmiddelen van Neerland-Indie* (*The Financial Administration of the Dutch East Indies*) (Amsterdam, J. H. de Bussy, 1881)

Keys, David, *Catastrophe: An Investigation into the Origins of the Modern World* (London, Century, 1999)

Krafft, Maurice, *Volcanoes* (New York, Harry N. Abrams, 1993)

Kuitenbrouwer, Maarten, *The Netherlands and the Rise of Modern Imperialism* (Providence, RI, Berg Publishers, 1991)

Kumar, Ann, *The Diary of a Javanese Muslim: Religion, Politics and the Pesantren 1883–1886* (Canberra, Australian National University, 1985)

Legge, J. D., *Indonesia* (New York, Prentice Hall, 1964)

Levelink, Jose, *Four Guided Walks through the Bogor Botanic Garden* (Bogor, Bogorindo Botanicus, 1996)

Lewis, Bernard, *The Middle East: 2,000 Years of History from the Rise of Christianity to the Present Day* (London, Weidenfeld & Nicolson, 1995)

— *What Went Wrong? The Clash between Islam and Modernity in the Middle East* (London, Weidenfeld & Nicolson, 2002)

Lucas, E. V., *A Wanderer in Holland* (London, Methuen & Co., 1905)

Merrillees, Scott, *Batavia in Nineteenth-Century Photographs* (London, Curzon Press, 2000)

Milton, Giles, *Nathaniel's Nutmeg: How One Man's Courage Changed the Course of History* (London, Hodder & Stoughton, 1999)

Money, J. W. B., *Java, or, How to Manage a Colony* (London, Hurst & Blackett, 1861)

Multatuli [Dekker, Eduard Douwes], *Max Havelaar, or The Coffee*

Auctions of a Dutch Trading Company (London, Heinemann, 1967)

Naipaul, V. S., *Beyond Belief: Islamic Excursions among the Converted Peoples* (London, Little, Brown, 1998)

Netherlands Royal Mail Line, *Java the Wonderland* (Arnhem [n.d.])

Nieuwenhuys, Rob, *Mirror of the Indies: A History of Dutch Colonial Literature* (Hong Kong, Periplus, 1999)

— *Faded Portraits: E. Breton de Nijs* (Amherst, MA, University of Massachusetts Press, 1982)

Oey, Eric (ed.), *Java* (Singapore, Periplus, 1997)

Oosterzee, Penny van, *When Worlds Collide: The Wallace Line* (Ithaca, NY, Cornell University Press, 1997)

Oreskes, Naomi (ed.), *Plate Tectonics* (Boulder, CO, Westview Press, 2001)

Ponder, H. W., *Javanese Panorama* (London, Seeley, Service & Co. [1942])

Poortenaar, Jan, *An Artist in the Tropics* (London, Sampson Low [1927])

Pope-Hennessy, James, *Verandah: Some Episodes in the Crown Colonies 1867–1889* (London, George Allen & Unwin, 1964)

Preger, W., *Dutch Administration in the Netherlands Indies* (Melbourne, F. W. Cheshire, 1944)

Quammen, David, *The Song of the Dodo: Island Biogeography in an Age of Extinctions* (New York, Scribner, 1996)

Raby, Peter, *Alfred Russel Wallace: A Life* (Princeton, NJ, Princeton University Press, 2001)

Raffles, Sir Thomas Stamford Bingley, *The History of Java* (London, Black, Parbury & Allen, 1817)

Read, Donald, *The Power of News: The History of Reuters 1849–1989* (Oxford, Oxford University Press, 1992)

Reitsma, S. A., *Van Stockum's Travellers' Handbook for the Dutch East Indies* (The Hague, W. P. van Stockum & Son, 1930)

Ross, Robert, and Winius, George, *All of One Company: The VOC in Historical Perspective* (Utrecht, HES Uitgivers, 1986)

SarDesai, D. R., *Southeast Asia, Past and Present* (Boulder, CO, Westview Press, 1989)

Scarth, Alwyn, *La Catastrophe: The Eruption of Mount Pelée* (Oxford, Oxford University Press, 2002)

— *Vulcan's Fury: Man against the Volcano* (New Haven, CT, Yale University Press, 1999)

Schama, Simon, *Patriots and Liberators: Revolution in the Netherlands 1780–1813* (London, Collins, 1977)

Schoch, Robert M., *Voices of the Rocks: A Scientist Looks at Catastrophes and Ancient Civilizations* (New York, Harmony Books, 1999)

Scidmore, E. R., *Java, the Garden of the East* (New York, The Century Co., 1897)

Severin, Timothy, *The Spice Islands Voyage: The Quest for Alfred Wallace, the Man Who Shared Darwin's Discovery of Evolution* (New York, Carroll & Graf, 1997)

Shepard, Jim, *Batting against Castro* (New York, Alfred A. Knopf, 1996)

Shermer, Michael, *In Darwin's Shadow: The Life and Science of Alfred Russel Wallace* (New York, Oxford University Press, 2002)

Sigurdsson, Haraldur, *Melting the Earth: The History of Ideas on Volcanic Eruptions* (New York, Oxford University Press, 1999)

Sitwell, Sacheverell, *The Netherlands: A Study of Some Aspects of Art, Costume and Social Life* (London, B. T. Batsford, 1948)

Soebadio, Dr Haryati, *et al.* (ed.), *Indonesian Heritage Encyclopedia* (10 vols. pub., Singapore, Editions Didier Millet, 1996 et seq.)

Standage, Tom, *The Victorian Internet: The Remarkable Story of the Telegraph and the Nineteenth Century's Online Pioneers* (London, Weidenfeld & Nicolson, 1998)

Stephens, Mitchell, *A History of News: From the Drum to the Satellite* (New York, Viking, 1988)

Suárez, Thomas, *Early Mapping of Southeast Asia* (Hong Kong, Periplus, 1999)

Taylor, Jean Gelman, *The Social World of Batavia* (Madison, WI, University of Wisconsin Press, 1983)

Thornton, Ian, *Krakatau: The Destruction and Reassembly of an Island Ecosystem* (Cambridge, MA, Harvard University Press, 1996)

Turner, Peter (ed.), *Java* (Melbourne, Lonely Planet, 1995)

Umbgrove, J. H. F., *Structural History of the East Indies* (Cambridge, Cambridge University Press, 1949)

Vandenbosch, Amry, *The Dutch East Indies, Its Government, Problems and Politics* (Berkeley, University of California Press, 1941)

Vissering, G., *Geweldige Natuurkrachten (Nature's Power)* (Batavia, G. Kolff & Co., 1910)

Vlekke, Bernard M., *Nusantara: A History of the East Indian Archipelago* (Cambridge, MA, Harvard University Press, 1945)

— *The Story of the Dutch East Indies* (Cambridge, MA, Harvard University Press, 1945)

Wallace, Alfred Russel, *The Malay Archipelago. The Land of the Orang-utan and the Bird of Paradise. A Narrative of Travel, with Studies of Man and Nature* (London, Macmillan, 1869)

Weyer, Robert van de, *Islam and the West: A New Political and Religious Order Post September 11* (Alresford, Hants, O Books, 2001)

Wilkinson-Latham, Robert J., *From Our Special Correspondent* (London, Hodder & Stoughton, 1979)

Williams, Stanley, and Montaigne, Fen, *Surviving Galeras* (Boston, Houghton Mifflin, 2001)

Woodcock, George, *The British in the Far East* (New York, Atheneum, 1969)

Zebrowski, Jr., Ernest, *The Last Days of St Pierre* (Piscataway, NJ, Rutgers University Press, 2002)

Zeilinger de Boer, Jelle, and Sanders, Donald, *Volcanoes in Human History* (Princeton, NJ, Princeton University Press, 2002)

ACKNOWLEDGEMENTS,
ERKENNINGEN, TERIMA KASIH

To try to write an account of a long-ago explosion in a faraway place – far away, that is, when the volcano is to the west of Java and I live 9,944 miles from it, in the west of Massachusetts – requires a mule-train of helpers to bridge the distance, and a congress of libraries and librarians to compress the years. To meet both requirements I was exceptionally fortunate in finding the most congenial and knowledgeable legion of able and interested helpmeets, some of them old friends, many more of them brand new, without whose enthusiasm, skills and wisdom this story would have been much more difficult to relate. As I list them here, with gratitude and pleasure, I must none the less reassure each and every one that though all did their very best to guide, advise and warn me, such errors and misjudgements as may appear in the book – and I would like to think there are few – are my fault alone and should not, to any degree, be laid at their door.

In the early stages of my research I was lucky enough to be directed, by courtesy of Atlas, my Dutch publishers, to the delightful Alicia Schrikker, a graduate student of Dutch colonial history at the University of Leiden. Alicia, whose professional area of interest encompasses the Dutch possessions in the East Indies, Ceylon and Japan, leapt at the chance of working on the story of Krakatoa, and in short order led me to sheaves of long-forgotten papers and archives and introduced me to battalions of long-overlooked and little-known players in the drama, fast making herself my most indispensable ally in the entire endeavour. While I owe much to many, my debt to Alicia is singular and incalculable; I wish also to thank her partner, Job Westrate, for his forbearance during the many days she worked with me, and for his later practical help when Alicia took off for her own studies in Colombo, Galle and southern Sri Lanka. Dr Wim van den Doel, a distinguished historian at Leiden, also readily gave of his advice. And I must record my personal gratitude to Hessel Stamhuis, a wise and kindly academic at the same university who came to stay with me in America: his death some months later was a sad shock.

In Indonesia, where I travelled several times, my old friend Toni Tack, whom I had met some years before when we were exploring little-known Hindu temples in central Java, was enormously kind and helpful, and accompanied me to Jakarta on several occasions, as well as to those coastal communities of west Java that were worst affected by the calamity of 1883. Toni is a game and courageous lady – and, unhappily, she needs to be even more so nowadays, since the island of Bali, her chosen home for the past many years, is no longer so peaceful a place as once we all supposed – but she wisely elected not to come with me to climb the scorchingly hot slopes of Anak Krakatoa on those occasions when I felt so moved. Instead it was left to the redoubtable and engagingly named Boing, a guide from Anjer, to haul me up the ever growing mountain – a duty he performed with agility and eternally good spirits.

Also in Indonesia I was given much help and hospitality by the British Ambassador, Richard Gozney; by Professor Sartono Kartodirdjo, the renowned historian at Jogjakarta's Gajah Mada University (who, in addition to offering his advice on the nature and meaning of the Banten Rebellion of 1888, also kindly gave me a pot of his wife's homemade Balinese nutmeg jam in return for the jar of TeaTogether's incomparable Lemon with Earl Grey Tea marmalade; which I sometimes use – as when turning up at teatime at Professor Kartodirdjo's house – as my calling-card); by Father Adolf Heuken, Jakarta's kindly (and Jesuit) urban

historian; by George Benney and the staff of the Mandarin Oriental Hotel Jakarta; by Trina Ebert and the staff at the Amanjiwo
resort, close by the temple of Borobudur; by the Jakarta-based
writers Scott Merrillees and Mark Hanusz; by the Indonesian
bookstore owner and Krakatoa enthusiast Richard Oh; by my
long-time friend Hannah Postgate, whose fondness of, and
enthusiasm for, all things Javanese is inextinguishable and wonderfully infectious; and by Robert Hall of the University of
London's Southeast Asia Research Group, whose expertise in the
arena of the tectonic evolution of the region that includes Java
and Sumatra – and thus Krakatoa – is well-nigh unrivalled.

Others whose gave generously of their particular knowledge
of the geology and geophysics of the region include Professor
John Dewey, now at the University of California, Davis, and
formerly Professor of Geology at Oxford; Rob McCaffrey and
David Wark at the Rensselaer Polytechnic Institute in Troy,
New York; Charles Mandeville; Stephen Self; Vicky Bruce. John
Rucklidge, who led the 1965 Oxford University Expedition to
east Greenland, of which I was the most junior member, and
who is now at the University of Toronto, was most helpful in
reminding me of the scientific purpose and value of that remark-
able adventure. Richard Fiske, of Washington's Smithsonian
Institution and of the Global Volcanism Program – and with
Tom Simkin author of the incomparable and near-definitive 1983
Smithsonian Press study of Krakatoa – was also generous with
his time and insights.

My friend Andrea Hsu, in Washington, DC, was as helpful with
answering the more arcane research questions for this project as
she has been in connection with similarly obscure queries for the
last three of my books, and I cannot fully express in print my
deepest gratitude to her. At rather longer distance, Penny van
Oosterzee, Robert Cribb and Nicholas Pounder (in Australia),
Eloise Van Niel (in Hawaii), Rob Whittaker and Professor Ceri
Peach (in Oxford) all gave valuable advice on matters that ranged

from the dietary preferences of nineteenth-century Batavians to the story of the botanical repopulation of the ruined islands around Krakatoa. I would like also to acknowledge the help of Adrian Beeby of Lloyd's, of Gina Douglas of the Linnean Society, Stephen Gillies, Amanda Green of the Foreign and Commonwealth Office Library, Ann Kumar, Laila Miletic-Vejzovic, Zyg Nilski, Margaret O'Clair, Vanessa E. Raizberg and Paula Szuchman. The newly formed Gieben-Wulf Cultural Research Centre in London answered a single question that had long been nagging me, and they did so accurately, efficiently and very, very quickly – a trinity of attributes that I think all would agree augurs well for their success: I do wish Emma and Andrea well. My son Rupert Winchester performed yeoman service on my behalf at the London Library (whose staff were unfailingly helpful) and at the Public Record Office, and in his dealings with Cable & Wireless.

Norah O'Donnell, a wonderful old friend at the Humanities Division of the University of Chicago, helped me by borrowing on her staff card, and *for two full years*, a pair of extremely rare and crucial books from the university's Joseph Regenstein Library. I owe the very tolerant librarians there a great deal for not asking for the volumes to be returned (though both are now quite safely back on their shelves).

Sophie Purdy kindly read and made most useful comments on the early drafts of the book: she deserves the very warmest of thanks.

In London I wish once again to record my deep gratitude to my agent and friend Bill Hamilton. My new editor at Viking, Mary Mount, handled my rather less than elegant first telling of this complicated story with consummate brilliance, managing first to spot, with an uncanny and instinctive ability, all of the inconsistencies and structural flaws and infelicities that littered the submitted script, and then to iron them out and so save me, at the very least, from the critical mauling I am certain I at first deserved. Mary would not be surprised to learn that I truly cannot find words adequate to describe my pleasure in working with and for her: I hope that we may team up for many more fascinating projects like this in the years to come.

Mary Mount's assistant, Julie Duffy, also made major contributions, most notably when it came time to find the pictures and other illustrations with which to leaven the text: I am most grateful to her. Soun Vannithone drew the line illustrations once again, and, as with the last book, he did so perfectly and exactly on time. Natacha du Pont du Bois coordinated with an almost terrifying efficiency what was the complicated and linguistically challenging task (since Soun is from Laos, and many of the pictures are from sources in Holland) of seeing that all the illustrated material was prepared properly and to a very demanding schedule.

Once again Donna Poppy, surely the ablest of the world's copy editors, took on with an unstinting good cheer the monumental business of keeping the devil away from the details in a book that ranged through unfamiliar complexities of science and history, religion and sociology, where there were litanies of names in Dutch and Javanese that all needed checking, checking, checking. To Donna and to her colleague in New York, Sue Llewellyn: a thousand thanks and *stet!* to all you do.

And in New York I owe eternal thanks to my robustly splendid agent Peter Matson, and to his colleagues Saskia Cornes and Jim Rutman; and to Krista Stroever, a most wonderful editor.

Finally: if there was ever to be a *primus inter* all these distinguished *pares* above – and I realize there should not be, since all who helped should be equally blessed – then my vote would have to be for that most deservedly legendary of New York publishers and a valued friend for the past six years, Larry Ashmead. Larry was the inspiration, the champion and the encourager-in-chief: I only hope he finds that this slender book is worthy of all the many hopes he once entertained for it.

ILLUSTRATION ACKNOWLEDGEMENTS

Van Linschoten's 1595 map, published by the Hakluyt Society (by permission of David Higham Associates).

Jan Pieterszoon Coen and Governor-general 's Jacob are from F. W. Stapel, *De gouverneurs-generaal van Nederlandsch-Indie in beeld en woord* (The Hague, Van Stockum, 1941).

Straw-hat maker from H. J. de Graaf, *Batavia in oude ansichten*, *Zaltbommel* (Europese Bibliotheek, 1970).

Alfred Russel Wallace and Charles Darwin (© Natural History Museum, London).

Alfred Wegener and '*Agamemnon* Laying Cable' (by permission of Mary Evans Picture Library).

John Webber's drawing (by permission of the British Library).

Batavia city scene and Concordia Military Club photograph taken from *Batavia in Nineteenth Century Photographs* by Scott Merrillees (Curzon Press, 2000).

Photograph of Rogier Verbeek and his great-grandson from biographical memorial of Verbeek by N. Wing Easton (Druk de Bussy, 1926).

Captain Ferzenaar's map of Krakatoa appears as Figure 21 in Verbeek's *Atlas*.

Telegraph map (© National Maritime Museum, London).

Samuel Morse (by permission of New York Public Library/ Science Photo Library).

Trace from Batavia Gasworks; before and after Admiralty charts of Krakatoa; Batavia tide-meter trace; and tide-gauge trace from Socoa, France (© The Royal Society).

The tsunami appeared in Alwyn Scarth, *Vulcan's Fury* (Yale University Press, 1999).

The *Berouw* stranded, etching by T. Weber from a field sketch by M. Korthals. From Edmond Cotteau, and W. Korthals, '1884 Mission Francaise au Krakatao' Comptes Rerdus des Séances de la Société de Géographie (Paris), 15.

British Admiralty map reproduced from Admiralty chart 2056 (by permission of the Controller of Her Majesty's Stationery Office and the UK Hydrographic Office, *www.ukho.gov.uk*).

Anak Krakatoa photograph by the Kraffts from *SEAN Bulletin* (December 1979).

Spider: *Nephila maculata* (© Premaphotos/naturepl.com).

Shell with seedling photograph by C. C. Reijnvaan (Doctors van Leeuwen, 1936).

Modern photograph of vegetation on Krakatoa (© D. Walsh of La Trobe University).

Photograph of Surtsey by Sturla Fridriksson.

Chapter heading and text line drawings copyright © Soun Vannithone, 2003

Every effort has been made to trace or contact all copyright-holders. The publishers will be pleased to make good any omissions or rectify any mistakes brought to their attention at the earliest opportunity.

INDEX

Figures in italics indicate captions.

Chacana volcano, Ecuador 308
Chamberlin, Thomas 76
Champa Kingdom, Vietnam 128
Channel Four 133n, 395
Charles Bal (cargo-carrying barque)
    220, 246, 299
Chaumont Bay, Lake Ontario 283–4
Chefoo (later Yantai), China 287
Chelsea, London 284, 290, 291
chemistry 305–6
chemolithoautotrophic
    hyperthermophilic
    archaebacteria 367n
Cherbourg 282
Chile 13n, 289, 308, 309
China, Chinese 22
  and spices 10
  rule of Macau 19
  mapping 23, 24
  coolies 42, 213, 228
  merchants 42
  Coen and 42–3
  Batava population 44, 144, 215
  and tectonic plates 111
  and possible eruption of AD 535
    131
  records of sea captains 131–2
  anti-Chinese riots (1998) 138
  and the 1883 eruption 215, 246–7,
    250
China Overseas Shipping Company
    (COSCO) 381
Christianity, Christians
  and the 1883 eruption 163
  and Muslims 32
  Protestant 44
Christie, Mr (in Ceylon) 264
Christmas Island 89, 114
Church, Frederic Edwin 283–4
  Niagara 283
  Sunset over the Ice on Chaumont
    Bay, Lake Ontario 284
  Twilight in the Wilderness 283
Ciliwung River 34, 38, 39
cinnamon 18, 31, 330
Ciparis (Sylbaris), Louis-Auguste
    243n
Claw, Iceland 82
Cloos, Hans 75–6

cloves (*Syzygium aromaticum*) 10, *11*,
    18, 29, 31, 65, 297n, 330
Cochin 11
cochineal 330
cockatoos 55, 65, *65*, 66, 68, 137n
'cock's tail' jets 352
Cocos (Keeling) Island 114, 190n
Coen, Jan Pieterszoon *33*, 142
  appearance 32
  personality 33, 35
  founder of the Dutch East Indies
    33–4, 36
  governor-general of the East
    Indies 33, 34
  decides to eject the British 34
  and the Chinese 42–3
coffee 10, 141, 148, 182, 188, 238–9
Cold War 106–7, 266, 275
Coleoptera 58
College of Delft 156n
Collocalia 21
Cologne Cathedral 297
Colombia 308, 309
Colombo 288
Columbia University 107
Compagnie van Verre 15
Concordia Military Club, Batavia
    147, 153, 172, 202, 203–4, *203*
Conrad (Dutch mailboat) 157, 167–8
Conrad, Joseph: *Lord Jim* 12–13
conservative plate boundary 113
Constantinople 10
continental drift 171
  Wegener's theory 71–8
  in basalts of east Greenland 87
  and convection 90, *91*, 97–8
  and earth's magnetism 92, 97
  dating of 97
  and plate tectonics *91*, 101, 315
  reacceptance of 101, 102
  Wilson's conclusions 104–5
  Jeffreys opposes the concept 304n
continental plate collision 112–13,
    307
continental shrinking 73
continental tectonic material 112,
    113, 114
controllers 156
convection 90, *91*, 97–8, 109, 302

418 INDEX